Seat of Wisdom

Seat of Wisdom:
An Introduction to Philosophy in the Catholic Tradition

James M. Jacobs

The Catholic University of America Press
Washington, D.C.

∞

Library of Congress Cataloging-in-Publication Data

Names: Jacobs, James M. (Seminarian), author.
Title: Seat of wisdom : an introduction to philosophy in the Catholic
   tradition / James M. Jacobs.
Description: Washington, D.C. : The Catholic University of America Press,
   [2021] | Includes bibliographical references and index.
Identifiers: LCCN 2021048746 (print) | LCCN 2021048747 (ebook) | ISBN
   9780813234656 (paperback) | ISBN 9780813234663 (ebook)
Subjects: LCSH: Catholic Church and philosophy.
Classification: LCC BX1795.P47 J33 2021 (print) | LCC BX1795.P47 (ebook)
   | DDC 261.5/1--dc23/eng/20211014
LC record available at https://lccn.loc.gov/2021048746
LC ebook record available at https://lccn.loc.gov/2021048747

This book is dedicated to all my students
who have patiently worked with me
as I have tried to come to understand what is written here.

Table of Contents

Acknowledgments

I want to thank the Administration and Faculty of Notre Dame Seminary for their encouragement and support of this project. In particular, I thank all those who helped in arranging a sabbatical during which this book was begun: Fr. James Wehner, Thomas Neal, Rebecca Maloney, Mark Barker, David Liberto, Fr. Philip Neri Powell, OP, and Caitlin Gilson. Gregory Vall was indispensible in assisting me with a variety of issues concerning Scripture. I thank all my friends and colleagues in the American Maritain Association, whose wisdom constantly inspires me to broaden and deepen my philosophical vision. I thank Sr. Dulce Flores, HMSS, for her encouragement to take up this project. John Martino from The Catholic University of America Press deserves special thanks for invaluable suggestions, as well as shepherding this book to completion. I likewise thank the anonymous readers whose insightful comments helped to make this a much better book, though any remaining deficiencies are my own. Most of all, I thank my wife, Laura, who has patiently supported me for many years.

Through philosophy's work, the ability to speculate that is proper to the human intellect produces a rigorous mode of thought; and then in turn, through the logical coherence of the affirmations made and the organic unity of their content, it produces a systematic body of knowledge. . . . Faith intervenes not to abolish reason's autonomy nor to reduce its scope for action but solely to bring the human being to understand that in these events it is the God of Israel who acts. Thus, the world and the events of history cannot be understood in depth without professing faith in the God who is at work in them. . . . This truth, which God reveals to us in Jesus Christ, is not opposed to the truths that philosophy perceives. On the contrary, the two modes of knowledge lead to truth in all its fullness. The unity of truth is a fundamental premise of human reasoning, as the principle of noncontradiction makes clear. . . . The fundamental harmony between the knowledge of faith and the knowledge of philosophy is once again confirmed. Faith asks that its object be understood with the help of reason; and at the summit of its searching reason acknowledges that it cannot do without what faith presents.

—Pope Saint John Paul II, *Fides et Ratio*

Religious and philosophical beliefs are, indeed, as dangerous as fire, and nothing can take from them that beauty of danger. But there is only one way of really guarding ourselves against the excessive danger of them, and that is to be steeped in philosophy and soaked in religion.

—G. K. Chesterton, *Heretics*

Introduction:
Catholicism and Philosophy

PHILOSOPHY: THE HANDMAID TO THEOLOGY

While Paul was waiting for them in Athens, he was deeply distressed to see that the city was full of idols. So he argued in the synagogue with the Jews and the devout persons, and also in the marketplace every day with those who happened to be there. Also some Epicurean and Stoic philosophers debated with him. Some said, "What does this babbler want to say?" Others said, "He seems to be a proclaimer of foreign divinities." (This was because he was telling the good news about Jesus and the resurrection.) So they took him and brought him to the Areopagus and asked him, "May we know what this new teaching is that you are presenting? It sounds rather strange to us, so we would like to know what it means." Now all the Athenians and the foreigners living there would spend their time in nothing but telling or hearing something new. (Acts 17: 16–21; NRSV-CE translation)

When the Apostle Paul stepped into the heart of Athens, the epicenter of Greek philosophy, he encountered people whose idea of wisdom was already shaped by certain habits of thought very different from the Jewish tradition of wisdom in which he had been trained. Paul's Jewish wisdom was based on God's revelation of the Law. This Greek wisdom, in contrast, was based on a rational analysis of evidence observed in nature and formulated in arguments. The Greeks called those who pursued this rational wisdom *philosophers*. These philosophers had diverse notions of reason and so fell into feuding camps about how to read the book of nature: not only the Epicureans and Stoics encountered by Paul but also followers of Plato, Aristotle, and others. However, according to the author of Acts, they did agree on one thing—they loved philosophical debate, for they "would spend their time in nothing but telling or hearing something new." And although they saw Paul, who was not a philosopher, as a "babbler," his teaching was, at the very least unlike what others before him had taught.

1

Then Paul stood in front of the Areopagus and said, "Athenians, I see how extremely religious you are in every way. For as I went through the city and looked carefully at the objects of your worship, I found among them an altar with the inscription, 'To an unknown god.' What therefore you worship as unknown, this I proclaim to you. The God who made the world and everything in it, he who is Lord of heaven and earth, does not live in shrines made by human hands, nor is he served by human hands, as though he needed anything, since he himself gives to all mortals life and breath and all things. From one ancestor he made all nations to inhabit the whole earth, and he allotted the times of their existence and the boundaries of the places where they would live, so that they would search for God and perhaps grope for him and find him—though indeed he is not far from each one of us. For 'In him we live and move and have our being'; as even some of your own poets have said, 'For we too are his offspring.'

"Since we are God's offspring, we ought not to think that the deity is like gold, or silver, or stone, an image formed by the art and imagination of mortals. While God has overlooked the times of human ignorance, now he commands all people everywhere to repent, because he has fixed a day on which he will have the world judged in righteousness by a man whom he has appointed, and of this he has given assurance to all by raising him from the dead." (Acts 17:22–31)

To bring the gospel to the Athenians, Saint Paul modifies his usual preaching so as to conform to the customs of the Greeks: he appeals not to Scripture but to the Greek religious practice (the altar to the unknown God), traditional Greek poetry, and above all to a philosophical discussion of the nature of the Deity as creator of the universe. He uses these points to critique the sacrifices offered to idols in Greek religion and to move his audience to an appreciation of the true nature of God. Many of those listening to Paul would have shared his criticism of typical pagan religion as illogical or irrational. Yet, Paul then goes further, teaching how the true Deity made himself known in the one whom he had raised from the dead. Here Paul engages philosophers not only with reason but also with the revelation of Christ that extends and completes their rational speculations. Predictably, though, this arouses a less than enthusiastic reaction:

When they heard of the resurrection of the dead, some scoffed; but others said, "We will hear you again about this." At that point Paul left them. But some of them joined him and became believers, including Dionysius the Areopagite and a woman named Damaris, and others with them. (Acts 17:32–34)

"Some scoffed; but others said, 'We will hear you again about this.'" Paul's experience in Athens is not unlike our own today. When people are presented with the Gospel, it elicits the mockery of some, while from others it evinces a modest curiosity. Christians have often been judged by the mockers to be "babblers," promoting a doctrine akin to superstition. But this reaction misses the profound wisdom of Paul's own witness. Paul's preaching does not neglect reason; rather, he shows how the Gospel builds on reason by going beyond it. Paul integrates faith and reason, providing everyone access to a truth that is at once the most fundamental—and so "not far" from any rational person—and yet also the most exalted, revealed fully only in the person of Christ. Those who frequent our modern-day Areopagus—whether university lecture hall or internet forum—are like the Athenians: Many are resistant to faith because they see only that faith goes beyond reason. Yet others are intrigued by the fact that faith does not conflict with reason but is rather an essential complement to it and eventually come to believe. For this reason, Paul, in some ways, can be said to be the godfather of Christian philosophy.[1]

Later Christians, following in Paul's footsteps, would realize that integrating reason into faith was not merely a strategy for converting the philosophically inclined Athenians. On the contrary, Christians came to see that faith and reason are integrally bound together in the most profound way. The Prologue to John, drawing on the creation story from Genesis, refers to Christ as God's Word, for "In the beginning was the Word and . . . all things came into being through him" (Jn 1:13). This Word, the *Logos*, is signified by the same term the Greek philosophers use for reason. Thus, the revealed order of creation *is* the order known by reason: *wisdom is one*. This inspired the Church Fathers, from the earliest centuries, to embrace philosophy for theological purposes, finding it an invaluable tool for communicating the faith to all people with reason.[2]

---

[1] Yet Paul's revealed wisdom remains resolutely different from philosophy; see the essay by Søren Kierkegaard, "On the Difference between a Genius and an Apostle," in *The Present Age: On the Death of Rebellion*, trans. Alexander Dru (New York: Harper Perennial, 1962), 63–87.

[2] For a discussion of the appropriation of philosophy by the Church Fathers, see Étienne Gilson, *History of Christian Philosophy in the Middle Ages* (New York: Random House, 1955), 9–64.

We might wonder, though, whether this approach is still relevant today, given the pluralistic nature of our culture. The differences between Epicureans and Stoics that Paul encountered seem quaint compared with the disagreements among the philosophy faculty at one university, to say nothing of the vastly different worldviews professed in contemporary society. Some would therefore see Saint Paul's genius in speaking to the Greeks merely as a case of "inculturation," in which he made use of the particular idiom of the local people—in this case philosophy—to bring them to Christ. Hence, whereas Hellenistic philosophy was once the dominant culture, today we should try to integrate the faith into other more modern ways of thinking. Greek philosophy was good for Saint Paul, but it should be left in the past since it is no longer relevant for us.

This view, however, fails to appreciate the importance of Greek thought for the Christian tradition. As Pope Benedict XVI argues, this legacy of Hellenistic philosophy is a gift of divine providence for the propagation of the Church universally, in time and space. As the German pope said in his famous Regensburg Lecture, "biblical faith, in the Hellenistic period, encountered the best of Greek thought at a deep level, resulting in a mutual enrichment"[3] of both Greek philosophy and Christian belief. This is not to say that faith cannot encounter new ideas and be enriched anew. But Greek philosophy is unique because of the way in which it framed wisdom in terms of the most fundamental realities—being, truth, goodness, and beauty—thereby unveiling the universal and unchanging principles that provide human life with meaning from the perspective of both reason and faith. Thus, we see that God, who is being itself (Ex 3:14) reveals himself in Christ, who is the truth (Jn 14:6), and who shares in the goodness of the Father (Mt 19:17), and who is the model of beauty and justice (Phil 4:8). The truths of philosophy and revelation, therefore, grow together to form the Christian tradition. Both paths enrich one another and lead to a more profound appreciation of a single reality. The incorporation of philosophical reason into Christianity, then, is useful not only for the Greeks but also for all who aim to appropriate the fullness of truth.

The philosophy that emerges from the encounter of biblical faith and Greek philosophy has come to be known as the perennial philosophy. It is perennial because it is a continuously developed tradition whose principles

---

3 Benedict XVI, *Faith, Reason, and the University: Memories and Reflections*, September 12, 2006. See also John Paul II, Encyclical Letter *Fides et Ratio* (September 14, 1998), 72.

transcend any specific cultural context. These principles reflect no single sectarian theory or historical epoch; rather, they are grounded on the most fundamental principle of reality—being—as the foundation for truth and goodness. The origins of this tradition lie in the thought of Plato and Aristotle, but its highest expression is found in the thought of Thomas Aquinas, who integrates philosophy and faith into an organic manifestation of the living truth.

This widespread usefulness of philosophy to theology is recognized in the Catholic tradition, where philosophy is frequently referred to as "the handmaid to theology," while theology itself—a divine gift of wisdom—is "the queen of sciences."[4] Just as the queen can only rule well with the help of her handmaid, doing theology well requires a deep grasp of philosophy. This is why knowledge of the perennial philosophy is so crucial, for many heresies arise from what are in reality philosophical errors. Pope Saint John Paul II pointed this out in his great letter on philosophy, *Fides et Ratio* (Faith and reason): "It is an illusion to think that faith, tied to weak reasoning, might be more penetrating; on the contrary, faith then runs the grave risk of withering into myth or superstition."[5] Bad philosophy can lead faith into error for the simple reason that bad philosophy distorts one's way of thinking and so obscures the true nature of reality. If you do not understand creation, you have little chance of coming to know the Creator.[6] Philosophy and theology—handmaid and queen—must work together.

THREE USES OF PHILOSOPHY IN THEOLOGY

Theology makes use of philosophy in three ways in particular. First, as the Church Fathers discovered, the revealed faith needs to be articulated in a way so that it can be preached. Philosophy is called upon to provide the terms and ideas with which we frame the doctrinal statements and creeds

---

4 Theology is queen of the sciences since, as Thomas notes, it is the noblest of all sciences (*ST* I.1.5) and can be equated with wisdom itself since "he who considers absolutely the highest cause of the whole universe, namely God, is most of all called wise" (*ST* I.1.6). Thomas likewise notes philosophy's status as handmaid (*ST* I.1.5.ad 2). See the bibliography for the method of citation and translations used.

5 *Fides et Ratio*, 48. This is why the United States Conference of Catholic Bishops' fifth edition of *Program for Priestly Formation* mandates no fewer than thirty academic hours of philosophy for all seminarians. Similar preparation would seem to be desirable for all who wish to study theology. See also *Fides et Ratio*, 60–62.

6 *SCG* II.3.6: "For error concerning creatures . . . spills over into false opinion about God, and takes men's minds away from Him."

in which the Church states what she believes. This is known as *auditus fidei*.[7] This is necessary even for the most fundamental Christian beliefs. For example, the Gospels command us to baptize all nations in the name of the Father, and the Son, and the Holy Spirit (Mt 28:19). Are these three Gods? Of course not. But how can we talk about this so as not to imply that there are three Gods? Similarly, Jesus Christ is affirmed to be truly human and truly God. This appears to be contradictory; how do we make sense of this?

Therefore, in order to express the faith clearly, the early Church Fathers made use of philosophical language in order to correctly signify what Christians believe. Philosophical notions like nature and person, and substance and accident, were adopted and used in the formulation of the doctrines and creeds. Common theological terms like *consubstantial* and *transubstantiation* are constant reminders of how theology employs philosophy for articulating its truths.

Once the faith is articulated, however, it invites us to deepen our understanding by means of reasoning. Memorizing the Creed is not *understanding* the faith; what is needed is a rigorous rational analysis to construct a coherent body of doctrines. This is the work of *intellectus fidei*, or understanding the faith.[8] In fact, since humans have a natural drive to understand the world, they naturally seek to think deeply about that which they believe. This curiosity about the faith is epitomized in the classic definition of theology given to us by Saint Anselm (1033–1109): *fides quaerens intellectum*, or faith seeking understanding. But this understanding of the faith depends on philosophy, for philosophy defines the rules of human reasoning; it provides the principles by which we are able to argue from evidence to further conclusions. This is why the Church has been open to using different philosophies: inasmuch as different philosophies illuminate different aspects of human experience, theologians can continually draw on new ideas to deepen our understanding of the faith.[9]

The third way theology utilizes philosophy actually precedes these others. This is because philosophy, in discovering the most basic principles of reality, gives people a common knowledge of God even prior to faith. For

---

7 *Fides et Ratio*, 65.

8 *Fides et Ratio*, 66.

9 We note, however, that the use of new ideas must be an organic development of the traditional faith or else the new idea fails in its orthodoxy; see John Henry Newman, *An Essay on the Development of Christian Doctrine* (Notre Dame, Ind.: University of Notre Dame Press, 1989).

example, reason, properly used, can tell us that the world must have been created, and so there must be a Creator; moreover, in order to be the Creator, this being must be perfect. Thus, reason alone can prove the existence of a perfect God. (This argument is developed at length later in the book.) Proving truths like this is inestimably beneficial for preaching the Gospel, since knowing *something* about God is a necessary prerequisite to believing that God became flesh in the Incarnation. The tradition calls these truths about God that are knowable by reason "preambles to the faith" because they establish the rational foundations upon which are built the dogmas of the Gospel. In other words, philosophy makes God available through reason to all people. This knowledge provides the preconditions for all later considerations of God in terms of faith.[10]

From the start, then, Christians made use of the philosophies of their day to help make arguments in defense of the faith. Indeed, Augustine likens the use of pagan philosophy to the Israelites appropriating the treasures of the Egyptians:

> If those who are called philosophers, especially the Platonists, have said things which are indeed true and are well accommodated to our faith, they should not be feared; rather, what they have said should be taken from them as from unjust possessors and converted to our use. Just as the Egyptians had not only idols and grave burdens which the people of Israel detested and avoided, so also they had vases and ornaments of gold and silver and clothing which the Israelites took with them secretly when they fled, as if to put them to a better use.[11]

Thus, theology makes use of the wisdom of pagan philosophy, transforming it in the process, creating a Christian philosophy in service to theology. For this reason, in the Catholic tradition, faith is inextricably intertwined with the rational truths known by philosophy. As has been well said, "Faith and reason are like two wings on which the human spirit rises to the contemplation of truth."[12]

---

10 It must be noted that this purely rational knowledge of God is rather limited and subject to error and so needs to be perfected by revelation. I develop this point more fully in chapter 1.

11 Augustine, *On Christian Doctrine*, II.40.60. Thomas applies this analysis to Augustine himself (*ST* I.84.5): "Consequently whenever Augustine, who was imbued with the doctrines of the Platonists, found in their teaching anything consistent with faith, he adopted it: and those things which he found contrary to faith he amended."

12 *Fides et Ratio*, epigraph.

This relation of philosophy and theology is, in the end, providential. The use of philosophy for the faith is not only a historical necessity but in fact enriches the operation of both faith and reason. Pope Saint John Paul II describes their interaction as a kind of spiral in which the truths of one continually lift the other to a higher plane of understanding:

> In the light of these considerations, the relationship between theology and philosophy is best construed as a circle. Theology's source and starting-point must always be the word of God revealed in history, while its final goal will be an understanding of that word which increases with each passing generation. Yet, since God's word is Truth, the human search for truth—philosophy, pursued in keeping with its own rules—can only help to understand God's word better. . . . It is as if, moving between the twin poles of God's word and a better understanding of it, reason is offered guidance and is warned against paths which would lead it to stray from revealed Truth and to stray in the end from the truth pure and simple. Instead, reason is stirred to explore paths which of itself it would not even have suspected it could take. This circular relationship with the word of God leaves philosophy enriched, because reason discovers new and unsuspected horizons.[13]

CHARACTERISTICS OF A CATHOLIC PHILOSOPHY

The Church has always acknowledged that, because of the resplendent complexity of creation, it should employ a variety of philosophies. Augustine and Bonaventure make use of Plato; Pseudo-Dionysius exploits Plotinus; Aquinas "baptizes" Aristotle; Karol Wojtyła, before ascending to the papacy, adapts Husserl's phenomenology. Each of these adds to the treasury of Christian wisdom. John Paul II, drawing on his experience as a philosopher, affirms that "the Church has no philosophy of her own nor does she canonize any one particular philosophy in preference to others."[14] It must always be remembered that the truth of creation is inexhaustible and that there will always be innovative paths of inquiry that reveal something new about creation to the believer.

---

13 *Fides et Ratio*, 73. Some may object that as a handmaiden philosophy is utterly subordinated to theology. Yet John Paul II is careful to defend the legitimate autonomy of philosophy as a discipline; what he insists on, though, is that reason alone can never be wholly self-sufficient without the higher light of revelation (see *Fides et Ratio*, 75–79).

14 *Fides et Ratio*, 49.

Nevertheless, in order to be a faithful handmaid to theology, in order to attain the truth of creation and lead us to the Creator, we must recognize that not all philosophies are consonant with revelation. If a thinker's assumptions or methods are inimical to the truth, then any attempt to use that philosophy can only end up in debasing the faith.[15] Such was the fate, for example, of liberation theology, which tried to use Marxism, an atheistic and deterministic philosophy, to express Gospel truths.

I would suggest, then, that any Catholic philosophy must have three characteristics if it is to be a faithful handmaid. These characteristics guarantee that a thinker will be able to know reality as it is in order to come to knowledge of God through his creation.

The first characteristic is that it must accept the most fundamental rule of reason, the *principle of noncontradiction*: a thing cannot be and not-be simultaneously in the same respect.[16] With respect to philosophy, this means that a belief cannot be both true and false. A truth is always true, and so one truth can never contradict another truth. This is a guiding principle for Catholic thought, since the truths of reason can never contradict the truths of faith. The God who created the natural world and gave people reason to know it is the same God who reveals himself to us in Scripture. So, what is true according to reason must coincide with what is true according to faith. There cannot be, as some medieval thinkers suggested, a "double-truth," where faith and reason simply contradict each other: faith being true from the perspective of religion and reason being true from the perspective of philosophy.[17] This idea that a belief can simultaneously be both true and false is impossible, for it is an incoherent vision of the world.

Consequently, any Catholic philosophy has to be able to accommodate truths of faith, especially the existence of God, the immortality of the soul, and the objectivity of morality. It is for this reason that Christian thinkers, from

---

15 Thus, the passage cited in the previous footnote continues: "Yet history shows that philosophy—especially modern philosophy—has taken wrong turns and fallen into error. . . . [It] is the Magisterium's duty to respond clearly and strongly when controversial philosophical opinions threaten right understanding of what has been revealed, and when false and partial theories which sow the seed of serious error, confusing the pure and simple faith of the People of God, begin to spread more widely."

16 I further elucidate the principle of noncontradiction in chapter 3.

17 This notion was revived by the great evolutionary biologist Stephen Jay Gould in his feckless attempt to resolve the so-called war between religion and science. He insisted they were "nonoverlapping magisteria," denoting that each is true in its own field but this in the end simply denies the principle of noncontradiction in cases where they really do conflict with one another. See Stephen Jay Gould, "Nonoverlapping Magisteria," *Natural History* 106 (March 1997): 16–22.

Justin Martyr and Augustine to Aquinas and Wojtyła, always *adapt* a philosophy as much as they *adopt* it. Since this adaptation conforms the philosophy to a more ultimate truth, that philosophy is elevated in the process. In light of this principle, it is obvious that a philosophy can contradict the faith only when it fails to use reason correctly; as Thomas argues, "If anything . . . is found in the sayings of the philosophers contrary to faith, this is not philosophy but rather an abuse of philosophy arising from faulty reasoning."[18]

The second characteristic of a Catholic philosophy is that it must be *realist*. That is, it must accept that there is a stable order of reality that people can know directly as the basis for both science and moral reasoning. In other words, we are really in contact with the world as the foundation for our principles of being, truth, and goodness. This rejects the widespread modern assumption that, because we have no unmediated access to reality, people are responsible for determining what is true and good. This modern position is called, broadly, *idealism*, not because it presents an ideal world, but because "reality" is the result of our own thinking and ideas, as opposed to reflecting the objective world.

Denying our direct access to reality is related to an array of problematic philosophical positions. If the true and the good arise from our thinking and not reality itself, then this may result, on the one hand, in *relativism*, the idea that each person's perspective defines truth and goodness for that individual. On the other hand, it may also lead to *skepticism*, which asserts that truth cannot be attained about anything at all. These positions are inherently problematic, because they evacuate life of meaning: if we can never know any truth as objective or be certain about the goodness of any act, the act of choosing is pointless, since it would never make any difference.

The most perennially pernicious of these philosophical assumptions, however, is *nominalism*. Realist philosophy arises from wonder at the intelligibility and goodness of the world, an awe that drives reason to discover the source of truth and goodness. Nominalism assumes that there is no objective order in creation. It reflects not a wonder or awe at cosmic goodness but rather a pessimistic doubt about reality that demands that people impose order on an otherwise unintelligible creation. This entails that the concepts of truth and goodness are ultimately arbitrary constructs the philosopher creates to prescribe an order for a fractious world. From the perspective of a realist Catholic philosophy, denying the inherent order and

18 *BDT* II.3.

intelligibility of nature makes nominalism a sort of "universal acid" that disintegrates the coherence of philosophy in every area: metaphysics, epistemology, ethics, politics, and aesthetics. Because it assumes the world has no intelligible order, any attempt to find meaning in human existence is in the end futile.[19] Pope Francis, in an address to the United Nations,[20] found the source of many of the world's problems to be a "declarationist nominalism"—the idea that a person believes he can change the nature and moral status of things simply by declaring them to be what he wishes. For this reason, nominalist assumptions are a constant foil for the realism of the perennial philosophy in the chapters to follow.

The third characteristic of a Catholic philosophy is that it must recognize that creation is exuberantly complex, so philosophy has to be sufficiently nuanced to capture this complexity. An adequate philosophy, therefore, will always oppose *reductionism*, the notion that all of reality can be reduced to one limited principle. For example, many modern scientists assume that the universe is made only of atoms, a point that theists must deny since God is immaterial; yet we also deny that God is the *only* being in the universe, as pantheists assert, for this deprives creatures of real independent activity. Therefore, a Catholic vision must encompass the reality of both atoms and God; it has to accept both physics and theology without running into contradiction. C. S. Lewis cleverly labelled reductionism as "nothing but-tery,"[21] as in "reality is composed of atoms and *nothing but* atoms." Lewis nicely exposes the dogmatic impulse behind reductionist theories: in assuming one principle alone is sufficient to explain reality, they are forced to ignore or explain away all the evidence that indicates its true complexity.

The problem of reductionism—favoring one principle or explanation to the exclusion of others—is so pervasive that the template for my own arguments is to frame Catholic truth as a response to the errors of overly simplistic philosophies. Each chapter addresses a different area of philosophy in which it is shown that the reductive answers of other philosophies,

---

19 Richard Weaver famously traces all modern ills to nominalism, for it undermines the authoritative nature of truth and goodness, making each person authoritative for himself—as he puts it, each person is his own priest and his own professor. See Richard Weaver, *Ideas Have Consequences* (Chicago: University of Chicago Press, 1984), 2–3. I explain nominalism more completely in chapters 2 and 3.

20 On September 25, 2015; available at http://w2.vatican.va/content/francesco/en/speeches/2015/september/documents/papa-francesco_20150925_onu-visita.html.

21 See the essay "Transposition" in *Weight of Glory and Other Addresses,* rev. ed. (New York: Harper One, 2001), 113–15.

while true in part, are nonetheless inadequate because they fail to account for all the evidence of experience. The Catholic position, by contrast, will be a "both-and" position, avoiding reductionism in order to account for the complexity of the reality we experience. Catholic philosophy can be seen to be learning from theology here, for since the time of Nicaea the Church has acknowledged the irreducible complexity of the truth. While it would have been easier to affirm that Christ is *either* God or human, in truth he is both; it would be easier to affirm God is *either* One or Three, but in truth he is both. It would be easier to talk about only nature or grace, but the fact is that they work together. The truth of reality requires that we have an expansive vision that accommodates all the facts; only this both-and approach can do justice to a cosmos whose abundance induces awe and wonder in thoughtful people.

It is for this reason that the philosophy of Thomas Aquinas presents itself as the most adequate voice for articulating the Catholic tradition. Embodying the collective wisdom of the tradition of the perennial philosophy (which I sometimes shorthand as the *perennial tradition*), he had a unique ability to synthesize the insights of other philosophers and to balance the both-and claims of whatever issue he was considering. His creative genius and insightful reasoning are well summarized by G. K. Chesterton:

> The Church is more immortally important than the State; but the State has its rights, for all that. This Christian duality had always been implicit, as in Christ's distinction between God and Caesar, or the dogmatic distinction between the natures of Christ. But St. Thomas has the glory of having seized this double thread as the clue to a thousand things; and thereby created the only creed in which the saints can be sane. . . . St. Thomas exalted God without lowering Man; he exalted Man without lowering Nature. Therefore, he made a cosmos of common sense; *terra viventium*; a land of the living. His philosophy, like his theology, is that of common sense. He does not torture the brain with desperate attempts to explain existence by explaining it away.[22]

OUTLINE OF THE BOOK

This antireductionist strategy provides the structure of each chapter. After introducing the problem to be investigated, I present two positions, drawn from prominent philosophers in the Western tradition, postulating answers

---

22 G. K. Chesterton, "St. Thomas Aquinas" in *The Spectator* (February 27, 1932).

that are in some way reductive and that pull in opposite directions. I then reply by articulating the "both-and" position from Thomas that integrates and synthesizes the best insights of the opposing resolutions. I demonstrate that this integrative position is the best answer, because it alone accounts for the true breadth of human experience.[23]

This procedure allows me to show how Thomas would engage the most important figures in the history of philosophy, especially seminal figures of modern thought like Descartes, Hume, and Kant. The ideas of these modern thinkers permeate contemporary secular society, and, while containing much truth, because their assumptions in some way obscure the breadth of reality, they have become impediments for the reception of the Catholic truth. This engagement, then, is critical for restoring the perennial philosophy to her proper place as handmaid to theology.

In order to properly defend the principles of a realist philosophy, the order of the chapters themselves must be determined by the order of reality. The order of reality, in its most fundamental principles, is discovered by considering the *transcendental properties*. The transcendentals are the necessary characteristics of everything that exists, and so they are the primary concepts under which people think about the nature of reality. (I address the transcendentals more fully in chapter 1.) These properties are the following: being, truth, goodness, and beauty. Accordingly, the discussion begins with *what is* (being) and how *being is known* (true) and progresses to what *should be done* (good) and what *should be made* (beauty). The book concludes by showing how these properties reveal their eternal source and cause, God, who is Being, Truth, Goodness, and Beauty.

Beginning with the fact that philosophy is handmaid to theology, chapter 1 addresses the relationship between faith and reason as understood in the Catholic tradition. The proper relationship is critical, for many religious believers disdain reason and argue that faith alone is sufficient; in contrast, secularists not only reject faith, but they often reject any use of reason apart from science. Both of these extremes—fideism and scientism—eviscerate the intellectual life by illicitly reducing the range of reason and fragmenting our experience. As Jesuit philosopher Norris Clarke comments, "With no integrating vision of reality and human life as a whole to balance off this

---

23 This is in conscious imitation of the disputation method employed by Thomas himself, as exemplified in the *Summa Theologiae*. By presenting the partial truths of opponents first, one can incorporate these insights while avoiding the problems they encounter.

piecemeal approach, we tend to become fragmented people, with our lives 'in pieces.'" [24] Philosophy is the solution to this fragmentation of life. Instead of seeing knowledge as a hodgepodge of unrelated facts, a philosophical understanding of reason integrates the truths of science and faith into a coherent vision of reality leading to an orderly way of life. Moreover, this rational understanding of the order and goodness of creation prepares the mind to receive the Gospel, so that the faith completes what reason is incapable of knowing. In this way, nature is perfected by grace. Thus, we need both science and religion, both faith and reason, if we are to realize the human capacity for wisdom.

Philosophy, like any field of study, has its own vocabulary and methods. Consequently, chapter 2 is a brief history of Greek philosophy as encompassing the basic principles that would be developed by the Christian tradition as the common heritage of the perennial philosophy.

Chapter 3 begins our analysis of the specifically Catholic philosophical tradition. The most basic lesson of philosophy—one that in fact trips up overly subtle minds—is that, apart from being, there is only non-being; however, since non-being is *nothing*, we cannot say anything, or even coherently think, about it. Therefore, everything we know must fall under the notion of being. For this reason, being is the first thing we study, since this idea of reality establishes the parameters for all other discussions. This branch of philosophy is known as *metaphysics*, the study of being inasmuch as it is being. But one thing that is obvious about being is that, while all beings are similar in having existence, each being must be distinct from all the rest. In other words, being is simultaneously one and many. The problematic reductions in metaphysics arise from accepting one truth so as to minimize or exclude the other. Either the philosopher emphasizes the sameness of being (a position known as *monism*) and reduces all differences to a mere illusion or he emphasizes the difference between beings (a position known as *pluralism*), which ultimately makes the universe unknowable because there is no common principle of intelligibility. Because a philosopher's idea of being is the foundation for all subsequent philosophical analyses, these inadequate theories of being become the wellspring for problems permeating every field of philosophy. In order to account for the obvious truth that beings are both similar and different simultaneously, we need to

---

24 W. Norris Clarke, *The One and the Many: A Contemporary Thomistic Metaphysics* (Notre Dame, Ind.: University of Notre Dame Press, 2001), 3.

employ Thomas's doctrine of the analogy of being as caused by a common act of existence.

This analysis of being also inevitably points to the need for a source of being, which is the philosophical notion of God. While other chapters will rely on this initial argument for God's existence, only in chapter 8 is God's existence and nature explored in depth.

Corresponding to the question of being is how we know this being. Therefore, chapter 4 takes up the part of philosophy known as *epistemology*, the theory of knowledge. The subject of epistemology is the apprehension of being in terms of its truth. Since we know reality by sense-experience and by reason, the reductive extremes are those philosophies that limit truth to reason alone (*rationalism*) or sense-experience alone (*empiricism*). Neither of these can capture the complete intelligibility of reality, and so Thomas would insist that we employ both, an approach called *realism*. Incidentally, since modern thought diverges from the perennial philosophy by giving precedence to epistemology over metaphysics, this chapter critically assesses many of the foundational presumptions underlying modern philosophy, including those of Immanuel Kant.

We then complete our discussion of human capacities by examining theories of human nature in chapter 5. Many thinkers have wanted to reduce a person to being a soul or mind alone, marginalizing the incarnational reality of the body (*dualism*); more scientific thinkers want to eliminate the soul as a primitive myth, leaving the body alone (*materialism*). However, Thomas argues that a human being is the intimate union of body and soul, for we are both animal and spiritual. This analysis will, moreover, confirm the scriptural teaching that people have a unique dignity and destiny not shared by other animals.

After establishing the reality of human nature, we then turn to what people ought to do in order to realize their potential in acting and making. In acting, we seek to become good people. Thus, chapter 6 is the study of ethics whose topic is the good. Some ethical theories tend to view people only as animals and see them as being motivated by desire alone; this reduces the good to happiness in terms of pleasure (*utilitarianism*). Other theories view people as an intellect motivated by reason alone, which reduces morality to a dutiful obedience to a moral law so that happiness is irrelevant (*deontology*). An adequate notion of the good includes both, that only by following the moral law can we attain happiness. This is the natural law tradition of Thomas.

In the last part of chapter 6, we consider the special kind of goodness associated with another kind of human activity: making objects. While we make tools to be used, our most significant productions are those things that have no use but are made simply because they are to be enjoyed as beautiful. This fact allows us to consider controversies about the nature of beauty as an objective reality and the duty of art to embody it.

Chapter 7 extends this analysis of the good, for we can only attain happiness in the context of human community. Thus, we consider the principles of political philosophy, that which is good for the community. Since an individual exists in a larger community, some err by subordinating the individual to the ends of the state (*collectivism*); others react to this and say that the role of the state is to guarantee the unbounded freedom of the individual (*liberalism*). But since the human individual *must* live in community for personal perfection, we need to balance the ends of both the community and the person by recognizing the spiritual nature of the common good. This is the school of Thomistic personalism.

Finally, having scrutinized the presence of being, truth, goodness, and beauty in creation, in chapter 8 we turn our attention to the Creator. While the theologian starts off by accepting the existence of God, the philosopher can only know God on the basis of the evidence from nature. This evidence points to the need for a Creator who is outside of the world, or *transcendent*; yet, if we are to know God, he must be present in the world in some fashion, or *immanent*. Simplistic theories reduce God in one way or the other: either he is in the world, but then he cannot be the cause of it; or, he is outside the world, but then he cannot be known, an ignorance that leads to agnosticism and finally atheism. Therefore, we need to accept both and see that God is the primary cause of nature in giving being to the world, but that his causal activity is necessarily evident in nature itself.

The final chapter is an application of these philosophical principles to the important problem of evil. The fact of evil has always been the greatest impediment to faith in a good and omnipotent God. The Christian response to the problem of evil is convincing, but it must draw from all the areas of philosophy we have discussed. The problem of evil, then, presents a good opportunity to see how philosophy can solve a real-life problem that people face every day.

CONCLUDING APOLOGETIC POSTSCRIPT

Clearly, each of these chapters necessarily is brief and introductory. While each of these topics deserves to be addressed at length on its own, I aim to demonstrate the coherence of wisdom by presenting them together in light of common metaphysical principles. Thus, our discussions are highly condensed and unavoidably simplified, and there are many important philosophers and ideas who will not be discussed in this book.[25] I also acknowledge that my analyses of various thinkers—and even of Thomas—would be challenged by other philosophers. Therefore, it is sincerely hoped that the reader uses this book to *begin* the study of philosophy and not as the final word.

Second, the Catholic tradition in philosophy is, indeed, catholic, inclusive of many diverse perspectives and schools. However, I focus on Thomas Aquinas because of his unique ability to synthesize and lucidly order the insights of his predecessors (both pagan and Catholic) in light of principles that continue to be fruitful in philosophical investigations.[26] This book does not claim to be a systematic presentation of the work of Aquinas.[27] I draw on Thomas as the best representative of that tradition whose principles pre-

---

25 I must acknowledge, however, the absence of the dominant school in contemporary philosophy, analytic philosophy. *Analytic philosophy* is a highly technical approach developed in the twentieth century focused on discerning the logical structures of language and arguments. The problem with analytic philosophy is that its method makes its research of purely academic interest, utterly unrelated to the search for wisdom as traditionally understood. In particular, I see three problems with its approach: it is nominalist (it argues about words and not reality; as has been noted, it is not talking about the world but only talking about talking), ahistorical (it ignores the contexts that make philosophical arguments meaningful), and anti-sapiential (it eschews the larger questions of being that make life meaningful). The puzzles analytic philosophy tries to solve are those philosophers have created for themselves; they are not the philosophical problems that have driven humankind in its search for wisdom for the past three millennia. As an illustration of this point: W. V. O. Quine, longtime chair of philosophy at Harvard and perhaps the greatest analytic philosopher of the postwar period, rejected all but the most drily technical use of philosophy, opining that the student who "major[ed] in philosophy primarily for spiritual consolation is misguided and is probably not a very good student." Cited in Bruce Kuklick, *A History of Philosophy in America: 1720–2000* (Oxford: Clarendon Press, 2001), 267.

Nevertheless, because analytic philosophy *is* the dominant approach in the Anglosphere, many Thomistic thinkers have engaged it directly and extensively, with varying degrees of sympathy for that approach; see, for example, the work of G. E. M. Anscombe, Brian Davies, Edward Feser, John Haldane, Anthony Kenny, Fergus Kerr, Gyula Klima, David Oderberg, and Eleonore Stump, among many others.

26 See Leo XIII's Encyclical Letter *Aeterni Patris* (August 4, 1879), 17–18, where he explains Thomas's eminence in terms of how his thought contains the "seeds of almost infinite truth."

27 For a list of some notable surveys of Thomas's thought, see the suggestions for further reading at the end of this chapter.

vent the thinker from falling into error due to oversimplification. The great Thomist Étienne Gilson compellingly explains the fruitfulness of this approach:

> All that is true in any other philosophy can be justified by the principles of Thomas Aquinas, and there is no other philosophy that it is possible to profess without having to ignore, or reject, some conclusions that are true in the light of these principles. Speaking in a more familiar way, one can be a Thomist without losing the truth of any other philosophy, whereas one cannot subscribe to any other philosophy without losing some of the truth available to the disciple of Thomas Aquinas. It is therefore of capital importance to concentrate on the meditation and ceaseless consideration of the principles.[28]

As Thomas himself noted, a small error in the beginning leads to a big error in the end.[29] If the world today seems to be embracing big errors, it is likely due to the fact that our philosophical principles are inadequate, reducing and distorting truth and goodness so that they no longer reflect the nature of reality. We must therefore rediscover the right principles to correct all the errors, small and large, that impede us from embracing the fullness of human existence.[30] This book is a humble attempt to point out what those principles are, for the wisdom of the perennial philosophy is never foreign to a human being in search of truth.

Accordingly, this book tries to establish that being is the only adequate foundation for our idea of reality; that reason's insight into the causes of being is the only adequate understanding of truth; and, that reason's insights into the natural dynamism of being are the only adequate basis for what ought to be done as good. From all these it follows that the source of being—and by extension the source of truth and the source of goodness—is naturally the supreme object of contemplation for humankind, for in light of that alone do all other truths attain full meaning. It is for this contemplative act, finally, that we exist.

---

28 Étienne Gilson, *Elements of Christian Philosophy* (Garden City, N.Y.: Doubleday and Company, 1960), 278.

29 *OBE* prologue.

30 Saint John Paul II recognizes this problem with contemporary philosophy in *Fides et Ratio*, 81: "To be consonant with the word of God, philosophy needs first of all to recover its *sapiential dimension* as a search for the ultimate and overarching meaning of life."

FURTHER READING

I recognize that a number of the positions I defend, including my interpretations of Thomas Aquinas, are contested, even for those within the Catholic tradition of philosophy. Therefore, at the end of every chapter, I provide a brief list of those secondary sources that most inform the positions defended in that chapter or are representative discussions of the topic. They include a mix of introductory and more advanced discussions. A complete list of references is in the bibliography.

Brock, Stephen L. *The Philosophy of Saint Thomas Aquinas: A Sketch*. Eugene, Ore.: Cascade Books, 2015.

Davies, Brian. *The Thought of Thomas Aquinas*. Oxford: Clarendon Press, 1992.

Gilson, Étienne. *The Christian Philosophy of St. Thomas Aquinas*. Translated by L. K. Shook. Notre Dame, Ind.: University of Notre Dame Press, 1994.

Pieper, Josef. *Guide to Thomas Aquinas*. Translated by Richard and Clara Winston. San Francisco: Ignatius Press, 1991.

Torrell, Jean-Pierre. *The Person and His Work*. Vol. 1 of *Saint Thomas Aquinas*. Translated by Robert Royal. Washington, D.C.: The Catholic University Press of America, 1996.

Wippel, John F. *The Metaphysical Thought of Thomas Aquinas: From Finite Being to Uncreated Being*. Washington, D.C.: The Catholic University of America Press, 2000.

Chapter 1

Wisdom and Faith:
The Relation between Reason and Revelation

THE PROBLEM

The importance of philosophy to the Catholic tradition is trenchantly illustrated by the fact that Thomas Aquinas begins his massive *Summa Theologiae* with a discussion of the relation between faith and reason.[1] Somewhat surprisingly, however, the saint and doctor of the Church does not assume the validity of faith and question the need for philosophy. On the contrary, he asks whether in addition to philosophy any other knowledge is needed. In other words, philosophy, reason's ability to attain wisdom, appears to be so complete a knowledge that not even faith can add to it. Thomas's reply is to show that true wisdom, the highest knowledge available to humankind, requires religious faith to complete what is known in philosophy. Thus, philosophy and revelation are seen to work in harmony with one another.

Today, both faith and reason, and the relation between them, are viewed very differently. One popular position argues that faith is not knowledge at all; it is a personal opinion about things that are simply unknowable, like God and the true nature of justice. This position defines knowledge very narrowly, for it presumes that science alone constitutes what we can know, thereby displacing the vague speculations of philosophy. Thus, adherents of this position would insist that Thomas's question ought to now be framed as whether in addition to science—empirical science, like physics, chemistry, and biology—any other knowledge is needed. Their reply would be that science is the sole reliable pathway to knowledge because it can prove all its claims through observation. This position entails that, for something to be known, it must be reducible to science and its method of experimentation. It also implies this corollary: if something cannot be reduced to the

1 *ST* I.1.

scientific method, then it cannot be known and so must be mere opinion. This supposed fate has driven many thinkers to try to make their own field more "scientific." Economists, psychologists, and even artists have tried to justify their ideas in terms of scientific theories like evolution or neuro-chemistry. For example, we are told that our ideas of God and justice are merely the result of a chemical reaction in the brain that arose because of natural selection. This position, that science is the sole source of certain knowledge, is known as *scientism*.

Others react against this scientism. Surely, they say, God and justice are real in themselves; for, if they were the result of chemical reactions, they would be meaningless fictions. But, since they are inherently significant ideas that are not knowable by science, there must be a way other than science by which we are able to know them. One obvious source of this knowledge is religious faith, since religion is the source for transcendent truths like God and moral judgments like justice. Moreover, since this religious faith is utterly independent of the scientific method, our knowledge of these truths is impervious to rational investigation or criticism. In the end, they say, we trust God more than we can trust reason and science. This position, that the most important truths are known by faith alone, is called *fideism* (from the Latin word for faith, *fides*).

And so we have today the so-called war of science and religion, implacable enemies locked in irresolvable conflict. On the one hand, God is not observable, so science denies his existence (and, indeed, the existence of all transcendent values); on the other hand, while science discovers facts, believers hold that those facts cannot be trusted if they appear to contradict the ultimate truths of religion. Since these positions lack a common perspective, one side will never be able to convince the other.

It is clear that if we are to resolve this conflict, we need to find a common ground between the two. This common ground can be discovered if we recognize that both scientism and fideism err by simplistically reducing all knowledge to only one method. The problem is that the magnificence of reality can never be reduced to one limited perspective. While scientism and fideism are wrong, it is equally obvious that both science and faith are indispensable in themselves. What is needed is some way to harmonize the two approaches, a rational worldview that can unite the truths of science and of faith into a coherent whole. Here we see that Thomas was onto something, since this is precisely the job of philosophy.

Indeed, philosophy is necessary because it provides those rational principles that unite and justify all other beliefs about the world. Philosophy unites all our beliefs by investigating the foundational principles of being and truth so that the world, in all its diversity, makes coherent sense. Philosophy investigates what it means to assert that something *is*, that it really exists in continuity with all other beings. Philosophy also shows that one truth can never contradict another truth. Therefore, all the sciences have to harmonize with one another: physics cannot contradict math and the discoveries of biology cannot violate the laws of chemistry. More significantly, though, the insights of science and of religion, as well as of art and literature, must all ultimately point to a coherent understanding of reality. It is philosophy that provides this encompassing framework for knowledge.

Equally significant is the fact that, in discovering the principles underlying our diverse ways of knowing, philosophy also justifies those beliefs. The ultimate principles of reality—being and truth—establish the criteria for evaluating the reasonableness of beliefs. In this way, philosophy can provide a corrective to ideas in science and religion that contradict the fundamental nature of reality. Furthermore, our beliefs need to be justified in this way, for without this there is no reason to believe them. A rational person has to find some degree of certainty in the way he thinks about the world. Our worldview holds together only under the light of philosophical analysis.

Because human beings philosophize to unite and justify our beliefs, all people must have a philosophy, whether they know it or not, for without it that person's mental life would be incoherent and meaningless. The problem with so many people today is that they are simply not fully aware of the philosophy they use to structure their beliefs.

WHAT IS PHILOSOPHY?

To understand what philosophy is, it is helpful to begin with its etymology. *Philosophy* comes from the Greek, and it means "the love of wisdom" (*phil-* means love; *sophia* is wisdom). Notice, first, that where other sciences are "-ologies," the study of something, philosophy is a love, a needed and profoundly desired kind of knowledge. This difference is explained by its object: wisdom. We are curious about all things, and so we want to study; but in order to live well, in order that our lives not be wasted, we need wisdom.

But what is wisdom? We all have an idea of what wisdom is, but many find it difficult to precisely define. Clearly it is some sort of knowledge, but not all knowledge is wisdom: people who know a great deal of trivia are often not wise; our society is not ruled by *Jeopardy!* champions. Unlike trivia, wisdom must be, in some way, a practical sort of knowledge because it helps guide you through life. Yet not all practical knowledge counts as wisdom: plumbing and auto mechanics are great things to know, but no one would say they constitute wisdom. Wisdom also is a knowledge that is hard to attain: the comic strip cliché of the ancient hermit living atop a mountain exemplifies this, and we value the wisdom of those who have a great deal of life experience.

Maybe we can find a clearer answer by looking at the object of wisdom. What is it the wise person knows that sets him apart from other people, even very knowledgeable people like scientists? What the Greeks saw is that wisdom is knowing the highest causes of reality, what Aristotle calls the "first principles" of reality.[2] First principles are the ultimate explanations as to why the world is the way it is. All our inquiries are in the end directed to finding a first principle, for if we know the ultimate explanation for all things, we implicitly know everything—just without the details that the other sciences give us.[3]

Philosophical inquiry, exemplified in metaphysics, is the natural consummation of the fact that all human beings by nature desire to know.[4] It is natural for human beings to be curious. But what do we desire to know? Above all else, we want to know why. If I am sick, I do not simply want to know what my symptoms are, I want to know why I have those symptoms. I want to know the cause or explanation why I am suffering from those symptoms. In fact, other people will likely share that curiosity—witness the popularity of hospital dramas on television. Similarly, if my computer is malfunctioning, the IT department might tell me how to fix it; but I really want to know why the problem occurred so I can deal with it myself in the future. Humans, therefore, in asking *why* are looking for a causal explanation for the events that we experience. Behind every event there must be some causal principle that explains why it happened in that way. Knowing these causes allows us to make sense of the world, both as individuals and as a race united in investigation: instead of accepting what happens as an inexplicable mystery, knowing the causes gives us an understanding and certainty about events.

In fact, not just philosophy but all sciences seek these sorts of causal

---

2 Aristotle, *Metaphysics* I.1 (981b27). Significantly, for the perennial philosophy, wisdom is also a habit (*Nicomachean Ethics* VI.1 and VI.6); that is, it is a constant disposition to approach the world through the prism of this principle, so that it brings unity and intelligible order to all experiences.

3 Aristotle, *Metaphysics* I.2 (982a10).

4 Aristotle, *Metaphysics* I.1 (980a22).

explanations. (*Scientia* is just the Latin word for knowledge, as opposed to opinion.) Medicine asks why I am sick, and, once it discovers the bacterial parasite, it can then seek to cure the illness. Physics and astronomy ask why the planets orbit the sun, and, having grasped the law of gravity, they can calculate eclipses well into the future. Indeed, while Darwin's discovery of evolution by natural selection was a brilliant inference, it was difficult to accept until Mendel's discovery of genetic inheritance could explain why it occurs.

Philosophy, though, seeks a causal explanation on a different level. Philosophy seeks the first causes or ultimate explanations. Instead of asking about specific kinds of beings, like biology or astronomy, it asks about everything. It asks the highest questions and seeks the most universal answers: Why does anything exist at all? Why does the world function with such regularity and order? How are we able to have any knowledge of the world? Why do certain things make people happy? Philosophy, then, unlike other sciences, is not just problem-solving; rather, it is finding the meaning of the universe so that those other problems are worth solving. If we did not recognize that our existence is orderly and meaningful, there would be no reason to solve problems of medicine or physics.

These are obviously a special type of question, but one that is natural and unavoidable for the human race. Plato and Aristotle, the founders of Western philosophy, agree in pointing out that philosophy begins in wonder: wonder at the existence, beauty, and intelligibility of the cosmos.[5] There is something awe-inspiring about the whole of reality; philosophy is the attempt to translate this awe into understanding by means of rational analysis.

THE NECESSARY USELESSNESS OF PHILOSOPHY

At this point, many pragmatically minded people might question the usefulness of philosophy: what good is all this wondering? After all, the other sciences—medicine and physics and computer science—are useful because they solve problems. Should not philosophy be held to the same standard? Indeed, philosophy majors in college (including this author) have been ridiculed for the apparent uselessness of their studies. (As one old joke goes, the engineering student learns to ask, "How does it work?" The philosophy major learns to ask, "Do you want fries with that?") There are three answers to this, each of which is crucial for appreciating the significance of philosophy.

---

5 See Plato, *Theaetetus* (155d1–4), and Aristotle, *Metaphysics* I.2 (982b12–28).

First, the idea that knowledge must be useful in some purely pragmatic sense is an idea that stems from the seventeenth century, especially in the writings of Francis Bacon (1561–1626). Bacon called his philosophical project "The Great Reconstruction" of knowledge and summed up his goal this way: "Human knowledge and human power meet in one. . . . Towards the effecting of works, all that man can do is to put together or put asunder natural bodies."[6] This idea that knowledge is power over the natural world represents a great shift in humankind's relation to nature. While there are obvious benefits to gaining greater control of nature—disease, hunger, and poverty have all been enormously reduced in modernity—it is nevertheless true that modern thinkers[7] tend to ignore ancient wisdom as if it were simply irrelevant. Prior to Bacon's time, thinkers believed that wisdom was found in accepting the way nature actually is and in subordinating our desires to that reality. As Jacques Maritain observed, for life to be meaningful, "What we need is not truths that serve us but a truth we may serve."[8] With modernity, on the contrary, knowledge is seen to lie in the ability to bend nature to our will.[9] Replacing theology as the highest kinds of knowledge are those that give us the greatest control over nature, like atomic physics or genetics. Each chapter will discuss in detail why this modern turn is problematic, but at this point I simply note that for the perennial philosophy there is no need for knowledge to be restricted to that which is useful in providing control of the environment.

Second, even Aristotle admits that philosophy is useless, but that it retains its value nonetheless. He says, "All the sciences, indeed, are more necessary that this, but none is better."[10] The other sciences are more necessary because we cannot survive without them. For example, we need agriculture and mathematics and architecture and engineering if we are going to live in a civilized fashion. If these sciences are successful, we no longer

---

6 Francis Bacon, *Novum Organum* (1620), bk. 1, aphorisms 3–4. Across the Channel, seventeen years later, René Descartes encouraged a similar shift: knowledge will "make ourselves, as it were, the lords and masters of nature" (*Discourse on Method* VI, 62).

7 The era of modern philosophy is traditionally understood to have begun about the year 1600. For a timeline of philosophers discussed in this book, including divisions into standards eras (ancient, medieval, modern, contemporary), see the first appendix.

8 Jacques Maritain, *Distinguish to Unite, or The Degrees of Knowledge*, trans. Gerald B. Phelan. (Notre Dame, Ind.: University of Notre Dame Press, 1995), 4.

9 This is why theology is no longer seen to be the queen of the sciences, for theology is ultimately about accepting a power greater than ourselves that must be obeyed.

10 *Metaphysics* I.2 (983a10).

have to struggle to survive. But this success would then raise a very different problem: what should we do with free time, with leisure, so as to not waste it? Because we are curious, in our free time we would naturally begin to wonder about the bigger questions and find the meaning of life. For this reason, Aristotle says philosophy is the fruit of leisure.[11]

To fully appreciate this point, we need to understand what leisure really is. This is something our own society has great problems with, not unrelated to our neglect of philosophy. Leisure can be defined in contrast to work. We have to work in order to get those things we need to live. This is farming, or building, or practicing medicine, or going to war; these provide food, shelter, health, and peace. Because there is a certain amount of pain involved in work, we do it only because we have to; in fact, the word for *work* in many European languages is associated with pain or even torture.[12] In contrast to this labor, free time or leisure is glorious: we have everything we need, so we do something simply because it is good in itself. For this reason, true leisure cannot simply be rest or amusement,[13] since we rest only so that we might be able to work some more. If leisure were simply rest, life would be a vicious circle since it would have no point other than work. The idea of "working for the weekend," where we play so that we can work again on Monday, is a life bereft of purpose. (This is—perhaps—one explanation for the high rates of depression in industrial society.) If life is to have meaning—if there is some point to all the struggle of work—then there has to be something other than work that is done for its own sake because it is simply good.

What are these things that are good in themselves? Friendship and familial love are obvious, but we also like to read and learn, enjoy art and music, and simply celebrate the goodness of creation with holiday (holy-days or the Sabbath or other days set aside to worship God) observances.[14] Another of

---

11 *Metaphysics* I.1 (981b20–25).

12 Hannah Arendt lists a series of sobering examples in *The Human Condition* (Chicago: University of Chicago Press, 1958), 48n39 and 80n3.

13 Aristotle, *Nicomachean Ethics* X.6 (1176b28–1177a1): "Happiness, therefore, does not lie in amusement; it would, indeed, be strange if the end were amusement, and one were to take trouble and suffer hardship all one's life in order to amuse oneself. . . . Now to exert oneself and work for the sake of amusement seems silly and utterly childish. . . . Relaxation, then, is not an end; for it is taken for the sake of activity."

14 The inability to enjoy the gratuitous goodness of creation is the sin of *acedia*, or spiritual sloth, which wallows in self-interest rather than recognizing the incomprehensible blessing of the gift of existence itself. Acedia can be seen to be the sin motivating the culture of death. One philosopher described the debilitating effects of acedia in this way: "The thing's authentic otherness

these basic goods is philosophy, something we do naturally because we have a drive to know why, to understand the universe. Thus, it is true that in a way philosophy is useless, but as Aristotle insists, there is no science that is better because it is the activity we pursue when nothing else needs to be done.[15]

My third reply to the accusation that philosophy is irrelevant today because it is useless is to insist that, despite its apparent uselessness, knowing these highest truths is actually the most important thing we can know. Thomas Aquinas defines the wise man—the philosopher—as one who, by knowing the highest truths, can put all things in their correct order.[16] Understanding the cause of the universe, knowing why all things are the way they are, allows us to place man in right relation to all other creatures and, more importantly, to God as Creator. Knowing the correct order of all things allows us to properly assess our experience and evaluate information. It is practical but on a completely different level than other kinds of knowledge. The daily news is obsessed with economics and politics; they are important, but to assume man exists simply to make and consume things or to engage in pointlessly perfervid debate is to misunderstand both man and the true place of economics and politics. Knowing the correct order of things empowers us to live life as we ought to. In short, philosophy makes a good life possible. In this way, philosophy is the most useful science.

FIRST PRINCIPLES

Philosophy, then, in seeking ultimate explanations, does not investigate any specific area of creation. That is what each of the sciences do. For example, physics studies the world in terms of fundamental laws and forces, while chemistry studies it in terms of molecular structure, and biology in terms

---

is obscured, for when objects are forced to stand over against us before submitting to us, their interiority, goodness, and beauty are vacated. . . . Objects become beautiful if they please us, according to our subjective taste, rather than demanding our delight as a matter of justice; objects become good if they serve us, according to our subjective purposes, rather than demand our willing them in keeping with God's own judgment and instruction." R. J. Snell: *Acedia: Metaphysical Boredom in an Empire of Desire* (Kettering, Ohio: Angelico Press, 2015), 83.

15 The argument in this paragraph is a very terse summary of Josef Pieper, *Leisure, the Basis of Culture,* trans. Gerald Malsbary (South Bend, Ind.: St. Augustine's Press, 1998). As Pieper points out, this contemplative appreciation of the goodness of the universe is a profound point of connection between philosophy and religion: "When separated from worship, leisure becomes toilsome, and work becomes inhuman" (54).

16 *SCG* I.1 and *ST* I.1.6.

of organic life processes. In fact, these sciences can all study the same thing—a tree, say—and yet make different discoveries because each science investigates it from its own specific perspective. Philosophy, too, investigates the same realities as the other sciences, but its perspective is higher; it seeks explanations that provide the foundations for all these other sciences.

One way of explaining this is to say that philosophy investigates the "conditions for intelligibility" in the universe. What I mean by this is that philosophy seeks the answer to the question, why does the world make sense at all? Why is my experience of the world intelligibly ordered and not a chaotic confusion? Notice, first, that this is the sort of question that no science can answer—or even ask. Any specific science must assume that the world exists with an intelligible order. If a science did not assume the world really existed and that it operated in an orderly way, there would no reason to even begin an experiment. Science only works because it assumes the laws it discovers will be universal (at work everywhere) and necessary (at work always); but to prove that the world is this way cannot be the job of science. Yet to assume with no proof is to build your house on sand; there needs to be some reason for believing that reality really has this intelligible universal order. Thus, behind every science are the discoveries of philosophy that make its investigations possible.[17]

This is how philosophy justifies our knowledge. If we never attempted to justify our knowledge, to go beyond the information collected by the sciences, we would be stuck with mere opinions. There is an old philosophical dictum that whatever is freely asserted is freely denied. If you make a claim but cannot provide some reason for why it should be taken to be true, then others can simply deny your claim. In fact, this is really a moral imperative. Each of us—individually and as a society—needs to justify our beliefs to ourselves. We ought not simply assume our opinions are true—that is a mindless and unserious existence. Rather, we need to constantly evaluate our ideas to make sure we are living the truth. This is the Socratic

---

17 In other words, science discovers *proximate* causes and explanations, while philosophy discovers *ultimate* causes and explanations. For example, a biologist will explain life in terms of the life processes associated with cells. A chemist will insist that those cellular processes are explicable in terms of the laws of chemistry. A physicist, in turn, will insist that chemistry can be explained in terms of atoms and fundamental forces. These are all proximate causes, because they are empirically observable as the direct cause of the effect. But why do atoms and forces—and the laws of chemistry and biology—even exist as intelligible principles in the universe? This is what philosophy asks. The cause of existence and intelligibility, then, is the ultimate cause behind the operations of all the proximate causes.

injunction at the origin of Western philosophy: "An unexamined life is not worth living."[18]

The ultimate justification for our beliefs, then, would be to determine why the world exists as it does and how it is intelligible; if we know these principles, we have the foundations that would enable us to understand the entire universe. So, we must ask, what is it about the world and about humankind that enables the universe to make sense to us? The answer would provide a foundation for all our other beliefs. But this question really implies three related questions, for there are different things to consider about the intelligibility of our experience: one about the world, one about human nature, and one about human action. Each of these three is the basis for an important area of philosophy.[19]

First, there must be objective conditions for intelligibility. That is, if the world is to make sense, there must be something about the nature of reality itself that enables it to be understood. The American philosopher William James once described the world, as perceived in naïve sensation, as a "blooming, buzzing confusion."[20] In one sense this is true. At the level of sense-experience, we experience things that are constantly changing, so there appears to be nothing stable at all in our experience. Furthermore, every individual we experience is utterly unique: no two snowflakes are the same, after all. Yet, in spite of this chaos of change and difference, we nevertheless are able to interpret that chaotic experience as an orderly and regular whole. Despite the fact there are changes, we know that things, like trees and people, exist continuously from moment to moment and over great lengths of time. Despite the fact that no two persons are identical, we recognize that they both belong to the human species and are similar for that reason.

So, in spite of the apparent instability and uniqueness of the objects of our experience, we discover intelligible principles of the world in the nature of being. The principles of being determine what really exists. This part of philosophy is *metaphysics*, which can be defined as the study of reality behind appearance or, as noted earlier, the study of beings *as being* (as opposed to a *certain kind* of being). At the level of appearance, the world may be a bloom-

18 Plato, *Apology* 38a4.

19 Although he argues for this in a very different way, the same general approach is in Jacques Maritain, *A Preface to Metaphysics* (London: Sheed and Ward, 1943), 130–31.

20 William James, *The Principles of Psychology*, ed. Robert Maynard Hutchins, vol. 53 of *Great Books of the Western World* (Chicago and London: Encyclopaedia Britannica, 1952), 318.

ing, buzzing confusion; behind it, though, what really exists is stable and orderly because of the principles of being. Metaphysics, then, investigates being to find those principles that enable us to make coherent sense of the world.

Second, there must be subjective conditions for intelligibility. That is, we have to explain how a human being is able to understand the world. It is non-sensical to say that the world makes sense to a rock. It is doubtful that it makes sense to a fly or a fish. Human beings, in contrast, are able to make sense of the world by coming to understand the principles of being. This investigation of man's ability to know the world is *epistemology*, the theory of knowledge. Epistemology investigates what we can know and how we can know it. In other words, epistemology uncovers the principles of being inasmuch as they are known to be true. The nature of truth, then, is the first principle or ultimate explanation for the subjective intelligibility of the world.

Third are the *intersubjective* conditions for intelligibility. Among all our experiences, interactions with other human beings have a unique criterion for intelligibility. If a tree limb falls on my head, or a dog bites me, I strike that up to bad luck. But if you hit me on the head, or if you bite me, I am rightfully outraged, since I believe people should not behave like that. We naturally expect our interactions to make sense, to be characteristically human. The rules for these interactions establish a criterion of goodness. This branch of philosophy is *ethics*, which seeks to define the good as the principle that makes sense of human actions in the world.

There are, then, three main parts of philosophy, each of which pursues a different first principle that explains why the world is intelligibly ordered. Metaphysics explores the principles of being, epistemology seeks to justify knowledge in terms of truth, and ethics seeks to explain human action as good. However, we must note that if truth and goodness are to be real—if they really exist—then they must be described in terms of being. For that reason, being has primacy among these principles. This crucial point will inform the way these transcendental and primary properties are argued in the rest of the book.

FOUR IMPLICATIONS OF FIRST PRINCIPLES

There are four important consequences of this idea that philosophy seeks explanatory first principles in the form of being, true, and good. These are fairly technical issues, but they are critical in establishing the nature of philosophical argumentation.

First, while all philosophers must acknowledge these fundamental concepts, they can nevertheless define them in diverse ways. When this happens—and this is at the crux of most modern social problems—people end up with completely different worldviews. For example, many people, under the influence of scientism, identify being with whatever is made of atoms (a position known as *materialism*). But this definition simply assumes that there can be no immaterial being. Notice that it does not prove that God or souls do not exist; rather, they are defined out of existence. This becomes problematic, however, for when there is evidence for immaterial beings (which there is, as we see later in this book), materialists have to explain that evidence away. Therefore, we need to be sure that the philosophical definition of being can adequately account for all our experiences; errors arise when our notion of being is too narrow and thereby distorts reality.

Similar problems arise when people define truth and goodness in different ways. If truth is only what science can know, then most of what is valuable in human experience—love, beauty, justice—no longer counts as "true." Perhaps this problem is most obvious with respect to divergent definitions of the good. For example, some people define the good as that which maximizes pleasure (*hedonism*); others define it as fulfilling God's law. These people can act in utterly contradictory ways, yet each would consider himself a "good" person.

This disagreement over the meaning of first principles is why so many debates have devolved into pointless chatter.[21] It is as if people were speaking different languages, with no common terms to begin communication. People literally talk past one another, since what is obvious to one is seen to be impossible by the other. One cannot prove to a scientist that God exists if the scientist assumes that there is no immaterial being. One cannot prove to a hedonist that adultery is wrong if he does not recognize a good other than pleasure. This problem is particularly acute with respect to being, since being is *all that is*; if someone defines being incorrectly, he will be wrong about everything.[22] Therefore, philosophy is needed as the first step to

21 This is one of the principal insights of Alasdair MacIntyre's critique of contemporary ethics in his seminal work, *After Virtue*, 3rd ed. (Notre Dame, Ind.: University of Notre Dame Press, 2007).

22 Leo XIII, in *Aeterni Patris*, 2, commenting on the political revolutions of the nineteenth century, says, "Whoso turns his attention to the bitter strifes of these days and seeks a reason for the troubles that vex public and private life must come to the conclusion that a fruitful cause of

engaging people whose worldviews differ from our own: recognizing and critiquing inadequate first principles, not simply rejecting their conclusions, is how dialogue becomes conducive to truth.

The second consequence follows from this. A first principle is the foundation for all other arguments and proofs: the reason the materialist rejects God, or the hedonist approves of narcotics, is because it follows from the first principle. But as the foundation for all other arguments, the first principle cannot itself be proved by argument. This is because arguments cannot involve an "infinite regress" of proofs. If you ask me to prove A, I can point to B; if you ask me to prove B, I can point to C. But this cannot go on forever, or else we could never really prove anything. There must be some truth that is simply evident and is the basis for all these other arguments. Consequently, there can never be an argument that proves a first principle is the correct first principle.

This might seem to condemn us to relativism. This is not the case, though, since we can test first principles indirectly, or by *dialectical* argument. We do this by provisionally accepting a first principle and then playing out all the consequences. If those consequences lead to a contradiction, or if they blatantly violate what we know about the world, we know that there must be something wrong with the principle. Let's take two examples from Descartes.[23] Descartes insists that reality is made of two kinds of being—minds and bodies—that are mutually exclusive—what is one cannot be the other. Yet, in order to explain how we know sensations, he suggests that the mind is *in* the brain. This is a direct contradiction of his premise that mind and body are completely distinct. There must be something wrong with his definition of being if it leads to such a contradiction. Similarly, Descartes's definition of mind means that only rational beings—humans—are conscious of the world. Other animals, lacking minds, are not conscious but are simply like robots who act without awareness. From this he concludes animals do not feel pain! This conclusion flies in the face of

---

the evils which now afflict, as well as those which threaten, us lies in this: that false conclusions concerning divine and human things, which originated in the schools of philosophy, have now crept into all the orders of the State, and have been accepted by the common consent of the masses." It is clear that today's political divisions often mask deeper moral and metaphysical divisions based on incommensurable definitions of being, true, and good.

23 Both of these arguments are in the Sixth *Meditation* (at 86 for the first example and 84 for the second); I discuss these in greater length in chapters 4 and 5. While these are common interpretations, every interpretation is inevitably contested by some philosophers. For this reason, I always include references to the primary text, so that the readers can assess the arguments for themselves.

universal human experience, as any child with a puppy can attest. So, we can again conclude that there must be something wrong with his definition of being and that his first principle is unacceptable.

I use such dialectical arguments to argue against inadequate definitions of being, true, and good in the rest of the book. The best principle is one that leads to neither contradiction nor implausible conclusions and so best accounts for our experience of the world.

The third significant point concerns the fact, as mentioned in the introduction, that being, truth, and good are the *transcendental* properties. They are called "transcendental" because they transcend all differences between kinds of being and so apply to all things.[24] More limited aspects or kinds of being—like blue, or chemical, or living—cannot be first principles, since they would not account for everything. However, everything is a being, is true, and is good. (I explain this more fully in chapter 3.) One immediate implication is that the cosmos cannot be considered to be just atoms floating in space; the world is not simply a set of brute facts that we impose meaning upon. Rather, the universe exists endowed with value, with a truth and goodness that we must accept as a fact about the world.

Finally, as philosophy discovers the principles of being, truth, and good, it will eventually discover the One True Good Being: God.[25] God is the source of all the properties of being because he is Being itself, Truth itself, and Goodness itself. That is why contemplating these ultimate principles brings people to some knowledge of the God who is revealed in Jesus Christ. As Jacques Maritain perceptively observes, "Once we touch a transcendental, we touch being itself, a likeness of God, an absolute, all that ennobles and makes the joy of life: we enter the realm of the spirit."[26]

Philosophy, then, can never start off assuming the existence of God. Rather, philosophy explores nature, finding the first principles that are the

---

24 It is important at this point to note that certain words used in philosophy take on drastically different meanings in different contexts. The word *transcendental* is a good example. It is used in the perennial philosophy as defined here. But to Immanuel Kant and German Idealism it means something very different; and, as used by Ralph Waldo Emerson and the American Transcendentalists, it means a third thing altogether. I note other terms that suffer similar fates as they are introduced. But it is always important to understand what a particular philosopher means by a term and to never assume it is used synonymously by different thinkers.

25 This insight is developed with great acuity in Alice M. Ramos, *Dynamic Transcendentals: Truth, Goodness, and Beauty from a Thomistic Perspective* (Washington, D.C.: The Catholic University of America Press, 2012).

26 Jacques Maritain, *Art and Scholasticism*, trans. J. F. Scanlan (New York: Charles Scribner's Sons, 1930), 32–33.

necessary conditions for intelligibility, and only in the end does our knowledge ascend to God as the necessary cause for all other realities. It is for this reason that this book addresses natural theology—our knowledge of God from a purely rational perspective, independent of all revelation—only after exploring being, truth, and goodness in nature.

But, if contemplating the principles of being is in some way getting to know the God of Jesus Christ, we must now address a more fundamental issue: philosophy's relationship to the Catholic faith.

PHILOSOPHY AND FAITH

The defining difference between philosophy and theology can be stated briefly: philosophy begins with nature and eventually ascends to God as the ultimate cause of the world; theology begins with the revelation of God in Scripture and then views all of creation in relation to him. Both are ways of coming to know God and creation, but they employ two different methods. Since they employ different methods, like physics and biology investigating the tree, they will discover different aspects of God's nature and of his creation, though the object is the same.

Thomas Aquinas explains this difference clearly in laying out his aims in the *Summa Contra Gentiles*:

> There is a twofold mode of truth in what we profess about God. Some truths about God exceed all the ability of the human reason. Such is the truth that God is triune. But there are some truths which the natural reason also is able to reach. Such are that God exists, that He is one, and the like. In fact, such truths about God have been proved demonstratively by the philosophers, guided by the light of the natural reason. . . .
>
> Now, from what has been said it is evident that the teaching of the Christian faith deals with creatures so far as they reflect a certain likeness of God, and so far as error concerning them leads to error about God. And so they are viewed in a different light by that doctrine and by human philosophy. For human philosophy considers them as they are. . . . The Christian faith, however, does not consider them as such; thus, it regards fire not as fire, but as representing the sublimity of God . . .
>
> For this reason, also, the philosopher and the believer consider different matters about creatures. The philosopher considers such things as belong to them by nature—the upward tendency of fire, for example; the believer, only such things as belong to them according as they are related to God—the fact, for instance, that they are created by God, are subject to him, and so on . . .

> But any things concerning creatures that are considered in common by the philosopher and the believer are conveyed through different principles in each case. For the philosopher takes his argument from the proper causes of things; the believer, from the first cause . . .
>
> Hence again, the two kinds of teaching do not follow the same order. For in the teaching of philosophy, which considers creatures in themselves and leads us from them to the knowledge of God, the first consideration is about creatures; the last, of God. But in the teaching of faith, which considers creatures only in their relation to God, the consideration of God comes first, that of creatures afterwards.[27]

It is important to note that the primary dividing line Thomas draws between philosophy and theology is that theology properly deals with truths that are revealed because they are beyond the ability of human reason to grasp on its own. Without revelation, we could never know such truths as the Trinity, the virgin birth, the Incarnation, and the Resurrection; these truths are known as the *mysteries of the faith*. Because they transcend the power of reason, these dogmas are accepted by virtue of our faith in the revealed Word of God.

Philosophy, on the other hand, knows truths based on reason alone. This applies even to some truths about God that, since they are known by reason, do not require faith. As a result, these truths are known as the preambles to the faith.[28] They are preambles because they are truths known by reason that faith builds upon and completes. For example, the preambles of the faith include that God exists, that there is one God, that he is perfect, good, wise, loving, and provident. Reason can know all this about God; but reason cannot know anything about Jesus being the Word made Flesh or God as Trinity. In other words, philosophy can show that God exists, but it cannot fully grasp Who he is.[29] However, knowing that God exists and that

---

27 *SCG* I.3 and II.4. John Wippel nicely summarizes the distinction: "[I]n metaphysics, one begins with one's discovery of being as being or being in general; in the course of one's efforts to understand this, one should ultimately discover the principle or cause of that which falls under it, God. In the teaching based on faith, however, one first turns to the study of God and only thereafter examines created reality insofar as it in some way imitates or represents the divine reality," John Wippel, "Metaphysics," in *The Cambridge Companion to Thomas Aquinas*, ed. Norman Kretzmann and Eleonore Stump (Cambridge: Cambridge University Press, 1993), 87.

28 *ST* I.2.2.ad 1.

29 *ST* I.2.2.ad 3. Another way to put this is that, while philosophy can provide true propositions *about* God, it alone cannot provide a personal relationship *with* God; that requires knowledge of the person of Christ. John Henry Newman makes a similar point in distinguishing notional assent from real assent in chapters 3 and 4 of *An Essay in Aid of a Grammar of Assent* (Notre Dame, Ind.: University of Notre Dame Press, 1992).

he is loving and provident, makes it possible to recognize that he is at work in the revelation of the Gospels. Faith is not an irrational "blind leap," as some skeptics of religion assert. Rather, through reason we have a fair idea of what God is like, and then revelation fills out this picture, in continuity with reason but certainly going beyond reason. In this way, grace perfects nature: the truths of revelation complete the truths we can attain on the basis of reason.

Some, especially in the Protestant tradition,[30] might object that this idea of the preambles of the faith diminishes the relevance of the Bible. But this is not true, for the biblical revelation is indispensable for knowing the mysteries of God's nature that reason cannot grasp on its own. In fact, there are three reasons why the preambles of the faith known by reason are actually necessary augmentations for what we believe from the Bible.

First, evangelization would seem to be impossible if there were no common rational truths to act as a starting point. You cannot preach the mysteries of Christianity—that the Son of God became flesh—unless your audience already accepts that God exists. For this reason, being able to establish through reason that God exists and that he is a loving creator makes the Gospel itself a compelling sequel fulfilling the expectations of reason.

Second, the Bible itself recognizes the importance of this rational knowledge of God. For example, the Book of Wisdom proclaims, "For all people who were ignorant of God were foolish by nature; and they were unable from the good things that are seen to know the one who exists" (Wis 13:1). Some might object that the Book of Wisdom, as deuterocanonical, is not authoritative.[31] However, Saint Paul makes a similar point (likely offering a summary of the earlier text): "For what can be known about God is plain to them, because God has shown it to them. Ever since the creation of the world his eternal power and divine nature, invisible though they are, have been understood and seen through the things he has made" (Rom 1:19–20). Thus, the capacity to know some things of God is itself a revealed

---

30 The Protestant tradition tends to fideism because of its founding doctrines of the depravity of human nature and *sola fides*. In assuming that original sin corrupts human nature itself, reason becomes inherently unreliable and the will inherently distorted; thus, we can have no part in cooperating with grace in order to attain salvation but simply blindly believe and abjectly hope in God's mercy (cf. *ST* I-II.85.1 for the Catholic rejoinder to this).

31 Most Protestant traditions have, since the time of Luther, either marginalized these texts (KJV and RSV) or simply ignored them by excluding them from editions of the Bible (NIV and ESV).

truth that is also accessible by reason. This ability to know God on the basis of reason was affirmed as a universal teaching of the Church by the First Vatican Council.[32]

Third, the preambles to the faith establish a criterion by which to judge different "revelations." In a religiously pluralistic world, we frequently come upon different faith traditions that claim to possess the "true" revelation of God. But these are often profoundly inconsistent with the Bible. Therefore, both revelations cannot be true. How can one assess the probable validity of these divergent teachings? We need some criterion outside of the various scriptures themselves. The preambles of the faith provide this rational criterion by which to judge whether a book is the true revelation of God. For example, if someone were to claim that God is a material being, or that God is not omniscient, or that he does not love creatures, we can use the truths of reason to evaluate these claims and conclude that that supposed revelation is false, not because it opposes the Christian faith but because it opposes the rational truth of what God must be like.[33]

So, if philosophy is able to know so much about God, then why is faith needed at all? Is knowledge of the mysteries of faith really that important? To this, there is a simple answer: "It was necessary *for man's salvation* that there should be a knowledge revealed by God."[34] The ultimate goal of human existence is to be united to God in heaven. In order to attain this end, it is necessary that truths about God be revealed. We need to know not only *that* God exists; we also need to know who he is through the revelation of Jesus Christ, for only the grace given by Christ can lift us to the Beatific Vision.

That is clear enough. But there is an additional nuance, for there are in fact two ways in which revelation makes salvation available to humankind. First, as I have said, revelation is necessary for people to know the mysteries of faith that are simply beyond the competence of reason. Knowing Christ, and participating in his grace, is required for salvation, and this is available only through the Gospel accepted on faith.

But second, even the preambles to the faith known by reason need to be revealed so that they might be known by all people. Since the truths about

---

32 Vatican Council I, Dogmatic Constitution *Dei Filius* II (April 24, 1870): "The Holy Mother Church holds and teaches that God, the beginning and end of all things, may be certainly known by the natural light of human reason by means of created things."

33 We might note that Thomas does this with respect to Islam in *SCG* I.6.4.

34 *ST* I.1.1, emphasis added; cf. II-II.1.5 and II-II.2.3.

God are the hardest things to know, the last truths philosophy attains,[35] they will be known by very few people and even then will not be perfectly correct. As we will see, even men as brilliant as Plato and Aristotle, who dedicated their whole lives to contemplating truth, still had very problematic ideas of God (though they were not completely wrong). But most people have to work for a living; they cannot spend their days in contemplation. Therefore, as Thomas concludes, "in order that the salvation of men might be brought about more fitly and more surely, it was necessary that they should be taught divine truths by divine revelation."[36] So, even the most humble Christian can know more about God than does the greatest philosopher.

In the end, the relation between reason and faith can be represented as a pair of overlapping circles:[37]

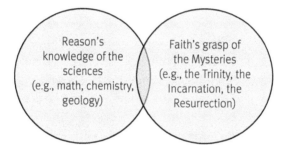

On the one hand, there are many subjects that are known by reason and about which the faith says nothing. These are topics like math, chemistry, biology, geology, and astronomy. There is a dignity to reason and to purely secular knowledge; all truth deserves respect. Therefore, we should not try to subordinate these sciences to the truths of revelation; the truths of science are about the world and so are not directly concerned with salvation.[38] This

---

35 See *SCG* I.4.3: "In order to know the things that the reason can investigate concerning God, a knowledge of many things must already be possessed. . . . This means that we are able to arrive at the inquiry concerning the aforementioned truth only on the basis of a great deal of labor spent in study. Now, those who wish to undergo such a labor for the mere love of knowledge are few, even though God has inserted into the minds of men a natural appetite for knowledge."

36 *ST* I.1.1. This is developed in *ST* II-II.2.4.

37 We should acknowledge that God can reveal all types of knowledge, but only those related to salvation are specified here. Moreover, the preambles are normally accepted on faith prior to being able to be grasped by reason, but they are either believed or known by a person at any one time.

38 There is a tradition within Christianity, stemming from Augustine, that does subordinate all learning to the goal of salvation. When done well, as in Saint Bonaventure's *On the Reduction of the Arts to Theology*, it is a subtle reflection on the relation between Creator and creation. When it is not done well, it is a crude fideism that leads to fundamentalist reading of Scripture.

is not impious—on the contrary, appreciating the order of creation is in fact appreciating what God has done.

On the other hand, there are the mysteries of the faith, truths necessary for salvation, but which reason can never attain. These are the dogmas that structure the theological tradition of the Church: the Trinity, the Incarnation, the virgin birth, the Resurrection, and so on.[39]

Finally, there is a set of truths that are knowable by reason but also given in faith for the sake of salvation. These truths fall into three main areas: truths about human nature, about ethics, and about God. (This book considers each of these areas in order.) Let us consider these truths that fall under both reason and faith.

To understand salvation, we need to understand the nature of a human being. Thus, Scripture reveals that humans are made in the image of God and that they are destined for an afterlife. Yet both of these points—that humans have a unique dignity among creatures, and that the rational soul is immortal—can be proved by philosophy. Even pagan philosophers have argued for immortality, and many modern atheists defend the unique dignity of humankind, so they are not uniquely religious teachings, but truths relevant for all humans.

An integral aspect of religion is the moral code by which we are to live. In the Bible, this is exemplified by the Ten Commandments. But to say that the prohibitions on killing and stealing are known only by revelation is absurd; indeed, no society could survive unless murder and theft were somehow controlled. Therefore, we can know by reason that certain actions are wrong. It is important to see that morality applies to all people, not just those who accept the Bible. Therefore, we will be able to demonstrate that the Ten Commandments are wholly rational;[40] they are, therefore, appli-

---

39 In fact, Thomas insists that since these truths transcend reason, any attempt to prove them will necessarily fail and so will only induce "the ridicule of the unbelievers: since they suppose that we stand upon such reasons, and that we believe on such grounds" (ST I.32.1; cf. DP 4.1).

40 There is a corollary to this that is important for Christians to remember. Since the precepts of the Decalogue apply to all people, no matter where or when, the giving of the commandments in Exodus 20 cannot be a moral revelation. These precepts, as applying to every human being, must have been known as a binding moral law prior to being revealed on Mount Sinai. This is evident in light of the fact that murder and adultery are condemned in Genesis. To assume that the giving of the commandments instituted moral rules is a great misconception known as divine voluntarism, which asserts that morality is not based on the facts of human nature but on God's arbitrary command. This presumes that there is no rational basis of morality; rather, the law is the result of God's capricious will that must be servilely obeyed. Christians should avoid this at all costs, for it is a radical form of relativism, since it implies that only those who accept revelation are morally bound by those laws.

cable to all people and not just to religious believers.[41]

Finally, as has been discussed, there are the truths about God known by reason, or *natural theology*. This is in contrast to revealed theology, which comes to an understanding of God on the basis of his self-revelation in Scripture and accepted on faith.

WHAT IS FAITH?

Our picture of the relationship between faith and reason highly esteems faith, for it tells us most directly about God. Yet many people object to this; they would argue that, since faith is not an act of reason, it must be inherently irrational, and so there is no reason to accept its propositions as true. They would insist that religious faith has no more gravity than a personal opinion, like preferring chocolate ice cream to vanilla. Moreover, since it is simply a personal opinion, every individual is free to believe whatever he wants to about God: Yahweh, Zeus, and the Flying Spaghetti Monster are equally plausible objects of belief. This position, however, seriously misconstrues what the act of faith is. These misinterpretations of faith obscure the fact that statements of faith are claims to objective truth. They are claims about reality, and so it is presumptuous to dismiss them as merely opinion or feelings or fictive projections. Therefore, one of the first steps to defending the Christian faith is to arrive at a correct understanding of faith itself.[42]

To clarify this, let us consider Thomas's understanding of faith. He sees faith as a mean between knowledge and opinion.[43] A person has knowledge when a proposition is known with certainty. It is certain because the rational evidence utterly convinces the mind it is true. For example, on the one hand, the proposition that a thing cannot exist and not-exist simultaneously convinces reason immediately because it is a self-evident rule of metaphysics. On the other hand, sometimes reason is convinced by the proof of logical

---

41 See Rom 2:14–15: "When Gentiles, who do not possess the law, do instinctively what the law requires, these, though not having the law, are a law to themselves. They show that what the law requires is written on their hearts."

42 Significantly, when Thomas defines faith, he defines it, like wisdom, as a habit (*ST* I-II.62 and II-II.1). That is, it is a constant disposition to see the world through the prism of this truth, thereby ordering all experience according to faith in Christ. It is different from wisdom, though, since it is a gift of grace and not something we attain by our natural powers.

43 *ST* II-II.1.2.sc. and II-II.1.4.

reasoning: I might be speaking to Joe right now, but I can know that, because all men are mortal and Joe is a man, he will someday die. Since the truth of these propositions is undeniable, the mind is convinced, and there is no need to "believe" the conclusion. We simply know it to be true.

Opinion is very different. We hold something as an opinion if we are uncertain about it. This uncertainty arises because, while there may be evidence, the proposition is neither self-evident nor proven absolutely. Because there is no proof, a person has to weigh the evidence for-and-against to see how likely something is. The amount of evidence will determine the strength of one's opinion; but since it is only probable, we always admit that we might be wrong. For example, that it will rain tomorrow or that my favorite team will win the championship are both possible; if evidence is strong for these propositions, then my opinion will be equally strong. Nevertheless, because an opinion is ultimately uncertain, no one would ever bet his life on it.

Faith is different from opinion, for we do stake our lives on the propositions of faith: believers are to live their lives for and, if necessary, die for Christ. This conviction arises because, like knowledge, we have certainty that it is true. But faith is different from knowledge because there is no rational proof for these beliefs. The obvious problem here is this: how can we be certain about something if there is no proof? The answer is that the certainty of faith comes from an act of the will, from a decision to believe it with certainty even though we have no proof.

But this is still problematic. Can we just will ourselves to believe anything? Clearly that is not so—we cannot believe that a dime is worth a hundred dollars. So why do we believe some things and not others? There are two elements that move the will to commit to believe a proposition. First, we agree to believe because we see that it is *good* to believe certain things; life is more complete, more coherent by believing some things even if we cannot prove them. It is the goodness of belief that moves the will to act. Again, though, we do not thereby believe whatever we want just because it is good. The second part, then, is that belief is directed not primarily to the proposition, but rather to the one who is telling me. We must have trust in a *person*, and there must be reasons for that trust; so even if we cannot prove what they are telling us, we agree to have faith in what they say.[44]

---

44 For an analysis, see Josef Pieper, *Faith, Hope, Love*, trans. Richard and Clara Winston (San Francisco: Ignatius Press, 1997), 19–85.

For example, prior to genetic testing, no one could *prove* their mother was their mother; yet the acts of love continually give evidence that it is good to believe what your mother says even in the absence of proof. We trust a restaurant is clean if we see the health commissioner's license in the window. Very few, even today, can actually prove the earth revolves around the sun;[45] yet there is near universal acceptance based on the authority of scientists and the value of accepting that idea.

It is the same for revelation. We cannot prove what God reveals as objects of faith (that he is Three-in-One, that he is incarnate in Jesus Christ, etc.). Yet, we can know—by rational proofs—that God exists and that he is loving. Moreover, because we are not completely happy unless we know who God is,[46] we naturally desire to know more than what reason can tell us. Thus, based on the knowledge of the preambles,[47] we realize it is good, for the sake of our salvation, to accept that that knowledge is completed and perfected by revelation. Because the certainty of faith arises from the confidence in the one whom we believe, we should be willing to bet our lives on its being true. Many martyrs, even to this day, provide evidence of the certainty to be found in faith.

The propositions we accept on faith then become the basis for a whole new science: theology. Theology uses the truths given in revelation and then develops arguments to show the consequences of that which is contained in Scripture and tradition.[48] The arguments and conclusions of theology are beyond the scope of this book,[49] but we should note one way in which it is very similar to philosophy. Just as philosophies that define their first principles in different ways end up with different worldviews, faiths that derive from different "revelations" have different religious worldviews.

---

[45] Although proposed by Copernicus in 1543 and given evidential support by Galileo, Kepler, and Newton, heliocentrism was only proved in 1838 by the German scientist Friedrich Bessel.

[46] *ST* I-II.3.8: "Man is not perfectly happy, so long as something remains for him to desire and seek. . . . If therefore the human intellect, knowing the essence of some created effect, knows no more of God than 'that He is'; the perfection of that intellect does not yet reach simply the First Cause, but there remains in it the natural desire to seek the cause. Wherefore it is not yet perfectly happy. Consequently, for perfect happiness the intellect needs to reach the very Essence of the First Cause."

[47] As mentioned above, these preambles also act as a set of rational parameters for what can be accepted as a valid revelation.

[48] *ST* I.1.2 and II-II.1.7.

[49] A good book to start the investigation of theology is Aidan Nichols, *The Shape of Catholic Theology: An Introduction to Its Sources, Principles, and History* (Collegeville, Minn.: The Liturgical Press, 1991). Nichols' argument has influenced my approach in this book.

So, the Christian accepts the Bible and the Muslim accepts the Koran, but since they have different starting points, different worldviews follow. Moreover, since real debate is only possible if there is some common starting point, we can only persuade people about the truth of the faith if they accept the same starting point, that is, Scripture and tradition.[50] In this way, Catholics and Protestants can argue about the truths of Christianity; for example, the real presence in the Eucharist in light of John 6. However, if others do not accept our revelation, then we cannot convince them of the truth of the faith. Rather, the best we can do is to demonstrate that our own beliefs are internally consistent with what is revealed and with the preambles of faith given by reason. Thus, we are once again directed back to the need for philosophy to provide the common ground to assess divergent claims to truth.

PHILOSOPHY OVERCOMES THE REDUCTIONISM OF SCIENTISM AND FIDEISM

The most adequate way to understand the world, then, is not with reason alone or faith alone. On the contrary, we can know the fullness of reality only by using faith and reason together. And this is where philosophy, with its unique relations to both religion and science, is indispensable. It mediates and integrates these two sources. In essence, scientism and fideism both fall into error because they eliminate this mediating role of philosophy.

First, philosophy shows a natural kinship with religion, since they both seek ultimate explanations, principles that show that life has a transcendent source of meaning.[51] Yet religion and philosophy are radically different because they use different methods to grasp these principles. Religion accepts these ultimate principles on faith; philosophy establishes them

---

50 *ST* I.1.8.

51 This similarity has led many modern secularists to condemn both religion and metaphysics as "comprehensive doctrines" that must be rejected in order to guarantee the freedom of the individual to define reality as he wishes. Without a comprehensive doctrine, though, there is no way to evaluate the value of disparate facts. Leo Strauss described it this way: "We are then in the position of beings who are sane and sober when engaged in trivial business and who gamble like madmen when confronted with serious issues—retail sanity and wholesale madness." *Natural Right and History* (Chicago: University of Chicago Press, 1950), 4. Chesterton, too, over a century ago in the introduction to *Heretics*, noted the absurdity: "There is one thing that is infinitely more absurd and unpractical than burning a man for his philosophy. This is the habit of saying that his philosophy does not matter. . . . [Today] a man's opinion on tramcars matters; his opinion on Botticelli matters; his opinion on all things does not matter. . . . Everything matters—except everything."

through reasoning about the natural world. This is why their conclusions are compatible but never identical with one another.

It is, however, precisely this use of reason that unites philosophy with science. Both philosophy and science methodically explore the data of the universe and draw only those conclusions warranted by evidence. Yet clearly they reach different types of conclusions: philosophy discerns ultimate explanations, while science discerns more proximate and limited explanations.

Therefore, the key difference between philosophy and science lies in the distinctive ways they use reason. Science begins with some observable effect and tries to discover a cause that can be verified in sense experience. For example, if an apple tree is not growing apples (an effect), scientific tests might reveal the presence of some parasite (the cause). This cause is always one that can be observed and tested in further experiments so that we are certain it is correct. Thus, science looks for a physical cause to explain the observed effect.

Philosophy likewise begins with some observable effect, yet it seeks to discover a cause that is rationally necessary, even if it can never be directly observed. For example, I have often heard my wife read poetry but never my dog; indeed, all people can read poetry, but no dog can. That universal effect must be attributable to some cause. Biologically, mammals are remarkably similar. Yet, there are obvious differences between the species that require some explanation. Traditionally, that difference is explained by the presence of a rational soul in human beings.[52] This rational soul is the cause of all those differences—language, art, society, religion—that distinguish us from all other animals.

Some partisans of science would object that philosophers are just "making things up," since they do not prove their theories in experiment. In fact, the accusation that philosophers are full of hot air is one that goes back to its beginnings in ancient Greece.[53] But this is to misunderstand the nature of philosophical proof. Where science relies on observation, philosophy relies on rational necessity. As mentioned earlier, there are two rational criteria philosophy uses to evaluate the adequacy of a philosophical explanation. First, it must be *internally consistent*: the theory cannot lead to a conclusion that contradicts itself, for this would show that the

---

[52] That this difference cannot be accounted for by the brain, as some suppose, is explained in chapter 5.

[53] For an entertaining rendition of this accusation, see Aristophanes' play *The Clouds*, which satirizes Socrates. Socrates makes note of this fact in his trial defense in the *Apology* (19c).

theory is untenable. Second, it must be *externally cogent*, that is, it must account for the totality of a person's experience. If there are obvious facts in the world that the theory cannot account for, then it must be given up in the face of a more adequate principle. These criteria will be used throughout the book to critique the inadequacy of reductive first principles. While these principles articulate a partial truth, they are incapable of presenting the complete truth and so end up in contradiction or failing to account for an evident truth of human experience.

Therefore, to schematize the relation among the three:

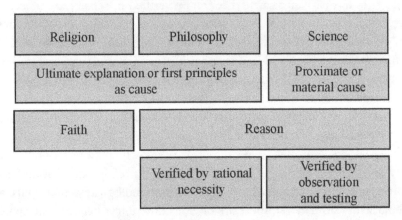

Philosophy, then, is the bridge uniting faith and science as sources of truth. This is crucial, for as Pope Benedict XVI argued in his Regensburg speech, when these are separated, we end up with two fundamentalisms.[54] On the one hand, if science is separated from philosophy and religion, we get technical skill to manipulate the world, but we have no sense of the moral value of those actions. This will lead to the assumption that, if something can be done, it should be done. On the other hand, if religion is separated from reason, then one's conception of God does not reflect the principles of being, truth, or goodness. The result is a God who acts in completely capricious ways, unlimited by the demands of truth and goodness. Such a God is not one who can be loved but only feared.[55]

---

54 As John Rist perceptively suggests, a fundamentalist is a person who accepts one "saving truth" but is then indifferent to truth per se; John Rist, *What Is a Person? Realities, Constructs, Illusions* (Cambridge: Cambridge University Press, 2020), 145.

55 This is characteristic of some aspects of contemporary Islam; yet similar effects are visible in the Christian tradition, especially in Protestantism influenced by medieval nominalism. I return to this in chapter 2.

In both cases, scientism and fideism deny the breadth of truth and goodness; they are irrational dogmatisms that eviscerate life of meaning. Since knowledge cannot be reduced in either way, philosophy takes on a crucial role. It is the bridge that imparts human value into the sciences and grounds religious faith in the necessary principles of reason. This enriches both, and it provides the foundation for a truly integrated understanding of all that we can learn about creation.[56]

FURTHER READING

Gilson, Étienne. *Reason and Revelation*. New York: Charles Scribner's Sons, 1938.

Jones, Brian. "Breaking Free of Our Metaphysical Winter: On Why Christians Must Study Philosophy." *Homiletic and Pastoral Review*. January 12, 2015.

Klima, Gyula. "*Ancilla Theologiae vs. Domina Philosophorum*: St. Thomas Aquinas, Latin Averroism and the Autonomy of Philosophy." Available at http://faculty.fordham.edu/klima/ANCILLA.HTM.

Maritain, Jacques. "The Majesty and Poverty of Metaphysics." In *The Degrees of Knowledge*. Translated by Gerald B. Phelan. Notre Dame, Ind.: University of Notre Dame Press, 1995.

———. "Philosophy and Theology." In *An Introduction to Philosophy*. Translated by E. I. Watkins. Lanham, Md.: Rowman and Littlefield, 2005.

Morerod, Charles. *Ecumenism and Philosophy: Philosophical Questions for a Renewal of Dialogue*. Translated by Therese C. Scarpelli. Ann Arbor, Mich.: Sapientia Press of Ave Maria University, 2006.

Pieper, Josef. *In Defense of Philosophy: The Power of the Mind for Good or Evil, Consists in Argumentation*. Translated by Lothar Krauth. San Francisco: Ignatius Press, 1992.

———. *Faith, Hope, Love*. Translated by Richard and Clara Winston. San Francisco: Ignatius Press, 1997.

———. *Leisure, the Basis of Culture*. Translated by Gerald Malsbary. South Bend, Ind.: St. Augustine's Press, 1998.

Wippel, John F. *Medieval Reactions to the Encounter between Faith and Reason*. Milwaukee: Marquette University Press, 1995.

56 John Henry Newman nicely lays out how the unity of faith and reason finds its natural home in the traditions of the Church: "Jerusalem is the fountain-head of religious knowledge, as Athens is of secular. In the ancient world we see two centers of illumination, acting independently of each other, each with its own movement, and at first apparently without any promise of convergence.... Each leaves an heir and successor in the West, and that heir and successor is one and the same. The grace stored in Jerusalem, and the gifts which radiate from Athens, are made over and concentrated in Rome. This is true as a matter of history. Rome has inherited both sacred and profane learning; she has perpetuated and dispensed the traditions of Moses and David in the supernatural order, and of Homer and Aristotle in the natural. To separate those distinct teachings, human and divine, which meet in Rome, is to retrograde; it is to rebuild the Jewish Temple and to plant anew the groves of Academus." *The Idea of a University: Defined and Illustrated*, ed. by Martin J. Svaglic (Notre Dame, Ind.: University of Notre Dame Press, 1982), 199.

Part I

What Is

Chapter 2

Origins of the
Perennial Philosophy

The search for philosophical wisdom—for the principles of reality behind appearance and grounding knowledge—is an arduous intellectual endeavor. Scientific discoveries can be made through careful observation; the laws of nature spontaneously reveal themselves to an attentive observer. In that sense, they are easier to know than are philosophical truths, which usually emerge only from many generations of shared inquiry and dialogue. For this reason, philosophy—unlike science—can progress only through a self-conscious reflection on its tradition in which the ideas of great thinkers are critically developed in order to explain more adequately the whole of human experience.

To enter into this dialogue, though, it is necessary to become familiar with the vocabulary and practices of philosophy. In this chapter, I consider the origins of Western philosophy in Greece. The principles discovered by these first philosophers, and the methods of analysis they developed, constitute the foundations of the perennial philosophy inherited by the Catholic tradition.

This historical overview has two goals. One is to introduce the vocabulary that philosophers use. As with any field of study, we cannot appreciate the arguments unless we first understand the specialized jargon.[1] The second is to expose the reader to a "laboratory" for philosophical arguments. While the specific theories of the early philosophers are clearly rudimentary, their logical critique and reformulation of ideas is a great witness for how philosophical argument works. This introduction, however, will be

---

[1] A frustration arising from much contemporary philosophy is that thinkers ignorant of the tradition will coin new terms to express ideas that had already been discussed at length in the past. At the turn of the twentieth century, C. S. Peirce recognized the dangers of this when he wrote an "Ethics of Terminology" (*Collected Papers* 2.226) specifying that if a term for an idea existed in Greek or Latin, that should be used before creating an unneeded and potentially confusing neologism.

necessarily brief and selective, restricted to those points requisite for later discussions.[2]

The study of philosophy is like an apprenticeship: you observe a master, learn to imitate him, and eventually you can do it well yourself. For this reason, following the debates of the founders of philosophy in Greece remains the best way to immerse yourself in the dialogue that they originated.

THE BIRTH OF PHILOSOPHY

The human race began a remarkable period of spiritual awakening starting around 600 BC. Other notable changes had preceded this. The agricultural revolution of about 10,000 BC had marked a great advance over primitive hunter-gatherer societies. True human civilization took another significant step forward with the political organization of people in cities from about 5,000 to 3,500 BC. This process also gave the impetus for the invention of writing, with which humans enter the historical period. But the change that occurred around 600 BC reoriented humankind away from survival and worldly prosperity and instead focused their attention on the heavenly realm of eternal things.

Karl Jaspers has labelled this the "Axial Age."[3] This designation suggests a change in the axis of human experience to a new set of values (Greek, *axia*): away from purely temporal concerns to more ultimate realities. We are perhaps most familiar with the developments in Judaism during this period. With the political crisis in the kingdom of Judah, which came to a head with the destruction of the First Temple in Jerusalem in 586 BC and the subsequent exile in Babylon, Judaism underwent a self-examination that caused its adherents to rededicate themselves more fully to their spiritual relationship with Yahweh. This reawakening of the Jewish spirit is best epitomized by the great prophets of the era: Jeremiah (ca. 641–ca. 585 BC), Ezekiel (ca. 622–ca. 570 BC), and the writings of Deutero-Isaiah (ca. 540 BC),[4] culminating in the rebuilding of the Temple (515 BC) and the revivification of Jewish life under Ezra and Nehemiah (ca. 450 BC).

---

2 For a complete history of philosophy, see Frederick Copleston, *A History of Philosophy*, 9 vols. (Garden City, N.Y.: Image Books, 1985).

3 Karl Jaspers, *The Origin and Goal of History*, trans. Michael Bullock (New Haven: Yale University Press, 1953), 1–21.

4 These compose chapters 40–55 of the Book of Isaiah and contain both a robust sense of monotheism as well as the universalizing of Yahwism through Israel's vocation as "a light to the nations" (Is 49:6).

But Israel was not the only people to be inspired by new religious ideas during this time.[5] In China, Lao-tzu (604–ca. 540 BC) wrote the work that became the foundation for Taoism and a little later Confucius (551–478 BC) established the school of philosophy that was to shape Chinese culture for millennia. Meanwhile, in India, Buddha (563–483 BC) was spreading his own insights into attaining enlightenment. Slightly to the west, Zoroaster (died ca. 550 BC) originated the religion that was to be the official faith of the Persian empire.

It was in Greece, however, that this awakening to the transcendent aspects of the universe would take a different form and set Western civilization off on a path different from the other great cultures of the ancient world. For just as sages were preaching new religious ideas, between 600 and 400 BC a series of Greek thinkers would turn not to religion but to reason to discover the fundamental principles of the cosmos.

Prior to this awakening of reason, when faced with the awesome mysteries of the universe, the Greeks would have constructed stories or myths to explain their experience. Why did the tide rise? Because Poseidon moved the waters. Why did the seasons change? Because of Persephone's abduction by Hades. But these myths were of very limited value, since they do not explain why things happen with necessity. The unpredictable acts of capricious gods could not be the basis for genuine knowledge. Some people began to realize that better answers might be discovered by using logic or reason to analyze the evidence and to formulate explanations that provide a true understanding of how the world functions. This transition is recognized as the birth of philosophy: when a person wonders why things happen and finds answers not by resorting to myths but by using reason. This monumental turn from *mythos* (myths) to *logos* (logic or reason) would prove to be a seminal innovation for the entire human race.

THE PRE-SOCRATICS (CA. 600 BC TO CA. 400 BC)

The Problems of Change and the One and the Many

The curiosity of the first philosophers was piqued by a pair of closely related questions that needed to be answered if the world were to make sense: the

---

5 The experience of Israel was significantly different, though. It must always be kept in mind that Judaism was formed in response to the call of God's revelation to humankind, whereas other religions are human traditions manifesting the human thirst for transcendence by trying to reach up to God.

problem of change and the problem of the one and the many. As mentioned in the first chapter, at the level of sense-experience, every being appears to be in a constant state of change; furthermore, every being is a unique individual and so different from every other being. If this were all there was—every individual not only different from everything else but even different from itself from moment to moment as it changes—then the universe would be unintelligible. There would be nothing solid to grab onto. We can make sense of the world only when we recognize continuity and similarity. Behind change, there must be stability; behind difference, there must be some unity. Let us consider this more closely.

The fact of change in the world is indisputable. Yet, also indisputable is the fact that most of this change is regular and predictable: although the world is constantly changing, we are rarely surprised because we understand there are underlying patterns behind the change. Even the myths tried to capture this regularity, but since the gods are so erratic, any pattern might abruptly end. However, a rational explanation for change finds a cause of the regularity built into nature herself, so that that pattern would be both necessary and certain. Reliable knowledge like this gives us a true understanding of the world. No longer subject to capricious gods, we can use these causal patterns—like weather or ocean currents—for our own advantage, ultimately allowing us to understand our place in the world.

We see, then, that to understand change, we must be able to grasp the stable principle that causes the regular pattern in change. That principle remains the same while causing other things to change. Thus, behind the apparent instability—the changing things—there is a stability in a principle that can be rationally understood even if it was not immediately apparent. Indeed, if there were nothing stable behind the change, the world would be nothing but flux and we would not know anything at all. For example, if I place an ice cube into a pan on the stove, it first melts, then it boils into vapor, which then condenses on the ceiling. There has to be something that explains all these changes; we know it is the constant chemical structure of H_2O that explains each change in phase. But if we failed to detect the common principle behind this, we would only perceive an unintelligible chaos where things go from one state to another with no apparent order.

In fact, we can conclude that the very concept of *change* itself implies a certain duality, since we must be able to grasp some aspect that remains the same while another changes. I only recognize change if I simultaneously see that the object before me is the same as what used to be there, yet in some way different. Thus, change implies that something is simultaneously same-and-different. For example, my childhood friend is very different from when we first met, yet I recognize something in him that is the same; for if I did not, I would not recognize him to be my old friend. Or, when we burn a log, we later recognize the ashes as being the same stuff as composed the log—even in spite of the dissimilarity in appearance. As a point of contrast, consider what happens when we do not see any similarity between two things. If we see a bird on a fence and a moment later see a squirrel in that same place, no one concludes that the bird changed into a squirrel; rather, we recognize that they are two different things that are not the same at all.[6]

The problem of change is just an instance of the larger problem of the one and the many. In both cases, the problem is finding intelligible similarity despite manifest differences: how is it that one thing can appear in many different ways, yet in fact be the same thing? The problem of the one and the many considers not changes over time, but diverse instances of the same species at the same time. We must acknowledge that every being is unique; no two snowflakes are the same. Yet, if every being were utterly different from all other things and with no similarity, we would not be able to understand anything at all. We would have no reason to call two things by the same name: you could not have two "snowflakes." For this reason, we understand things only by grasping similarities, by seeing a thing as a member of a class of related things or an individual as an instance of a species. In other words, we understand a thing when we know what kind of thing the individual is. There must be a reason why we can call two things by the name "snowflake," if that is the kind of thing they truly are. Therefore, in spite of all the individual differences, there is a real similarity that justifies us calling two things by the same name.

To see why recognizing classes is so important, imagine this case. An archeologist discovers an ancient script in an unknown language; he will not be able to decipher it until he discerns some similarity with a known language (a point proven by the Rosetta Stone). Or imagine an astronaut finds an egg on an alien planet; dare we predict what sort of life-form will emerge if it is unrelated to any earthly species?

---

6 If we could schematize this, change would be something like this: $Xa \rightarrow Xb$. That is, object X with property a changes when that same object X takes on property b. If there were not that common underlying thing X, then we would just perceive a and then b, with no apparent connection between the two objects at all, thereby suggesting that it was simple difference as opposed to change.

This shows us that the intelligibility of the world depends on our ability to assign individuals to their proper universal class. Our experience affirms this. Say you are taking a chemistry class and are given a petri dish with some green glob in it. The assignment is to determine what that green glob is. Initially, it is clear that there is an individual object in the dish, but you do not know what it is. You can know aspects of it in limited ways: see it, taste it, smell it, touch it. However, you only really know what it is when you can put a label on it and declare, "This is an X." That X is a universal class, a name by which you associate this individual with an entire group of things. This name pointing out the similarity between individuals is a universal term, since it applies to many particular individuals of the same kind. These terms help to solve the problem of the one and the many, since they enable us to go behind the unendingly diverse world as it appears to us and instead describe reality in terms of a common nature or principle that they all share. Common natures, then, allow us to comprehend experience, since they explain why different individuals behave in predictably similar ways: a chihuahua and a Great Dane can both be dogs, since in spite of their differences they are the same kind of thing. It is true that every thing is unique; but it is equally true that it must be similar to other things if we are to understand it at all.

The quest of the earliest philosophers was to use reason to discover this common nature behind all things in order to make difference and change intelligible. This rational understanding of the intelligible principles of nature frees us from the capricious explanations of myths.

The Philosophical Solutions

The first philosophers in Greece had two general approaches to discover the principle of stability behind change, and unity behind difference.[7] Some said that there must be some basic stuff of which everything is made, so that no matter how different things were, or how they changed, that common stuff was the underlying reality that enables us to make sense of the change and diversity. This line of thought is still with us in those physicists who argue that beneath all the different elements there must be one common subatomic reality whose properties will completely explain the

7 The information about early philosophers, such as their dates and arguments, is somewhat uncertain because of the fragmentary nature of the evidence. The sources are collected in G. S. Kirk, J. E. Raven, and M. Schofield, eds., *The Presocratic Philosophers*, 2nd ed. (Cambridge: Cambridge University Press, 1983).

physical universe. For example, string theory hypothesizes that all matter is ultimately made up of strings of energy vibrating in fourteen dimensions; once we fully understand how these strings work, we can unite all other scientific theories into a coherent whole.

In contrast, some Greek philosophers argued that there are many kinds of stuff in the universe, but that they are ordered by the mathematical structure of reality. Behind plurality and change, we understand the harmonious order of these mathematical principles. This line of thought is still current in those physicists who seek to reduce all phenomena to mathematical formulae, as in the famous $e = mc^2$.

The best answer, I would suggest, is to combine both ideas. To pick one or the other would be reductive. Rather, as Plato and Aristotle would argue, matter must be structured by a rational form. In fact, it is the great discovery of Aristotle to see that the answer to both problems, entailing simultaneous similarity-with-difference, requires a composition of distinct but complementary principles. But this discovery is only possible because it builds on the arguments of earlier thinkers. Let us take a look at those who prepared the way for Aristotle's breakthrough.

The first group of philosophers, referred to as the Milesians (since they hailed from the city of Miletus, in modern-day Turkey) offered theories about the basic stuff of reality. Thales (ca. 625–545 BC), one of the Seven Sages, is normally considered the first philosopher. He thought the common principle uniting all things must be water. While saying that "all things are made of water" might seem odd to us, Thales's reasoning takes account of evidence and is a rational conclusion. First, water appears to be everywhere: it comes down from the sky and wells up from the ground. Second, water is vital for life, since living things cease to exist without water. Third, bodies of water have a constant and fluid motion, which might explain why there is a constant process of change in all material things. Finally, water occurs readily in three phases—solid, liquid, and gas—and so can account for the variety of the things in the world. Water, then, unites all beings and can explain the appearance of change.

It is instructive to see how the next two generations of philosophers from Miletus respond to Thales's speculations, for they clearly illustrate how philosophical argument works. The first reply comes from Anaximander (ca. 610–545 BC), whose argument relies on the traditional Greek belief in four basic elements: earth, air, water, and fire. Each element is characterized by properties: hot, cold, wet, and dry. Fire is hot and dry; air is hot and wet;

water is cold and wet; and earth is cold and dry. It is here that Anaximander sees problems for Thales. Water is cold and wet and so can explain other things that have those properties (earth as cold and air as wet). But water can never account for the existence of something hot and dry; yet this is what fire is. Water and fire have no common property, and it is obvious that fire exists. Since Thales's theory cannot explain fire, it cannot be correct. Anaximander's logic, in fact, leads him to conclude that none of the four elements could be the basic stuff of reality, since any one element would not be able to explain its opposite. Anaximander reasons that there must be a common principle behind the elements, a stuff he calls *apeiron* or the Unlimited (in contrast to the elements, each of which is limited to a specific kind). It is the unseen movements of the Unlimited, always operating behind our experience of the elements, which explain change in this world.

Anaximander's conclusion opens him up to a serious objection from his successor, Anaximenes (ca. 580–500 BC). Anaximander had suggested that there must be some unexperienced principle that is the ultimate stuff of reality. The problem is obvious: how can he claim to know the existence of something that we can never directly experience? Moreover, if we cannot know the operations of the Unlimited, is this theory any better than a myth? Anaximenes, therefore, returns to the four elements. His reasoning tells him that air is the foundational element, since it can account for all properties. He observes that as air condenses, it gets colder and denser; and as it rarified, it gets hotter and sparser. (For a simple empirical proof, blow on your hand with pursed lips and then with a wide-open mouth.) As a result, air can account for all things in a continuum between the coldest, most dense stuff (rocks and earth) through the cold but less dense (snow, then mud, then water) to the warm (air) and finally the hottest (smoke, then fire).

In the Milesians' combination of rational inference evaluated in light of empirical experience, we see the beginnings of the philosophical method. Though they seek an ultimate explanation, it has to be logically sound and able to account for the breadth of human experiences.

At the same time, at the other end of the Greek world in Southern Italy, philosophers sought not a basic material stuff but a rational mathematical order as the ultimate causal principle. This is the school of Pythagoras (ca. 580–500 BC). While familiar from the theorem bearing his name, the Pythagorean School also had wide-ranging philosophical influence stemming from its arguments that all truth had a mathematical foundation. Math is appealing to philosophers because of its certainty and stability: 2 +

2 will always equal 4, for everyone everywhere. The Pythagoreans pointed to a truly universal and unchanging principle when they argued that a mathematical harmony and proportion lay behind the world.

This concentration on math also opens up a new horizon for human reason. This is because numbers are not things that are observed by the senses; rather, they are pure ideas. If I see three apples, I perceive separate individual objects; that there are "three" is an idea arising in my mind.[8] Since numbers are ideas, the ultimate reality for Pythagoras is known by reason and not merely observation. We perceive a complex material world; in reality, though, that complexity can be reduced to geometric relations based on points, lines (connecting two points), planes (composed of three points), and three-dimensional solids (four points). No matter what the material world is made of, it is intelligible because of this mathematical order underlying its structure. That is, the world is intelligible as quantities and not primarily in terms of perceivable qualities. Even the universe as a whole exhibits this mathematical structure in the "harmony of the spheres," an intelligible order similar to the way music is based on fractional proportions.

The next pair of philosophers propose more problematic accounts, for they reject the attempt to reconcile change and stability or plurality and unity. While both make good arguments, they are reductive and their assumptions are diametrically opposed. As a result, they end up advancing contradictory visions of the universe. Even though this brings philosophy to something of an impasse, it is a great lesson about philosophical method, since it shows that a reductive method impedes the philosopher's ability to pursue truth.

Heraclitus (ca. 540–475 BC) took as the starting point of his method the obvious observations of his sensations. This tells him there is one irrefutable fact: the world is in a constant state of change and the only thing that does not change is change itself. He finds an explanation for this in the element fire, which always consumes and changes reality. Since experience tells us all things are in a constant state of flux, there is no stability in this world. He says, famously, that you cannot step in the same river twice, since everything about it will have changed. To avoid utter skepticism, Heraclitus theorizes that there is some rationale behind this change, which he refers to by the Greek word *logos* (reason or word). This *logos*, a kind of divine

---

8 If this is not convincing, consider how we easily manipulate large numbers—billions of miles, trillions of dollars—that can never be counted by observation.

mind, determines the order of change, but it cannot be known based upon our experiences of a constantly changing world.

Since sense-experience gives evidence of change but not stability, perhaps starting with reason, pure logical analysis, is better suited to discover the principle of stability. This is the insight of Parmenides (ca. 515–450 BC). Parmenides eschews sensation and uses abstract rational analysis to determine the nature of reality. His starting point is to see that logically the one thing that all existing things have in common is that they exist. In other words, no matter how different things are, they all necessarily are being. From this, Parmenides frames two irrefutable premises: being is that which is and not-being is that which is not. That is, being is whatever exists and not-being simply does not exist. He then draws the unlikely conclusion that change is impossible. The problem is that change, or becoming, is a *coming-into-being*: a property that was not there before comes into existence. For example, if I become tall or tan, then I previously was *not* tall or tan. But here is the problem: if something new is to come-into-being, it must either come from being or from not-being, since those are the only two possibilities. But neither of these is possible. It cannot come-to-be from being, because then it would already exist, since it is already being. Neither, however, could it come-to-be from not-being, because there is no not-being from which to arise; not-being is nothing. Since you cannot get something from nothing, then change cannot arise from nothingness. Thus, being is everything that is and there can be no change. Parmenides's pure logic leads him to say that the world is only stability and unity; there can be no difference, no change or variation, at all. Because there is no change or difference, that which exists—being—must be eternal, unchanging, one, and everlasting.[9] Change, it turns out, is a mere illusion of sense-experience.

Heraclitus and Parmenides represent the earliest version of the dichotomy between two important epistemological methods that entertain different types of evidence: empiricism and rationalism. Empiricism says that all knowledge comes from sense-experience; but as Heraclitus finds, this leads mainly to a knowledge of flux and diversity in which it is hard to find stability. Rationalism says all knowledge is derived from logic and rational deduction; but, as Parmenides discovers, this leads to a world that is like

---

9 Odd as this might sound, it might help to point out that the reader likely accepts Parmenides's argument, though in a slightly qualified form. Theists would say that God alone is the Supreme Being and so he is eternal and unchanging and one; everything other than God needs to be created and so is not wholly being and can therefore change. I return to this in chapter 8.

abstract logic: static, unchanging, unresponsive to our experience. If we are to know the world, our philosophical method needs to accommodate both our experience of change and diversity as well as reason's need for stable, unifying principles.

The logic of Parmenides's argument is unassailable. Yet the fact of change, as Heraclitus points out, is equally obvious. Since change implies difference, the only way out of this impasse is to admit that Parmenides's definition of being is correct—because you cannot get something out of nothing, being is eternal and unchanging—but that there are different *kinds* of being that can combine and separate to account for change and difference. This is the insight of the generation of philosophers collectively known as the *pluralists*. To assume a variety of beings is again a great step forward. It is as if a painter who had been restricted to a palette of only the color white, with which he cannot change the canvas at all, suddenly finds himself with a palette of many colors, which allows him to change the canvas in myriad ways. Importantly, the pluralists also recognize that, in addition to different kinds of being, there has to be, like the painter working on the canvas, a cause for the change if it is to happen according to an intelligible regularity. That is, in addition to passive material principles, there had to be an active principle causing order. Thus, for some pluralists, such as Empedocles (ca. 495–435 BC) and Anaxagoras (ca. 500–428 BC), change in the world is caused by an active mind, often associated with the divine, which causes the motion of a variety of passive material elements.

The great exception to this was the school of the atomists, whose founder was Democritus (ca. 460–370 BC) but whose influence was to persist until after the time of Christ, especially in Lucretius (ca. 99–55 BC). The atomists accept that the world is composed by a great number of tiny indivisible (*a-tom*) particles of matter that move through a void.[10] However, the atomists deny the existence of a moving cause. Rather, atoms move randomly through the void coalescing in various ways to form different kinds of objects depending on the shape and arrangement of the atoms. As Aristotle would point out, the atomists only explain *how* change happens (atoms being rearranged—which is itself a kind of change) but not *why* this happens, thus leaving the universe largely unintelligible in the end.[11]

---

10 This void is in fact a sort of non-being, but it is necessary to allow for the movement of the atoms.

11 *Metaphysics* XII.6 (1071b32–37); cf. *On the Heavens* III.2 (300b9–30).

Atomic theory would have a long life and would return in many different ways over the centuries. There are, however, two important implications to be found in later versions of atomism: materialism and determinism. *Materialism* is the belief that the entire universe is made up of nothing but matter; that is, there is no spiritual reality at all. Thus, human life has no intrinsic superiority to any other agglomeration of atoms. Furthermore, to avoid the unintelligibility of random motion, later materialists would argue that change is caused by physical laws. This philosophy of *determinism* entails that all changes are determined strictly in accord with those laws.[12] A consequence of this is that there can be no freedom, since everything is matter and matter functions according to determinate laws. The idea that we are free is simply an illusion caused by our ignorance of the laws of science. These aspects of materialism and determinism are alive and well in modern scientific and philosophical theories, yet the basic reasoning is no different from what it was 2,500 years ago.

THE SOCRATIC REVOLUTION

The practice of philosophy was approaching its bicentennial and the speculations of the *cosmologists*, those investigating the nature of the universe, seemed to have hit a dead end. Since there was little agreement as to how to explain change, it began to look as if we could not know the nature of the universe at all.

In response to this, a new generation turned their focus from the universe to the place of humankind in the universe. This attention to our self-awareness is evident in the explosion of creativity in Athens in drama, history, sculpture, as well as philosophy. While this newfound appreciation of the human perspective has great benefits, it also brings the risk of overshadowing the objective realities of being, truth, and goodness. Indeed, whenever philosophers are tempted to place the human being at the center of reality, they are faced with the challenge of *relativism*, the presumption that a person's perspective defines reality for that individual.[13]

In philosophy, this turn to the subject was initiated by a group of loosely related thinkers called the *sophists*. For them, the focus on the human reflected a skepticism about our ability to know the truth, a skepticism that

12 For example, Pierre-Simon Laplace, an eighteenth-century exponent of atomism, asserted that if one knew all the laws of physics and the location of all the atoms, we could predict all future events.

13 There is a systematic critique of relativism in both chapter 4 and chapter 6.

arose for two reasons. First, the failures of earlier philosophers to come to agreement about the nature of the world brought into question the reliability of reason. Second, as the Athenians became increasingly aware of the religions and customs of other societies, they began to doubt whether their own religious and moral customs were really true: Can we be sure our gods are real if the Egyptians worship a different pantheon? Why should we presume our moral beliefs are correct when other peoples have different laws and customs? From the fact that people have different customs, they draw the simplistic conclusion that there is no universal truth. For them, truth is relative to the person (or society) who believes it.[14]

This position is most clearly articulated by Protagoras (ca. 490–415 BC), who said, "Man is the measure of all things: of those things that are, that they are; of those things that are not, that they are not." We determine truth, we are not measured by it. If a bucket of water feels cool to me, it is cool; if the same bucket of water feels warm for you, then it is warm for you. If our society thinks cannibalism is wrong, it is wrong for us; if another society practices cannibalism, then it is right for them. Other sophists build on this, questioning whether it is possible to attain any objective idea of truth, goodness, justice, or beauty; that is, they question the possibility that there are standards by which to evaluate our beliefs. Concluding that there are no objective standards, the sophists argue that each person's opinion is true simply because he believes it. This teaching reflects a social revolution in Athens against traditional values, similar to that which shook America in the 1960s. Plato describes the era as one in which "the written law and the customs [of our fathers] were being corrupted at an astounding rate."[15]

This social turmoil inspires a response from Socrates (470–399 BC), who emerges as the seminal figure in ancient thought. Against relativism, Socrates insists that there are objective standards that can be known, especially moral values. While disagreements about whether water is warm or

---

14 This is an object lesson against easy answers, for contradictory beliefs cannot both be true. A thing cannot be both living and dead or round and square. The fact that people disagree in no way implies that there is no truth. In fact, to deny this is fatal to reason and logic, because, if contradictories are both true, there can be no coherent understanding of the world. This is why the foundation for all philosophical inquiry is the principle of noncontradiction: a thing cannot be and not be simultaneously or a proposition cannot be true and false at the same time. Aristotle says that if someone denies this principle, then you should treat him as a vegetable since there is no use in trying to have an intelligent discussion with him. *Metaphysics* IV.4 (1006a12–15).

15 *Seventh Letter* 325d4.

cool are trivial, disagreements about moral issues will destroy society. After all, murder cannot be justified simply because someone claims "it is right for me" or "I do not consider the victim fully human." Social cohesion requires that there be universal standards of truth and goodness accepted by all people.

Socrates grasps the existential importance of universal standards in asserting that the point of living is not simply to survive but to live a just and righteous life. But to be just, we must know and live in accord with that moral standard against which we constantly judge our acts. As noted earlier, he famously proclaims, "An unexamined life is not worth living."[16] By his example, Socrates directs philosophy to a new goal: the care of the soul. Philosophy is attaining wisdom so that we might live a good life.[17]

Socrates sought these objective truths by means of what became known as the Socratic Method. He would ask a person to define some important topic, like justice (or goodness, or piety, or beauty); Socrates then criticizes that definition, showing it to be inadequate, and then continues investigation for a better definition. The crucial insight in Socrates's argument against relativism is his search for a *definition*. Definitions are universally true: the definition of a horse applies not just in Athens but in Egypt and Rome; the definition of justice applies not just in 400 BC, but also in the thirteenth and twenty-first centuries AD. A universal definition, then, is the objective standard used to evaluate beliefs and actions; it is the truth to which we should conform. While Socrates himself never claimed to have finally formulated any definition, his recognition of the objective truth of universal standards discovered by reason permanently shapes the direction of Western philosophy.

Unfortunately, Socrates's incessant questioning had another effect on the people of Athens: it annoyed them greatly. Athens had been through a series of terrible wars with its archenemy Sparta, and Socrates's constant questioning caused many to view him with suspicion. Finally, in 399 BC, he was convicted on trumped-up charges and executed by the government of Athens.[18] Socrates's execution inspired his pupil, Plato, to dedicate his life to philosophy in an attempt to vindicate the wisdom of his misunder-

---

16 *Apology* 32d1–3 and 38a1–4.

17 *Apology* 28b-c and 29d. Indeed, in the *Crito* (48b5), Socrates refuses an opportunity to escape his own execution, saying that the really important thing is not merely to live but to live justly.

18 This fails to communicate the dramatic nature of the events; but I would not deprive anyone of the sublime experience of reading the whole story in Plato's *Apology*, *Crito*, and *Phaedo*.

stood teacher, whom he called "of all the men of his time . . . the wisest and justest and best."[19]

PLATO: THE DISCOVERY OF TRANSCENDENT TRUTH

The philosophy of Plato (427–347 BC) is one of the landmarks of Western civilization. Indeed, the twentieth-century philosopher Alfred North Whitehead said that all of Western philosophy is but a series of footnotes to Plato.[20] After the death of his teacher, Plato begins his philosophical career by writing dialogues that present Socrates's search for definitions. The nature of these dialogues takes a noticeable turn after 387 BC. Though Socrates will remain the main character, Plato begins to go beyond his teacher by articulating philosophical doctrines of his own. The inspiration for this new approach came as a result of a trip Plato made to the Greek colonies in Sicily where he came into contact with the Pythagoreans.[21] Socrates had sought definitions because they were universal and unchanging. The Pythagoreans, for their part, saw that mathematics is a science that unquestionably presents truths that are universal and unchanging. Putting the two together, Plato realizes that mathematics can be in some way the model for discovering universal and unchanging definitions. These truths, then, would be the standards by which to assess our worldly experience. Moreover, this insight allows Plato to solve the impasse into which Heraclitus and Parmenides had driven philosophy, for it is possible for both their ideas of unceasing change and immutable being to be true. By integrating the insights of his predecessors, Plato becomes the cornerstone of what would become the perennial philosophy.

The intuition that drives Plato's philosophy from that point forward is that, like numbers, the universal and unchanging standards are ideas that are known by reason alone. Definitions are universal and unchanging because they point to these ideas, not to the changing, specific objects of the material world. Here he is taking up Parmenides's use of reason to grasp

---

19 *Phaedo* 118a17 (Jowett translation). For his integrity and courage, Socrates has come to be something of a secular saint. Indeed, John Stuart Mill wrote (in chapter 2 of *On Liberty*), "Mankind can hardly be too often reminded that there was once a man named Socrates." Quoting this line, the biblical scholar Adolph Harnack then comments: "That is correct; but it is even more important to remind mankind that a man named Jesus Christ once stood in their midst."

20 Alfred North Whitehead, *Process and Reality: An Essay in Cosmology*, corrected edition, ed. David Ray Griffin and Donald W. Sherburne (New York: The Free Press, 1978), 39. Mortimer Adler cheekily commented that most of those footnotes were written by Aristotle.

21 Plato describes this and subsequent trips to Sicily in his *Seventh Letter*.

an unchanging world of being. Yet, against Parmenides, he did not denigrate the material world of change as mere illusion; rather, Plato also accepts Heraclitus's argument that sense-experience tells us about a world of flux, a world of becoming. This material world, however, is made up of a great variety of examples of any quality (e.g., beauty or justice) that are also changing (susceptible of becoming ugly or unjust). For this reason, this world cannot be a source of stable knowledge; rather it only gives rise to unstable and unreliable opinions about the nature of any quality. Thus, our experience of the changing world—a beautiful song or a just politician—always has to be judged by those eternal standards known by reason. In other words, reason grasps the ideal standard in order to provide stability and unity for assessing the ephemeral experiences of sensation. Plato calls these ideal standards the Ideas or Forms. He would spend forty years developing this theory in his school, the Academy. As a memorial to his mathematical inspiration, he posted over the front door of that school a sign saying, "Let no one ignorant of geometry enter."[22]

The fundamental insight behind the theory of Forms is the recognition that a definition must define some thing. A definition defines a real being—it cannot refer to nothing at all. Plato reasons, then, that, since a definition is unchanging and universal, the thing that is defined must be similarly unchanging and universal. The definition, then, must point not to any material being, which is particular and changing, but to an idea known by reason alone, the Form. He concludes that behind every experienced quality in this world there is an unchanging Form that is the essence of that quality. Plato's own example is that, while there are "many beautiful and many good" things perceived by our senses in the world, we can only call them that because they imitate an "absolute beauty and an absolute good" that we know by reason.[23] It is only because the thing imitates the unchanging and universal Form beauty that we call it beautiful. Further, since a material thing's beauty is partial and apt to change, it can never be confused with the essence of beauty.

Because the Form is an unchanging essence, it is the necessary basis for knowledge. Knowledge is distinguished from opinion—which can be false—in two ways: knowledge must be "of that which is" and it must be infallible. First, knowledge must reflect what really is the case: if I say Washington is

---

22 Many great philosophers (Descartes, Leibniz, Husserl, Russell, Whitehead) start out as mathematicians and, inspired by math's certainty, try to make philosophy like math. As we will see, this is not without problems.

23 *Republic* VI (507b).

the capital of the United States, that really is so, and so I have knowledge. If I say New York is the capital, that is not really so, and so I am ignorant. Further, knowledge cannot be a lucky guess; it requires that I know with infallibility, in such a way that it cannot be wrong (like $2 + 2 = 4$). Knowing the Form meets these criteria because it is a real essence that, as unchanging, I cannot ever fall into error about. The Form, as the defining universal essence, is therefore the standard used to make sense of sense-experience. Whenever we use a common name to refer to a number of different, imperfect and changing instances—blue things, or good things, or beautiful things—there has to be some essence that justifies this usage of the word.

As a corollary, the Form, as the universal essence, is also what determines things to be what they are. Plato would say that a material object in the world is what it is, or has a certain quality, because it *imitates* or *participates* in a Form. For example, the reason this animal is a dog is because it imitates that essential Form; if the dog were to die, however, it would cease to imitate the Form of dog and would instead imitate the Forms of water, carbon, flesh, and so on. Note that the Forms themselves do not change; rather, things change because objects imitate different Forms.

These principles lead Plato to a dualistic vision of reality, combining Parmenides's idea of being with Heraclitus's idea of becoming. There is a world of Forms, a transcendent, eternal realm of unchanging universal essences known by reason; this is the source of true knowledge, articulated in definitions. Then, there is the material world of changing particular things as given by sense-experience; since this is changing, it can only be the basis of opinion.[24] Here we have Plato's solution to the problems of change and the one and the many. While things in this world—dogs, cats, birds—are always changing, the Form of the thing remains the same. Further, while there are many dogs, birds, and cats in this world, we can identify each species according to their common essence of a shared participation in a universal Form.

We might still wonder why the essence cannot be known from our experience of things in the world. Plato argues that this is simply not possible. Consider, for example, a geometric formula. We all know that the area of a circle—of all circles—is πr^2. But of what is this formula true? Circles in the material world are all imperfect because of imperfections of ink and

---

24 Though this notion runs throughout all of Plato's philosophy, the clearest illustrations of it are in a famous series of extended metaphors—the Analogy of the Sun, the Simile of the Line, and the Allegory of the Cave—in *Republic* VI–VII (505–18).

paper. And yet, the formula is true. The truth of this formula cannot point to any material instance, yet it is fundamental to geometry. Plato would conclude that this formula can only arise from our idea of a perfect circle, known by reason; this is what allows us to apply that formula to all circles we encounter in the world, no matter how imperfect or changing they are. The same applies for all essences: things in this world are imperfect, and so the standard must be in the realm of Forms.

Indeed, because things in the material world are both changing and imperfect, the greatest error we can make is to assume that sensation gives us knowledge. On the contrary, sensation only gives opinion—uncertain, ungrounded beliefs that may or may not be true. The only thing worse than relying on mere sensation is basing our beliefs on reproductions, or images, of material things—pictures, reflections, shadows, and today television and the internet—which only distantly participate in the Form and so are not reliable at all. This is the perennially relevant lesson of Plato's famous Allegory of the Cave in which people tied to poles can see only shadows on the wall in front of them and mistake those shadows for reality. His point is that we only attain truth by turning away from sensation and opinion (the shadows) and to the truths known by reason (reality in the Forms).[25]

In sum, for Plato the Forms play two important roles: they are *what is*, being that is unchanging; and they are *what is known*, the essence that is grasped by reason in judging experience. The thrust of Plato's argument, then, is to pull us away from relying on sense-experience and to use reason to know unchanging truths, the Forms. But this leaves an unsettling division of reality into world of sense-experience and the transcendent realm of Forms. It is this division of reality that motivates his greatest student Aristotle to take a different approach. Aristotle spent twenty years in the Academy, but, upon Plato's death in 347 BC, he went on his own. He then spent the rest of his life criticizing Plato's dualism as a useless doubling of reality.[26] For Aristotle, *this world*, the material world of sense-experience, is the world we live in, so this is the only world that we need to explain. This basic difference between Plato and Aristotle, conspicuous in every branch

---

25 *Republic* VII (514a–517b).

26 In *Metaphysics* I.9, Aristotle presents a number of criticisms of Plato, but the idea of the Forms as being a useless doubling of the world is the one he leads off with (990b1–3): "Firstly, in seeking to grasp the causes of the things around us, they introduced others equal in number to these, as if a man who wanted to count things thought he would not be able to do it while they were few, but tried to count them when he had added to their number."

of philosophy from metaphysics to politics, is memorably captured by the Renaissance master Raphael in the painting *The School of Athens*. Plato and Aristotle stand together at the center of the painting. Plato points skyward, to the unchanging world of Forms, while Aristotle resolutely points to the earth, the material world of common-sense experience.

ARISTOTLE: THE MASTER OF THOSE WHO KNOW

The primary philosophical reason Aristotle (384–322 BC) rejects this doubling of the world has to do with questions concerning how the Forms,[27] existing in a separate realm of intelligibility, can act as essences and causes of things in this world. First, Aristotle asks, how can the essence of anything exist apart from the thing of which it is the essence? If I am essentially a man, then that essence must be in me. It seems obvious that, for any object, its defining essence must be in that object. It is simply implausible to say that what makes an object to be what it is exists somewhere other than in the object itself.

A similar problem arises with Plato's notion that the Forms in some way cause things to be what they are by "participation" or "imitation." Plato never really explains how this works or why things begin to or cease participating in a Form. Recall that philosophy began with the aim of explaining why change happens, but unchanging Forms in a transcendent realm just cannot explain the reality of change in this world.[28]

In fact, Plato's problems arise from his failure to accept the full reality of change. Plato was so convinced of the need for truth to be universal and unchanging that he assumed that objects of truth—the beings that are known—must themselves be universal and unchanging. Since every material thing in this world is particular and changing, this led him to separate the world of change (becoming) from the realm of the Forms (being). This obscures a very obvious point: that changing things exist and so must themselves be beings. Plato, then, is left with a great puzzle: not all real things are beings—a paradoxical conclusion indeed. This problematic notion of being is in need of resolution.

Aristotle was able to avoid these puzzles because he was more open to the reality of change. This was, perhaps, due in part to an accident of history: his father had been a doctor. This means that Aristotle tended to view the

---

27 Aristotle is called the "master of those who know" by Dante in *Inferno*, canto 4.

28 *Metaphysics* I.9 (992a24–29).

world, including change, through the lens of biology and not math (as Plato had done). In biology, change is not only natural; it is good because it represents development and maturation. So, Aristotle's fundamental response to Plato is to define *being* in a different way so as to allow for change. Where Plato identifies the basic kind of being as Forms, which are unchanging, Aristotle defines being in terms of *substances* that have the capacity for change built into them. By focusing on substance, Aristotle can explain this world as it really is: both stable and changing.

Act and Potency: Explaining Change

It is in explaining change that Aristotle takes a giant leap over not just Plato but over all his predecessors. While others looked for one underlying principle to explain change, Aristotle recognizes that change must be explained in terms of a simultaneous similarity-with-difference. Accordingly, change can only be explained if we understand substance (being) to be a composite of two distinct but complementary principles, one of which will ground similarity, while the other allows for difference. This allows for one thing to become different. Aristotle describes these underlying principles as a composition of act and potency.[29] *Act* is the principle determining what something is now; *potency* is the principle that has the ability to be something different, what the thing can become. Incorporating the principle of potency (the capacity to take on difference) into being (what is) is Aristotle's ingenious discovery that enables him to explain the reality of change.[30] This enables Aristotle to do justice to the perceived dynamism of reality without denying an underlying intelligible stability.

The first obvious instance of change is exemplified in the fact that every organism, while remaining the same organism, goes through a great deal of development in the course of its life. An oak tree begins as a germinated acorn and becomes a sapling then a mighty tree. A human being begins as a single-cell zygote, develops as an embryo and fetus, and then through infancy and adolescence into adulthood. There is obviously one thing that is underlying this change, for that change is the development and growth of that thing. It is the tree or the person who by nature continuously grows.

---

29 This is the topic of *Metaphysics* IX.

30 It is a truly brilliant discovery, since we only ever experience what something currently is. To be able to grasp that a being is now one thing but can be something else and to isolate the principle responsible for that tendency to otherness requires a great mental abstraction. That is why it took Greek philosophers over two centuries to identify it.

Aristotle calls this underlying reality *substance*. A substance is defined as that which exists in itself and not another.[31] That is, substances are the independently existing realities in the world, the things that we point to as objects in our experience. The substance is the principle of identity and stability underneath the change. Yet, as we shall see, because it is able to change in various ways, because it is the subject of the process of development, it is also the source of the dynamism that is manifested in the changes.

There is a great variety of changes that a substance may undergo. It can grow in size and weight; it can change color and attain new abilities; it may move location; it might act in different ways. Aristotle calls these changing properties *accidents*. Accidents are most easily distinguished from substances because they exist only in substances and never on their own. (They are real, but they exist in a dependent fashion.) Redness exists but only as a property of the apple that is red; a hundred pounds exists but only in a rock or a dog that weighs a hundred pounds. Accidents like color and weight only exist as properties of substances. The substance's accidental properties, though, always have the potential to change: I gain and lose weight, I sit then stand then I walk, I move to a new place, I learn something, I grow in virtue. These changing properties, however, can exist only because the substance is both stable over time and yet dynamic in causing these changes.

This first kind of change, which Aristotle calls accidental change, is possible because substances always exist in composition with accidents. The thing that primarily exists is the substance; the accidents have potency to come and go. When a certain accident exists, though—say I am pale or weigh two hundred pounds—that complexion and weight also exist. But to distinguish the primary existence of the substance from the accidental actualities it has at any moment, we refer to the substance as *first act*, the primary existence of things in the world, while accidents are a *second act*, a real property, but one whose existence is dependent on the substance. It should not be thought that accidents are unimportant. Substances cannot exist without them. Indeed, though these accidents depend on substance, they are in fact the first thing we notice about anything: we perceive size, shape, color, and activity and recognize them as manifestations of the substance's reality. Only because an apple has a particular color, shape, and flavor do I recognize it as an apple.

31 *Categories* 2 (1b3–5) and 5 (2a11–13).

Aristotle famously lists nine kinds of accidental properties:[32]

1. Quantity (how much in size: five feet, ten pounds)
2. Quality (what sort of property: red, musical, pretty)
3. Relation (how it is related to other substances: taller than, father)
4. Time (when: 3:00 p.m.)
5. Place (where: in the kitchen, in New York)
6. Habit (what does it have on or possess: wearing shoes, being virtuous)
7. Posture (how is it positioned: sitting, standing)
8. Action (what it is doing: running, speaking)
9. Passion (what is being done to it: being spoken to, being rained on).

For Aristotle, therefore, any real being must be one of ten categories of being: it is either a substance (Fido, Socrates, this tree) or it is one of the nine accidents (which are always secondary because they are dependent on substances). These are the only ways things can exist in the world: as perduring substances that develop and grow in terms of constantly changing accidents.

Substantial Change

There is another and more fundamental sort of change evident in our experience. This is the fact that substances themselves come into existence and go out of existence. Organisms are born and they die. Artifacts are built but will someday fall apart.[33] This kind of change is generation (substances coming to be) and corruption (substances ceasing to exist). To distinguish this from accidental change, we refer to this as *substantial change*.[34] In order to account for this kind of change, we must once again find a composition of act and potency. That is, substance itself must be composed of two principles, one of which is a principle of actuality, determining what the substance is, and another of which is a principle of potentiality, with the capacity to become something else. Taking his cue from Plato, Aristotle calls the principle of actuality the form because it determines what something is.[35] But that form

---

32 *Categories* 4 (1b25–2a4). Aristotle is sometimes accused of not providing logical justification for this particular list of accidents. However, Thomas gives a very clear logical deduction of the accidents in *CP* III.3.5.322–25.

33 Though often used as examples, artifacts are not technically substances, as we see in chapter 5.

34 *Physics* I.7–9.

35 Customarily the word *form* is capitalized when used with respect to Plato's theory of Forms but left in lowercase when discussing Aristotle's theory.

exists only in composition with *matter*,[36] a principle that has the potency to lose one form in order to take on another. In other words, when matter loses one form, a substance is corrupted; but, in taking on a new form—a new principle of actuality—that same matter underlies the generation of a new substance.[37] This is substantial change.

Let us illustrate this relation of form and matter with an example of substantial change. A human being begins to exist at conception. Prior to conception there was matter with the form of sperm and matter with the form of ovum; at conception, that matter merges, loses the form of sperm and egg, and takes on the new form of human. The matter provided by the sperm and egg has the potential to receive a new form and become a new human being. Of course, this same process explains corruption or death: when a substance loses its form and ceases to exist, the matter takes on a new form and becomes something different. Thus, when a human being dies, the body remains. It is no longer properly a human being but simply organic compounds of the no-longer-alive body. Similarly, I can cut down a tree to get logs and then burn the log and find a pile of ash. In each of these changes, the matter underlying the change had the potential to possess the form of tree, the form of log, and the form of ash, which results in three distinct substances.

Here we see Aristotle's most important development of Plato's thought. Where Plato saw the Forms as existing apart from this world, for Aristotle forms are *immanent*, existing in composition with matter to constitute a particular substance. This helps to resolve the puzzles left from Plato's theory of Forms. As immanent, Aristotle's forms can be the essence of the substance, since they define what kind of thing it is. Yet the immanence of forms also explains change, since the potency of matter to take on a new form means that new substances come to exist when that matter is deprived of a previous form. In short, Aristotle's discovery of potentiality allows that being (substance) is always capable of becoming; this more profound capacity for change is not just accidental change of second act, but the substantial change of first act—the primary existence of things—through generation and corruption.

---

36 The English word is from the Latin *materia*, which is derived from *mater*, or mother, that which is the source of new beings.

37 An important consequence of this is that, since forms are principles of actuality, they can exist without matter; but without matter, they would be unchanging. This is how Aristotle approaches the existence of God in *Metaphysics* XII (see chapter 8).

The theory that defines being as substances composed of the complementary principles of form and matter is known as *hylomorphism*. Every
changing being is a composition of stuff (*hyle*) with a shape (*morphe*). (Aristotle allows that there are unchanging beings that are pure forms; however,
for now, the focus is on material substances since these are the principles
of change in the world. I discuss the immaterial causes of being in the next
chapter.) Central to this theory is the fact that form and matter are complementary *principles*, not themselves *things*. A thing exists on its own; but
form and matter only exist with one another.[38] We can see this point in considering that there cannot be a shape without some stuff to be shaped, nor
can there be stuff without any shape at all. For example, a chalk circle is
equally composed chalk (stuff) and circle (shape). If I try to take away either
the shape or the chalk, the other also will cease to be.

In substances, then, form is the principle of actuality that determines
what the substance is. While one might say the effect of the form is giving
the substance its shape in the most general sense—we can distinguish dogs
and cats and birds by their bodily appearance—we need to be more precise
in formulating this. As the principle of actuality, form simultaneously gives
to matter a pattern of organization required for that substance to exist and
to carry out its characteristic activities. For example, every atom is made of
protons, neutrons, and electrons; but the form of carbon will order them
so that a carbon atom exists and is able to behave as carbon is expected (and
not as iron would). Similarly, all animals are made of organic tissues like
flesh and blood; but the form of a person will order that into complex
anatomical systems so that the person can carry on activities characteristic
of persons (but not those of a fish).

Thus, we can say that the form gives three things to matter. It (1) orders
the matter, (giving the matter its identifiable shape or sensible pattern indicative of a kind of thing), (2) causes the substance to exist (it gives existence
or first act), and (3) endows that substance with the capacity to act in certain
ways (it gives the potential for certain second acts). The form and the existence of the substance are therefore coextensive with determinate power for
accidental development. The dynamic potential of substances to change in
accidental ways is thus grounded in the form. This is a crucial principle for

---

38 Philosophers will discuss matter with no form at all as a principle of pure potentiality to take
on form; this purely hypothetical state (for without form it has no actuality) is called *prime
matter*. On this, see Aquinas's *PN*, 14–17.

the intelligibility of change in the world: what something is (first act, form) determines what something can do (second act, accidents).[39] For example, a human being cannot (naturally) turn green, fly, or grow to be fifty feet tall. Rather, how humans look, their size and actions, manifest the reality of their human form. And the same can be said of all other natures: the accidental properties and activities of any substance are indicative of the form that makes that substance what it is.

If form is the principle of actuality, then matter is the principle of potentiality. But the potentiality of matter not only accounts for the difference of substantial change. Rather, because the actuality of forms is limited when it is present in matter, matter is also the principle of individuality. Matter allows the universal form to become instantiated as a *particular* substance. That is, while all people have the form of human, and all dogs have the form of dog, each particular person or dog is different and unique. The differences between individuals arise from their material distinction—their size, actions, histories, habits, and so on. Thus, there can be many distinct individual substances that share the same universal nature.

This happens, again, because of the potentiality of matter, which limits each individual substance to one time and place and set of accidents and actions—that is, it makes it unique. Thus, the form of human is wholly in both Plato and Aristotle, yet their matter makes them unique individual persons, since they have different accidents: properties, talents, and histories. The form of dog is in both Fido and Rusty, but again they are particular substances because matter allows for distinct sets of accidents—size, color, playfulness—by which they can be distinguished. Nevertheless, because action (second act) follows from being (first act), all people will be broadly alike and all dogs will have intelligible similarities. (Conversely, we are able to distinguish species because of these characteristic accidents: a cat and a skunk might appear similar initially, but their accidents reveal that there is an essential difference between them.)

It is the union of form as act and matter as potential that allows for there to be many individuals of one thing. Both the problem of change and the problem of the one and the many are solved by this composition of principles.

---

39 This crucial point about the dual nature of act and potency is nicely summarized by Aquinas in *DP* 1.1.

Essence

A consequence of the presence of form as the principle of actuality is that it determines the essence of the substance as a universal kind of being.[40] The form of human makes Socrates a *human being*, and so he is similar to all other humans and distinguishable from nonhuman animals. The form of dog makes Fido a dog: he is like all dogs and distinguishable from cats and horses. To call Socrates a "human" and Fido a "dog" is much more significant than describing them by their accidental properties, since these names indicate the *essence* of the substance, its whatness. Accidents change constantly; I grow fat, get tan, go bald, yet I still exist. But an essence cannot be lost without the substance ceasing to exist. I am a human—that is my essence—and the only way I can cease to be human is by dying.

This difference between accident and essence is marked by saying that accidents are *in* substances, but essences are *said of* substances. While these statements may look similar grammatically (Socrates is *x*), they are very different statements, for the essences that are said of a substance are the most fundamental description of its being.

In determining what a substance is, the essence determines the nature of the substance, and so is the basis of that substance's definition. For Aristotle, the word *nature* indicates an internal principle of movement and change; nature is the essence considered as a principle for dynamic activity.[41] In other words, because the form organizes matter so as to act in a determinate way, each substance has a determinate nature that causes that substance to act in a certain way, to develop accidents indicative of that kind of being. It is obvious that, since there are a great variety of ways of acting in the world, there are a great number of different natures. The nature of an apple tree is to grow apples; the nature of a lion is to live in prides and hunt. We can say, then, that activity is a self-revelation of the essence of a being.[42]

The characteristic activity of a substance reveals an intelligible pattern that becomes the basis for classifying that substance in terms of its species,

---

40 Aristotle also refers to these essential predicates as "second substance" in *Categories* 5 (2b15–35). I note this primarily because it plays a role in early Christian theology: Gregory of Nyssa and other early Church Fathers would adopt this terminology in their theologizing about the Persons of the Trinity.

41 *Physics* II.1 (192b15). Notice that *nature* is etymologically derived from the Latin *natus*, meaning birth; thus, nature implies the kind of biological development that is expected for living things. Of course, each kind of living thing has a different pattern to its development.

42 W. Norris Clarke, *The One and the Many*, 31–36.

or universal kind of being. Here Aristotle is taking up Socrates's quest, for this is the basis for the definition of the substance. Thus, Socrates is a human, which describes his material appearance and characteristic activity as common to all humans. But each species, or kind, will then be definable according to its genus, or what larger grouping of similar species (the human is an *animal*), and difference, or what distinguishes that species from others in that genus (the human is a *rational* animal). All these aspects of essence that define *what* a substance is—species, genus, difference—can be truly *said of* any particular substance. In this way, we can affirm that each substance is particular and yet knowable in terms of a universal essence that defines that substance as a specific kind, or class, of being.

The Four Causes: Why Change Happens

As we have seen, the basic unit of reality for Aristotle is the substance. But that being is characterized by becoming: substances change. A substance comes to be when form and matter come together; the form determines the nature of the substance and the matter makes it a unique individual of that species. But, because the substance is of a certain nature, it will act and change in a predictable way, characteristic of that nature, throughout the course of its existence. When that substantial form is lost and the matter takes on a new form, then the thing ceases to exist and a new substance comes to be.

We have explained *how* things change by two compositions of act and potency: form and matter explain substantial change, and substance and accident explain accidental change. However, we have not yet explained *why* change happens. Remember, our natural curiosity will necessarily inquire why change is happening—why new substances come to exist and why those substances develop through a process of accidental change. To explain why things change with regularity and in an intelligible pattern is crucial. Aristotle's answer lies in his theory of the *four causes*.[43]

For the perennial philosophy, a *cause* is an explanation of why something comes to be the way it is. To be able to point to why an event happens, to know the causal principles that explain a course of events, is to truly understand how nature works. Without the cause, the thing in question would not exist. But Aristotle's understanding of causes is broader than our modern idea, because the scientific method can account for only causes directly observable in experience. Aristotle accepts these, but he sees that

---

43 *Physics* II.3 (194b16–195a2).

the mechanical actions of matter are not self-explanatory,[44] and so the most important causes are metaphysical explanations for change.

In explaining substantial change, we have already become familiar with two *intrinsic causes* of change: matter and form. These are the principles of potency and act required for change to happen. The material cause is stuff from which a being is made; the formal cause is the principle that determines what it is. As we have seen, this means that the form gives the matter its intelligible pattern, its existence as a kind of thing, and ability to act in ways typical of that nature. Matter, in contrast, causes the individuality of the substance in terms of the uniqueness of its accidents.

These are causal principles because they can come together in different ways to explain the ultimate effect. For example, bricks and mortar are matter with a potential to take on many different forms. You can make a house, or a church, or a barbeque pit with the same material stuff. It is the pattern that determines what sort of thing exists and what can be done with it. Similarly, the nucleic acids ACGT compose the DNA of every living thing; yet, depending on the form that orders those nucleic acids, we get very different genomes creating different organisms with unimaginably diverse capabilities.

Yet matter is equally important, for it has to be the right sort of matter if it is to be properly disposed to receiving the form. You could have two things in the shape of a human, but if one is bronze and the other is flesh and blood, only one is human. Indeed, the story of the Three Little Pigs epitomizes the importance of the material cause with respect to the same formal cause. Therefore, the material cause is a real explanation for why something is what it is.

A substance comes into being with this composition of form and matter. But what brings them together? And why do substances act and develop in predictable ways? In other words, why do these changes happen? To these questions, Aristotle posits two extrinsic causes: the *efficient cause* and the *final cause*. Both of these are instances of a fundamental principle of reasoning, the principle of sufficient reason: there must be an adequate reason for what happens in the world.[45] If we deny this, if we assume the change

---

44 This was Aristotle's critique of the early materialist thinkers, but it applies just as well to modern science. To describe nature by finding laws is not an explanation: to find a regularity (a law) implies that there must be *some reason why* that law correctly describes the experienced events.

45 The principle of sufficient reason is discussed more fully in chapter 3.

can happen without any cause whatsoever, we destroy the intelligibility of our experience. Therefore, it is necessary that we discover these causes as explanations for our experience of change in the world.

The efficient cause is a substance (or substances) whose activity produces change, bringing an effect into existence. This is particularly evident with respect to the generation of new substances, since nothing can cause itself to exist. (Accidents require efficient causes, too, but here we focus on substantial change.) For a substance to cause its own existence, it would have to exist before it even came into being, which is logically impossible. But there has to be some reason for this new union of form and matter in generating a substance. The efficient cause is the cause whose activity contributes to the real existence of substances by bringing form and matter into composition. Bricks and mortar become a house only if there are workers to give shape to them. Sperm and egg only conceive a new person if there are people engaging in conjugal union. Thus, the efficient causes are necessary to explain how new beings, especially new substances, are generated.

Substances, though, are characterized by activity. They develop in predictable patterns as manifest by their accidental changes. The fetus develops on her own according to a known pattern, a pattern that continues throughout maturation and throughout life. The cause of this regular development of a substance is the *final cause*. The final cause is the end-state that a substance tends to as determined by its nature. It is the goal of the natural process of development; for this reason, that end-state can be said to be the purpose for which the substance exists. Apple trees sink roots, grow leaves, bud, in order to grow fruit (for it is by this that its seeds are spread). Thus, the tree exists for the purpose of growing apples, and all its other activities and changes are subordinated to that goal. In other words, that end is the primary potential of the plant to which all other potentials are ordered. If there were no final cause, there would be no reason for a substance to act, let alone act according to a predictable and ordered pattern directed to attaining that final cause.

One consequence of this notion of final causality is that, since it is the state of being that a substance naturally seeks, we can assess whether a substance is good or bad by the extent to which it fulfills its purpose. For example, a house is built for the sake of providing shelter from weather; a house with thin walls and a leaky roof is, then, a bad house. An apple tree exists for the sake of growing apples; a barren apple tree is, therefore, a bad apple tree.

A second consequence of finality is that it motivates all activity of substances, including their activity as efficient causes. For this reason, final cause is called the cause of causes.[46] It is the ultimate explanation of dynamic change in the universe.

A third consequence, which we have already seen, is that there is an integral relation between formal cause and final cause. The form determines the essence, and the essence determines the nature of the substance, moving it to act in certain regular ways. Implicit in the form is the state of being to be sought as the perfection of substances of that nature. In abstract, this seems an abstruse philosophical point; however, it is really the commonplace observation that what something is determines what it does. Clay made into a vase holds flowers; clay made into a pipe plays music. Flesh and blood in a dog give certain abilities, while in a fish there will be different abilities. This fundamental doctrine is often stated as the principle that action follows from being (in Latin, *agere sequitur esse*). It is one of the most basic rules for grounding the intelligibility of this world, since second act always flows from first act.

In fact, so tightly united are the formal and final causes of a being, that we normally identify a thing's essence wholly through its activities. To go back to the green glob in chemistry class: in order to discover what it is, we need to test it. We weigh it; we mix it with water, acid, and other chemicals; we try to burn it. We discover its nature based on how it acts under all these conditions. This activity reveals the essence, so this heretofore unknown stuff becomes a definable substance. In fact, Thomas says that we know the form of no substance directly but only by means of the sensible activities and accidents by which the form is made manifest.[47]

LATER PHILOSOPHICAL DEVELOPMENTS

Later chapters take up in more detail other arguments and ideas from Plato and Aristotle, since their thinking provides the foundation for both how we see philosophical problems and strategies for solving them. Here, though, we must attend to their notion of form. Forms are crucial for both Plato and Aristotle, because forms are the stable reality behind the flux of activity, as well as a universal essence uniting disparate individuals. Moreover, for both Plato and Aristotle, because the form is the stable universal behind

---

46 Thomas makes this point in *PN* 29.
47 *ST* I.77.1.ad 7.

appearance, it is also what is known and so makes reality intelligible. As the grounding of both being and truth (as well as the good), the discovery of form shows that the world has an order independent of humans, an order that we must bow to if we are to claim to be wise. For this reason, the rejection of the concept of formal cause—and, by implication, of final cause—is the defining aspect of philosophy as it developed in the modern era.

However, before turning to those modern developments, let us first consider a couple of the more important thinkers who contributed to the perennial philosophical tradition by cultivating the interplay of Platonism and Aristotelianism.

The last major contribution to the perennial tradition in the ancient world is that of Plotinus (AD 204–270), the founder of Neoplatonism. Neoplatonism is explicitly part of the perennial philosophy since its aim is to synthesize the ideas of Plato, Aristotle, and Stoicism.[48] Plotinus's main insight is that neither Plato nor Aristotle ever really answered the problem of the one and the many. Both explain how individuals are united into *kinds*, or species, by their common forms, but neither give a convincing explanation as to how the different forms are united. Plato had suggested that the Form of the Good is a "Superform" above all other Forms that in some way causes everything.[49] However, this idea was never fully developed. Aristotle's highest cause, the Unmoved Mover, only causes the motion of all the substances but cannot account for their existence.[50] Plotinus tries to answer the problems of the one and the many and change by integrating these Platonic and Aristotelian causes in a new way.

Plotinus articulates a subtle and intricate vision of reality. Since there must be one principle uniting all things, Plotinus posits a source of being called the One (or the Good). The One is not God but rather a philosophical principle that causes beings by natural necessity, like fire causing heat. This occurs by means of a series of "emanations" in which being flows down, like a champagne fountain, from the One through intermediate stages that constitute a

---

48 Stoicism was the dominant philosophy during most of the Hellenistic era (200 BC–AD 200). It argued that the world is deterministically ordered by a divine Reason that is identical with Nature; consequently, the most virtuous form of action is to live in harmony with that order by disciplining one's emotions and desires so as to not be disturbed by events outside of one's control.

49 See the three overlapping arguments for the Forms in *Republic* VI–VII (505–18). Plato also identifies the Good with Beauty in the *Symposium* (200d–212c).

50 *Metaphysics* XII.7 (1072a18–1073a13). Since Plato's Good and Aristotle's Unmoved Mover are in some way analogous to the Christian idea of God, I consider them more fully in chapter 8.

dyad then a triad, finally ending in a multiplicity when being fills the potency of matter and becomes many different things.[51] The first emanation from the One constitutes the Mind, and so there are now two things. The Mind looks back and contemplates the One and conceives of the many ways things can exist, and in so doing constitutes the Platonic Forms. The second emanation now comes from the Mind and causes a World Soul, an active force that, in turn, implants Forms into a passive material substrate. This third emanation actualizes hylomorphic substances of form and matter. Since matter is at the opposite end from the One or the Good, matter becomes associated not just with plurality but also with evil and unintelligibility.[52]

Since the One is perfectly good, all beings desire to be reunited with it. A person can accomplish this ascent by purification from matter: by ascetically rejecting the material world, we turn to the Forms and unite with the Mind. But this is as far as reason can go. Like Plato and Aristotle, for Plotinus the Forms are the principles of being and intelligibility. The One, however, cannot be any one form, since it has to be the source of *all* Forms. Therefore, Plotinus insists that the One is "beyond being" and so beyond rational comprehension. Union with the One can only be attained by a kind of mystical union (which Plotinus claimed to have experienced a handful of times).[53]

While the details of Plotinus's philosophy might appear strange, its basic structure is vaguely similar to certain Christian doctrines: The world comes forth from a transcendent source of being that is Good, and we humans seek to return to the divinity by a certain ascetic lifestyle. Moreover, this transcendent being has three parts to it (The One, Mind, and World Soul). It was for this reason that Saint Augustine (354–430) found Neoplatonism an important aid on his way to conversion. Augustine had two great stumbling blocks in accepting Christianity: he could not imagine the existence of an immaterial being and he could not excuse God from the existence of evil in the world. Neoplatonism pointed the way to solutions for both problems.[54] First, it showed him how this changing material world could only be caused by an unchanging immaterial reality that was in fact more real.

---

[51] The most concise statement of this is in *Enneads* V.2.

[52] This depreciative conception of matter is not restricted to Neoplatonism; it is common in the Gnosticism that informs heretical sects, from the Manicheans to today, that doubt the goodness of material creation.

[53] There is a tradition that Plotinus was familiar with Buddhism, which may account for this mysticism.

[54] See *Confessions* VII.9.13–14.

Second, it showed him that evil is not caused by God but is a disruption in the order caused by God. In other words, evil is a lack of being, like a cavity in a tooth. This intellectual conversion prepared the way for his religious conversion in embracing Christianity.

Augustine played a critical role in the advancement in the perennial philosophy, for his adaptation of Platonism would become the foundation for Western Christian philosophy for almost one thousand years. He converts Plato's Forms into the Divine Ideas by which God freely creates the world out of love. Since the world is a manifestation of God's love, it is necessarily good; evil, therefore, can only be the result of free will.[55] Thus, Augustine's great contribution to philosophy is the discovery of free will and an accompanying emphasis on love—not only in God, but in humans— as a complement to the intellect's grasp of truth. He argues that the most important aspect of the moral life is to direct one's will to love the appropriate object, since happiness lies in loving the highest good, in union with God: "For Thou hast made us for Thyself and our hearts are restless till they rest in Thee."[56] Evil, then, is the result of a disordered love, where we desire something that cannot bring us happiness.[57]

Saint Augustine is a transitional figure, for with him the rational wisdom of the Greeks is assimilated into the Judeo-Christian revealed wisdom. Symbolically, we can take the year 529 as a signal of this change, for in that year Emperor Justinian closed Plato's Academy and Saint Benedict founded the monastery of Monte Cassino. The engine of intellectual life was no longer Greek philosophy but rather Christian theology. Philosophy in this era was inevitably concerned with the reconciliation of faith and reason, two sources of wisdom pointing to the same truth.

During most of this era, Christian philosophy was Platonist. This is because it is, with its emphasis on the transcendent, amenable to Christian doctrine. It is also the case, though, that Aristotle's philosophy, aside from his logical treatises, had been lost to the Latin-speaking West.[58] However, after 1085 when Christians reconquered Toledo (where Aristotle's works had

---

55 This is developed at length in chapter 9.

56 *Confessions* I.1.1.

57 Augustine, *On Free Choice of the Will*, Bk. I.

58 Boethius (AD 480–525)—known for his important theological writings as well as *The Consolation of Philosophy*—had begun translating Aristotle into Latin but was executed by the emperor after having completed only the first part of Aristotle's works, those on logic. These works were enough, however, to imbue Aristotle with a certain authority.

been studied by Muslims and Jews) from the Muslims, Aristotle's thought became the focus of Christian philosophers and theologians. But Aristotle was not so easy to assimilate, since his thought contradicted Christian doctrine in fundamental ways. For example, Aristotle denied the creation of the world, the personal immortality of the soul, and the providential love of God. However, Aristotle's philosophy presented a more adequate interpretation of the natural world than did Plato's, and so he could not be ignored.[59]

This was the situation into which Thomas Aquinas (1225–1274) stepped, and it is why his philosophy is the apex of the perennial tradition. He synthesizes into a coherent philosophy all the strands of wisdom available to him: not only the truths of Plato and Aristotle but also the Christian Neoplatonism of Augustine and the perfect Wisdom of revelation. In particular, his use of Aristotle's idea of potency allows him to see the radical contingency of creation, implying as a corollary that God alone is the ultimate cause of all that is. But, by giving being to creatures, God also endows them with a power to act, so that natural substances exercise real causal activity, especially with respect to the generation of substances, knowledge, and virtue.[60] This causal activity of nature means that there is an intelligible order in creation itself, even though all creatures depend on God for their existence. If wisdom is to understand the causal order of the universe, then wisdom lies in appreciating both God and nature.

We have seen that a common thread running through all the great figures of the perennial philosophy—Plato, Aristotle, Plotinus, Augustine, Thomas—is a tendency to synthesize diverse sources of wisdom into a coherent doctrine. This fact highlights an important aspect of the perennial philosophy. This is its respect for authority and tradition. These philosophers understood that the search for wisdom involves every member of the human race. Wisdom cannot be discovered alone or anew by each generation; rather, we can grow in wisdom only if we appreciate the accomplishments of those who came before us. However, since wisdom is a search for truth, this respect for authority is a not a blind repetition of the past but a critical assessment in light of ever-growing knowledge.[61] This practice

59 About this time, the monastery was replaced as the primary center of intellectual life by the newly founded universities; for this reason, this era in philosophy is referred to as *scholasticism* (from the Latin for school, *schola*).

60 *DV* 11.1.

61 See C. J. F. Martin, *An Introduction to Medieval Philosophy* (Edinburgh: Edinburgh University Press, 1996), 16–44.

embodies a careful balance of humility and pride, for it recognizes the debt to the past without being imprisoned by it. As Bernard of Chartres (d. ca. 1130) said, "We are like dwarves seated on the shoulders of giants. We see more things than the Ancients and things more distant, but it is due neither to the sharpness of our sight nor the greatness of our stature, it is simply because they have lent us their own."[62] To forget the hard-won wisdom of the past is to sentence oneself to a self-incurred darkness since one has turned away from the light.

THE REJECTION OF THE PERENNIAL PHILOSOPHY

This synthesis of faith and reason in the perennial philosophy did not last. In fact, on March 7, 1277, three years to the day after the death of Thomas Aquinas, the bishop of Paris condemned 219 propositions related to Aristotelian philosophy.[63] The impetus for these criticisms was the theological need to defend the omnipotence and freedom of God. Earlier philosophers had assumed that the intelligible order of creation revealed how God *had to* be; but, if God really is omnipotent and free, what actually exists tells us nothing about God, since he could have created something different. This emphasis on unlimited divine omnipotence and freedom is intellectually corrosive, though, since the more one emphasizes the power of God to do *anything*, the less necessary anything in creation is. That is, if God is free and omnipotent, there need not be any necessary connections in nature—between substance and act or between cause and effect; therefore, there is no real intelligible order to nature, since at any time God might make *anything* else happen. An omnipotent God overwhelms natural causes and makes them pointless.[64]

Consider an example. Science tells us that only apple trees can grow apples. However, if God can do anything, then the tree with apples on it

---

62 Quoted in Étienne Gilson, *The Spirit of Medieval Philosophy*, trans. A. H. C. Downes (Notre Dame, Ind.: University of Notre Dame Press, 1991), 425–26. Isaac Newton was famously to use this same trope in a letter to fellow scientist Robert Hooke in 1676.

63 This drew heavily on the arguments of Saint Bonaventure, *Collationes in Hexaemeron* (e.g., VII.8–12). For an overview of the controversy, see Étienne Gilson, *History of Christian Philosophy in the Middle Ages*, 387–410.

64 This is what happened in the Muslim tradition, which had for four centuries developed a lively philosophical culture, after the Asharites came to dominate their intellectual life in the twelfth century; see Robert R. Reilly, *The Closing of the Muslim Mind* (Wilmington, Del.: ISI Books, 2010). As Chesterton comments, the problem with this approach is not that it believes in God, but that it believes in nothing but God.

might be a lemon tree onto which God put apples. In fact, God could make apple trees grow Big Macs. In a world like this, we can never infer anything from our experience of nature. A more ominous example is that we believe that reason tells us that murder is wrong because it destroys life. Yet if God can do anything, he could make it good to murder. In religion, we believe grace is necessary for salvation; but an omnipotent God could save people without the mediation of grace. If this were the case, however, then there would be no point in going to Church or receiving the Sacraments. In all these examples, the infinite power of God undermines the logic of what happens in creation—in science, morality, and religion. This assumption dissolves both faith and reason, since there are no predictable patterns of activity in the world.[65]

This overemphasis on divine omnipotence is also related to the rise of nominalism. For if God can do anything, it is not necessary that God use forms as universal causal principles in the creation of the natural world. And if there are no forms, there are no universal natures; on the contrary, every being is a radically unique individual that might act in any conceivable way. This is precisely what nominalism holds. In nominalism, because there are no universal forms or natures, common words that point to an entire group of things—dog, human, bird—do not indicate a real nature or essence but are merely names (Latin, *nomina*) we use for our convenience to indicate things that appear similar to us. However, since there is an observable regularity in nature—all dogs act like dogs, all oranges taste like oranges—there must be something (other than forms) to explain this. Thus, recursively, nominalists will invoke divine omnipotence, for it is God himself who directly causes regularity in nature. This is still problematic, though, for, if God is free, this regularity is not necessary and he could change the way these things act tomorrow. For this reason, nominalism undermines the certainty of knowledge.[66]

This elimination of forms of universal natures is perhaps the best example of Ockham's razor. This principle is named after English Franciscan William Ockham (ca. 1285–ca. 1349),[67] who is the primary exponent of nominalism in the Middle Ages. Ockham's razor asserts that beings should not be multiplied without necessity. If we can explain creation without using

---

65 In fact, no experience is trustworthy, since God could make us perceive things that are not even real. I return to this very problematic possibility in chapter 4.

66 We return to the problem of nominalism in all subsequent chapters.

67 The razor in fact goes back to Aristotle, but Ockham wielded it with particular savagery, and so it bears his name.

universal forms, it is always better to do so. Since God is omnipotent, we do not need common forms—indeed, Ockham gets rid of almost all metaphysical distinctions—and so all we need in the universe is the individual material thing that is known by direct sense-experience.

Ockham's nominalism became a seminal moment in the history of philosophy, limiting the range of reason and severing faith from reason completely. First, nominalism destroys the possibility of metaphysical knowledge, since without necessary causal relations there is no way to know reality behind appearance. That is, while we can witness events happening in the world, since we can never infer a necessary cause for that event, our knowledge remains only at the most superficial level of experience. This rejection of causal inference entails, too, that neither can we know the existence of God. This doctrine gives birth to dichotomous revolutions.

On the one hand, turning the perennial tradition on its head, knowledge is no longer about universal forms, which are assumed not to exist.[68] Knowledge is now focused on material individuals, which are best known by direct sense-experience and not by rational inference. In particular, since the objects of sense-experience are always material, and matter always has quantity, the best way to know the world is by a mathematical analysis of material bodies. This development leads to Galileo and Newton. Thus is born the scientific revolution.

On the other hand, since God is no longer approachable by reason, we have to conclude that we have access to God by faith alone. Indeed, everything having to do with salvation, including morality, is the result of God's arbitrary will, which can be known only on the basis of what God has chosen to reveal to us and not by reason at all. Religion, therefore, is relegated to the realm of subjective faith, utterly separated from reason. This eventually inspires the Protestant Reformation, the modern idea that a person works out his own salvation through an unmediated personal faith.[69]

---

68 Descartes explicitly advocates this rejection of tradition in a letter to the famous priest Marin Mersenne: "I hope those who read [the *Meditations*] will get used to my principles without noticing and recognize their truth before realizing that they destroy those of Aristotle" (letter of January 28, 1641).

69 Luther proudly called himself a "terminist," the fifteenth-century name for nominalism. The intellectual genealogy from Ockham to the scientific revolution and the Reformation, and thereby the modern world, is laid out in Brad S. Gregory, *The Unintended Reformation: How a Religious Revolution Secularized Society* (Cambridge, Mass.: Belknap Press of Harvard University Press, 2012) and Michael Allen Gillespie, *The Theological Origins of Modernity* (Chicago: University of Chicago Press, 2008).

Whatever the benefits of these two revolutions, it is nonetheless clear that nominalism is ultimately a destructive force, since it inculcates skepticism both about the objective order of the world and about our ability to know it. Since universal categories are not real but are instead mere conventions created for our convenience, there is nothing necessary about them. This has significant consequences: "Human" might be construed to include chimpanzees or exclude people who have disabilities, according to the whim of the speaker. Any knowledge based on such arbitrary classifications can only produce confusion and discord in the end.

This emerging skepticism from nominalist philosophy was unfortunately reinforced by a number of historical events. The Age of Discovery, in which new lands and new peoples shattered previously settled views of the world, destroyed the confidence of Europeans in traditional learning. The attacks on Aristotle undermined trust in metaphysical judgment. The Reformation eroded faith in the Church herself. There seemed to be no trustworthy authority. This confluence caused a profound anxiety about human knowledge, which is well illustrated by John Donne in his poem "An Anatomy of the World" (1611):

> And new philosophy calls all in doubt,
> The element of fire is quite put out,
> The sun is lost, and th'earth, and no man's wit
> Can well direct him where to look for it.
> And freely men confess that this world's spent,
> When in the planets and the firmament
> They seek so many new; they see that this
> Is crumbled out again to his atomies.
> 'Tis all in pieces, all coherence gone.[70]

This sense of intellectual dislocation led to a resurgence of skepticism among intellectuals.[71] To fight this, philosophers of the era searched for a way to guarantee certainty in knowledge. Some thinkers, like Galileo (1564–1642),

---

[70] This passage is cited in Stephen Toulmin, *Cosmopolis: The Hidden Agenda of Modernity* (Chicago: University of Chicago Press, 1990), 65. To offer an interpretation: Science had banished the old elements (such as fire) and the stability of their formal causes; in their place the telescope and microscope revealed a disconcertingly infinite vastness and multiplicity. All sense of intelligible order and contextual horizon was thereby undermined.

[71] The best representative of this is Montaigne's famous essay, "An Apology for Raymond Sebond."

follow Plato's great insight in recognizing that the one science that is immune to skepticism is mathematics. In fact, Galileo said that the universe is written in the language of math, and so by using math we can know the world with the same kind of certainty as God: "The human intellect understands some propositions, namely those of the mathematical sciences, quite perfectly, and in these it has as much absolute certainty as Nature herself.... [In these propositions] I believe its knowledge equals the Divine in objective certainty."[72]

Galileo made great discoveries based on this assumption. Yet, it carries a problematic corollary: where does this leave things not reducible to math, like the soul, ethics, and theology? If we cannot know these things with confidence, it is hard to see how we are to avoid falling into the most vicious form of skepticism about our place in the universe.[73]

This is the problem taken up by René Descartes (1590–1650), called the father of modern philosophy. Descartes tries to reconcile Galileo's science with religion by asserting that, while the material world obeys the laws of physics, the human mind is completely distinct from the body and so is free and immortal. Moreover, his proof for this separation is possible only on the condition that the mind is created by God, thereby rescuing theism.[74]

However, this response to skepticism impacts philosophy in three significant ways, turning it decisively away from the perennial philosophy. First, in order to attain certainty, Descartes explicitly rejects all traditional philosophical beliefs. He begins not with the nature of the universe but with the certainties of his own mind. Because he starts with his own ideas, epistemology displaces metaphysics as the primary interest of philosophers. Moreover, this privileging of the human mind over the material universe introduces problems that have entranced philosophers since then. This leads to the second significant impact: the veil of perception. If we only have direct contact with our ideas, how can we ever prove that they conform to

---

72 Galileo Galilei, *Dialogue on the Great World System*, ed. Giorgio de Santillana (Chicago: University of Chicago Press, 1953), 114.

73 One should consider the so-called Galileo Affair—the Church's condemnation of his teaching—in light of this. It is absurd to assert that the Church is opposed to science per se, since the Church prepared the way for science by emphasizing the intelligibility of reality and the dignity of human knowledge. As others have noted, to claim that the Church is opposed to science because of Galileo is like claiming that ancient Athenians were opposed to philosophy because they executed Socrates. On the true relation of the Church to science, see Christopher T. Baglow, *Faith, Science, and Reason: Theology on the Cutting Edge*, 2nd ed. (Woodridge, Ill.: Midwest Theological Forum, 2019).

74 I examine his argument in greater detail in chapters 4 and 5.

reality? I know my ideas, but then it follows I never know the world itself, since my ideas always intercede between my mind and reality. This distancing of human knowledge from being will be a constant issue in modern thought. The final problem is tied to this: because we are certain only of the operations of the mind, it becomes plausible to say that a person is nothing other than the mind or consciousness. This implies that a person is not his body at all. Although this flies in the face of common experience, philosophers since then have deemed the "mind-body problem," the relationship between the mental realm of consciousness and the physical realm of bodily activity, one of the premier problems in philosophy.

The subsequent course of modern philosophy is determined by the assumptions of nominalism and the Cartesian method. Since Descartes's own solutions were so problematic (as I later show), there follows after him an eruption of divergent schools, each of which promises to have *the* solution but which in turn only create new problems for the next generation to solve. While some see this huge flowering of diverse schools as a sign of health in philosophy, it can also be seen as a sign that philosophy is seriously off track. The ancients had begun philosophy out of wonder for the intelligible goodness of creation and by sustained inquiry based on increasing that wonder; modern philosophy, following Descartes, begins by doubting whether we know anything at all and sustains itself by fostering greater doubts about our ability to know reality.[75] Modern philosophy's preferred solution is to put greater emphasis on human powers as the source of intellectual coherence; but this is ultimately futile, since it only affirms the solipsistic experience of the self:[76] I know how *I* relate to the world, not how the world is in itself. The fault in all this lies not in God's creation, but in we who refuse to see it correctly; as Chesterton said, "The world will never starve for want of wonders; but only for want of wonder."[77]

History has shown that, once the principles of the perennial philosophy were rejected, philosophy was destined to lose coherence. Philosophers could

---

75 Whereas wonder invites us to revel in mystery and to uncover the knowable, doubt replaces mystery with unknowability and darkens the intellect by celebrating the adamantine limits of rationality. See Josef Pieper, *Leisure, The Basis of Culture*, 102–4.

76 Jonathan Swift, in his *Battle of the Books* (1704), metaphorically characterizes the difference in terms of bees and spiders. The ancients, like bees collecting pollen to make honey and wax (sweetness and light), work on nature and produce wisdom. Moderns, however, are like spiders, who spin out from their own minds webs in which to trap unsuspecting passersby.

77 G. K. Chesterton, *Tremendous Trifles*, chapter 1.

barely speak to one another, let alone to the average person. New methods passed in and out of fashion: rationalism, empiricism, idealism; subjective idealism, objective idealism, absolute idealism; historical materialism, positivism, existentialism; pragmatism, logical positivism, phenomenology— and this just brings us to the early twentieth century! This quagmire was noted by Jacques Maritain: "Modern philosophies grow out of what has gone before . . . by way of contradiction; the scholastics by way of agreement and further development. The result is the philosophy in our day is like a series of episodes simply stuck end to end, not like a tree where each is organically related to each and all to the roots."[78] To begin to remedy this Babel of philosophical confusion, let us return to that most fundamental principle, being. This is the shared foundation of the perennial philosophy, and this alone can serve as an adequate basis for knowing reality as it truly is.

FURTHER READING

Collins, James. *A History of Modern European Philosophy*. Milwaukee: Bruce Publishing, 1954.

Copleston, Frederick. *A History of Philosophy*. 9 vols. Garden City, N.Y.: Image Books, 1985.

Gilson, Étienne. *The Spirit of Medieval Philosophy*. Translated by A. H. C. Downes. Notre Dame, Ind.: University of Notre Dame Press, 1991.

———. *The Unity of Philosophical Experience*. San Francisco: Ignatius Press, 1999.

Guthrie, W. K. C. *The Greek Philosophers: From Thales to Aristotle*. New York: Harper and Row, 1975.

Hadot, Pierre. *What Is Ancient Philosophy?* Translated by Michael Chase. Cambridge, Mass.: Harvard University Press, 2002.

Rist, John M. *Plato's Moral Realism: The Discovery of the Presuppositions of Ethics*. Washington, D.C.: The Catholic University of America Press, 2012.

Sullivan, Daniel J. *An Introduction to Philosophy*. Milwaukee: Bruce Publishing, 1957.

Veatch, Henry B. *Aristotle: A Contemporary Appreciation*. Bloomington, Ind.: Indiana University Press, 1974.

---

[78] Jacques Maritain, *Theonas: Conversations of a Sage*, trans. F. J. Sheed (New York: Sheed and Ward, 1933), 5.

Chapter 3

The One and the Many: The Search for Being in Metaphysics

THE PROBLEM:
KNOWING REALITY BEHIND APPEARANCE

The most fundamental question addressed by philosophy is the question of the nature of reality. Humans have a desire to understand not just this event or that part of reality; rather, we have a natural drive to understand the whole of reality, for unless we understand the order of all reality, we can never form a coherent vision of the whole of human experience. This quest carries significant consequences, for any erroneous beliefs about the order of reality are likely to lead to further errors in specific areas of investigation. Nevertheless, it is obvious that people have radically different ideas of reality. How is it possible for us to disagree about this most fundamental truth? The problem arises because we live in a world of appearances: a world of superficial phenomena and continuous change. It is the task of intelligence to get behind this superficial flux and to discover the principles and causes that allow us to make sense of those disparate appearances. Since this is not easy—in fact, disciplining the mind in this way is difficult—people tend to grasp at some partial aspect of reality. This error, taking some part as an adequate explanation for everything, is the reason why people understand reality in radically divergent ways. But a partial explanation of reality will always be reductive and inadequate. For that reason, our own approach will be to find the most adequate notion of being, one that accounts for the whole spectrum of human experience.

There is a general rule in philosophy that says in order to discover the truth, we need to start with what is most evident to us and progress to what is most evident in itself. In other words, we begin by examining evidence that is presented to our senses, since that is obvious to us, but from that evidence we form conclusions about the causes for those experiences, even though we do not experience them directly (since we experience the effect).[1] Reason's job, then, is to discern those causal principles that give regularity and predictability to the apparent chaos of experience. For example, the weather can seem as capricious as the gods, but in meteorology we learn the natural causes and so understand the changes in weather as predictable. Once we discover these causal principles, we no longer experience the world as a series of disjointed events, but rather we see the world's regularity as meaningful. These principles are more *evident in themselves* because, as laws of nature, they are necessary for the effect even to exist, and they are the universal cause of all the distinct particular events. Since they are not subject to change, they are more obvious to reason. It is in light of these laws that unique and singular events can be understood to be an instance of a universal pattern; a chemical reaction in a laboratory that might have been unexpected becomes a perfectly comprehensible event or an unknown illness can be diagnosed to be the result of a virus. Oftentimes, though, reaching these principles of intelligibility takes quite a long time and hard work because they are not *evident to us*: singular events can remain puzzles or partially understood for many generations.[2]

Let us now apply this. What is most obvious to us, and the source of all our evidence, is the natural world. Although the natural world is populated by unique substances in a constant process of change, we have already seen that Aristotle's philosophy—based on the distinction between act and potency and the dual compositions of form and matter (underlying substantial change) and substance and accident (underlying accidental change)—reveals the stable principles of reality for making sense of the natural world. The perennial philosophy will accept as a foundational truth Aristotle's analysis of nature. We presume, then, that the basic unit of being is a substance, in which the form determines the nature (what it is) as well as the activity (what it does) of the substance. The four causes—form and matter, efficient and final—are therefore the causal principles that explain

---

1 Aristotle, *Physics* I.1 (184a16–21): "The natural way of [discovering causal principles] is to start from the things which are more knowable and obvious to us and proceed towards those which are clearer and more knowable by nature." Cf. *ST* I.2.2: "When an effect is better known to us than its cause, from the effect we proceed to the knowledge of the cause. And from every effect the existence of its proper cause can be demonstrated, so long as its effects are better known to us; because since every effect depends upon its cause, if the effect exists, the cause must pre-exist." See also *CBDT* 6.1.

2 In 2011, the Nobel Prize in Physics was awarded to researchers for the discovery of dark energy, an as-yet mysterious phenomenon. We see the events it causes, but not enough evidence has been collected to completely understand the nature of dark energy as a cause. Yet, even as partially understood, it is accepted as a scientific truth worthy of the highest honor.

change at the level of nature. This solution to the problem of the one and the many as well as the problem of change will be presupposed in our further analyses of nature in other branches of philosophy.

There is, however, another question that can now be brought forward: what are the causal principles behind nature itself? We say that substance exists as first act and accidents are second act; we say that the causal principles of material substance are form and matter. But these arguments assume that that all these principles—substance, accident, form, and matter—already exist. The philosophy of nature assumes the existence of the natural world in which these principles operate as explanations of change. However, we must now ask the question, what does it means to say of something that it is a *being*?[3] This is the topic of metaphysics. Literally, this is the study of that which is "behind nature" (*meta-physis*); where the philosophy of nature deals with why things change, to ask what is "behind nature" is the question of why those changing things exist at all.[4] The question of being is the question of why there is *something* rather than nothing at all.

Thomas warns that this is a difficult science, since people are inclined to accept as real only what they can picture in their imagination. This is why so many people are inclined to assume all of reality is like the material universe. This has caused many philosophers to fall into a great error concerning being: since nature is obvious to us, they think it is obvious that there is nothing other than nature, that there is nothing supernatural (or above nature) behind this world. But this illegitimately limits the extent of being: we need to be open to the possibility that some being is immaterial.[5] The correct idea of being is crucial, of course, since it affects how a philosopher interprets everything.[6] As Aquinas points out, since being is the foundation for all other notions of reality, "When the errors made about being and nonbeing have been removed, the errors made about truth and falsity and rest and motion will then also be removed."[7]

---

3 Aristotle, *Metaphysics* IV.1 (1003a 20–32), calls metaphysics the study of being-*qua*-being, the study of everything under the aspect of its existence.

4 *CBDT* 5.1.

5 Thomas notes, in *CNE* VI.7.1210–1211, that metaphysics and theology are the hardest subjects to learn because they "exceed imagination and require a sharp mind."

6 For a history of philosophy written from the perspective of erroneous ideas of being, see Étienne Gilson, *Being and Some Philosophers*, 2nd ed. (Toronto: Pontifical Institute of Medieval Studies, 1952).

7 *CM* IV.17.736.

It is important to reiterate Thomas's warning that metaphysics is a difficult science. Because these are the most fundamental principles, they can seem inordinately abstract. There is a temptation to skip this material and move on to those issues more tied to our everyday lives: knowing, moral actions, politics, even our relation to God. However, all those later arguments will be built on the principles we lay down in this chapter. I ask the reader for patience; some of the arguments might appear overly recondite. But getting the principles of being correct will allow our later labors to be more fruitful.

REDUCTIVE EXTREMES

The most obvious fact that any adequate metaphysics must account for is the simultaneous similarity-and-difference among beings. First, all things that exist have in common the fact *that they exist*. This point is the primary metaphysical truth. *Being*, then, is the principle of unity that underlies the intelligible order of the cosmos. Yet equally obvious is that every individual being is different from all others; indeed, if it were not different, it could not be an *individual*, since two identical beings would be the same thing. Thus, the problem for metaphysics is to hold together the apparently contradictory truths that all beings are the same and that every being is unique. To do justice to reality we need to respect this "both-and" of similarity and difference. The common philosophical errors about being arise from grasping on to one of these truths and defending it to the exclusion of the other.

Unity without Diversity: Monism

One reductive strategy is to emphasize the fact of the unity of being to the exclusion of difference. This perspective is known as *monism*: that reality is essentially composed of only one thing. In its most extreme version, it claims that, because all reality is being and there is nothing other than being, being must be one complete whole. Therefore, any appearance of difference or change is simply an illusion. The most famous representative of this school of thought is Parmenides, as we saw in the previous chapter. This is a clearly inadequate position, though, since if there are no differences in reality, then good is the same and bad, and a human is the same as a horse.[8] This, obviously, reduces reality to nonsense.[9]

8 Aristotle, *Physics* I.2 (185b17–23).

9 Many Eastern religions, such as Buddhism, might be described as monistic in this sense. See Benedict M. Ashley, *The Way toward Wisdom: An Interdisciplinary and Intercultural Introduction to Metaphysics* (Notre Dame, Ind.: University of Notre Dame Press, 2006), 385–402.

This conclusion is so contrary to common experience that very few philosophers will accept the logic without adapting it in some fashion. A more common form of monism is seen in the various forms of *pantheism*. This is the position that since God is a supreme being, everything else is dependent on God for its existence and so must be ultimately merely a part of God. Influential versions of pantheism can be found in the ancient world in Stoicism, which identifies God with nature, and in the modern world in the Absolute idealism of G. F. W. Hegel (1770–1831), who sees history as a manifestation of an Absolute mind's coming to self-knowledge. Perhaps the most famous example of monism in modern philosophy, though, is that of Baruch Spinoza (1632–1677).[10] He starts with the definition of substance bequeathed to him by Descartes: a substance is that which exists in need of nothing but itself.[11] But, since all creatures depend on God the Creator for their existence, it follows that God must be the only substance. Since creatures cannot be independent substances, Spinoza concludes that they are merely attributes of God, and so there is no real distinction between God and the universe. As he famously concludes, God is nature and nature is God.

Pantheism is a constant temptation for theists, who believe they give greater glory to God by erasing the distinction between Creator and creation. In reality, it does the opposite. To say that creation is really part of God implicitly denies his ability to call forth from nothingness a creation that is truly other than himself. More problematically, if there are no acting substances other than God, then God is responsible for the evil that occurs in the world. This is clearly a diminution of God and a position unacceptable for traditional theists.

Another common example of monism, especially for those who identify science as the only way to know the world, can be found in some forms of materialism. Although many materialists accept that there is a variety of kinds of matter, it can become a monistic metaphysics when it insists there is nothing but a material principle behind nature. This faces an immediate problem, though: if all being is matter, why do material beings act in such different ways? It is clear that a rock and a human being are both made of

---

10 This argument is in Spinoza's *Ethics*, pt. 1.

11 Descartes's definition is in *Principles of Philosophy* I.51, though it is implicit in the *Sixth Meditation*'s definitions of mind and matter. This is an instance where a term, when given a different definition, has radically different philosophical implications. Aristotle had defined substance in contrast to accident: that which exists in itself and not in another. This does not imply that substance is not dependent on God, or other creatures, in some way. For a critique of modern redefinitions of substance, see W. Norris Clarke, *The One and the Many*, 133–34.

the same atomic elements; then why should the human be able to do so many more things than the rock can? In fact, the periodic table itself shows how even different elements composed of the same subatomic particles are characterized by their natures and actions (that is, by their form) and not merely their material composition. Thus, it is impossible to reduce reality to matter alone. In spite of these problems, materialism remains popular due to its association with science. We revisit this theory in our discussion of human nature in chapter 5.

Diversity without Unity: Nominalism

At the other end of the spectrum are those philosophies that emphasize the diversity of being to such an extent that they cannot find a principle of unity or similarity. This position is called *pluralism* to indicate the many-ness of being. We have already met the extreme version of this position that denies any principle of unity: nominalism. According to nominalism, every being is radically unique. Universal kinds, or species, are not objectively real and exist only in name. They are merely words we impose on individual beings to point out some superficial similarity we want to accentuate. This is the position of most modern philosophers who reject the Aristotelian tradition of forms.

To see how problematic this position is, recall that to know what something is means that you can name the universal class to which that thing belongs. You can be said to know something when you can state, "This is an X," where X is a class of being to which the individual belongs. This universal class indicates the nature of the object, which reveals how that thing will regularly behave. For example, if I point to a round, red object and identify it as an apple, this leads us to expect it to have certain properties common to all apples and different from, say, a rubber ball. The nature, as a universal class uniting individuals, makes those objects meaningful for us.

Since nominalists hold that everything that exists is a radically unique individual, there are no real universal classes. Since we must use words to communicate, those words do not refer to a real nature; rather, they are merely names that we use to classify these objects for our benefit. Two apples appear sufficiently similar to group them together; but there is no real unity behind the two objects. Moreover, since these groupings are wholly man-made, they are completely arbitrary: a green apple might not count as an "apple" for some people, while a sour apple might not count for others. Still others would be happy to group the red apple, because of its appearance, with the rubber ball.[12] Nor is this of purely academic significance: historically, human beings of the wrong complexion or IQ have been denied human nature and deprived of their rights. This tendency is also evident in the frequent attempts to redefine reality to conform to our wishes. More broadly, nominalism's denial of nature erodes confidence in science since it is impossible to predict how an object will act. Universal statements based on the nature of a thing are always suspect.

A clear illustration of this sort of nominalism is David Hume (1711–1776), one of the greatest influences on contemporary philosophers. He explicitly denies that we can know natures:

> It must certainly be allowed, that nature has kept us at a great distance from all her secrets, and has afforded us only the knowledge of a few superficial qualities of objects; while she conceals from us those powers and principles on which the influence of those objects entirely depends. Our senses inform us of the colour, weight, and consistence of bread; but neither sense nor reason can ever inform us of those qualities which fit it for the nourishment and support of a human body. . . . It is allowed on all hands that there is no known connexion between the sensible qualities and the secret powers; and consequently, that the mind is not led to form such a conclusion concerning their constant and regular conjunction, by anything which it knows of their nature. The bread, which I formerly eat, nourished me; that is, a body of such sensible qualities was, at that time, endued with such secret powers: but does it follow, that other bread must also nourish me at another time, and that like sensible qualities must always be attended with like secret powers? The consequence seems nowise necessary.[13]

Thus, on the basis of nominalism, while we call two loaves by the same name, "bread," we cannot know that they are alike at all and so we can never be rationally sure that bread will nourish us. This sort of uncertainty leaves the entire world subject to skepticism.[14]

We have, of course, seen the havoc nominalism plays in the philosophy of nature already, for, if there are no universal natures, there would be no

---

12 The comedian Steven Wright has a joke that perfectly lampoons the arbitrariness of nominalism: After someone points out that he is wearing two different color socks, he replies, "Yeah, I know, but to me they're the same because I go by thickness." The fact that we see this as ridiculous points out the inadequacy of nominalism as a principle for ordering reality.

13 David Hume, *An Enquiry Concerning Human Understanding*, sec. 4, pt. 2, para. 29.

14 This was in fact Hume's conclusion. We examine his argument in greater detail in chapter 4.

explanation for its regularity; there would be no intelligible order in nature. In this chapter, we must explore the problem at another level. Jacques Maritain succinctly indicates the issue: "A deep vice besets the philosophers of our day.... It is the ancient error of the *nominalists*.... The reason [for their incapacity to know reality] is that while having a taste for the real indeed, they nevertheless have no sense of being. Being as such ... for them is only a word."[15] Just as nominalists deny universal natures, so they also deny a universal principle of being that unites all things. Being for them is simply a brute fact; there is no common principle to explain why things exist. But this would leave the universe without a principle of order and intelligibility; it would leave us with no answer to the most important questions.

This nominalist rejection of being leads many contemporary philosophers to assert that *being* only indicates that "there is one instead of zero"; it makes no real difference in our analysis of concepts. This, in turn, leads them to analyze concepts with no reference to reality at all. One example of this is the popularity of using "possible universes" as a basis for discerning the nature of reality. Yet, reflecting on our own lives, we know that being—our existence—is the most relevant fact of all, for it is the reality that is evident to us at all times.

THE ACT OF EXISTENCE

The resolution to this dichotomous reductionism requires that we acknowledge that there is a common principle or cause of being that can be diversified so that it appears to be many different things. Our analysis demonstrating this relies on two principles that direct all reasoning: the principle of noncontradiction and the principle of sufficient reason.[16] These philosophical principles are the foundation for all intelligibility, for to deny them is to make it impossible that the universe will make sense at all. Since these principles are the foundation for all rational argument, they must be self-evident. As such, they cannot be proved directly. Yet, they are indirectly proved, for without them there can be no rational argument about anything.

The principle of noncontradiction says that a thing cannot be and not-be in the same way at the same time. At one level, this is the most obvious fact communicated in any experience, for an object either exists or it does not. This applies also to natures: something is one nature and cannot be

15 Jacques Maritain, *The Degrees of Knowledge*, 1.
16 See Ashley, *Way toward Wisdom*, 72–74, and Clarke, *The One and the Many*, 19–23.

something else; the animal exists either as a cat or not-cat. This is the principle underlying the static intelligibility of being, for at any one point in time a being is what it is. (Note, though, that this does not exclude the fact of change over time. Also, note that this allows distinct parts of the same substance to have different qualities: my arms can be hairy, while my palms are not.)

The principle of sufficient reason, in contrast, underwrites the intelligibility of change, allowing us to make sense of being inasmuch as it is becoming. This principle states that, for every fact in the world, there is a sufficient reason for its existing either in itself or in another being. Thus, for any effect, there must be a cause to account adequately for the nature of the effect. That effect can be explained either by the nature of the subject or, if not, by some other being adequate to account for the effect.[17] For example, the fact that hair is growing on my arm is explained by my nature as a mammal. However, if I turn green, there is nothing in human nature to explain that; there must be some extrinsic cause—a disease or paint—that would be able to explain why I have turned green. In both cases, it is important to see that the cause has sufficient power to account for the effect. This principle rules out the possibility of "uncaused" events; if something happens, there must be a reason for it. To reject this principle would be to allow for inexplicable events, things that happen with no cause at all, and so the universe simply would not be intelligible. Although children take delight in uncaused events, seeing them as *magical*, adults know there is no magic and that there must be a logical explanation for everything.[18]

Therefore, metaphysics must develop a theory of being able to account for similarity and difference among beings, as described by the principle of noncontradiction, as well as providing a sufficient explanation for why things come to be in the first place. We will see that Thomas Aquinas's doctrine of the act of existence is the best foundation for metaphysics, for it fulfills both these criteria as the cause of being.

A problem for many philosophical novices is that in English the word *being* can be pretty vague. To appreciate Thomas's argument, we need to make a distinction between two uses of it that are clearer in Latin. *Being*

---

17 Because the principle of sufficient reason allows that the sufficient reason may be in the nature of the being itself, we can see that the question of what causes God to exist is an ill-formed question. We return to this in chapter 8.

18 Miracles conform to this principle, for when nature cannot account for an event it is reasonable to attribute that event to the creator of nature, God. We take this up in chapter 8.

can indicate either (1) *that which is*, rendered by the Latin participle *ens* (a thing having being) or (2) *that by which a thing is*, rendered by the Latin infinitive verb *esse* (the action of being, to-be as a verb).[19]

In the former sense, being as *ens*, we might talk about things as a human being, a canine being, a bovine being, and so on. This names an existing thing, a substance (or accident, existing dependently on the substance, as in *blue thing*). It is in this sense, as we will see, that everything is a being, for if it were not, it would be nothing at all, and a being either is or is not. But this does not get to the heart of the issue, for we want to know *why* things exist, how they came to be. To answer this, we need a principle to supply an explanation for why some things are beings and many things— like golden mountains and flying pigs—are not. This is why *esse*, the act of existence, is the more important usage for our analysis. It is the causal principle that explains why something is; moreover, as we will see, it is also uniquely capable of explaining how there can be many different kinds of being. Since understanding lies in knowing the cause, then to understand reality requires that we grasp the cause of being. Let us illuminate this point by considering Thomas's reasoning.[20]

Thomas begins by asserting a version of the principle of sufficient reason: that whatever properties a thing has are caused either by that thing's essence, or else by some extrinsic cause. As I argued in the previous chapter, the form determines the essence or nature of every being. That essence, then, is the cause of all those properties that are characteristic to that nature. Human beings have all sorts of properties that flow from our essence: we are mammals, and so have hair; we are rational, and so can speak and read; we are social, and so belong to families and political society. However, I might have other properties that do not arise from my essence. If I am green, that must be due to the poison I ingested.

Thomas then notes that one thing that does not follow from the essence of a man is his *existence*. Think of an individual human: as human, it is necessary that he is mammalian, social, rational, and so on, but it is not nec-

---

19 This distinction is mentioned in *SCG* II.54.8 (italics in original): In creatures there is "the composition of substance and being, which by some is said to be *of that which is* and being, or of *that which is* and *that by which a thing is*."

20 I follow the argument in *OBE* c. 4, with briefer parallels in *SCG* II.54 and *ST* I.3.4. Helpful commentaries can be found in Gilson, *Being and Some Philosophers*, 154–89; and John F. Wippel, *The Metaphysical Thought of Thomas Aquinas: From Finite Being to Uncreated Being* (Washington, D.C.: The Catholic University of America Press, 2000), 132–76.

essary that he exist. This truth is borne out by the fact that every person is born and will die; existence is an utterly contingent fact, and so it cannot be explained by his essence. Moreover, this contingency applies to the entire human race: human nature as a whole did not have to exist; it evolved only very late in the history of the planet. Again, this truth is evident when we consider all those creatures that could have existed but in fact never did: dragons, unicorns, and griffins.

We can extend this reasoning to *any and all* species or natures. None of the elements had to exist, as they were the result of the Big Bang and subsequent atomic fusion; no species of plant or animal had to exist, as they were the result of evolution.

From this, Thomas concludes that there is a real distinction between essence and existence. No essence can explain the existence of that thing—hydrogen has to have one electron, but it did not have to exist; water has to be a solvent, but it did not have to exist. It follows that existence must be given to these essences by something outside of them. In other words, while essence accounts for *what* something is, it cannot account for the fact *that* it is. Thus, the existence of an essence must be caused by something other than the essence itself.[21]

Now, logically, there could be one exception to this argument: a being whose essence is existence itself. But if there is such a thing, there could only be one of them, and it would be the "first being," the cause of the existence of other things. Let me explain. First, there can only be one being whose essence is existence: there can be two beings only if there is *some* difference between them, distinguishing one from the other. The only way to be distinct from a being whose essence is existence, however, would be for the second being to have an essence that is *not existence* itself. But in that case, it would be like all the other things whose essence does not include existence. As such, it would need to be given existence by that being whose essence is existence. This leads to the second point: the being whose essence is existence is the first cause of other beings. This is again implied by the principle of sufficient reason: the only being capable of giving existence

---

21 This is a point both Plato and Aristotle miss because they recognize no distinction between essence and existence, attributing both to form. Thomas indicates their error by pointing out that no form *has to* exist: "Because every form is a determination of *esse*, none of them is *esse* itself" (*CBDH*, c. 2). This crucial insight of Thomas is tied to the Judeo-Christian idea of creation, which makes the existence of the universe itself a contingent fact based on the will of the Creator.

would be one whose essence is existence.[22] But since there is only one being whose essence is existence, then all other beings—whose essences are something other than existence itself—would be *created* or given being by that first being.

Building on Aristotle's insight about the relation of form and matter, this relation of extrinsic cause to essence is described in terms of act and potency. In general, everything that receives a property from another is in potency to that property. For example, a cold object is in potency to heat, since it can become hot. However, since it is as cold, it cannot make itself hot; rather, it must be given heat by something that is already hot. Thus, only something in actuality can affect something in potency. In the same way, essences are in potency to existence; existence is that which actualizes the essences, which only have potential to exist. Thus, existence is the principle of actuality for all essences that did not have to exist. This is the distinction that makes some things real and others merely imaginary: humans are real because they have been given existence, and unicorns are fictional since they have not been given existence.

This leads Thomas to a consequential conclusion: "*Being*, as we understand it here, signifies the highest perfection of all. . . . Wherefore it is clear that *being* as we understand it here is the actuality of all acts, and therefore the perfection of all perfections."[23] Without the act of existence, nothing would be at all; therefore, the act of existence is the ultimate cause of all being, substance and accident, and form and matter as the principles of substance. The act of existence, then, is the principle of unity that unites all forms; and it is the explanation for both being and becoming since nothing exists without it.

Significantly, this argument also provides an explanation for how we get many different beings. Here we take guidance from the principle of noncontradiction: nothing can be similar and different in the same way. All things are similar in possessing the act of existence, in *being* (for without it they would not exist at all); however, to get different beings, there must be another principle to account for the difference. That principle is essence, which causes the differences between natures and individuals. Thus, existence and essence are the two principles whose composition is necessary to

---

22 *DP* 7.2.

23 *DP* 7.2.ad 9. Cf. *ST* I.4.1.ad 3: "Existence is the most perfect of all things, for it is compared to all things as that by which they are made actual. . . . Hence existence is that which actuates all things, even their forms."

account for the unity of being and the diversity of beings. Again, just as with form and matter, existence and essence are principles, not things, for they always occur in composition with one another.

This raises a puzzle: if nothing exists without the act of existence, what are essences that they can receive the act of existence? Does this not seem to imply something like the eternal uncreated Forms of Plato to which existence is added?[24] But how can existence be *added to* anything, for the thing must already exist if something is to be added to it?[25]

This can be answered by introducing one of Thomas's crucial metaphysical principles: act is not self-limiting, and so act is limited only by *receptive potency*. First, recall that the act of existence is an *act*—it is an activity, it is a verb. Pure actuality is pure activity, and there is no limitation to it. So, this activity can only be limited when it is received into something; it is the potency of the receptive principle that determines how the activity is limited. Thomas frequently invokes, in a great variety of circumstances, this rule: "what is in another is in it according to the mode of the receiver."[26]

A few metaphors might help explain this. If I have three glasses of different sizes—four ounces, eight ounces, and twelve ounces—they have different potencies to receive milk. If I fill them all, they would all be actually full, yet the twelve-ounce glass has three times the amount of milk as the four-ounce glass. The potency of the cup to receive the milk determines how much it will *actually* have.

Similarly, consider an electrical line supplying energy to three light bulbs: forty watts, sixty watts, and one-hundred watts. The same electricity is given to all three bulbs, but the forty-watt bulb has much less potential to illuminate because its potency to receive electricity is more limited. The *act* of electricity is the same; yet the results differ because of the different potentials of the bulb.

Third, if I am giving a talk about philosophy and the audience contains high school students, college students, and other professors, while the information that is being given is the same for all, it is received only according to the capacity of the listener. The professors would get more out of the talk than the college students, who would get more than the high school stu-

---

24 Some medieval philosophers, such as the Muslim Avicenna and the Franciscan Duns Scotus, held a position similar to this.

25 *SCG* I.26.3.

26 *SCG* I.43.5.

dents. It is the capacity (or potential) of the receiver that determines how the act is received.

Thomas applies this to the act of existence: "Considered absolutely, being is infinite, since there are infinite and infinite modes in which it can be participated. If, then, the being of some thing is finite, that being must be limited by something other that is somehow its cause."[27] The act of existence, in itself, is infinite; but it can be received by an infinite number of essences whose variable potential to receive existence explains the many different kinds of being. The act of creation, then, is the simultaneous creation of essence as a limiting principle by giving it the act of existence; thus, in created things, being is always limited to a determinate mode of being. Essence does not exist before creation; rather creation is bringing potential, limited modes of existence into being. We therefore have different kinds of beings, that is, different species or natures, based upon the degree to which the essence of that nature constricts the act of existence.

Participation

In explaining the relationship between essence and existence in terms of act and potency, Thomas is relying on an Aristotelian concept. But to explain how this works, he adapts a very different principle from Plato: participation.

Plato had used the idea of participation to explain how the Forms as essences relate causally to changing material things: brown things participate in the Form of brown; tall things participate in the Form of tall; just things participate in the Form of justice. One of the problematic assumptions in this argument is that Plato assumes that the Forms of brown, or tall, or justice necessarily exist. It is clear, though, that none of these finite realities *has to* exist. Indeed, the only thing that *must* exist is existence itself. Consequently, Thomas argues that things that do not have to exist (such as the Forms) only exist by virtue of *participation in existence*. This clarifies how there can be diverse kinds of being, for the potency of the essence determines the degree to which it participates in the act of existence. Things that participate in existence more intensively can be said to exist more; this explains the variety of beings. Let me explain this further.

Thomas defines participation as "when something receives in a particular way that which belongs to another in a universal way."[28] Thus, there are

27 *SCG* I.43.8; see also *SCG* II.52.1–2.
28 *CBDH* c. 2; see also *SCG* I.40.3.

three elements in participation: one substance that has a property necessarily and from its essence, a second substance that has that same property
contingently and partially, and a causal connection between the two so that
the contingent property is dependent on the substance that has that property by necessity. Thomas's typical example for this is fire. Fire's essence, its
defining property, is to be hot; other things are hot when fire communicates
heat to them. Thus, broccoli in a steamer is hot because of the water, which
is boiling because the pot is hot because it is heated by the fire. All the heat
in these objects, then, really depends on the fire, for if we remove them from
the fire they soon cool down. Moreover, the amount of heat depends on
how much the thing participates in the heat of the fire: the pot on the fire is
very hot; other utensils and pots are further from the fire, and so are pro-
portionally cooler since they have less participation in the heat. Also, since
heat is the essential property of fire, fire itself is never diminished in communicating heat to other things; it remains the source of all heat for those
things being warmed.[29]

It is part of Thomas's genius that he is able to combine this Platonic idea
with the Aristotelian doctrine of act and potency, so that the source is the
principle of actuality for the property of which the receiver is in potency. This
is a fundamental insight with regard to being, for the act of existence is the
cause of being in which all finite and created essences necessarily participate.

Unlike Plato's Forms, though, all things must participate in being. If
they did not, they would not exist at all. Thus, there is really only one cause
of all substances and all properties: that is the act of existence. Further, there
must be a first cause whose essence is existence that gives being to all other
essences: "Being itself belongs to the first agent according to His proper
nature. . . . Now, that which belongs to a thing according to its proper nature
does not belong to other things except by way of participation, as heat is in
other bodies from fire. Therefore, being itself belongs to all other things
from the first agent by a certain participation. That which belongs to a thing
by participation, however, is not that thing's substance."[30]

Thus, while there is only one principle, *Being*, that is the cause of all
being, participation is the crucial mechanism for explaining how we have a

---

29 I note this because the paradigmatic example of causation in modern thought is Hume's
example in section 4 of the *Enquiry Concerning Human Understanding* of two billiard balls col-
liding, in which the kinetic energy of one is completely transferred to the recipient. This is misleading since it misrepresents the real nature of efficient causality.

30 *SCG* II.52.8.

plurality of *beings*. Just as things closer to the fire are hotter because they participate more in the heat, things can participate in existence to greater or lesser degrees. Since essences are in potency to existence, they are nothing until given existence; but the more potency an essence has to participate in existence, the more being it will have when actualized.[31] The degree of this participation, then, is determined by the essence: "Participated existence is limited by the capacity of the participator."[32] So the differences in beings should be understood as things existing more or less; we return to this in discussing the ladder of being later in this chapter.

Participation by essences in the act of existence, then, solves the problem of the one and the many. All real things are existent; yet their essential potency causes them to participate in being in different ways. By this composition, being (*esse*) and essence are necessary intrinsic principles of each substance. In this composition, essence explains the differences among beings, while the act of existence is the universal intrinsic cause of being, since nothing can exist without it. However, it is evident from what has been said that the presence of that intrinsic cause implies an *extrinsic* cause of being, the source of the act of existence. As might be expected, this source of existence is identified with God.

A Preliminary Argument for God as First Cause

While we discuss God in greater depth in chapter 8, it is necessary to introduce him now in order to complete this argument. We have seen that knowing is knowing a cause. In metaphysics, we seek to discover the highest first cause. Yet, for Thomas, this metaphysical argument can happen in two ways.[33] On the one hand, we can discern the most universal *intrinsic* principle of being; this is the act of existence, without which nothing can exist. But we can also ask where that act of existence, as the universal intrinsic cause, comes from. This leads us to consider the *extrinsic* source of being, since the act of existence is given to essences by another being.[34] As we have seen, this has to be a being whose essence is existence, of which there can

---

31 *DV* 2.3.ad 16. But not all possible modes of being are given existence. God has ideas of everything that *can be*, even though creation itself is finite. These uncreated possibilities are called *virtual* practical ideas in God's mind since he never gives them being in reality (*DV* 3.3).

32 *ST* I.75.5.ad 4.

33 Prologue to *CM*; see also *CBDT* 6.1.

34 Just as the composition of form and matter in substances requires an extrinsic efficient cause, even more so does the composition of essence and existence require an extrinsic cause of being.

only be one and whose existence is primary insofar as it is the cause of all other things. This extrinsic cause of being is God, who creates the universe by delimiting being to multitudinous modes through the receptive potential of the essences he creates to receive existence. Metaphysics, therefore, is able to attain knowledge of God, albeit indirectly and limitedly: He is known insofar as he is the cause of existence.[35]

This indirect knowledge of God is possible because of the fact of creation, the relation of participation between God as extrinsic cause and the contingent reception of being by creatures:

> It must be said that every being in any way existing is from God. For whatever is found in anything by participation, must be caused in it by that to which it belongs essentially, as iron becomes ignited by fire. . . . God is the essentially self-subsisting Being. . . . Therefore all beings apart from God are not their own being, but are beings by participation. Therefore it must be that all things which are diversified by the diverse participation of being, so as to be more or less perfect, are caused by one First Being, Who possesses being most perfectly.[36]

Since God is the primary being who is the source of existence for all creatures, his essence is existence itself.[37] Since act is not self-limiting, God's existence is infinite.[38] Therefore, everything else that exists does so by participation in existence. As substances are created, they are differentiated from other kinds of substances according to their diverse essences, which receive existence in limited and diverse ways, like glasses receiving milk in diverse amounts. In this way, although creatures share existence with God, they are nonetheless truly *other than* God, with an essence distinct from his and activity independent of him.[39] We thus avoid pantheism and nevertheless uphold the intrinsic unity of all being.

---

35 The exact relationship between the science of metaphysics and God as an object of knowledge was greatly controverted in the Middle Ages with a variety of positions being held by different thinkers.

36 *ST* I.44.1.

37 *ST* I.3.4.

38 *ST* I.7.1.

39 An important technical point here is that this participation in being is not in God directly but in *esse commune*, the common being that is the foundation for the existence of things other than God. See *DP* 7.2. ad 4: "God's being which is his essence is not universal being, but being distinct from all other being: so that by his very being God is distinct from every other being."

This unity of being in God's causal activity is reflected in the Christian transformation of Plato's Forms into the divine ideas. God knows himself as the infinite act of existence. But he therefore also knows in his Ideas all the finite ways things can participate in existence.[40] These divine ideas are a transcendent model for the forms intrinsic to particular things and so can be seen to be an *exemplar* cause (a fifth cause in addition to Aristotle's four) that connects the forms in this world with God. These divine ideas, conceiving all the ways things can be, are the basis for the diverse essences as limitations of the act of existence producing a great variety of beings.

On Essence

The idea that essence is the created principle that limits existence to a determinate mode—like milk being poured into glasses or electricity lighting up bulbs—illustrates how the Thomistic idea of essence develops that of Plato and Aristotle. For the Greek tradition, essence, or form, determines both *what* something is and, because it is the principle of actuality, *that* it is. Thomas distinguishes contingent essences from the act of existence. We may now ask, what is this essence to which existence is given?

To define essence, Thomas first considers a number of ways in which essence identifies what a thing is. (This *whatness* of a being is commonly rendered with the Latinate term *quiddity*).[41] In one way, essence signifies what is common to all members of a particular nature, so that we can identify those animals that are dogs and distinguish them from cats and cows. Because it defines a common species, essence will also identify their nature in the sense of those activities that are characteristic of a fully mature instance of that species: lions hunt antelopes, and apple trees grow apples. Since essences identify groups, they are also the basis for defining things in terms of species and difference. Because an essence defines things, it is also the crucial object that must be grasped for us to truly know what an individual is. After considering all these aspects, Thomas then epitomizes them all by describing essence in terms of its limitation of existence. Essence, he says, is "that through which and in which a thing has real being." Essence is not a *thing*, but it is the principle by which existence is limited into a determinate kind; and since action follows from being, that limited mode of

---

40 *ST* I.15.2. In *SCG* I.54.4, Thomas notes that this limited mode of existence is an "imitation" of God's being that "falls short of its perfection."

41 In this paragraph, I follow *OBE* c.1.

being will act in a predictable way. Different natures, then, are really modes of being and acting: being in a dog way means acting in a dog way; being in a human way entails acting in a human way. The *act* of existence, then, not only makes the substance exist but also overflows from that first act into second act.[42] The universe is essentially dynamic, and the activity of a substance is the self-revelation of its being.

In sum: Being is both that by which a thing exists—*esse*, or the act of existence—as well as what exists—*ens*, the being in the world. It is both because any being (*ens*) is an essence that constricts the act of existence into a determinate mode of actuality. This metaphysical truth grounds the certainty of scientific laws, for actions, as a manifestation of a determinate mode of being, are related necessarily to the essences and natures of the substances from which they arise.

It is now clear how wrong the nominalists' idea of being is. They assert that existence adds nothing to a concept. But this is to miss the point: existence does not add to essence, for neither is a *thing* to begin with. Rather, existence and essence together constitute the reality of a substance. Existence makes a thing real by giving it being, but essence, as the principle that limits existence to a determinate mode of being, specifies the kind of being the substance is, distinguishing it from other kinds of being. In this way, essence is the determinate "carrier" of existence, both being integrally united to give substances an active presence in the world. If we fail to see the common causal necessity of the act of existence, reality dissolves into an aggregation of unrelated brute facts with no unifying intelligibility.

The Double Composition of Act and Potency

Existence and essence are co-principles for every substance, determining that it is and what it is. In the previous chapter we saw that Aristotle said that form and matter are the intrinsic principles of any material substance. In both cases, these are relationships of act to potency. Are these asserting the same thing? In order to clarify this, we need to consider the relation of essence to form in substances.[43]

An individual material substance is composed of matter and form. The essence of the substance, then, must be identified either with matter alone, or with form alone, or with both together. First, it is clear that essence

---

42 *SCG* III.97.4–5.

43 My argument in the section follows *OBE* c. 2–3.

cannot be identified with matter, for essence specifies the nature of the thing, while matter is the principle of potency to become various natures. However, neither can we identify essence with form, as Aristotle did.[44] If essence is the defining whatness of a thing, it would be absurd to leave out the fact that some things are essentially material objects. You cannot define furniture without considering that it must be a material reality. More seriously, you cannot define a man without reference to the fact he is an animal, for a rational being without a material body is an angel, but men and angels are not the same being at all!

Thus, for material creatures,[45] the essence is *both* form and matter taken together. This raises a possible problem, though: since matter is the principle of individuation, it seems that to take form and matter together would always point to an individual substance. But an essence is supposed to be the basis for a *universal definition* that unites many disparate individuals. "Rational animal" points to the essence of a human and so applies to every human being who has ever existed. To resolve this puzzle, we need to distinguish two ways of using the idea of *matter*. On the one hand, we can take it as a specific chunk of matter—this thing here—and in that case it is a principle of individuation. (This can be called *designated matter*.) Or we can take is as pointing to a generic sort of matter common to a species—as "animal" indicates anything composed of "flesh and blood." (This can be called *nondesignated matter*.) It is this latter sense of matter that is employed in a universal definition. That generic matter is common to animals made of flesh and blood but can be determined into a species by the form, which indicates what kind of animal it is by providing the unique bodily patterns and powers associated with each species. All animals are flesh and blood, but humans, dogs, and cats look and act in their own way. In particular, a human as a species is the kind of animal (genus, matter as flesh and blood) who is specifically rational (the form that distinguishes a human being).

The result of this relation of form to essence is that in material creatures there is a *double-composition* of act and potency.[46] In both cases, act is limited and diversified by the potency that receives that act. All real things share the act of existence, but existence is limited by the essence to a particular

---

44 Aristotle, *Metaphysics* VII.17 (1041b9).

45 In immaterial creatures, essence is form alone (*OBE* c. 5). Angels are distinguished from God by the fact that their essence is not existence, and so they need to be created.

46 *OBE* c. 5.

kind of being: to be human implies not being dog or bird or tree. In material creatures, this species—indicated by the form—is then received into matter, so that there are many different individuals of the same kind. Socrates, Plato, and Aristotle are all fully human beings; they all possess the essence of humanity, and yet each is a unique individual due to his accidental material differences (size, color, talents, history).

Four important corollaries follow from this double-composition (existence-essence and form-matter) in material substances.[47]

First, since an individual is a limitation of a species' form, no one individual exhausts all the possibilities of the essence of a species. Humanity is artistic and athletic and scientific, but these talents are apportioned out to different individuals, so that the great singer might not be a great physicist, and vice versa; yet each is fully human.

Second, since essence is that through which and in which a thing has real being, and essence (in material substances) is a combination of form and matter, it must be that form and matter are *concreated*, constituted at once.[48] As Thomas notes: "This single act of being is that in which the composite substance subsists: a thing one in being and made up of matter and form."[49] Moreover, because they are created together as a single essence, we can also say they are *commensurated*, or measured out to one another: *this* form is made for *this* matter, and this matter is for this form.[50] In other words, God creates the form and the matter for one another; this has important implications for human nature, since the body and soul are created for one another.[51]

Third, an essence is both universal and individual.[52] This is crucial, for, in the words of one philosopher, this breaks the Gordian knot of the problem of universals.[53] This ancient problem notes that, if a universal is shared by many individuals, the universal is either divided, and so not really universally

---

47 We should recall that there is actually a third composition in material substance, that between substance and accident. The first act of the substance underlies all the accidents that manifest its nature in second act.

48 *ST* I.45.4 and 8.

49 *SCG* II.68.3.

50 *SCG* II.81.7.

51 We return to this in chapter 5.

52 *OBE* c. 3.

53 Jorge J. E. Gracia, "Cutting the Gordian Knot of Ontology: Thomas's Solution to the Problem of Universals," in *Thomas Aquinas and His Legacy*, ed. David M. Gallagher, 16–36 (Washington, D.C.: The Catholic University of America Press, 1994).

the same for all; or it remains the same for all, but then you cannot really have individuality.[54] Thomas's solution is that essence can be considered as either individual or universal. The essence of a human *must be* rational, social, mammalian, and so on; but that essence *can be* individual, when it is in concrete matter, or it *can be* universal, when taken as a definition (with non-designated matter). This leads to the fourth important corollary.

An essence will be individual or universal depending on its manner of existing. As actually existing in reality in a material human being, the essence is always individual; but when that essence is known—when we grasp the definition or form an abstract concept of it—the essence exists in the mind and is universal. That the same essence is in the thing and in the mind guarantees that our knowledge reflects the world as it really is. *What is* identical to *what is known.* This point plays a central role in the discussion of knowledge in chapter 4.

We now can explain how reality is both one and many because of compositions on three distinct levels. First, the objects of perception are accidental differences that are constantly changing; yet we know those must exist in some stable being, a substance. For example, every time I see myself in the mirror, the ravages of age reveal themselves as I change; yet I have no problem recognizing that it is I at each moment. Second, each substance is a unique individual, different from all others; yet each substance is of a certain formal nature, and so is the same as many other individuals of that species. Although I am a unique human person, I easily see that I am the same as all other people, with the same rights and capabilities. Third, the variety of forms means that there are a multitude of different essences, yet all essences are united in the act of existence that makes them real. So, even though humans alone have rights, I recognize every creature is a gift from God, since it exists only by his giving the act of existence. The act of existence, then, permeates all levels, causing natures to be, individuals to be, and accidents to be (if fleetingly), and so it truly is the "act of all acts."[55] Being is simultaneously both absolutely one and astoundingly many. Only at the level of sensation is this a "blooming, buzzing confusion" for under each level is a principle of stability the provides layers of intelligible order. In other words, the universe is full of dynamic and unique beings, which are all united according to the stability of substance, of essence, and of existence.

54 The classical source for this widely debated problem is Porphyry's *Isagoge*, written in AD 270.
55 *DP* 7.2.ad 9.

THE TRANSCENDENTAL PROPERTIES OF BEING

The great metaphysical insight that we have relied on so far is that the one property that all existing things have in common is that they exist. They all share in the act of existence that gives them being. One significant consequence of this is that we must define all things in terms of *being*. To define something as non-being would be to admit it is nothing, and such a thing cannot even be thought.

But defining things in terms of being presents a problem. As Thomas frames it, "All the other conceptions of the intellect are had by additions to being. But nothing can be added to being as though it were something not included in being—in the way that a difference is added to a genus or an accident to a subject—for every reality is essentially a being."[56] To define something cannot be done by saying "being-plus-this other element," for that other element must already be a being (since it would be pointless to add some characteristic that was nothing).

Therefore, there are two ways of looking at being in order to define concepts: either a concept represents *a division* of being or it is *convertible* with being. A division of being is when you indicate a determinate kind of being that applies to only some things but not all: human, blue, tall, living—all these describe some things in the world but certainly not all (since there are non-humans and non-blue things). The most familiar divisions of being, as we have already seen, are Aristotle's categories: substance and the nine kinds of accidents. These are the limited kinds of being caused by forms.

In contrast, those concepts that are convertible with being must be applicable to *all* things. Because these properties can be applied to all beings, they are said to transcend the categorical divisions of being and so are known as the *transcendental* properties. The transcendental properties are those properties that belong to all things simply because they exist. Being, obviously, is the first transcendental property, since everything is a being and there is nothing other than being. There is no more basic term than *being* by which to describe things, since everything is a being of some sort.

Nevertheless, if we approach being from a certain logical perspective, the other transcendental properties make themselves known. These perspectives are neither adding to being nor dividing it into limited kinds but rather viewing being in terms of some notion that is implicit in being itself.

---

56 *DV* 1.1; this section follows this text and its parallel in *DV* 21.1.

These notional aspects are the result of considering being in terms of its richness, which allows us to make logical affirmations and negations that draw out an aspect of being, and also to consider being in terms of its relations to other beings, whereby other aspects are made manifest. In other words, the richness of being allows it to be understood according to these various aspects that apply to all beings.

Considering being, first we can affirm that its existence is the existence of a *thing* (Latin, *res*). By saying a being is a thing, we understand this to mean that every being is of a certain nature. This point reflects the composition between existence and essence, for every being must have an essence that defines it.[57] We can then, by logical negation, see how a being *cannot* be: a being cannot be other than itself. From this we take the idea that every being must be undivided or that it is one (*unum*), for if it were divided it would be two things. While this is obvious at one level, it is an invaluable guide for determining whether an object is one complex being—an organism like a dog—or simply an amalgam of different things acting similarly— like rocks in an avalanche. If there is one essence, there is only one final cause, so all activity will be ordered to that end. If there is not one focused center of activity, it is not a real substance. This will defuse many pseudo-problems philosophers have stumbled on when they confuse groups of things for single substances.

However, when a being is considered in its relations with other beings, more significant aspects are revealed. When seen in community with other things, the first fact that emerges is that this thing is *not* that thing. Thus, each being is an *individual* being. Thomas describes this by saying each thing is *something* (*aliquid*) in distinction from other individuals. (Note that *thing* implies essence or nature, while *something* implies individuality; this corresponds to the composition of form and matter.)

More important than these brute physical relations are the relations of beings to a soul. Souls relate to objects through their ability to know (by the intellect) and to desire (by the appetite). In knowledge, there is a "conformity [or adequation] of thing and intellect," and the being is seen under that aspect of *true* (*verum*). When the being elicits the desire of the appetite, it is because the being is seen under the aspect of *good* (*bonum*). It is part of the richness of being that allows it to be known and to be desired. Because

---

57 *CM* IV.2.553: "The term *thing* [is derived] from the quiddity only; but the term *being* is derived from the act of being."

true and good belong to being, they are part of creation as constituted by God: in giving existence, he makes things true and good. One consequence of this is that it is not for people to determine what is true or what is good. The objective reality of truth and goodness is the foundation for the argument for philosophical realism in epistemology and ethics (chapters 4 and 6, respectively).

Because these properties are convertible with being, the more being participates in existence, the more unity, truth, and goodness it possesses. It follows that God, as the perfect Being who creates all other things, will also be perfect Unity, Truth, and Goodness.[58] Although *thing* and *something* are transcendentals, since the ideas of nature and individuality follow immediately from being, the other transcendentals are of more substantive interest. In the perennial tradition, then, the canonical list of transcendentals is this: every being is one, true, and good.[59]

We can see again how nominalism undermines the intelligibility of creation. If we cannot know *being* as a universal causal principle, then true and good are also obscured. Since there is no objective reality to ground these principles, the nominalist will infer that it is a person's duty to decide for himself what is true and what is good. This leads ineluctably to relativism. To illustrate how this relativism can be avoided, we need to demonstrate *how* the transcendentals are objectively grounded in reality. These arguments are further developed in later chapters as we consider truth as the object of epistemology and goodness as the object of ethics.

The first thing to note is that, since the transcendentals are convertible with being, they can never be properly defined. To define a concept is to limit it to a kind of being; *de-fine* implies a finite mode of being as indicated by genus and species. Being itself, as including all species, cannot be defined; but it follows that neither can those properties convertible with being be defined.

Nevertheless, the transcendental properties are distinguished from one another insofar as they indicate different logical aspects under which we consider being. Being, as I have argued, is primarily an act, it is actively present to us; this is how we distinguish being from non-being (such as illu-

---

58 See *ST* I, questions 11, 16, and 6, respectively.

59 It should also be noted that, while many Christian thinkers, including Pseudo-Dionysius and Saint Bonaventure, argue that beauty is a transcendental property, Thomas understands beauty to be a species of the good (*ST* I-II.27.1.ad 3 and *ST* I.5.4.ad 1). We consider the place of beauty in chapter 6.

sions). In turn, each transcendental marks out a particular experience of being as actively present to us that causes in us a distinct reaction: as there is a single center of activity in any being, we recognize unity; as the mind can be conformed with any being, we recognize truth as a transcendental; as desire can be elicited in the appetite by any being, we recognize the presence of the good.

But this active presence to us once again illustrates the importance of understanding being in terms of the act of existence, for it is the act of existence that grounds each of the transcendentals. Truth is the knowability of being, but being makes itself knowable to us only inasmuch as it is active and not as mere potency.[60] That is, we know things actively present in the world; inert things would remain unknown, and even potentiality can only be inferred from what is actively present. Goodness is the desirability of being; but anything is good only if it is perfect, and perfection is the result of the act of existence.[61] It is existence that perfects, or actualizes, the potential of any essence, and the more perfect a thing is, the more desirable it will be. Therefore, in both cases, the act of existence is at the root of the intelligibility of the transcendental properties. (I defend this claim more fully in chapters 4 and 6.)

THE DIVISIONS OF BEING

The transcendental properties, then, are very few. Most often when we talk about being, we do so in terms of the various divisions of being, that is, when we indicate a specific *kind* of being that describes only some things and is not common to all things. As mentioned, the most familiar divisions of being are the ten Aristotelian categories. Every real being is either a substance, that which exists in itself and not in another, like a human or a dog or a tree; or it is an accident, one of the nine properties that exist in a substance, like tall or blue or running. These are necessarily divisions of being because any substance must be of one specific nature and category: a human cannot be a dog or a tree; but neither can it be an accident. And any one

60 *ST* I.5.2 and I.87.1. Thomas realizes that this definition of truth—"the conformity of mind and thing"—might seem to imply a relativism: since everyone's perceptions of reality differ, it might be argued that the thing conforms to my mind in one way and your mind in another. Thomas's reply is to note that the first mind is God's: things conform to God's mind, and that constitutes their truth. Human minds, in turn, conform to the things in the world, and that makes truth in our mind. Thus, our mind is dependent on the world, and the world is dependent on God's mind as the source of truth (*DV* 1.2 and *ST* I.14.8.ad 3).

61 *ST* I.5.1.

accident must be one determinate accident and category: blue cannot be white or green; but neither can it be a quantity or a relation. Thus, to name a substance by nature or accident is always specifying it according to determinate kinds of being and dividing it off from all that it is not.

In addition to the categories, though, other divisions of being help us understand the full spectrum of our understanding of being. We can appreciate these other divisions if we remind ourselves that accidents, although real, exist in a dependent fashion. This notion of dependent modes of being—dependent on substance, which alone exists in itself—can be amplified to discover other divisions of being that are even more dependent—and ultimately less real—than the accidents are. A caveat, though: if we ever forget this radical dependency on substance, philosophical analyses can quickly lead to great confusion.

The first additional division of being is between actual being and potential being. Substance and accident are both actual: they are present in the world. Yet substance and accident both have potential to change. This potency—what does not exist now, but what can be—is *real*, but not yet *actual*. It is real because the nature of the substance determines what accidental changes are possible (a person has the potential to be six feet tall and running but not twenty feet tall and flying), and the nature of the matter/form composition determines what substantial changes may occur (when a person dies, the corpse reduces to organic compounds but cannot become steel). This real potential is inherently present in the world as a possibility, as a change that might come about. This real potential is very different from the pure speculation of *logical possibility*—anything that is not a contradiction in terms and so might obtain in some possible universe—which is completely untethered from reality. While there is a logical possibility that pigs might fly, in this universe there is no real potential for that. Thus, potential being is dependent on the actual substances. For this reason, the first of the "24 Thomistic Theses" is that act and potency are a complete division of real being.[62]

But there is one other division of being, whose reality is even less actual and more dependent than potential being. In discussing the way in which we use the verb *to be*, Thomas frequently invokes this broadest division of being:

---

62 This list was drawn up by a number of professors in 1916 in response to various popes insisting on the centrality of Thomas for Catholic education. The list is available at http://www.catholicapologetics.info/catholicteaching/philosophy/thomast.htm.

> The term *a being* in itself has two meanings. Taken one way it is divided
> by the ten categories; taken in the other way it signifies the truth of prop-
> ositions. The difference between the two is that in the second sense any-
> thing can be called a being if an affirmative proposition can be formed
> about it, even though it is nothing positive in reality. In this way privations
> and negations are called beings, for we say that affirmation *is* opposed to
> negation, and that blindness *is* in the eye. But in the first way nothing can
> be called a being unless it is something positive in reality.[63]

The point here is that we frequently talk about things—meaningfully and
not nonsensically—even though they are not real *things*. Thus, this last division of being must be distinguished from real being—substances, with their
accidents and potency. Those unreal things we talk about are what the tradition calls beings of reason (*entia rationis*). A being of reason is anything
that we can meaningfully talk about even though it does not exist in reality
(as substance, accident, or potential). However, since it is meaningful, it
cannot be *nothing at all*, for then we would not be able to say anything about
them. These can be said to have existence only insofar as we think them—
they are, in other words, mind-dependent beings. This is the most dependent and least real division of being, for where potency might become actual,
mind-dependent beings are those things that exist only in the mind. But
this does not mean they are unimportant.

There are four very different types of beings of reason. First are fictions.
It is perfectly true to say that Harry Potter is a wizard at Hogwarts. Yet,
Harry does not exist; there are no such thing as wizards; and Hogwarts is
purely imaginary. But as a fiction—an idea made up by the mind—it is perfectly correct to say this (and indeed wrong if you deny it). To admit that
fictions have existence, but only as mind-dependent, solves many possible
puzzles that philosophers have faced with examples like unicorns and the
golden mountain.

Second are negations or privations. This is where the mind recognizes
the *nonexistence* of something. For example, if a dentist tells me that I have
a cavity in my tooth, he is not saying there is something there; rather, he is
saying that there is something missing from my tooth. This is mind dependent because we need to recognize what *ought to be* there to see there is a
lack of being (as Thomas's example of blindness illustrates). The most
important instance of privation, as we will see, is evil. If evil is a being, it

63 *OBE* c. 1.

must be created by God; if, however, evil is a lack of being, it is an absence of being in the universe contrary to God's will. This provides the first answer to all arguments concerning the problem of evil.

Third are universals. We say that Socrates is a human. We also say that the human species is a type of animal. But only the individual substance, Socrates, exists in the world. *Human* and *animal* are derived from Socrates's essence; they are universal categories that are predicated of Socrates's individual existence. There is nothing in this world that is just *human* or *animal*. Yet we talk meaningfully about the existence of species. This is because the mind can judge the nature of a substance and so assert the necessary relation between an individual and a universal class that is known when the essence exists in the mind. This kind of mind-dependent being is particularly important because it allows us to have scientific knowledge: it allows us to know individual members of a universal classes in terms of their necessary properties, so that the world is predictable and regular. For example, once I know Socrates is a human, I will also know that he is mortal, rational, mammalian, social, and so on. Had David Hume realized this, he would not have feared eating his bread.

Finally, there are cultural realities, those realities that depend on the common recognition of people. For example, does the border between the United States and Canada exist? You cannot see it from space, and it is often not physically marked on the ground. Yet, depending on which side one is on, you are subject to different laws. The border is real so long as people respect it as real. If people cease to recognize a border, it effectively ceases to exist. This is how the Roman Empire came to an end. The same can be said of the office of president; individual substances exist—people named Kennedy, Johnson, Nixon—but the office of president requires that people respect the authority. While there are people alive today with claims to be the king of France or the Holy Roman Emperor, these claims are (for the most part) ignored since the cultural realities behind them have disappeared.

THE ANALOGY OF BEING

To adequately understand reality, then, it is imperative that we distinguish independent being—substances—from all those modes of being that are dependent on substance—accident, potency, and beings of reason. We group these diverse uses of *being* under the notion of the *analogy of being*. In its simplest fashion, deriving from the Aristotelian distinction between substance and accident, the analogy of being is the idea that "'to be' is said in many ways."[64] That is, when we assert that something "is," we must admit that things exist in different ways. This truth is illustrated by the following set of statements:

1. Socrates is a man.
2. Socrates is pale.
3. Man is an animal.
4. This is a hole.

Here we have four instances of the verb *to be*, yet each is used in a different way: substantial being, accidental being, universal species, and privation of being. To ignore the different uses of being will be to fall into the error of Plato, who assumed every use of *is* implies a distinct Form.

Developing Aristotle's insight, Thomas summarizes the divisions of being.[65] The primary meaning of being is that which exists in itself and not in another. These are substances. This is the primary use of *being*. Other things can be said to be only because they are dependent on substance. We can say that substances are real, actual, and independent.

Substance is primarily divided off from accidents, which exist only in substances. Accidents are real and actual, but they are dependent for their existence on the substance in which they exist. Things like weight, color, hairiness, and intelligence exist only in a human being; should that human die, these would leave the world with him.

Both substance and accident are actual beings—they exist now. These are divided off from potential being, that which could be actual but is not actual now. In this sense, potency is dependent on actuality since what might be is always dependent on what is now.

Act and potency are real beings, and this is divided off from beings of reason, which are not real at all. As such, beings of reason have no essence (because essence is that by which and in which a thing has *real* being). The clearest way to identify beings of reason is that, since they are not real, they have no independent activity in the world. Dreams may haunt us at night, yet by day we know they are harmless. Monsters might scare us in books and movies; yet in reality they cannot harm us. This fact points us back to the act of existence as overflowing into activity, and so things without it cannot act on their own.

64 Aristotle, *Metaphysics* IV.2 (1003a33) and XI.3 (1060b32).
65 *CM* IV.1.539–43.

Therefore, to schematize this:

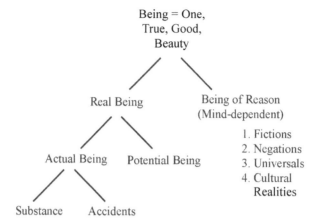

This illustrates the various ways being can be ascribed to something. Because these uses of being are not exactly the same (a *univocal* use of being), and neither are they utterly different (an *equivocal* use of being), we say that being is used *analogically*. In general, analogous predication occurs whenever a term can be applied to different things in such a way that its meaning is partially the same and partially different. For example, I can say that my dog loves me, my wife loves me, and God loves me. It is clear that love indicates one activity—the appreciation of something good as desirable—yet the way in which dogs love (based upon instinct for survival), humans love (based upon a rational appreciation of virtue as an excellence of human nature), and God loves (as the Creator who freely creates me out of his gratuitous generosity) are very different. A similar statement can be made about knowledge: dogs know only by sensation, humans by reason, and God as Creator of all that is; each knows, but in different ways.

More technically, Thomas defines *analogy* in terms of the thing signified as related to the mode of signification.[66] The thing signified is some quality or perfection; the mode of signification arises from the substance to which that perfection is attributed. In the examples given, love and knowledge are perfections; the mode is animal, or human, or divine. Since God is the Creator of all perfections,[67] the perfection signified—love, knowledge, life,

---

66 *ST* I.13.3 and 6. It should be noted that the topic of analogy is one about which there is a great deal of debate among Thomists. For a brief overview, see Clarke, *The One and the Many*, 46–57.

67 *ST* I.4.2.

being—always refers primarily to him; but since we only *know* the perfection though our experience of creatures, the mode is always finite and imperfect (from a person or a dog).[68]

The analogy of being, then, simply recognizes that being is an act that can be exercised by different things in different ways. The independent existence of substances is the primary use, and the dependent modes of existence of are diminishing qualifications of existence. This analogy of being, then, once more shows how being is simultaneously one—the act of existence—and many—the way that act is exercised by dependent kinds of being. Indeed, in this way *being* is the foundation for all true statements, since at the root of all predications is "one first non-univocal analogical predication, which is being."[69]

THE LADDER OF BEING

There is one last way in which the analogy of being explains the order of reality. Substances exist in themselves as independent, and so are the primary sense of being. Yet substances are not all the same; in fact, substances are differentiated by the degree to which the essence participates in the act of existence. In fact, difference in kinds necessarily implies a hierarchy to order those kinds.[70] Substances themselves exist in varying degrees, because their essences participate more or less intensively in the act of existence. Thus, the being of substance is itself analogical.

Some essences have very limited potency for existence, so their existence is itself limited; other essences have greater potency—as a metaphor, we might say they are "larger" essences—and so are able to participate in existence more intensively. The evidence for this lies in the principle that action follows from being: it is evident that some natures have a greater capacity for action—by moving, or sensing, or knowing—so they must *exist more* in order to *do more*. As an analogy, most adults can run; but the Olympic sprinter does the activity more intensively, more fully, than the jogger on the treadmill. In the same way, every being exists (else it is nothing); however, the way in which they exercise that existence points to real differences in the potential to exist.

---

68 *ST* I.13.6. I return to the topic of analogy in chapter 8.

69 *ST* I.13.5.ad 1.

70 *ST* I.47.2. Notably, there are two exceptions to this idea that difference is hierarchical: the Persons of the Trinity (*ST* I.39.1–2) and of man and woman (*ST* I.92.1 and 3). In people, sexual difference is complementary, as we see in chapter 5.

Interestingly, this hierarchy of substances' activity can be explained by employing the same criterion we used before: dependent being versus independent being.[71] Since being is made manifest in activity, any substance whose activities do not depend on other things can be said to exist in a more absolute fashion. The more dependent an activity is, the lower the being; the less dependent the activity, the higher the being. Based on this, we can say that at the bottom of the ladder of being are inanimate beings—atoms and inorganic molecules—that change only in reaction to external stimuli. A hydrogen molecule will form a chemical bond only in reaction to an atom in its environment, and a rock will roll down a hill only in reaction to an initial impetus. The activity of an inanimate substance is then completely dependent on other substances.

Living things are defined by the fact that they have within themselves a power to grow and change.[72] This intrinsic power to change on one's own lifts living things above inanimate substances. Plants exhibit this power, but they are dependent on their environment for water and nutrients in order to be able to grow. Moreover, the goal of a plant is to drop a seed into the soil to propagate the species. So, although the plant is active in itself, that activity originates and ends outside of it: it is dependent on its environment for its activity.

Animals are characterized by sensory consciousness. This is an act that is internal to the animal itself, and so it not dependent on something else for its consummation (like the plant dropping a seed). Moreover, this awareness of the environment allows them to instinctively react to things, which means their activity is more spontaneous and individualized than plants. Yet, animals are still dependent in two ways: their consciousness is of the material environment in which they live and their actions are not freely chosen but are determined wholly by natural instinct.

Human beings rise above animals by having free will, so these human acts are independent even of animal instinct. For this reason, each person has control over his actions. Nevertheless, humans are still dependent on their environment, the material world, to gain the knowledge upon which they exercise free choice. Moreover, they are, like all creatures, dependent on God for giving them their existence as defined by their essence. Angels are similarly dependent on God for their existence and essence, but as immaterial beings, their activity does not depend on the material world at all.

---

71 This argument summarizes *SCG* IV.11.

72 This is explained more fully in chapter 5.

The only truly independent being—the one who embodies the independence of substance in the fullest sense—is God. His action alone depends on no one but himself, and so he is completely free. Other substances possess independence in a more analogical fashion.

Putting these together, we get a ladder of being in which natures exist analogically, from the least active to the pure actuality: (1) atomic elements; (2) inorganic compounds (molecules, up to complex protein chains); (3) plants; (4) animals; (5) humans; and (6) angels. Indeed, within each of these kinds (except for humans), there are a multitude of species, such that "the lowest in the higher genus touches the highest of the lower species."[73] For example, the highest (most active) plant—a Venus flytrap, say—is close to the activity of the lowest animal, a sponge or, similarly, the highest animal, a chimpanzee or dolphin, is seen to have human qualities, while the worst person is condemned for being a brute.

Above all this, as the source of all being, is God, whose essence is existence itself, and so is not a *kind* of being. Indeed, even though God's infinite existence makes it appear as though creatures are nothing in comparison to him,[74] we nevertheless affirm that there is an analogical relation between God's existence and that of creatures because of the shared principle of being. Certainly, creatures are not beings in the same way God is; but, since he causes them to exist, the being they possess is a likeness—distant though it be—of God's.[75]

In spite of the central role that the analogy of being plays in solving the problem of the one and the many, we note that most modern philosophers do not think it is relevant. Modern philosophers will tend to see existence as a binary fact, that is, either something exists or it does not. Atoms exist, dogs exist, humans exist, God exists; these are distinct facts, and we cannot use the intensive participation in the act of existence to determine a hierarchy among them. This factual state of existence understands being *univocally*. Instead of an analogical act of existence as a principle in composition with essence, being will tend to be reified as a thing, one common property the accrues to things that are real. This reification of being, though, destroys the notion of ontological dependency that is the crucial insight of the analogy of being. As a result, reification extends to all aspects of being equally:

73 *SCG* II.68.6–12; see also *SCG* III.97.3.
74 *DV* 2.3.ad 16.
75 *ST* I.4.3.

accidental properties, logical possibility, and beings of reason (including evil) become topics of existential analysis independent of the substances on which they depend. This disrupts the orderliness of the natural world in numerous ways since cause and effect are isolated from one another. And God's existence, which had been inferred causally on the basis of this dependency, becomes much more difficult to establish, leaving open a path to fideism that sunders the union of faith and reason.[76] In the coming chapters, we examine these consequences more closely.

We have made a number of claims about the nature of reality. A reasonable question might be, how do we *know* this? The next chapter takes up the question of knowledge and demonstrates that we can come to know these metaphysical truths because being is convertible with the true.

FURTHER READING

Aertsen, Jan. *Medieval Philosophy and the Transcendentals: The Case of Thomas Aquinas.* Studien und Texte zur Geistesgeschichte des Mittelalters 52. Leiden, New York, and Cologne: E. J. Brill, 1996.

Ashley, Benedict. *The Way toward Wisdom: An Interdisciplinary and Intercultural Introduction to Metaphysics.* Notre Dame, Ind.: University of Notre Dame Press, 2006.

Clarke, W. Norris. *The One and the Many: A Contemporary Thomistic Metaphysics.* Notre Dame, Ind.: University of Notre Dame Press, 2001.

Feser, Edward. *Scholastic Metaphysics: A Contemporary Introduction.* Heusenstamm, Germany: Editiones Scholasticae, 2014.

Gilson, Étienne. *Being and Some Philosophers.* 4th ed. Toronto: Pontifical Institute of Medieval Studies, 1952.

Maritain, Jacques. *The Philosophy of Nature.* Translated by Imelda C. Byrne. New York: Philosophical Library, 1951.

———. *Existence and the Existent.* Translated by Lewis Galantiere and Gerald B. Phelan. Garden City, N.Y.: Image Books, 1956.

Oderberg, David S. *Real Essentialism.* New York: Routledge, 2007.

Pieper, Josef. *Living the Truth: The Truth of All Things* and *Reality and the Good.* Translated by Lothar Krauth and Stella Lange. San Francisco: Ignatius Press, 1989.

---

76 Karl Barth, the greatest twentieth-century Protestant theologian, sees this fideism as a victory. Arguing that the analogy of being was "the invention of the antichrist," he places God outside the capacity of reason and makes knowledge of him dependent on revelation alone. See the discussion of Barth's *Church Dogmatics* I/1 in Fergus Kerr, *After Aquinas: Versions of Thomism* (Malden, Mass.: Blackwell, 2002), 35–36.

Chapter 4

What Is Truth? Epistemology and the Extent of Knowledge

THE PROBLEM: WHAT CAN BE KNOWN?

We have seen that everything must be understood with reference to being. In other words, if something is real, it must be intelligible in terms of the principles of being that have been introduced in the previous chapter. This is the case even for *truth*. The tradition of the perennial philosophy defines truth as the state of conformity between a being (thing) and a mind.[1] Because truth is this state of being, it is explained primarily in terms of those principles that underlie all reality, like act/potency and existence/essence. In particular, human knowledge is the result of the act of existence in substances acting on the potency of humans to learn, so that the essence of a real being is grasped in the mind as a being of reason pointing to a universal essence that defines that object.[2] This grounding of knowledge in the principles of being means that the mind grasps reality as it is. For the perennial philosophy, then, since all being is characterized by existence and essence, all being can be known. Thus, truth is a transcendental property of being. In other words, the entire universe is intelligible. This claim is justified because metaphysics precedes and grounds epistemology.

The universal intelligibility of being is threatened, however, if we understand truth to be the result of a human operation and not grounded in being. This approach is typical of many modern philosophers who start, not with being, but with human experience. Beginning with human experience, they identify truth in terms of their sensations, or their intuited ideas, or an order imposed on reality by their minds. But to define knowledge in

---

1 *ST* I.16.1–3.

2 Note how many terms from the previous chapter are employed in this explanation: essence, existence, real being, being of reason, essence as a definition. This exemplifies why the principles of being, though difficult, must have priority in our analysis.

terms of one's subjective and limited experience means that truth will exhibit that same subjectivity and limitation. One consequence is that modern philosophers reject the universal knowability of being. Instead, they assume that some types of being are inherently unknowable and so the universe is not wholly intelligible. In short, modern philosophers invert the tradition and assert that it is knowledge that determines reality, not that reality determines knowledge. In other words, they place epistemology before metaphysics: they start with a theory about how we know the world and then deduce which aspects of reality are knowable.[3]

The assumption that some types of being cannot be known is, however, a dogmatic and arbitrary limit on knowledge. In fact, any epistemology— an explanation of how we can know reality—that imposes such an arbitrary limit seems to undermine the philosophical quest to understand the highest principle of reality: being. The attitude of the perennial philosophy, then, clearly has greater confidence in the powers of reason than do modern thinkers who toil in the shadow of the Enlightenment. By focusing on being, the perennial tradition recognizes two principles as immediately evident. First, the world is populated by active substances and, second, humans have the potency to be acted on by those substances. This receptivity to reality characterizes both sensation and intellect, each of which receives reality in distinct ways to make known the fullness of truth. In fact, these powers have the potentiality to "become all things" (as Aristotle puts it) by receiving the active presence of substances.[4]

If truth depends on this relation of human beings to reality, misjudging the nature of sensation or of the intellect will inevitably distort our conception of truth. This is precisely the problem with reductive epistemologies,

3 This is in fact a circular argument, since either they assume their method is reliable and use that as proof of what facts are known; or they assume which facts are known with certainty and use that data to defend their method. This circularity has become known as "problem of the criterion." This is discussed in Roderick Chisholm, *The Problem of the Criterion* (Milwaukee: Marquette University Press, 1973). The perennial tradition argues that only way out of this circularity is to start with metaphysics, not the act of knowing.

4 *De Anima* III.5 (430a14–15) and III.8 (431b20). In addition to sensation and reason, there is a third source of knowledge: testimony. Consider seeing a sign that says "Welcome to New Orleans" or reading a certificate from a health inspector asserting a restaurant is safe. Can we be said to *know* where we are, or that we are safe? In these instances, we take someone else's word for something, for it is impossible to prove all things for ourselves. Thus, there is in real life a great reliance on testimony of others; this is simply an instance of faith that applies more narrowly to revelation. However, those human authorities on whom we rely are in turn dependent on sensation and reason. Accordingly, I bracket questions of knowledge based on testimony, though it is an important element in human knowledge.

which give priority to sensation or reason and so end up obscuring reality because they cannot account for the fullness of our experience of reality as one and many, stable and changing.

Worse than these errors about sense and reason, though, are those who reject our ability to know reality at all. We need to address this before we can move any further into our defense of truth.

THE REJECTION OF KNOWLEDGE: RELATIVISM AND SKEPTICISM

An important goal of epistemology is to clearly distinguish knowledge that is certain from opinion, which may or may not be correct. Knowledge has this certainty about what is because we are able to provide reasons that ground our beliefs by guaranteeing their correctness.[5] So, traditionally, knowledge has been defined as "justified true belief."[6] From philosophy's earliest days however, some have challenged whether knowledge defined in this way is even possible. Instead of seeking wisdom, these thinkers either despair of the possibility of adequate justifications and so end up in skepticism or they despair the possibility of objective truth itself and so end up in relativism. These have been important challenges for anyone claiming to know the truth from the Ancient Greeks even to today.

Skepticism arises from the apparent inability to ever provide adequate justification for any belief. We have noted that human knowledge arises from either sensation or reason; but it is also immediately obvious that neither sensation nor reason are infallible. Sensation is frequently deceptive: we perceive sights and sounds that are not real, like the bent oar in the water. Reason, though, might appear to have greater certainty, since everyone knows $2 + 2 = 4$. Nevertheless, we commonly err in reasoning; we make mistakes in math and logic all the time. But if both sources of knowledge are susceptible to error, then we would never be justified in believing anything at all. This is the conclusion of Pyrrho (360–270 BC), the founder of Greek skepticism, who argues the only way to attain peace in one's life is to believe nothing, since then you can never be wrong.

Where skeptics question the notion of justification, relativists dispute the significance of "true" in the formula "justified true belief." Since it is

---

5 This is reflected in Aristotle's definition of truth, "to say of what is that it is." *Metaphysics* IV.7 (1011b26).

6 This definition goes back to Plato (*Theaetetus* 201c–d and 208b).

impossible to justify any belief, relativists assert that each person decides what is true according to his own perspective. Consequently, all beliefs are equally valid, and there is no objective truth that is universally binding for all people. For example, if a wall looks blue to me, and it looks white to you, then it is true for me that it is blue, and true for you that it is white.

Let us begin by answering the more extreme position, relativism. Two responses point out the problem with relativism. First, it violates the principle of non-contradiction. If it is true that the wall is blue for me and white for you, the wall is both blue and white in the same way simultaneously. But this is impossible; indeed, if reality lacked objective truth, the world would be unintelligible. We could not understand one another if everyone defined reality for himself; like Humpty Dumpty in *Alice in Wonderland*, our words would me whatever we wanted them to mean. Relativism, then, is internally contradictory, since it makes a claim about reality while making even talking about reality impossible.

A second argument, originating with Plato, is that relativism leads to a *performative contradiction*. That is, the one holding the belief contradicts himself in holding it. The relativist insists that there is no objective truth. But, if that is the case, his own claim that "there is no objective truth" *cannot* be true. If that claim is not true, then it *must be* the case that there is objective truth.[7] Again, relativism is shown to be internally inconsistent and so cannot be held with intellectual honesty. While these are decisive arguments against epistemological relativism, they have not prevented people from embracing the position.[8] We revisit the issue in chapter 6 when we look at ethics, where its influence has been of greater consequence.

Skepticism is more difficult to dismiss. It accepts that there may be true beliefs but finds that there is no way to justify them and be certain they are true, since both sense-experience and reason are susceptible to error. Even when they are correct, nothing signals the presence of accurate information against faulty information, so we cannot be certain when we are right. There is no siren or flashing light in the mind that lets us know we have arrived at truth. Indeed, the only way to confirm an experience is to repeat it—to look again or reason again—but that second experience is no more trustworthy

---

7 *Theaetetus* 171a–c.

8 A test for relativism: If you call a dog's tail a leg, how many legs does the dog really have? Many are tempted to say five. But this is the essence of relativism: to misname something does not change reality. The dog by nature has four legs. Yet humans are all too eager to misname things in the hope that reality will accord with our desires.

than the original is: if the two concur, they might both be deceptive; if they do not agree, there is no way to know which (if either) was correct. Nevertheless, the skeptic's solution—that that we should never hold *any* belief with certainty—although plausible in the abstract, is impossible to live by, for people cannot abide such universal doubt. We therefore need to find a different solution.

The only way out of this skeptical puzzle is to find something that cannot be doubted to act as the basis for justifying knowledge. This indubitable first principle, which defines truth and guarantees the reliability of facts, is the foundation for all certain knowledge. (This is known as *foundationalism.*[9]) However, different philosophers have suggested different foundations. Just as different ideas of *being* led to disparate interpretations of reality, different ideas of the foundation of truth lead to disparate epistemologies—different notions of what we can know. Some will argue that knowledge is founded on sense-experience alone; this is known as *empiricism*. Conversely, others will argue that knowledge is derived from reason alone; this is known as *rationalism*. Some others will recognize that the first principle for knowledge must combine both sensation and reason. Yet this can be done in different ways: one way argues that the mind constructs experience from the data of sensation, a problematic position known as *idealism*; the other way grasps being as it is, and this is the realism of the perennial tradition. We need to analyze the consequences of each of these foundational ideas of truth in order to ascertain which theory is the most adequate explanation of human experience.

---

9 The most common alternative to this foundationalism is *coherentism*, which argues that truth is guaranteed by the fact that all our beliefs form coherent system or web of beliefs. This is the position of American Pragmatism. As William James notes, this shifts the burden of justification away from the principle on which the belief is based to the results to which the belief leads: "The attitude of looking away from first things, principles, 'categories,' supposed necessities; and of looking towards last things, fruits, consequences" (*Pragmatism*, Lecture 2, in *Pragmatism and The Meaning of Truth* (Cambridge, Mass.: Harvard University Press, 1975), 32; he also refers to this idea of truth as beneficial consequences as getting the "cash-value" of an idea!). The main problem with this is that a person can have a coherent system of beliefs that in no way is anchored in reality: Think of someone with schizophrenia having a psychotic episode or someone following a conspiracy theory. Their ideas are usually internally coherent but are clearly not in conformity with reality.

FRAMING THE PROBLEM:
PLATO'S CRITIQUE OF KNOWING AS LOOKING

The questions of knowledge and truth were among the first with which philosophers had to deal. For this reason, it is helpful to consider the way in which Plato addresses them, for his thoughts frame the way all later philosophers approach the issue. As is memorably articulated in the Allegory of the Cave, in which people stare at shadows on the wall of a cave and confuse that for reality,[10] Plato is reacting to the fact that the average person's unreflective assumption is that we know something if we see it (or smell, hear, feel it). This is so deeply ingrained and invoked in naïve arguments against theological doctrine,[11] that it is best to begin by showing why this equation of knowing with looking is deficient. This critique of "knowing as looking" is a foundational insight that guides future developments in the perennial philosophy.

Plato gives a number of reasons why merely perceiving something can never lead to justified true belief. First, we all know we have perceptions that we *know* are not true, such as dreams and hallucinations.[12] Similarly, we often perceive things without knowing what it is we are perceiving, as whenever we react with, "What the heck is that?!"[13] It is clear, then, that we cannot equate knowing with perceiving.

If, however, perception *were* knowledge, this would have the disastrous effect of creating a solipsism, an extreme form of relativism that asserts that each person is utterly isolated in his own reality.[14] Since each person's faculties are unique—your eyesight and hearing are different from mine—there is no way to know how anyone else perceives things. Your perception of blue might not be mine. Worse, though, my own senses often function in inconsistent ways: think of how the taste of orange juice changes after brushing your teeth or how colors appear different under different lighting. It seems, then, that every perception is an utterly unique event. If this were the case, knowledge of the world could only be what each person perceives it to be—solipsism. This clearly is not the case,

---

10 *Republic* VII (514–18).

11 The well-known scientist Carl Sagan once said that if God wanted people to believe in him, he should have put a giant Decalogue on the face of the moon!

12 *Theaetetus* 157e1–158a4.

13 *Theaetetus* 163b2–c4.

14 *Theaetetus* 159e5–161e2.

though, since we regularly communicate and talk about a world we hold in common.[15]

Since knowledge is not mere perception, Plato argues that knowledge arises from the mind, or reason, making judgments about perceptions. It is these rational judgments that justify our knowledge by making them certain.[16] While our sensations reveal how the world appears to us, the mind's judgments grasp how the world really is in itself, the truth that lies behind those appearances.

Plato notes three kinds of judgments that only the mind can make: identity, essence, and being. Let us consider these as more general philosophical issues. *Identity* is the fact that the same thing exists over time, regardless of how its appearance may change. The important thing is to see that a judgment of identity can never arise from sensation alone: If I look at a tree, then turn away and look back a second time, what I have are two distinct perceptions of the tree. As perceptions they will always be distinct—the first is not identical to the second. Indeed, even if I look again and again, I just add to the number of perceptions; but a greater number of different perceptions can never lead to identity. What you need is something above sense-experience to judge the diverse perceptions and recognize the identity of the thing perceived, in spite of the differences between discrete perceptions. The mind, then, knows something different, something more, than the sense perceptions: that my diverse perceptions are of the same object.

A similar argument is made for essence, with the mind judging that different individuals share a common nature. Plato and Socrates appear very different; yet we can judge that they are both human beings. This cannot be done by sensation, since sensation perceives how different they are. Indeed, if we were to perceive all the billions of people on earth, those perceived differences would only multiply. The mind, however, is able to judge those perceptions and grasp the essence that unites all those different individuals into one nature.

The third argument concerns the judgment of being or reality against mere appearance. Animals will often react to statues or noises, unable to judge that the object is not what is appears to be. The human mind, in contrast, constantly judges these perceptions in order to ascertain a reality: that is a painting, not a real tiger; that car coming toward me will in reality turn

---

15 Plato sardonically concludes that, if a philosopher claims knowing is perceiving, then a pig or baboon would be as wise as that philosopher, since their knowledge would be just as true.

16 *Theaetetus* 184b3–186e6.

with the road; that frightening noise of thunder is just a discharge of ionized particles in the atmosphere. Thus, the mind grasps being—what really is—while the senses only report how things appear to be.

This is the key to distinguishing sense-experience from reason: sense-experience only perceives that world as it appears to be, but reason can grasp the real nature causing those appearances. All thinkers in the perennial philosophy retain this important distinction, even though the details change. Thus, *knowing* is not simply looking; rather, knowing arises from the justification of those beliefs by means of rational judgments about how the world really is—judgments about being.

We should briefly examine Plato's own solution to the problem of knowing. As you might guess, knowledge for Plato is grasping the Forms, the unchanging universal essences that cause our experiences. If we rely solely on sense-experience, we only have opinion, since the world of sensation is subject to change. Thus, the mind only has certainty when grasping the Form. Plato says we do this by recollection.[17] We know unchanging truths that can never be attained by sense-experience of the changing world, and so the fact we know them demonstrates we must have attained them prior to any experience of this world.[18] For example, we know what *equal* means, even though no two objects in this world are ever perfectly equal. Or we know what a circle is, even though there is no perfect circle available to sense-experience. We know we know these things because we use them as standards by which to judge the objects of sense-experience as being equal or circular. Further, Plato says, "Our present argument applies no more to equality than it does to absolute beauty, goodness, uprightness, holiness, and . . . all those characteristics which we designate in our discussions by the term 'absolute.'"[19] The term translated as *absolute* is bettered rendered as "the thing itself"; that is, there is a thing that is simply beauty itself or goodness itself; the pure subsistent instantiation of that quality that is the standard for the imperfect manifestations in this world. Since Forms determine what something is, we must know the Form *before* we experience any object in this world in order to be able to recognize it. This fact—that knowl-

---

17 *Meno* 98a1–4: "[True opinions] run away from a man's mind; so they are not worth much until you tether them by a working out of reason. The process . . . is recollection. Once they are tied down, they become knowledge."

18 *Meno* 80d–90a; I am following an abbreviated version of the argument in *Phaedo*, 72e1–76b2.

19 *Phaedo*, 75d1–3.

edge is re-cognition—leads Plato to conclude that our soul has knowledge of the Forms prior to our birth. Thus, he claims that knowledge consists in recollecting those forms as the unchanging standard of knowledge.

The obvious difficulties with this theory—which include preexistent souls, a transcendent realm of Forms, and the probability of reincarnation—lead most philosophers to search for another explanation for the nature of truth. Nevertheless, the perennial philosophy will always agree with Plato's seminal insight about the insufficiency of knowing as looking.

REDUCTIVE EXTREMES
Rationalism

Many philosophers other than Plato have questioned the value of sense-experience because it is prone to error. In order to avert all possibility of error, they argue we should rely on reason alone, which will guarantee certainty to our beliefs. This position is known as *rationalism*, and it dominated Continental European thinking in the first part of the Enlightenment. The three great rationalists are René Descartes (1596–1650), Baruch Spinoza (1632–1677), and Gottfried Leibniz (1646–1716). Unlike Plato, though, they reject the idea that reason has direct access to being; consequently, although they employ reason to know the world with logical certitude, they ultimately know only their own intuitive ideas. Thus, their arguments create as many questions as they do answers.

Descartes is explicit about why he adopts this method for his new philosophy:

> Some years ago I was struck by the large number of falsehoods that I had accepted as true in my childhood, and by the highly doubtful nature of the whole edifice that I had subsequently based on them. I realized that it was necessary, once in the course of my life, to demolish everything completely and start again right from the foundations if I wanted to establish anything at all in the sciences that was stable and likely to last.[20]

Therefore, Descartes subjects to doubt every belief that is less than utterly certain in order to discover an indubitable and necessary truth as a new foundation for knowledge.[21]

---

20 *First Meditation*, 17. Implicit in this is a rejection of the authority of past philosophers.

21 Descartes makes this general argument repeatedly: Part 4 of *Discourse on Method* (1637), *Meditations* (1641), and in *The Principles of Philosophy*, pt. 1 (1644).

His process is very methodical: at each step, he subjects to doubt some aspect of knowledge to discern what is certain; whatever survived the pervious step is then subject to doubt in turn. He has already doubted what he was taught; so, he does not take any truth on authority but accepts only what he can prove for himself.

Descartes begins by (1) doubting the reliability of sense-experience, because it can be erroneous. Nevertheless, even though I might err about the details of sense-experience, he might argue, it seems that it is for the most part reliable. The general reliability of sense-experience (2) can be questioned on the assumption that I may be hallucinating. If this is the case, then I cannot trust my sensations at all. Yet, even if I am hallucinating, I would still have to affirm that my sensations are caused by an external material world. The existence of such a world can be doubted, though, (3) if I am dreaming, for then the perceptions arise completely from my mind. Yet even at this point, it seems that the content of my dreams must reflect some material reality: maybe not in details like shape or color, since dreams can be fantastical, but in the fact that, in representing material objects, that material world is four-dimensional: it occupies space, and matter is extended in space (and time) in such a way that is can be objectively measured through mathematics.[22] It would be possible to (4) doubt the existence of this material world if I assume my "perceptions" of it are simply images in my mind projected by God (whom I know to exist as a perfect Creator).[23] If this were the case, I would nevertheless still trust mathematics because I would at least know those ideas come from God, who is trustworthy. Suppose, however, (5) that these ideas were not given to me by God, but by a demon—an evil genius—whose aim is to systematically deceive me. In that case, I could not trust any idea at all, whether from sensation or reason.[24]

22 That matter is characterized by extension that can be measured implies a correlation between matter and math, a point that is crucial to Descartes. This reflects his genius in mathematics in discovering analytic geometry, which reduces the spatial measurements of geometry to algebraic calculations.

23 This idea of God who could do anything he wishes is derived from Ockham and late medieval nominalism as discussed in chapter 2.

24 *First Meditation*. Note that such a scenario is the premise for the film series *The Matrix*. As Descartes implies in *Principles of Philosophy* I.5, this argument applies to *any* situation in which the mind is created by an imperfect being. His point is that the mind can be trusted completely *only* if it is created by a perfect God. This has consequences for strict Darwinism: if the brain is the result of a long series of random mutations, why should we trust its judgments about the nature of reality?

Through this thought experiment, Descartes has seemingly doubted away all knowledge.

In the face of this "hyperbolic doubt," Descartes must discover an Archimedean point, one solid truth to be the foundation for reason, from which to rebuild by logical steps our knowledge of the world. His discovery is that, even if all his ideas are deceptive, he knows he must exist in order to be deceived. Thus, the one thing of which he is certain is his own existence: as he famously declares, "I think, therefore I am" (*Cogito, ergo sum*).[25] But since he knows that he exists only so long as he is thinking and that he still doubts the existence of a material world, he next concludes that he is simply a mind, a thinking thing, and not a body, for a body cannot exist unless there is a material world.

This leaves Descartes with a very pointed problem. The one truth from which he has to rebuild knowledge is that he exists as a mind; consequently, if he is to prove there is anything other than his mind, he must do so by surveying his ideas, which is all he has access to. If he can find an idea that his mind cannot create, he knows it must originate from something else; this would prove there is something other than his mind in the universe. Descartes realizes his mind is finite and imperfect, but he also has an idea of an infinite and perfect being. Since an effect can never be greater than the cause, this idea cannot have been created by his mind, that is, it cannot be a fictitious idea. Indeed, the only thing that could have created the idea of a perfect being is in fact a perfect being itself.[26] Moreover, we know this perfect being *must* exist, for if it lacked existence, it would not be perfect.[27] Therefore, Descartes can now be certain that in addition to his mind there must be a perfect being, God. Moreover, since an idea of God can only come from God, we can know that the mind must have been created by God to have innate ideas in it.[28] We can tell which ideas are innate because they are not confused, like ideas from sensation; rather, they are clear and distinct.

---

25 *Second Meditation*, 25, though this precise formulation is from *Principles of Philosophy* I.7. Descartes is echoing a similar argument made by Saint Augustine to refute skepticism, though Augustine's formulation is *"si fallor, sum"* (If I am deceived, I am). See *City of God* XI.26, *On the Trinity* XV.4.21, and *On Free Choice of the Will*, II.3.7.

26 This argument comprises the *Third Meditation*.

27 This is Descartes's version of the controversial "Ontological Argument" from the *Fifth Meditation*. This argument has its origin in the thought of Saint Anselm (1033–1109). We return to this in chapter 8.

28 That is, ideas we are born with and known by intuition, as opposed to ideas that arise from experience of the world.

Moreover, since they are given to us from God, innate ideas cannot be wrong. For this reason, innate ideas are utterly reliable and so they are the basis for all our knowledge.[29]

The first innate idea is the *cogito*, Descartes's realization that he exists. The second is that he is a mind, a thinking thing. The third is that there is a perfect being, God, who creates him and his innate ideas. The fourth is mathematics, an intuitive ability to measure quantity, which thereby implies the existence of matter as dimensional. However, if the mind is immaterial, matter must be utterly distinct from mind. Descartes's reasoning is this: Since I do not have innate ideas of the material world, I can only know it through my confused sensations. These perceptual ideas, since they are not innate, must arise from something other than the mind. The only two possibilities are that they come from God or that a material world really exists. But since God is perfect, he is not a deceiver and would not mislead us about the existence of a material world.[30] We can conclude, then, that there is a material world; moreover, since matter is characterized by extension—by quantity—the material world can be known perfectly by mathematical science (such as had been pioneered by Galileo).

Descartes's argument has one outstanding merit: he reconciles traditional religious truths with modern science. On the one hand, we know both God and the immaterial mind (which would be free and immortal) must exist; and, on the other, the material world is separate from the mind and so knowable by a mathematical science and its deterministic laws of science.

There are, however, also some problems with this solution. For example, Descartes is clear that our knowledge of the material world is only certain with respect to quantity: "In many cases the grasp of the senses is obscure and confused. But at least they possess all the properties which I clearly and distinctly understand, that is, all those which . . . are comprised within the subject matter of pure mathematics."[31] This leaves purely qualitative aspects of experience—including colors, flavors, textures, tones, and smells[32]—out-

---

29 Descartes's position has been criticized as confusing human knowledge with that of angels, since it assumes our knowledge is innate instead of being learned from the world. This error of seeing a human as a disembodied consciousness would have great influence in modern thought, as we see in the next chapter.

30 *Sixth Meditation*, 78–80.

31 *Sixth Meditation*, 80.

32 Modern science has devised technology for quantifying many of these; nonetheless, the experience of color is not the same as the wavelength of light and the aesthetic character of music cannot be reduced to decibels and pitches.

side the realm of certainty. As such, all those qualitative sensations may not belong to the world at all. This doubt leads Descartes to divide our sensations into two sorts: primary qualities like size, shape, location, and duration, which we know to exist because they are measurable as matter, and secondary qualities, like color, flavor, and tone, of which we cannot be certain.[33] Since Descartes assumes that knowledge must come from reason alone, it cannot properly account for the qualitative aspects of experience. This problem, that we do not have direct access to the whole world as it is, is known as the veil of perception, a problem that was bequeathed to later philosophers to solve.

Descartes is to be commended for responding to skeptics who deny we can have certainty. His own use of reason, though, leads to the possibility that we cannot perceive being as it truly is. His successors in the rationalist tradition decide that the source of this weakness lay with an imperfect starting point. They agree with the method but want to discover a better foundation. Logical certainty can be had only if a person starts with an absolutely necessary premise. The *cogito*, the fact Descartes exists, is not an absolutely necessary truth, since his existence is contingent: he had to be created by God. Thus, these later philosophers look for a principle that is not contingent in any way. Spinoza, as we have seen, substitutes for the *cogito* the definition of substance: that which exists in need of nothing but itself. To exist in need of nothing but oneself implies that a substance must exist of necessity and that God is the only substance since he is the only necessary being. Moreover, since he is necessarily perfect, it follows that everything that flows from him does so of necessity. From this logical necessity, Spinoza would construct a compelling picture of an utterly rational world in which everything has to happen as it does. For his part, Leibniz begins with a purely logical principle, the principle of sufficient reason: all imperfect and contingent beings need a cause, which must be a perfect and necessary being.[34] Further, since God is perfect, everything he causes must be maximally perfect, and it cannot be otherwise. Again, this world is so rationally perfect that things have to be the way they are. What is common to both thinkers is that in pushing the logical perfection and necessity of the first principle,

33 This distinction between primary and secondary qualities would be picked up by other philosophers and is the source of the popular pseudo-problem, if a tree falls in the forest and there is no one there to hear, does it make a sound?

34 See, for example, *The Monadology*, nos. 38–48, and *Discourse on Metaphysics*, esp. nos. 1–15.

they eliminate contingency and freedom from creation. While this would make all knowledge utterly certain—since things cannot be otherwise—it achieves this by seriously misconstruing the nature of the world. These rationalists assume that there is no difference between their abstract logic and concrete reality of life.

The general lesson from rationalism, then, is that, if we derive all knowledge by looking inward to reason alone, we gain certainty only by eliminating contingency from the world. This does not do justice to the reality of a changing world.

Empiricism

Reason in isolation from sense-experience cannot tell us what the world is really like. Empiricism presents itself as the commonsense correction to the overreach of rationalism, since our senses put us in direct contact with facts of the world. This position is developed by the British Empiricists, the most notable of whom are John Locke (1632–1704), George Berkeley (1685–1753), and David Hume (1711–1776). We will see, however, that sense-experience alone—absent the judgments of reason—can never attain certainty about experience and so results in skepticism, not knowledge.

Modern empiricism adopts a handful of assumptions in reaction to rationalism. The first follows naturally from the principle that knowledge arises from sense-experience alone. If this is the case, there are no innate ideas: the mind in itself has knowledge of nothing apart from experience. On the contrary, the human mind is a blank slate, *tabula rasa*, and ideas arise from sense-experience. The first principle of empiricism—its foundational definition of truth—is that all truths must be traced to a direct sense-experience as the self-evident foundation for knowledge; correspondingly, any idea not traceable to experience must be rejected.[35]

This restriction of knowledge to sense-experience also reveals empiricism's dedication to Ockham's razor. Either there is proof in experience that something exists or the idea must be eliminated as extraneous. For example, Locke's argument against innate ideas is that they are simply not needed because we gain ideas by way of sensation.[36] Rationalism never recovers from this attack on innate ideas. However, Locke's successors apply Ockham's razor with increasing severity, reducing reality to the barest of

---

35 Hume, *An Enquiry Concerning Human Understanding*, sec. 2, para. 17.

36 Locke, *An Essay Concerning Human Understanding*, bk. 1, chap. 2, paras. 1–5.

experienced facts. Locke assumes our mind's ideas are caused by the material world, but Berkeley observes that all we can really know are the ideas
in the mind, and so we cannot prove there is a material world as the cause
of these ideas.[37] Hume, then, observes that we actually never perceive a
mind and so all we can know is an unconnected flow of ideas.[38] This is the
characteristic problem of empiricism: a theory that begins in common sense
has principles that erode our knowledge of all but the most superficial elements of reality.

Ockham's razor grounds two other shared assumptions: nominalism
and psychological atomism. Nominalism is the notion that only individual
things exist, and there are no universal natures. This naturally follows from
the principle that reason can never go beyond sense-experience: we perceive
only individual things, and it is impossible to perceive a universal, and so
there is no reason to suppose universals exist apart from names conceived
to represent individuals.[39] This focus on bare individuality is intensified in
psychological atomism, a theory that, in imitation of science, attempts to
analyze experience into its smallest components.[40] This means that we do
not experience things—substances—but rather we only have immediate
knowledge of "simple ideas," the discrete sensible elements that comprise
our experience of things. For example, we do not experience an apple;
rather, we see redness, feel roundness and hardness, taste sweetness, and
hear crunchiness. Each of these is an element of one or two sense powers.
We then imaginatively combine this set of experiences—red + round + hard
+ sweet + crunchy—into a complex idea that we label "apple."[41] Thus, our
mind creatively constructs both the individual as well as the universal collective term out of what really is known—simple ideas that are cognized in
isolation from underlying principle of unity. Indeed, Locke sees there has
to be *something* underlying these experienced qualities, but, since we only

---

37 Berkeley, *A Treatise Concerning the Principles of Human Knowledge*, I.3–7 and 18.

38 Hume, *A Treatise of Human Nature*, bk. 1, pt. 4, sec. 6. This process of Berkeley rejecting
matter and Hume rejecting mind is epitomized in the old quip, "No matter, never mind."

39 Locke, *Essay Concerning Human Understanding*, bk. 3, chap. 3, paras. 1–12.

40 Locke, *Essay Concerning Human Understanding*, bk. 2, chaps. 1–2; Berkeley, *Treatise Concerning the Principles of Human Knowledge*, I.1; Hume, *Enquiry Concerning Human Understanding*, sec. 2.

41 As an analogy for atomistic analysis, consider trying to analyze a line of poetry in complete
abstraction from the poem as a whole. This is perverse, since it is the poem that gives the line
its context, meaning, and its very reason for existing. Thus, to focus on properties in abstraction
from the whole will obscure the intelligibility of that property.

have access to these simple ideas, he concludes that this underlying stuff is entirely unknowable.[42] By focusing on psychological atomism, empiricism makes impossible any knowledge of united beings acting as causes of regular activity in the world. Since knowledge of this unity eludes pure sense-experience, empiricists offer no explanation for why sensible qualities appear together, or why distinct individuals appear to be the same sort of thing, or nature.

Psychological atomism points to one last assumption, perhaps the most baffling of all. Empiricists insist that we know ideas and not things.[43] That is, what we know is the image of a thing in our consciousness and not the thing in the world. Ironically, this assumption makes empiricist epistemology a nonstarter. For if we know only ideas, and ideas mediate all experience of the world, then there is no way to know reality itself. There is always an insuperable wall between the mind and reality. Thus, while the claim that we only know what we experience is a reasonable starting point, the way in which it is carried out ends in the inability to know the world in any meaningful sense. Instead of erasing the veil of perception, they make it an iron curtain.

The full implications of relying solely on sense-experience are seen most clearly by David Hume.[44] Hume understands that knowledge lies not just in singular experiences but in connecting ideas together with some necessity. But he also realizes that the psychological atomism of strict empiricism militates against this. Hume asserts that there are three principles by which we associate one idea with another: resemblance, contiguity in time or place, or cause and effect.[45] The first two—things looking similar or being adjacent to one another—are clearly arbitrary, playing on our imagination more than reason. However, we believe cause and effect reveals a *necessary* relation between ideas. Relations of cause and effect allow us to reason from what we experience to something we do not directly experience. We see a pile of

---

42 Locke, *Essay Concerning Human Understanding*, bk. 2, chap. 23, paras. 1–6. Locke calls this underlying substrate holding qualities together *substance* but can only describe it as "a supposition of he knows not what." Again, this departs significantly from Aristotle's usage.

43 Locke, *Essay Concerning Human Understanding*, bk. 2, chap. 1, para. 1; Berkeley, *Treatise Concerning the Principles of Human Knowledge*, I.1; Hume, *Enquiry Concerning Human Understanding*, sec. 2.

44 Hume's position is a valuable touchstone because it is very clearly argued, yet remarkably tendentious in its conclusions. His ideas remain influential and are widely shared by contemporary analytic philosophers.

45 Hume, *Enquiry Concerning Human Understanding*, sec. 3.

ashes and can know with certainty that there must have been a fire in the past as the cause of this effect we perceive; conversely, we see a match and know that if we apply it to the dry straw there will be a fire, with heat, in the future. These inferences are based on the idea that there is a necessary connection between a cause and its effect that enables us to grasp a past or future fact even if we cannot have sense-experience of it. Without this sort of reasoning, we would be completely ignorant of past events and of predictable future events, since we would only have access to the bare data of the present.

To assess whether this causal inference is valid, Hume introduces a distinction that will become standard for many later philosophers. This is the idea that all propositions are either relations of ideas or matters of fact.[46] Relations of ideas (also known as *analytic propositions*) are statements that are true with necessity because they simply define one idea in terms of a synonymous idea. Thus, "a bachelor is an unmarried man" or "2 + 2 = 4" are relations of ideas since the first term is identical with the second. Since they are identical, the test for whether a proposition is of this type is to see if its negation leads to a contradiction: "a bachelor is not an unmarried man" and "$2 + 2 \neq 4$" are both nonsensical. However, since these are merely relations of ideas, they tell us nothing about the world: we do not know if there are bachelors, or if they are happy, or if they have any other property in common.

This is contrasted to matters of fact (also known as *synthetic propositions*). These are facts about the world known on the basis of direct sense-experience. That "the pen is on the desk" or "it is raining" is knowable only by experience. However, unlike definitions, facts of this kind are always contingent, since they may or may not be true. Thus, contingent synthetic propositions can be negated and are still meaningful possibilities: "the pen is not on the desk" and "it is not raining" are unproblematic claims.

Hume then draws a rather strong conclusion from this division. If a proposition is neither a relation of ideas nor a matter of fact, he says it is meaningless and cannot be known at all. (Analyzing propositions in this way is known as Hume's Fork.) Hume declares that any book claiming to hold knowledge of something other than definitions or directly sensible facts must be "throw[n] in the fire, for it can contain nothing but sophistry and illusion."[47] This reduction of knowledge to the tautological/mathemat-

---

46 Hume, *Enquiry Concerning Human Understanding*, sec. 4, pt. 1, paras. 20–22.

47 Hume, *Enquiry Concerning Human Understanding*, sec. 12, pt. 3.

ical and the empirical bodes ill for metaphysics and theology; indeed, following Hume, many philosophers would see such enterprises as inherently meaningless. The contemporary tendency to scientism is a persistent echo of this Humean argument.

Hume then goes further and applies this reasoning to propositions concerning cause and effect.[48] The connection of cause and effect is meaningful because, if it is true, we can know that one event will *always* be connected to another, even if we do not perceive them. The problem is that we need to justify this belief that the connection will *always* obtain, and this is possible only if it is a relation of ideas or a matter of fact. First, it is clear that causal relations are not relations of ideas, since you need experience to know them at all. You could never guess that an acorn would grow into an oak, or a lemon would taste bitter, without direct sensation. Is this causal connection perceivable to sense-experience as a matter of fact? The problem here is that we must know the connection is always the case. If A really does cause B, then it must always be so. But we have no way to know this since we would have to know all future events will follow this pattern. It is obvious we do not (now) have sense-experience of the future. So, it appears that causal relations are neither relations of ideas nor matters of fact.

However, we might be able to connect the present to the future with a principle that allows us to extrapolate from the past to the future. So, let us presume as a principle that *the future will happen just like the past*; this would justify causal relations as a matter of fact. But we need to justify this assumption. Again, though, this principle itself is neither a relation of ideas (since we can clearly negate it and have a perfectly meaningful statement— the future will not be like the past) nor a matter of fact (since we cannot have sense-experience of the future). Therefore, since we cannot know that future cause-and-effect relations will be like the past, we cannot connect cause and effect with necessity. We cannot know that A causes B; the best we can have, for Hume, is a habit—a strong feeling of expectation—connecting one experience with another.[49] Cause and effect relations turn out to be as imaginary as resemblance: they lead to opinion, not knowledge.

Here again we see the corrosive effect of reductive empiricism's nominalism. Hume's rejection of causality arises from his rejection of universal natures. As has been argued, if we can know a nature, we can know those

48 Hume, *Enquiry Concerning Human Understanding*, sec. 4, pt. 2.
49 Hume, *Enquiry Concerning Human Understanding*, sec. 5.

properties and powers that are necessarily tied to that nature as their cause (such as fire being hot). But since Hume relies on sensation alone, which can know only individual things, Hume concludes that there is no necessary relation between what something is and what it does. Ultimately, any effect can follow from any nature: bread might not be edible; fire might not be hot; an acorn might grow to be a Big Mac tree. There is no way to predict what power or action will emanate from any given thing. Since causal relations are knowable by mere custom, not reason, there is never certainty in reasoning based on what we know from sense-experience. This is, as Hume admits, a skeptical conclusion that undermines not only metaphysics and theology but also threatens science itself, since it questions the reliability of inductive reasoning.[50]

To his credit, Hume takes seriously the premise that all we know is direct sense-experience. But in doing so he disregards what the intellect, true reasoning, can elicit from that experience. Again, any epistemology that results in skepticism is immediately subject to suspicion, since there is little use for an epistemological theory that concludes that knowledge is impossible.

The way forward, then, is to combine the partial truths of rationalism and empiricism, so that our senses and reason work together.

An Inadequate Resolution: Idealism

Hume's skepticism famously awakens Immanuel Kant (1724–1804) from his "dogmatic slumber,"[51] forcing him to rethink philosophy from the ground up. Kant accepts Hume's argument that we cannot know natures and so there can be no necessary connections in experience. Yet he is repelled by the skeptical conclusions. He is a man of the Enlightenment; he has witnessed science's success in discovering the necessary laws of nature. To resolve this apparent conundrum, he takes a cue from the rationalists, who recognize that, for knowledge to be certain, it must be grounded in

---

50 We should note at this point a classic refutation of Hume: Hume's Fork—that all meaningful propositions are either relations of ideas or matters of fact—is itself neither a relation of ideas (it can be meaningfully negated) nor a matter of fact (it is not known by sense-experience). It is, therefore, on Hume's own terms, meaningless. Again, this internal inconsistency shows that the philosophical theory is untenable even apart from its lack of cogency in explaining experience.

51 Kant, *Prolegomena to Any Future Metaphysics*, introduction, 260. This work is an abbreviated version of the argument in the *Critique of Pure Reason* (1781; revised, 1787). The most accessible way into Kant's thought is the preface to the second edition of the *Critique* (known as Preface B).

reason. Kant thus combines the two earlier approaches: sensation supplies the data that will inform knowledge with the facts of reality and reason connects those experiences with necessary judgments and turns the raw data of experience into a universal law of nature.[52]

Kant's innovative solution to the problem of skepticism would fundamentally change the way philosophers view the world. His approach is shaped by three principles he inherits from modern philosophy. First, he accepts Descartes's notion that knowledge has to be absolutely certain; second, he accepts Locke's position that we know ideas and not things; third, he is persuaded by Hume's arguments (based on nominalism) that we cannot know necessary relations based on our experience of nature. Kant's response to this is to focus philosophy not on the world but on the act of knowing itself as a way to justify our knowledge. Philosophy is not about things *per se* but is rather about our ideas. Metaphysics is thereby recast: it is no longer an investigation of the necessary conditions of existence, but it is instead about the necessary conditions for human knowing. Kant's use of *transcendental* as determining the "conditions for possible experience" reflects this. Whereas for the perennial tradition the conditions for the possibility of experience are the transcendental properties being and truth, for Kant it is the structure of the mind that is the key condition for the possibility for any experience. For this reason, Kant's philosophy is referred to as *idealism*. It is the structure of the mind—and not nature—that guarantees necessary relations in experience because the mind adds judgments of necessity to the data of experience. Thus, the mind has a role in actively constructing the world as we know it. While this is a brilliant resolution to the partial truths he inherited, it can be problematic insofar as it creates a chasm between our experience, constructed by the mind, and reality as it is. Kant saves truth but only by sacrificing our access to being. This momentous conclusion—that a human is responsible for constructing his experience of the world—has repercussions in all areas of contemporary thought. After Kant, humankind's relationship with the world would never be the same again.

Kant, recognizing the innovative nature of this change, refers to his new view of the world as a second Copernican revolution.[53] Copernicus's hypothesis that the earth orbited the sun, instead of the sun circling the earth, shifted the axis of reality and changed the way we look at everything

---

52 Kant, *Critique of Pure Reason*, B1.
53 Kant, *Critique of Pure Reason*, Preface B, xvi–xvii.

else in the solar system. Kant similarly shifts the axis of human experience. Up to his time, philosophers had always believed that knowledge was the mind conforming to the world (the objects of experience). Kant flips this and argues that knowledge is the world (its objects of experience) conforming to the mind. In other words, the mind does not fit reality, reality fits the mind. He thus overcomes skepticism and saves science by making the mind active in constructing the laws of nature instead of simply grasping reality as it is.

Let us consider this activity of the mind in more detail. Adapting the rationalist assumption of necessary innate ideas, Kant argues that the mind naturally has, not ideas, but logical structures. Information about the world is collected by the senses and given to the mind,[54] which then orders that information according to these logical structures. In this way, all experience conforms to the mind, since it supplies the necessary rules for interpreting that data. Because the data of experience conform to these structures, that experience will always be organized in the same way, according to the same rules, and so there *appears to be* necessity in what happens. This is how the mind actively constructs our experience by creating the appearance of necessity in experience due to the regular structuring by the mind.[55] Science is possible because of this activity of the mind constitutes a regularity that can generate laws.

Because the contributions of the mind to experience accompany every experience we have, it can be difficult to discover exactly what they are. Kant argues that we can uncover what they are by investigating the necessary conditions for the possibility of experience. If some judgment is necessary for us to even have experience, it must come from the mind, since there is nothing necessary in experience itself. As a necessary condition for experience, the mind will impart that judgment to all data in constructing our experience of the world, thereby giving the data the appearance of necessity. Kant would employ this insight in defense not only of the truths of math and logic, and the speculative knowledge of science, but also, as we see in chapter 6, the practical knowledge of ethics.

---

54 Note that in Latin *data* literally means "that which is given."

55 The classic metaphor for this is wearing a pair of rose-tinted glasses. These glasses impart a hue to everything experienced, so that we might assume that hue is part of reality itself. A more modern metaphor is to see the mind as a software program, say one that alphabetizes: no matter how the data are fed into the mind, the data always come out in the same order, so that it appears that the world is ordered by letter.

Thus, Kant's starting point (or first principle) for truth is the mind's ability to impart necessity to experience. He refers to these as *synthetic a priori judgments*. They are a priori because they are based in reason alone; but they are synthetic because they are capable of connecting two previously unconnected ideas with necessity so as to produce real knowledge. This is essentially where Kant corrects Hume: not all a priori judgments of reason are simply relations of ideas; some are productive of real knowledge of the world. For example, while Hume sees $5 + 7 = 12$ as merely a definition, Kant sees it as a conclusion whereby we learn something new. Similarly, while Hume rejected causal reasoning, Kant would insist the judgment "every change has a cause" is a synthetic a priori truth at the basis of scientific knowledge.[56] The foundation of all knowledge reflects the mind's ability to make synthetic a priori judgments by which necessary order is given to experience.

Kant investigates the possibility of making synthetic a priori judgments with respect to the three faculties of the mind: intuition, understanding, and pure reason.[57] The necessary conditions for these faculties reveal the nature of possible judgments and the kind of sciences that can be grounded on them.

Intuition is the ability to receive data from the world. The necessary conditions for even having this sense-experience are that they occur in space and time. If there were no space, all the objects of experience would collapse into a confused mass; if there were no time, all our experience would occur simultaneously and so be indistinguishable from one another. To even be perceivable, then, objects must be separated in space and dispersed over time. Space and time are the "forms of intuition," the necessary conditions for intuition to operate. As necessary, though, we can know that these forms of intuition arise from the mind. Consequently, all objects of experience conform to the mind's structure of space and time and so appear to exist temporally and spatially. Furthermore, as necessary qualities of all experience, space and time become the foundation for certain sciences: space is the basis of geometry (which considers the nature of absolute space apart from all content) and time is the basis of arithmetic (from the idea of pure succession of units). All experience, then, must be conditioned by the mind's adding the order of space and time to the data of the world.

---

56 For both examples, see the introduction to the *Critique of Pure Reason*, A1/B1-A16/B30.

57 This summary follows the argument of both the *Critique of Pure Reason* and the *Prolegomena to Any Future Metaphysics*.

Experience, though, is not composed of isolated bits of data in space and time, something like movie stills. On the contrary, experience arises when these bits of data are logically connected into a flowing and coherent whole. These logical connections are the necessary conditions for experience to be intelligible, and so again the mind must add this structure of logical order to the data of the intuitions. This is what the faculty of understanding does: it subsumes representations of sense-experience from the intuition according to determinate logical rules, connecting them into an intelligible whole.[58] Kant argues that there are twelve possible judgments regarding four aspects of experience (quantity, quality, relation, and modality—all derivable from time and so logically tied to the forms of intuition) by which intuitions are connected to one another.[59] He calls these logical judgments the "categories of the understanding"; they replace Aristotle's categories, the difference being that where Aristotle's categories indicated how things could exist, Kant's categories (or concepts) indicate how the mind can logically connect intuitions together so that they represent a coherent reality in our experience. They concern our ideas and the process of knowing. For our purposes, the most important of these categories are substance (i.e., the continued existence of things underlying accidents) and cause and effect, both of which had been denied by Hume's extreme empiricism. Since the mind will always interpret data according to these judgments of substance and causality, the physical sciences will have the necessity of the laws of nature. But again, this necessity arises from the mind's judgments that make the world appear to us as if the physical laws were in reality itself.

Experience for Kant, therefore, is composed of three necessary aspects: data are first given in intuition, which is then synthesized according to space and time into a representation, which is last made determinate by subsuming those representations according to categorical judgments. The mind's role in the construction of experience is epitomized in Kant's famous dictum, "Thoughts without content are empty; intuitions without concepts are blind."[60] That is, without intuitions to provide data there can be no thinking at all; but, if those intuitions were not ordered by the logical judg-

---

58 They are representations, since the data of sensation have already been determined according to the forms of space and time given by the mind and so are already unlike objects in themselves.

59 The argument for these categories is difficult; see the "transcendental deduction," *Critique of Pure Reason*, A84/B117-A130/B169.

60 Kant, *Critique of Pure Reason*, A51/B75.

ments of the mind, they would be completely incoherent (as in Hume's skeptical conclusion).

This leaves the third faculty: reason. Reason for Kant is that faculty that attempts to apply the categories of the understanding to that which is *not* experienced. Instead of applying a rule to that which is given in sense-experience, reason attempts to draw inferences to higher causes, things that are the unconditioned ground of all experience and that cannot be given in sense-experience. This has been the aim of metaphysics since the origin of philosophy—to know the principles of reality *behind* experience. Kant, however, thinks this is impossible; indeed, he thinks the lack of agreement among philosophers proves that "the procedure of metaphysics has hitherto been a merely random groping . . . among mere concepts."[61] Because these conclusions are not based in experience, no valid judgments can be made. Therefore, metaphysics as understood in the tradition cannot be science. Kant's argument, then, has two goals: first, to refute Hume's skepticism and establish the validity of math and science and, second, to redefine metaphysics to be about the limits of human knowing and not the objective state of being-qua-being.

For Kant, the problem with metaphysics is that it tries to apply the concepts of the understanding, which are applicable only to objects of possible experience, to that which is not experienced. The concepts allow us to subsume intuitions (given in time) according to rules that determine them according to necessary laws (which are derived from time). These concepts, then, are all derived from the structure of intuition, and so they can be applied only to intuitions, things that we experience. To try to apply them to things we do not experience, to generate conclusions merely out of our ideas, simply does not lead to valid knowledge. For example, cause and effect can explain the relation between fire and heat because I experience them; similarly, substance can explain why my dog continues to exist even when I am not with her. Metaphysics, though, tries to apply this to things we do not experience. Can we apply cause and effect in order to show the universe had to be created by God? Can we apply substance to show a soul continues to exist even after death? We are tempted to think this way— indeed, Kant says reason must draw these speculative conclusions about ultimate causes—but, since we cannot experience them, they are "transcendental illusions" and are not knowledge at all.

---

61 Kant, *Critique of Pure Reason*, Preface B, xv.

Although reason naturally thinks about these fundamental ideas—God, freedom of the will, and immortality—they can never be known because they transcend the limits of possible experience. Kant's understanding of metaphysics as concerning the structure and limits of human cognition leads him to separate these thinkable ideas—being as it is in itself, apart from the conditions of human knowledge—from reality as it is experienced by us.[62] The "thing-in-itself" can never be experienced because experience is always the data of reality as constructed by intuition and the judgments of the understanding. Because nothing in experience corresponds to these metaphysical speculations (like God and the soul), there can never be determinate judgments, or knowledge, of them. Kant calls this thinkable-but-unknowable reality behind experience the *noumena*. Knowledge of the material world is restricted to that which is experienced, the world of necessity and determined by the laws of science. Kant calls this *phenomena*: the world as it appears to us in our experience as ordered by the judgments of the mind.

The upshot of this, however, is that although there are things-in-themselves, we can never know them. While knowledge of the phenomenal world has scientific necessity, the realm of the noumena—where the soul, and free will, and God are speculated about—cannot be known. Nevertheless, reason is not futile in considering these ideas. Kant argues that, although they cannot be known, these ideas have a practical justification: they are the necessary conditions for ethics. (We return to this in chapters 6 and 8.)

Though Kant did rescue the sciences from Hume's skepticism, he did so at great cost. First, he limits theoretical knowledge to sense-experience and so makes it impossible to know ultimate principles or causes of sense-experience. By focusing on the structure of human knowing, being as the universal cause of experience gets obscured. The result is that he essentially separates truth from being. In this way, Kant's redefinition of metaphysics subtly opens the door to skepticism. Truth is the product of human knowing, and we can only have empty speculation about being as it is in itself. This leaves the most important things in life as unanswerable mysteries, frustrating our natural desire to know. This epistemology, then, is self-defeating, for it assumes some being is unknowable.

Second, Kant's response to Hume—that the mind constructs reality—lets a very malevolent genie out of the bottle. Because truth is a construct of the mind, we no longer grasp being as it is; this detaches all the transcen-

---

62 *Critique of Pure Reason*, A236/B295–A260/B315.

dentals from their objective foundation. Given the assumption that being in itself is unknowable, Kant's three *Critiques* delineate how the mind constructs the true, the good, and the beautiful.[63] Yet Kant's Enlightenment optimism in the power of reason allowed him to defend the universal objectivity of the mind's construction. He proclaimed, "*Sapere aude!* 'Have courage to use your own reason!'—that is the motto of enlightenment."[64] He assumed rational people would construct the same reality. Unfortunately, this assumption was itself not universal. After the close of the Age of Reason, many philosophers began to argue that each person is free to—indeed, obligated to—construct truth and goodness according to their own perspective. This relativistic constructivism of truth and goodness is manifested first in the counter-Enlightenment Romanticism, but it reaches its nadir in the nihilism of Friedrich Nietzsche (1844–1900). The consequences of both are still widely seen in the egoistic assumptions of identity politics and critical theory.

Kant is a rare philosophical genius. He found modernity mired in inadequate approaches to truth and reconstructed philosophy to guarantee the certainty of human knowledge. The problem, though, is that he inherited ideas that already distanced him from being, and so, despite his best efforts, he could never get back to the fullness of being. This is the moral of Kant's legacy: once the mind is separated from being, the objective nature of truth, goodness, and beauty is also obscured. This is why Kant's Copernican Revolution has had such mixed consequences for modern culture.

An adequate epistemology, then, must use both reason and sensation to grasp being as it is in itself. We have to let being speak for itself, so that the mind discovers the principles that are already there instead of imposing an order upon it. Accordingly, let us now turn to realism.

THOMISTIC REALISM: NECESSITY IN THE CONTINGENT

Modern approaches to epistemology are hampered by problematic assumptions about both the world and humankind. They share a metaphysical nominalism, which leads them to believe people must impose a regular order on the world, whether through God-given innate ideas, synthetic a

---

63 In addition to the *Critique of Pure Reason* (1781) on epistemology, Kant developed his ethical theory about the good in the *Critique of Practical Reason* (1788) and his aesthetics in the *Critique of Judgment* (1790).

64 From his short essay, *An Answer to the Question: What Is Enlightenment?*, 35.

priori judgments, or mere imagination. Moreover, to formulate the problem by asking whether knowledge is based on sense-experience or reason misunderstands the basic truth that a *person* knows the world.[65] It is a human person who has the powers of sensation and reason that cooperate in the pursuit of truth for the good of the person. Both sensation and reason are directed to knowing being, but they grasp different aspects of being: sensation is ordered to the individuality of substances, while the intellect grasps the universal nature of substances. Since sensation knows material individuals, those experiences are characterized by contingency and change, and so they are not certain. But, since intellect knows a universal form as the cause of the individual's accidents and activities, our knowledge can be certain at that level. It is the same existent thing that is known; it just reveals what it is in different ways to the senses and to the intellect. Therefore, this epistemology is rightfully called *realism*. Being is the foundation for knowledge in Thomas, for knowledge is just being as received by the mind.

In fact, acknowledging the complementary roles of sensation and intellect illuminates the conundrum at the heart of all epistemology. We have contact with the facts of the world through sense-experience. These are always individual facts conditioned by circumstances. Yet to be knowledge, those circumstantial facts must be understood in light of necessary truths—laws which show what is necessary about that event. For example, we all "know" that acceleration due to gravity is $9.8 m/s^2$. Yet if I drop a piece of paper, it floats gently in apparent violation of a law of nature. You will no doubt reply that the problem is that friction due to air resistance slows the paper. I grant that, but where do objects actually fulfill the law? In a vacuum. And where on earth is there a vacuum, apart from science labs? Nowhere. Universal laws are nice and neat; reality, in contrast, will always be riven with contingency due to the potency of matter. Similarly, we "know" water boils at 212 F. But this of course is true only at sea level and so this law is almost never literally accurate.[66]

Puzzles like these lead some thinkers, such as Plato and Descartes, to simply ignore sense-experience. Others, such as Hume, opted to accept the

---

[65] *DV* 2.6.ad 3: "Properly speaking, it is neither the intellect nor the sense that knows, but man that knows through both." Since the mind is a power of the person, it is an error to think of the mind as a thing; this reification of a power dissolves the unity of the person, as we see in chapter 5.

[66] This fact has, for some, serious consequences. British Airways had to reformulate their tea, since at cruising altitude water boils at too low a temperature to brew regular tea properly.

vagaries of sense-experience but concluded that no certain knowledge was possible. Still others, such as Kant, accepted this but insisted our minds impose order on the world, thereby altering the vagaries of reality in the process. What we need to do is meet the issue head on, accept the contingency of experience, and yet realize the mind can grasp the universal essences that cause the contingent events. We sense the event but know the cause that must necessarily be behind it. This is the solution of Thomas (largely following Aristotle). We therefore look first at Thomas's discussion of the sensitive powers and then his discussion of the rational powers.[67] We then see how these can be used to develop a complete array of sciences providing a full knowledge of the world.

Sensation

The crucial starting point for realism is to recognize that *faculties are distinguished by their object.*[68] That is, powers are different only when they know different things. For example, sight grasps light waves and hearing grasps sound waves. They are two different faculties. Conversely, if I had an organ on my knees that received sound waves—as crickets have—that would simply be another instance of hearing, not a sixth sense.

The most important application of this principle is that it allows us to clearly distinguish sensation from reason or intellect. The sensitive powers are able to know material individuals; the rational powers are able to know immaterial universals (universal forms or essences).[69] Thus, when a nominalist rejects the existence of immaterial universals, he is eliminating the object of the mind as distinct from sensation; but, if there is no separate object, then there is no reason to assume mind exists at all. For this reason, nominalists must grant that sensation is the sole source of knowledge. This is a confounding problem for empiricism, but one that Thomas solves persuasively by distinguishing sensation from intellect.

A second principle at work in this discussion has to do with the relative hierarchy of these powers. Thomas takes as a general rule that the higher the power is, the broader its capabilities. That is, higher powers can have

---

67 Terminological point: the rational powers include both rational cognition and rational appetite. Rational cognition is *intellectus*, intellect or understanding, but mind is another synonym. I use these interchangeably. Rational appetite, as we see in chapter 5, is the will.

68 *ST* I.77.3 and *DQDA* 13.

69 *ST* I.78.1.

access to more things. Implicit in this is the idea that the lower powers are more physical—requiring physical contact—while the higher powers are less physical. We see how this is applied below.

To Thomas, the sensitive powers are activated (or actualized) whenever they are stimulated by their proper object—the thing they are made to know. We are always capable of seeing, but we actually only see when there are light waves and colors to be seen; hearing is always possible, but we only hear when there is a sound wave in our environment. So, we have sensation when one of our senses is acted upon by something outside of us.[70] This change in sensation is not merely a physical change in the body. While there is always a bodily reaction in the process of sensation, the awareness of the object is a *spiritual* change—a change that cannot be reduced to matter alone but is something other than matter. In sensation, this change is the presence of an image in my consciousness.[71] Let us illustrate the difference between the physical and the spiritual change: if I put my hand and a rock in the fire, both will get physically hot, but the rock will never yell, "Ouch!" The physical change from fire is the same, but the rock never has an awareness of heat. The awareness of heat is a spiritual change in our consciousness. Sensation is a special faculty limited to higher substances, because it does something other than simple material changes. This is possible because sensation just *is* that power that allows a living substance to receive the form of another thing spiritually so that animals are aware of their environment. If we have an operation that requires a power, we should avoid a materialist reduction that would eliminate the existence of that power.

Thomas's theory is confirmed by observations of modern physiology. Bodily reactions to stimuli involve a great complexity of neurons, nerves, receptors, muscles, enzymes, and so on. All this may occur on a physical level, but, unless there is awareness—a spiritual presence of the object in the consciousness of the perceiver—then there is no sensation. A blind person might have a retina that functions perfectly well, but that neurochemical reaction alone, even if relayed to the proper part of the brain, does

---

70 Note that action follows from being, so, if my senses are to be acted upon, they can only be acted on by something real. This answers the hyperbolic doubt of Descartes, since it is impossible to have sensations unless there is a something real actualizing the potential of the senses to see, hear, taste, and so on. Because of the passive nature of sensation, the fact of the existence of an external world is self-evident.

71 *ST* I.78.3.

not guarantee visual awareness. Sensation is a spiritual change over and above these neurochemical reactions.

This awareness of the environment is necessary for the animal to survive. Consciousness of the environment causes instinctive reactions to things based on biological imperatives with respect to food, drink, sex, sleep, health, and so on. Since different animal species have different needs, their sense powers are similarly diverse; indeed, sense-experience of the world is always *species specific*. Each species has a way of sensing the world best adapted to its own mode of being: eagles see better than humans do so that they can hunt from great heights; bats hear better than humans do in order to navigate in the dark; dogs have more acute smelling than humans do so that they can use the fire hydrant as a sort of social network. Each species senses the world in its own way. This is important, for only reason will be able to get to the world as it really is, apart from the drives of biological imperatives. Reason's ability to grasp being behind the appearances of sensation is why human knowledge of the world is fundamentally superior to that of any other animal. (This is evident in the fact that we know of the existence of light waves and sound waves outside the narrow spectrum of our powers of sensation.)

There are five sense powers by which human beings are aware of different kinds of realities in our environment. Each is directed to a proper object, and each has special bodily organs constructed to be receptive to that object: eyes are built—lens, pupil, retina—to receive light waves and to see; similarly, ears are made to hear sounds as their proper object, noses to smell odors, the tongue to taste flavors, and the skin to touch textures. The lowest senses (taste and touch) are possessed by even the lowest animal species (such as sponges) but are limited in their ability because they require direct physical contact. Hearing and smell are higher senses and function more broadly since they need only be in the proximity of the object that is moving or decomposing. Sight is the highest sense since it functions at great distances with minimal physical limitations.

Because there is a physical object and physical organ at the basis of this mode of spiritual awareness, sensation will always be of very specific qualities: *this* lemon tastes very sour; *that* red is very bright. Sensation, as based in knowledge of material objects, will always be very particular. The specificity of sensation will give us great detail about the world, which is often what is needed for an animal to survive. (In addition to these proper objects of sensation, there are also common sensibles, things known by two or more senses, like size, shape, and distance, which are also necessary for an animal to succeed biologically.[72])

We are all familiar with the five senses. Yet the perennial philosophy insists there are *nine* sense powers. The five external senses gather information about the environment, but we need other powers to organize and interpret this information. This is the job of the four internal senses.[73] The first two—the formal interior senses—organize the information into a coherent image that can be thought about: these are the common sense and the imagination. (These are technical terms and should not be confused with the colloquial uses.) The five external senses feed us five different "lines" of information: color, sound, smell, texture, and flavor. This information needs to be united if it comes from one object or separated if it comes from different objects. This is the function of the common sense. On the one hand, if I smell something sweet and see a plate of cookies on the table, the common sense ties sight and smell together and grasps that the same object is the source of both sensations. On the other hand, if I see a blue jay and hear a jackhammer, the common sense informs me that these are from two different objects. If we did not have a common sense, the information of the senses would be a chaotic jumble of discordant information.[74] Once this information has been organized, the imagination forms an image or a *phantasm* (this important term will be crucial for Thomistic epistemology), which is the representation of the thing in our consciousness, the expression of the likeness of that object according to all the information attained about it by the senses. In this way even an animal can recognize what kind of thing the object is based on its physical appearance. (Crucially, though, this is not its true essence; it is more like Locke's idea of an "empirical universal"—a vague physical similarity built up by repetition of experience. Only reason can grasp a true universal essence as cause.)

Because animals have sensation in order to survive, animals must be able to react to what they perceive. Therefore, in addition to the formal internal senses, there are also two "intentional" internal senses that estimate the value of the object as beneficial, harmful, or neutral to the existence of

---

72 *ST* I.78.3.ad 2. It is worth noting that how the moderns inverted this, turning the proper objects into "secondary qualities" that were not real, while leaving the common sensibles as "primary qualities" because they were quantifiable by math.

73 *ST* I.78.4.

74 There is a perceptual phenomenon called synesthesia that has precisely this effect. It is a fascinating case-study in how sensation and the interior senses interact.

the animal. First is sense judgment (also called the *estimative power* or, in humans, the *cogitative power*), the instinctive evaluation of things in the environment: Is that object dangerous? Is it food? These judgments are natural for all animals, but the nature of the judgment reflects the biological needs of each species. For example, a sheep will flee instinctively from a wolf; a lion will naturally chase an antelope; a squirrel will run up a tree to escape a dog. Judgments of this sort play an important role in human life, too, since we have natural reactions—fears and desires—that drive us and yet need to be controlled (as we see in the next chapter). Finally, the survival of an animal also depends on its ability to be aware of things even when they are not in the immediate environment: a squirrel knows where it buried its nuts or a predator knows where prey congregate. The final internal sense, then, is memory, which is the ability to recall the value of objects and experiences. For example, a dog might remember his master's routine and so be able to "predict" when it is about to go for a walk or be given a bath.

One significant truth follows from this. As sensory powers, the internal senses need a physical organ, comparable to the eye or ear. That organ is the brain. The brain must not be confused with the mind. The brain is the seat of sensitive powers, while the mind is the immaterial intellectual power that knows universal forms. Brain damage causes harm not to the mind but to the interior senses.[75] Brain damage impedes the ability to form a correct image or make correct judgments about the environment. But brain damage never deprives a person of the immaterial power of rationality, nor can it be seen to deprive a person of the human rights that go with rationality. Since science alone cannot empirically discover this difference between the brain and the mind, contemporary medicine sometimes makes terrible errors in assessing the moral condition of patients.

Ignoring this distinction between brain and mind has led to two notable misconceptions. First, as mentioned, nominalists, by eliminating the object of the intellect, effectively do away with the mind as a separate faculty itself. But instead of giving up the word *mind*, these thinkers often redefine it in terms of the interior senses: common sense, imagination, judgment, and memory are now taken to be the operations of the mind. This reduction of human cognitive powers makes it impossible to get beyond the realm of appearance and biological instinct. A human being is thereby reduced to being simply an animal.

75 I.84.7.

The second error is more problematic because it is more pragmatic. If you define human intelligence in terms of the brain and its sensitive powers, this obscures human nature's relation to other animals. On the one hand, you can protect human uniqueness by denying that animals have any cognitive capacities. This was the solution of Descartes and was common in much modern philosophy until recently. But this is absurd: we see cats judging how to hunt a bird; we see dogs expressing emotions in the most heartwarming way. Animals have complex inner lives, and we have to respect that fact to make sense of creation. On the other hand, one might want to elevate animals to the same state as humanity as talk about "animal intelligence." But this is to underestimate what intelligence does. The solution is to appreciate the magnificence of sense powers and for that very reason give all the greater appreciation to the uniqueness of human intelligence in the world.

Intellect

There is a difference between perceiving an object and understanding what that object is. When we perceive a thing but realize that we do not know what it is, we naturally seek to know the form that is the essence of the thing. That formal essence provides real knowledge because it is the *cause* of all the accidental properties and actions we are perceiving. Thus, if we know that form or essence, we completely understand the nature of the thing we are experiencing. This relies on the metaphysical truth that action follows from being; the form is the principle of actuality that determines what a thing is and so is also the cause that gives matter its ordered structure, existence, and powers to act. While sensation has access to that structure and the activity, it is reason's job to grasp the cause behind those evident facts. Since this form is common to all the individuals of that nature, it exemplifies the entire class of beings. Knowing the form reveals what is *necessarily true* about the thing I am sensing. Thus, while all humans have peculiar accidents that make their appearances unique, reason grasps that the cause of their general structure and activity is the form of man and sees them as essentially the same.

In order for this form to represent an entire class or nature, it must be grasped by the intellect as an *immaterial universal*. Individuals are distinguished from one another by their material and accidental differences, but, when the form is considered without those differences, what remains is the common essence shared by diverse individuals. For example, an apple must be particular in a number of ways: red or green or yellow, sour or sweet, mealy or crunchy; yet the universal form of apple refers to all of these simul-

taneously and indifferently, including all the ways an apple can be. Therefore, even though they know the same thing, the object of reason must be
different from the object of sensation: sensation's object is the material particular, but reason's object is an immaterial universal—an essence or form
taken apart from any one individual of that nature. Reason works in conjunction with sensation by grasping the essence of apple that causes the particular redness and sweetness of *this* apple I am sensing. Because reason
grasps the essence—and not just the appearance—of things, Thomas says
that the proper object of intellect is being.[76] It is the actuality of being that
makes things knowable, and so reason can know something inasmuch as it
is *in act*.[77] Once again, it is the receptivity of the cognitive power to being
as active that assures us that we know reality as it is in the world.

Therefore, in order to know reality, reason must start with sense-experience. As Thomas frequently notes, there is nothing in the mind that is not
first in the senses.[78] Thomas, therefore, agrees with modern empiricists in
asserting that the mind is a blank slate, *tabula rasa*, prior to experience.[79]
This blank slate, in Aristotelian terms, means that not only the senses but
also the mind is *in potency* to receive the actuality caused by essences of
objects. Thus, we can only know the world if we have direct contact with it,
and the contact must begin with the senses.[80]

The primarily passive nature of the mind contrasts strongly with Kant.
The significance of this difference can be brought out by asking whether in
the act of knowing the world changes or I do. Kant argues that the act of
knowing changes the world (by adding to the data of sensation to construct
experience); Thomas sees the mind as receptive to reality, and so argues that
in knowing I change: it is my potential to know that is realized. Indeed, for
Thomas, only God's knowledge changes the world. Human knowledge is
the ability to become aware of reality as it is.

Beginning with sense-experience, though, presents a puzzle. Sensation
knows material particulars; how do we get the immaterial universal, the

---

76 *SCG* II.83.31 and II.98.9. Thomas also says that the proper object of the human intellect is
the "quiddity [i.e., whatness or nature] of material things" (*ST* I.88.2), another way of noting the
existential role of essence as that in which things have real being.

77 *ST* I.5.2 and I.87.1.

78 *ST* I.84.1 and I.117.1.

79 *ST* I.79.2.

80 This is true even for self-evident first principles, such as the principle of noncontradiction,
which is the most evident truth grasped in any and all experience.

essence of the nature, from that particular sensation? The mind must turn to the image, or phantasm, for all our thinking, since we must always be thinking about reality as experienced.[81] This phantasm (say, a particular red thing) which is *actually* sensed, is *potentially* intelligible in terms of a universal (say, apple). To be made intelligible, though, we need to consider the object in the phantasm apart from all its material accidents. In other words, it must be *made immaterial* so that the universal essence may come to light. This is the function of the "active intellect."[82] The active intellect—not a separate faculty, but a distinct function of the intellect—considers the phantasm and judges what form would cause all those sensible properties; it is the ability to make a judgment about the intelligible causes present in the flux of experience. In doing so, it separates a universal form as the cause from the accidental details of this particular matter. The mind therefore grasps the essence common to all individuals of a nature. My phantasm of Fido contains very particular size, shape, color, smell, sounds; yet, in judging that those sensible qualities must be caused by the form of dog, I separate the idea of dog from Fido and now understand all the possible ways a dog can be.

This process of the active intellect is called *abstraction*.[83] From this abstracted form we conceive the universal idea, which is then impressed in the passive or receptive intellect as the stable object of knowledge.[84] This concept is the essence as it exists in the mind and is formally identical to— the same form as—the essence as it exists in the real being. It is the same form that is the object throughout the process of sensation and intellection: it exists outside the mind as the principle of actuality in the object, received in its particularity by the senses, then abstracted from the phantasm by the active intellect, and finally grasped by the passive intellect as a concept of the universal essence.[85] This is why, even though every individual is unique,

---

81 *CBDT* 6.2 and ad 5. This is true even when we think about God, since we know him through his creatures; we return to this in chapter 8.

82 *ST* I.79.3; *SCG* II.77.

83 *ST* I.84.6 and 85.1.

84 *ST* I.85.2.ad 3. Thomas avoids the problems of moderns who say we only know ideas by emphasizing that the concept is not *that which* we know but rather that *by which* we know (*ST* I.85.2). Ideas—phantasms and our concepts of universal essences—are beings of reason that function as signs of the world outside of us. This dependence equally on the object and the mind means that ideas are a bridge between the mind and reality and not a wall as most moderns assumed.

85 See *ST* I.14.1, which argues that knowledge is the presence of a form in the mind. Thus, a form can be possessed in two ways: existentially, where it is the principle of actuality for a substance or accident, and intentionally, where a form is present in the mind as cognized.

we can define natures with certainty. This identity between individuals in the world and essential concepts in our mind becomes the basis for science. Indeed, in knowing the form or essence as the cause of the particular, we know a *more certain* reality than in merely knowing the individual itself which is characterized by all sorts of potency and contingency.[86]

Here we can reinforce the fact that the mind is not the brain. In order to abstract and understand the universal form, the mind must be immaterial and so cannot be a bodily organ. There are two reasons for this. First, separating form from matter is an immaterial job. Since action follows from being, if the mind is to do an immaterial job, it must be immaterial itself.[87] That is, just as wood, which is potentially hot, can only be made hot by fire, which is actually hot, in the same way the phantasm, which is potentially immaterial, can only be actually immaterial by something actually immaterial, the mind. If the mind were not immaterial, abstraction would be impossible, and there would be nothing other than sensation.[88] Second, unlike each of the senses, the mind is capable of knowing *all* things.[89] The senses have a particular biological structure that is ordered to one aspect of reality: for example, the rods and cones in the eye are able to perceive light and light alone. The mind, in contrast, can know any kind of being—from atoms to God—because it lacks a restrictive material structure. Its immateriality makes it capable of receiving the actuality of any being whatsoever. This immateriality of the mind is crucial for properly understanding human nature, since it underlies human dignity, ethics, and immortality, as we see in the next chapter.

Three Acts of the Intellect

The intellect's power actually encompasses three distinct operations by which we come to know the world as it is. The first step, where we form a concept as a sign of a thing's essence, is called *apprehension* of the form. This grasps the universal concept that allows us to understand a nature in

---

86 *ST* I.85.1. This is an important rejoinder to nominalists, who say we are only really certain about direct sensation, because their universals are conceived by blending individuals into a vague generalization. For realists, universals are not vague generalizations; rather, they are causal principles with necessary properties that grant certain knowledge to science in spite of the contingency of the material world.

87 *ST* I.79.3.

88 *SCG* II.77.

89 *ST* I.75.2.

terms of its necessary properties. This concept, on its own, can be neither true nor false. Simply to think "dog" is very different than making the claim, "Fido is a dog." While the concept alone is like an isolated word, the claim that something in the world embodies that reality is like a sentence, a proposition that connects an individual object with the concept we have formed. This second act of the intellect is called "composition and division," or, more simply, *judgment*.[90]

In judgment, we attribute real existence to the essence in a thing outside the mind. That is, we tie the essence as a conceptual being of reason to a real substance with *esse*, the act of existence, in the world. We do this by affirming that the individual object we are sensing is of a certain nature: "This is an X." So, "Fido is a dog" is asserting that the thing I perceive possesses the universal nature of dog. Similarly, we might associate the nature with one of its essential properties, as in "A dog is a mammal." Where abstraction separates essence from the existent substance, the act of judgment reunites the essence and the act of existence by saying the existent substance is of the essence I have conceived through abstraction.

This existential claim, though, also is a concrete claim about how the world really is, as opposed to how it appears to the senses. For example, I might exclaim after a mistaken reaction, "That appeared to be a snake, but that is just a stick." It is for this reason that judgments can be true or false. If I mistakenly pronounce a substance to be of a certain essence, then I am in error. A true proposition is one where there is a conformity between the concept in my mind and the essence of the thing I am experiencing. This is Thomas's definition of truth. This fact helps us appreciate that abstraction can be hard work. It is not a magical intuition, but it is a rational judgment based on evidence. Inadequate evidence, or undisciplined thinking, will lead to erroneous judgments. So, we must continually strive to refine our judgments by constantly checking our abstracted concept against the reality, confirming that the concept matches the evidence presented in experience.[91] There is, then, a constant interplay between apprehension and judgment, as we come to better understand both the universal concepts and the world as it exists.

---

90 *ST* I.16.2 and I.85.5; see also *CM* IV.6.605.

91 Indeed, Thomas says we can never fully know the essence of a flea (*Commentary on the Apostle's Creed*, prologue). Sense-experience knows truth imperfectly (*ST* I.84.5; cf. *ST* I-II.93.2). Consequently, learning must continue over our entire life, and every experience is an opportunity to learn something new. Only God, who creates the essence, knows truth perfectly because he is the measure of that truth (*ST* I.14.8.ad 3).

It is interesting to note how this intellectual judgment is a parallel to sense judgment. Recall that sense judgment instinctively reacts to a phantasm—how the world appears—as beneficial or harmful to our biological survival. Intellectual judgment, in contrast, allows us to react not to appearance but to the real essence of things, thereby enabling us to evaluate the object according to its objective goodness. In this way, humans are able to transcend the instinctive reactions of our animal nature: while a donut appears tempting, I know that in reality it is not good for my health. Judgments of this sort are the heart of ethics, as we see in chapter 6.

After apprehension and judgment, the third act of the intellect is where we string a series of judgments together, and by doing so we learn something new by logical inference that is not immediately evident in experience. This is *reasoning*.[92] Classically, this takes the form of a syllogism: A is B; B is C; therefore, A is C. For example, I know Socrates is a man; I know that all men are mortal; therefore, I can be certain that Socrates, too, is mortal, even if I am speaking with him right now. Against Hume, this allows us to know with certainty all sorts of things we never directly experience. The rules for creating valid syllogisms make up the science of logic, which is normally understood to be a propaedeutic to philosophy, since it tells us when our arguments adhere to the rules.[93]

The Three Degrees of Abstraction and the Diversity of Sciences

We have knowledge of the world because the mind can know the universal causes behind the particular contingent events we experience. In this chapter we have focused on the cause of the nature of the substance, the forms or essences of material beings. Yet as noted in the previous chapter, there are other causes that can be considered by the mind. The mind, therefore, is capable making a variety of abstractive judgments about one and the same experience. These different judgments focus on different causal principles, yet each one yields a legitimate science concerning necessary causal principles. These judgments are often referred to in terms of the three degrees of abstraction that are the foundation for those diverse sciences.[94]

---

92 *ST* I.79.8.

93 See Aristotle's *Organon*, or books on logic, esp. the *Prior Analytics* and *Posterior Analytics*.

94 *ST* I.85.1.ad 1 and *CBDT* 5.1 and 3. See also Jacques Maritain, *Distinguish to Unite*, or *The Degrees of Knowledge*.

Sciences are distinguished by the object of their study: biology studies living things and astronomy studies objects in outer space. This same principle can be taken more broadly in light of the degrees of abstraction. Since knowledge is attained by knowing something immaterial (which is therefore universal and necessary), Thomas distinguishes families of sciences according to the degree of immateriality, or separation from matter, of the object known. Let me explain.

First, some things depend on matter both for their existence as well as for the way in which they are understood. That is, some things must be material in order to exist. These are all the natures of material creation: elements, plants, animals. When we understand these *in light of this materiality*, we are focusing on matter as the principle of potentiality that enables them to change. In other words, we are considering material beings in light of their mutability. This first science, *physics* (from the Greek word for "nature" or *physis*), aims to grasp the material world as a changing reality. This is what philosophers since Thales have done and what we have been discussing: discovering the forms or essences as the causes that explain why objects in the world change with regularity and predictability. This broader science of nature can be subdivided between the natural sciences, which discover *empirical* causes of change, and the philosophy of nature, which seeks the more abstract/less material formal or final causes to explain change. (Thus, science and philosophy necessarily complement one another by discovering distinct causal principles that are all necessary for explaining the events we experience.) The abstractive judgment that characterizes these kinds of knowledge is attained by separating form from matter to grasp the universal nature.

Second, there are other things that depend on matter for their existence but not for the way in which they are understood. That is, we sometimes consider material things not in terms of *what* they are and how they might change but instead consider the intelligibility of matter itself. Matter considered apart from form has the characteristic of dimensionality, since the primary property of matter is that is takes up space (and, as we now understand, time).[95] In other words, we can consider material things purely in terms of quantity. In one way, we can consider abstractly the spatial aspect of matter; this is the science of geometry. Even more abstractly, we can consider pure quantity apart from spatiality; this is arithmetic. Collectively, this second level of abstraction is known as *mathematics*. The abstractive judg-

---

95 *OBE* c. 2.

ment that generates mathematics is to abstract the intelligibility of matter from the substantial form.

Mathematics occupies a very special place among the sciences. Because it is rooted in sense-experience, but nevertheless ignores the contingent nature of change, it is the most certain science.[96] This certainty of math is a siren tempting philosophers to think all sciences must be like math. But this is dangerous, since as the second degree of abstraction it is removed from reality as it really is. Indeed, Thomas says that philosophers who think that all knowledge should be like math commit a "sin" (*peccant*)[97] because they ignore the fact that we must approach the complexity of being with a variety of abstractive judgments in order to capture the fullness of being.

Finally, some things depend upon matter for *neither* their existence nor the way in which they are understood. These are immaterial objects, the unchanging principles behind the changing world. Knowing these ultimate causes is *metaphysics*. Unlike the first two sciences, which abstract one principle (form or matter) from the other, metaphysics employs a "negative judgment" (*separatio*) that aims to grasp how things utterly different from our material experience must be. We directly experience only material things but can know that there are causal principles that are not limited to material things, since they are the very foundations of being. Importantly, because these principles are not directly experienced as discrete substances, they cannot be captured in simple univocal concepts like substantial forms such as dog, man, or tree. They will be like material objects only analogically. Nevertheless, we can have knowledge of these causal principles because without them the world could not exist and operate as it does. These are the most universal principles of intelligibility: substance, act, being. Because of its distance from matter, metaphysics is the hardest science to know; but because of the necessity of the principles, it grasps the most fundamental truths and so has the highest degree of certainty when known.

Metaphysical reasoning subdivides into two kinds of causal judgments.[98] First, we discern the most universal *intrinsic* cause of being, that

---

96 *CBDT* 6.1. In fact, since the first accident of all material beings is quantity—since matter always gives size and location to the substance (*OBE* c. 2)—physical sciences lend themselves to mathematical formulation. But we should never allow those abstract formulations to obscure the qualitative essences that exist in the world.

97 *CBDT* 6.2. This recalls Aristotle's famous teaching that one should not seek the same kind of certainty in all sciences (*Nicomachean Ethics* I.3, 1094b12–15).

98 *CBDT* 6.1.

without which nothing could exist. This is *being*, or the act of existence. As an act, a verb, being cannot be conceptualized; yet we know it must be present to make things real. This act is the proper subject of metaphysics. We can also discern the most universal *extrinsic* cause of reality, the source of the act of existence; this is God, who in creation gives the act of existence to contingent entities. Because this knowledge of God is indirect and limited, we can never have a clear conception of him.[99] Nevertheless, we can be certain of his existence as a cause by means of this necessary rational judgment. This rational knowledge of God is natural theology, an indirect object of metaphysics.

The important point is that in *any* experience we are capable of making *all* of these abstractive judgments. A person is therefore capable of knowledge of all types of reality. For example, an ice cube melting yields as many kinds of knowledge as the mind cares to seek. I can explain the change in terms of the chemistry: a temperature in excess of 32° gives the water molecules energy to cause them break apart. This empirical explanation of causality is natural science. More abstractly, I could say it melts because the matter has the potential to lose the substantial form of ice; these causal principles are the subject of the philosophy of nature. I could measure shrinking space and disregard that is it ice; this is geometry. More abstractly, I can reduce it to pure numbers in terms of arithmetic and see that two is less than three. Finally, in order to melt, the ice has to first exist; it must have an act of existence by which the form and matter are united. This is metaphysics. But then I can ask where this existence comes from, and I can quickly see that there must be a Creator who is himself uncaused: this is natural theology.

One event, then, even the most trivial, can generate a great amount of knowledge, from science to metaphysics to theology. This is because any being reveals the principles and causes of being; the mind's openness to conform to those principles is truth. We should not allow the arbitrary and dogmatic assumptions of rationalists, empiricists, and idealists to artificially constrict knowledge to a small part of reality. Their prescribed methods fail to see how a person has the potency to receive all truth, both particular facts and universal laws. To deny that the mind is open to all being is to argue yourself into a skepticism, which makes all intellectual effort pointless because it separates truth from being.

---

99 As Saint Augustine said (Sermon 117.5), if you think you understand God, it is not God you are understanding.

If you have an inadequate approach to knowledge, then you will naturally misunderstand the objects of knowledge. This has urgent implications for our knowledge of human nature itself. It is our idea of human nature that is at the heart of the most fraught social debates today because it is the most widely misunderstood. Accordingly, let us now turn to human nature, a central question for philosophers ever since Socrates accepted the Delphic Oracle's challenge, "Know Thyself."

FURTHER READING

Deely, John. *What Distinguishes Human Understanding?* South Bend, Ind.: St. Augustine's Press, 2002.

Gilson, Étienne. *Methodical Realism*. Translated by Philip Trower. Front Royal, Va.: Christendom Press, 1990.

Maritain, Jacques. *Distinguish to Unite, or The Degrees of Knowledge*. Translated by Gerald B. Phelan. Notre Dame, Ind.: University of Notre Dame Press, 1995.

O'Callaghan, John. *Thomistic Realism and the Linguistic Turn: Toward a More Perfect Form of Existence*. Notre Dame, Ind.: University of Notre Dame Press, 2003.

Ross, James. *Thought and World*. Notre Dame, Ind.: University of Notre Dame Press, 2008.

Simon, Yves R. *An Introduction to Metaphysics of Knowledge*. Translated by Vukan Kuic and Richard J Thompson. New York: Fordham University Press, 1990.

Chapter 5

What Is Man That Thou Art Mindful of Him? Humans as Persons

THE PROBLEM: MAN, BETWEEN THE BEASTS AND THE ANGELS

Having lived through the brutal occupation of Poland by both the Nazis and the Soviets, Karol Wojtyła observed, "The evil of our times consists in the first place in a kind of degradation, indeed in a pulverization, of the fundamental uniqueness of each human person. This evil is even more of the metaphysical order than of the moral order."[1] This degradation of the human person has not abated, for our society still suffers from broad misconceptions of what it means to be human.

The future saint then argues that this error can be overcome only if we recover the "inviolable mystery of the person." Our current view of human nature is too often characterized by various tendencies to simplify it, which can only serve to obliterate the mystery of the human person. For example, it is true that a human is an animal; but reason raises human beings above other animals. It is true that a human is a spirit; but unlike the angels, he is anchored to the earth by his body. Any adequate idea of a human must admit both sides of this reality; to ignore either is to misconstrue human nature and to open the door to the degradations of the human person that have become too common in modern society.

A balanced vision of human nature, therefore, is one which recognizes a man is both a *human* and a *person*. To say we are human is to note our nature, the essence that unites humankind as one species and distinguishes us from all other creatures. As such, all people are the same as rational animals, and we are not free to change this objective fact. Yet being a member

---

[1] In a letter to the noted Catholic theologian Henri de Lubac from 1968; cited in George Weigel, *Witness to Hope: The Biography of Pope John Paul II* (New York: HarperCollins, 1999), 174.

of the human species also means that we are endowed with powers of intelligence and free will that enable each individual to be truly unique. This uniqueness of human substances is why we refer to ourselves as *persons*. Other creatures are more-or-less interchangeable; a pet, although beloved, can always be replaced. A person, though, has a dignity that means each deserves to be accorded rights and respect. This personhood, however, is explicable only in light of human nature, so it is a dignity that must be accorded to all human beings. Furthermore, that dignity can never be used as a pretext to ignore the truth of human nature that is its very source.

Problems arise when we dissolve this metaphysical unity and separate humanity and personhood. On the one hand, this leads some to say that not all humans count as persons, thereby depriving them of rights. For example, in 1981 the National Academy of Science affirmed that *human life* begins at conception but mystified the moral issue by claiming that *personhood* is a question for philosophy or theology.[2] This separation of personhood from human nature implies that not all humans are persons and so legitimizes the exploitation of some humans as mere things (as history all too often has proven). On the other hand, some will argue that not all persons are human; in recent years, Belgium has extended human rights to chimpanzees and Bolivia has granted rights to forests. Once we ignore how natures ground reality, we are liable to invent the most groundless fantasies.

Discovering the truth of human nature unavoidably builds upon the principles from earlier chapters. As a human *being*, the metaphysical principles of being provide the concepts needed to define human nature. And we have already seen how human knowledge demands that we account for the capacity for sensation and reason and how both must work together to come to know the essence of a human. For this reason, it is often the case that reductive approaches to metaphysics and epistemology impel philosophers to reductive understandings of human nature. A small theoretical error in the beginning might now become a very large atrocity in human history.

However, for both the perennial tradition as well as those who depart from it, philosophy's approach to human nature begins with Plato, for here, as in many other areas of philosophy, his arguments provide the framework for later thinkers.

---

2 In a flagrant instance of sophistry, authorities will then claim that the answers given by philosophy and theology are irrelevant since they are not scientifically verifiable. This circular reasoning is the foundation for an alleged unlimited right to abortion on demand.

THE PLATONIC FOUNDATIONS

Plato develops his theory of human nature while investigating the nature of justice. This is a fruitful strategy because there is an inherent relationship between the *descriptive* and the *prescriptive*. That is, in order to describe the nature of something, you invoke the best instance as a sort of paradigmatic example. For instance, to explain to someone what art is, you would point to the works in a museum and not the productions of an elementary school art class. Both are art, but the best instance better embodies the nature of the thing to be understood. (This, of course, reflects the fundamental insight of Plato's theory of Forms.) Similarly, to know what a human being is, we should discuss the just person—the excellent person—and not the couch potato, since the former better illustrates all that a human being ought to be.

On the assumption that larger things are easier to come to understand than are smaller things,[3] Plato begins by defining justice in a city and then applies this definition to an individual. He can do this because just things are essentially the same since they all participate in the same Form of justice.[4] A city is made up of different kinds of people who are all naturally suited to different jobs. A city is *just* when the right people do their appropriate jobs. This means the wisest people (guardians) will rule, the most courageous people (auxiliaries) will defend the city, and those dedicated to making consumer items (artisans) obey the leaders and pursue material pleasure with moderation.[5] Where each class has its own virtue (wisdom, courage, and temperance respectively), justice is the virtue of the whole city: each class doing its own job.

This definition presents an immediate difficulty, since it is not obvious that there are three parts in a human being to parallel the three classes in the city. So, Plato uses the principle of noncontradiction to argue that the soul is made of three parts: if a person has opposing attitudes with respect to the same object at the same time, then there must be distinct parts of the soul reacting to the thing in opposite ways.[6]

First, Plato notes that we can want something and yet decide against trying to get it. For example, if you are out fishing on a pond, you can be very thirsty and yet judge that you should not drink the brackish water. In

3 *Republic* II (368d–e).
4 *Republic* IV (435b1–2).
5 *Republic* IV (434a1–434d1).
6 *Republic* IV (436b4–c1).

this case, you simultaneously want to drink and don't want to drink. This indicates a distinction between the appetite, which simply desires, and reason, which judges about how that desire should be fulfilled.[7]

Next Plato observes that sometimes we have a desire that gives rise to a contrary emotion. He tells the story of Leontius,[8] who had a compulsion to gawk at corpses but acting on that desire filled him with revulsion. From this, Plato infers a distinction between the appetites, which simply desire, and the emotions, the spirited reactions to experiences. Finally, Plato points out emotions cannot be the same as reason, since children and animals both exhibit strong emotions but do not exhibit the use of reason.[9]

We can conclude, then, that the soul's three parts are the reason, the emotions, and the appetites. Applying the definition of justice as the virtue of the whole, we can see that the just person is the one in whom reason rules the appetites with the help of well-trained emotions.[10] (One proof of this theory is that those who give appetites free reign *over* reason are intuitively seen to be ridiculous; for example, Homer Simpson.) This just order of the soul has the force of moral obligation because the just person is not only interiorly well-ordered but is also happy because of that interior order.[11] Those who do not control their appetites become slaves to them and are never satisfied since there is always more to want. Reason, in contrast, knows the truth, an eternal and unchanging reality that can never be lost and that satisfies the soul permanently and more fully than does any bodily pleasure.

While Plato concludes that the soul has three parts, these parts are not equal. Because the reasoning part has access to the unchanging Forms, it is in some way more real than the body, which is subject to change. In fact, he says the tripartite nature of the soul in this life is like a statue that has been submerged for many years and has become encrusted with foreign accretions.[12] The true soul is discovered by chipping away those bodily accretions, leaving reason alone as the truest aspect of the soul. This true

---

7 *Republic* IV (439d3–8).

8 *Republic* IV (439e).

9 *Republic* IV (441a–c).

10 *Republic* IV (441e). In the *Phaedrus* (245–54), Plato develops a famous analogy of the soul with a chariot: The driver of the chariot uses a good horse to control a bad horse who wants to go off course. Therefore, the charioteer (reason) uses the good horse (emotions) to keep the bad horse (appetites) on track.

11 *Republic* IX (577d–587e).

12 *Republic* X (611c–612a).

nature of the soul explains how recollection of the Forms is possible, for it preexists our bodily nature. It follows, though, that if the soul really is just reason, the body must be an impediment to a person's true nature, since it obscures reason; Plato would even call the body a prison for the soul.[13] Fighting against the limitations of the body is the duty of the philosopher, for he seeks to free reason from this material realm. This ascetic rejection of the body is, in effect, to "practice dying," freeing oneself of the material world in order to grasp the eternal Forms.[14]

The desire to transcend the body underlies another important aspect of Plato's idea of the soul. This is the immortal nature of the soul. In the *Phaedo*, Socrates—who is awaiting execution—seeks to console his bereft students by proving the soul is immortal. Although he offers a number of arguments, let us consider the final one.[15]

Certain Forms have defining properties that always come and go with the presence of the Form. For example, with the Form of fire comes the property of heat. You cannot make fire cold, for if you eliminate either the heat or the fire, the other goes with it. The soul is defined as that which brings life to bodies. Therefore, the soul's defining property is life, for anything that has life has a soul. When a thing dies, it cannot be that the soul dies (just as fire cannot be made cold); rather, it must be that the soul departs from the body, taking life with it. The soul—life—cannot ever admit death. Therefore, he concludes, the soul is immortal.

This Platonic vision of the soul, especially the idea of a tripartite soul and its immortality, would have tremendous influence on Western civilization. What we must note, though, is that, although each aspect of his theory is necessary to account for the evident experience of human nature, these aspects are not perfectly compatible with one another. On the one hand, in emphasizing the soul simply as reason, Plato is able to clearly explain two important truths: how a person knows transcendent Forms and also how the soul, as separable from the body, is immortal. On the other hand, this makes reason's connection to the body—as well as its tripartite nature—tenuous: if I am really just my rational soul, how is the soul able to cause appetites and emotions in the body? Indeed, if the soul is immortal, how could it even *have* appetites like hunger once separated from the body? Moreover, if

---

13 *Phaedo* 82e–83a.

14 *Phaedo* 64a–67d; esp. at 67d.

15 *Phaedo* 100b1–107a1.

I am really an eternal soul, why am I in this body at all? Yet the alternative position, that the soul is inextricably tied to the body as the cause of my material existence, would compromise both its access to transcendent immaterial Forms as well as its immortality,[16] which is hardly more satisfactory.

Puzzles like these would lead later thinkers to emphasize one aspect over the other. Either a human being is really just a soul, and we can safely depreciate the body, or a human being is really just a body and the soul is an unnecessary myth. While the simplicity of these approaches makes them popular, they are also highly problematic for in reducing a human being to only one reality, they misrepresent the truth of human nature.

REDUCTIVE EXTREMES

To get human nature right, we must respect the fact that a man is an animal and simultaneously a spiritual person. Inadequate theories about human nature are reductive: he is only an animal, or, worse, chunks of matter, an amalgamation of atoms. Alternatively, a person is a spirit only, so his biological reality is irrelevant. Let us consider the development of this latter theory first.

Dualism

Dualism is the theory that a human being is composed of two distinct parts: a mind and a body. The conspicuous problem with dualism is that, since it assumes mind and body are utterly separate, it is impossible to explain how they can interact. Thus, as we saw with Plato, the tendency will be to emphasize that a person is primarily a mind or consciousness and to view the body as a mere appendage to be used. This subordination of the incarnational reality of a person ends up creating a false sense of liberty, as if we were no longer constricted by the limits of human nature.

The modern version of dualism is a by-product of Descartes's epistemological project. Recall that, in his search for certainty in knowledge, Descartes began by doubting everything that was in any way uncertain. He ultimately discovers that the one thing of which he is certain is that he must exist so long as he is thinking. From this he concludes that he is a mind, a thinking thing, and not a body (since he can still doubt the existence of a material world). Indeed, when he initially comes to knowledge of God as his creator, he can only be certain that he is a mind with certain innate ideas. It is because

---

16 This is the usual interpretation of Aristotle's position (see *De Anima* II.1 and III.5). Thomas integrates and corrects both approaches in articulating the most adequate position.

his innate ideas, including that of God, can only come from God as a perfect creator that he is able to free himself from the specter of the evil genius.

Descartes then continues his arguments by noting that, since he now knows that God is the "author of his being," he can trust all those innate ideas in his mind "concerning God himself and other things whose nature is intellectual, and also concerning the whole of that corporeal nature which is the subject-matter of pure mathematics."[17] That is, Descartes can now be certain not just that he is a mind and that God exists but also that his innate ideas of math—which he now knows are from God—are reliable. Because math measures quantity, this innate idea can be applied to the material world, since the primary attribute of matter is extension, that is, it is dimensional and quantitative. This mathematized measurement of matter would come to characterize much of modern science.

However, Descartes must first prove that there is a material reality to measure. His first evidence for this lies in the fact that he has distinct innate ideas of mind and body that are mutually exclusive of one another. His idea of a mind is as a "thinking, non-extended thing;" in contrast the "body . . . is simply an extended, non-thinking thing."[18] Since these innate ideas must be from God, he can conclude with certainty that what is thinking cannot be body and what is spatially extended cannot be mind. Thus, there are bodies distinct from the mind; but, because human existence is coextensive with consciousness (that is, mind), even if bodies exist, they cannot be essential to human nature.

Nevertheless, we can prove that we are present in bodies in a material world. First, Descartes knows that through his sensations he apprehends impressions of a material world. These perceptions cannot be innate ideas from God because they are not clear and distinct; rather, they are confused and complex impressions. Yet, since he cannot control these perceptions, he knows that they are not created by his mind and so must come to him from something outside of him. The only options are that they are caused by a real material world or God is deceiving him by making them appear real. But God is not a deceiver; consequently, Descartes concludes that these ideas are caused by his bodily interaction with a material world.[19] Thus, there is a material world in which minds have a body.

17 Descartes, *Fifth Meditation*, 71.

18 Descartes, *Sixth Meditation*, 78.

19 Descartes, *Sixth Meditation*, 78–80.

However, since these ideas are confused, they cannot be the source of certain knowledge. What, then, is their purpose? It is only to help us survive. Bodily sensations of pain and pleasure "inform the mind of what is beneficial or harmful for the composite [of mind and body] of which the mind is a part."[20] Moreover, since the body is distinct from mind, it is not capable of consciousness. Instead, Descartes explains that the body works as "a kind of machine equipped with and made up of bones, nerves, muscles, veins, blood and skin in such a way that, even if there were no mind in it, it would still perform all the same movements as it does now."[21] This machine-body can act without any consciousness or mind, like the elaborate automata of Descartes's era that could be programmed to perform remarkably complex movements. This affects the reliability of our sensations, since machines can break and a broken body will communicate faulty information to the mind. This is the source of erroneous sensations. For example, if I fail to perceive pain when I step on a nail because of some broken bodily mechanism, I will fail to act to protect the body from harm. This reemphasizes the need to put our trust in the innate ideas of reason alone. Thus, as a human I am really my mind, and the body is merely something of an appendage.

This argument, however, precipitates another puzzle, for it is still true that the mind receives sensitive information from the body. There must therefore be some place where this connection happens. The mind cannot be throughout the whole body because it is by definition unextended and indivisible, while the body is extended and divisible and so can be the source of error. Therefore, the mind must be directly tied only to "the brain, or perhaps just one small part of the brain, namely the part which is said to contain the 'common' sense."[22] Thus, mind and body interact at this point giving us consciousness of the material world. Again, sensations constitute knowledge only when they are subjected to the innate ideas of math, generating quantitative science. Qualitative sensations that cause pleasure and pain—color, flavor, sound, texture—never count as knowledge but are merely useful in helping the body survive.

Recall that one inspiration for Descartes was to reconcile mathematical science with traditional religious beliefs about the existence of God and the

---

20 Descartes, *Sixth Meditation*, 83.

21 Descartes, *Sixth Meditation*, 84.

22 Descartes, *Sixth Meditation*, 86. Notice Descartes's retention of the tradition's idea of common sense. Descartes would famously identify this with the pineal gland (*Passions of the Soul* I.34). That gland's true function is to produce melatonin to aid in sleep.

freedom and immortality of the soul. We can see here how his dualistic argument does save the soul: since it is other than the body, it is not determined by the laws of science and so free; since it is distinct from the mortal body, it is immortal. Nevertheless, the conclusion to his argument makes clear that it is an inadequate solution. In trying to connect mind and body, Descartes asserts that the nexus is in the brain. The problem is that if the mind is located *in* the brain, it has location, and so is extended. This directly contradicts his own definition of mind as unextended and exclusive of body. Without this conclusion, though, Descartes has no way to account for mind-body interaction, perhaps the most obvious fact of human existence: when I step on a nail, I am consciousness of pain; when I command my arm to lift, it obeys. Because of this contradiction, we can conclude that his theory is not tenable.

Nevertheless, Descartes's argument has exercised a dominating influence on the subsequent history of philosophy. The mind-body problem—how an immaterial mind can causally interact with a material body—has become one of the paradigmatic philosophical problems. The consequences of dualism are enormous. We have already discussed that it leads to the veil of perception in epistemology, a consequence of the claim that we can never have direct knowledge of the qualities of the material world. Equally disconcerting is that, in restricting consciousness to the rational mind, dualism also leads philosophers to believe that animals are merely mechanisms lacking awareness and emotion, an error that we are only recently overcoming.

The worst, and longest lasting, consequence of this dualism is the identification of the self with consciousness, so that it is freed from all natural determinations of the body. This opens the door to hedonism (since I am not my body, I can treat my body as I please), abortion (since fetuses do not appear to be rational, they are mere blobs of matter), euthanasia, and gender-identity ideology (I am what I believe I am, despite biological fact).[23] All of this follows from Descartes's method of rationalism, which introduced a division between mind and body that should never have been accepted.

Later thinkers inherit Descartes's dualism as a common point of departure and strive to resolve its evident problems. They agree with Descartes

---

23 These consequences, and others, are catalogued in Patrick Lee and Robert P. George, *Body-Self Dualism in Contemporary Ethics and Politics* (Cambridge: Cambridge University Press, 2008). A good historical critique of these philosophical developments is in John Rist, *What Is a Person? Realities, Constructs, Illusions* (Cambridge: Cambridge University Press, 2020).

that we are most certain of our own consciousness, which appears to be free, and so must be conceived of as distinct from the material world of bodies governed by the necessity of scientific laws. But the more the self is identified with consciousness, the less grounded in objective reality it becomes.

For example, following Descartes, John Locke assumes mind and body are distinct substances but adapts the details according to the needs of his empiricism.[24] Since we only know ideas caused by qualities, Locke postulates substance as a substrate to hold various qualities together. Thus, each substance functions as the foundation for sets of properties: body is the substratum underlying sensible qualities (size, shape, and color), while mind is the substratum for various mental operations (like thought, memory, emotion, and will). Locke refers to the body as a *man*, that is, the living organism with a human appearance. The same man continues to exist just so long as there is a continuous life animating the body that persists despite constant changes. Similarly, the *mind* is the mental substance that is the source of our thoughts, which also persists through constant change. But then he introduces a third category: *person*. Since we only directly know the acts of the mind, and not the mind itself—as a substrate, it is postulated to be there as an "I know not what," but never directly experienced—the person is those activities of the mind—thinking, perceiving, feeling—of which an individual is directly aware.[25] It is the train of consciousness that constitutes my self-identity at a given moment. But, because that consciousness might be transferred to other bodies—a premise we see in many bad movies—there is no necessary link between the man and the person. But neither is there a connection between the mind and person, since memories can be obliterated and consciousness can be interrupted (as in sleep). For example, my self-awareness and memories of myself as a teen are very different from my self-awareness and memories that I now possess.[26] While we assume the mind must have persisted as a substrate for all these acts, we nevertheless conclude that these diverse sets of memories would not be the same *person* at all. Personhood is reduced

---

24 Locke, *Essay Concerning Human Understanding*, bk. 2, chap. 23, para. 5.

25 Locke, *Essay Concerning Human Understanding*, bk. 2, chap. 27, para 16.

26 Thomas Reid uses this as an objection to Locke in his Brave Officer paradox: suppose there is an officer who was flogged as child, a hero in battle in his twenties, and a general in old age. The hero remembers being flogged, and the general remembers being a hero, but the general no longer remembers being flogged. Thus, the general simultaneously is and is-not the same as the boy who is flogged, which is impossible. See Thomas Reid, *Essays on the Intellectual Powers of Man* (Cambridge: Cambridge University Press, 2011), 3.6.

to the flow of memories that I identify as the self. With this argument, Locke invents the problem of personal identity: given that we cannot know the mind as a substrate, what really constitutes the self, and how do I identify my own personhood? Like the mind-body problem, this rather arbitrary separation of personhood from both the man (i.e., body) and the mind (i.e., underlying spiritual unity) creates a number of problems later philosophers would become preoccupied with.

Locke's position is exacerbated by David Hume.[27] Hume's genius is to show the real consequences of a strict empiricism. On this basis, Hume argues he never has sense-experience of the "self" or "mind" at all. Rather, he only experiences constantly changing perceptions "of heat or cold, light or shade, love or hatred, pain or pleasure. I never can catch *myself* at any time without a perception, and never can observe any thing but the perception." There is nothing constant in our perceptions, like a little red light or beeping sound, which might be interpreted as proof of the "self." Therefore, Hume is forced to affirm that persons are "nothing but a bundle or collection of different perceptions, which succeed each other with an inconceivable rapidity, and are in a perpetual flux and movement."[28] Moreover, since identity is defined as that which is *absolutely the same* from moment to moment, there can be no true identity in the person, whose perceptions are constantly changing. The self is unending change, with nothing stable from moment to moment. Hume concludes that personal identity is a mere fiction we create to try to make sense of our experience.

With this argument, the self dissolves into the ephemeral present with no abiding reality. The only things certain about the self are its desires; since there is no abiding goal for life over time, the only good in life is the immediate satisfaction of those desires. A person no longer thinks of himself in terms of the whole of his existence, of developing potential and growing toward perfection. Rather, each moment becomes an independent reality, and life is episodic with no chance of lasting happiness. Since there is no stable personal identity, each person is free to create a new identity from moment to moment.

One might argue, in response to Hume, that even if I do not recognize my own identity, others around me do. The self, if nothing else, exists in a

---

27 This paragraph follows Hume, *A Treatise of Human Nature*, bk. 1, pt. 4, sec. 6.

28 Notice that, because Hume rejects knowledge of cause-and-effect relations (as shown in the previous chapter), he cannot reason to the reality of mind as the cause of this flow of experience.

network of social responsibilities that tie me to a larger world. This position is attacked by Jean-Jacques Rousseau (1712–1778), who isolates the self by denying that human nature is a social animal. The perennial philosophy had always understood that human existence and happiness is inconceivable without social relations. Rousseau rejects this and argues that society is the source of human unhappiness. He argues that a person is essentially free. But when society imposes rules and norms on the individual, that natural freedom is compromised.[29] A man recovers freedom only by rejecting the artificial structures of society and following his untutored inclinations and unrestrained feelings. The consequence of this is that personhood is further atomized into one's subjective sense of self.

Rousseau's romantic view of the "noble savage" continues to inform contemporary ideas of human nature. This is witnessed in the belief that social roles are all oppressive constructs imposed against the will. We therefore need to reject social expectations and discover our most authentic self in maximizing personal freedom. Clarion echoes of Rousseau have resonated through the culture since the 1960s and have become a significant assumption for many in the West.

These various strains of argument liberating the person from the limits of human nature come to be epitomized in the existentialism of Jean-Paul Sartre (1905–1980).[30] He assumes there is no God who creates humankind and so there is no nature to limit our freedom. It follows, then, that each person exists with the freedom to choose for himself what he will be: "Not only is man what he conceives himself to be, but he is also only what he wills himself to be after this thrust toward existence." Since there are no standards by which to evaluate these choices, "we can never choose evil." A person is whatever he chooses to be, and the fact that he has chosen it makes that good for him. Sartre emphasizes that such a choice, in the absence of any values to guide us, is fraught with dramatic responsibility for a person's life. We are, he ironically intones, "condemned to be free"—we have a boundless freedom to be exercised with every choice we make.[31]

---

29 See his "Second Discourse," *Discourse on the Origin of Inequality*.

30 This argument is from Sartre's oft-reproduced essay, *Existentialism Is a Humanism* (1946), in *Existentialism and Human Emotions*, trans. Bernard Frechtman (New York: The Wisdom Library, 1957), 9–51; but especially 12–24). His thesis is summed up in the motto "existence precedes essence."

31 Nor can this freedom rightfully be constrained by other people; as he famously concludes in his play *No Exit*, "hell is other people" because their expectations inevitably limit us.

This liberation of the person from any natural restrictions brings us, paradoxically, to a point where human nature and ethics become meaningless. If my choices are utterly free, there is *no reason* to choose one thing rather than another; since it does not matter what I choose, free choice is without true significance. I can choose whatever I want, and it is never, in itself, good or bad, better or worse. This fact can only lead to despair.

We have reached the *reductio ad absurdum* of dualism. Once we separate mind from body, then mind will invariably lose contact with reality itself. Separating personal identity from past and future, and from the nurturing structures of human society, further distorts a man's self-image. This leads many today to believe a person is a free floating will that can be whatever he wants to be and whose identity is infinitely malleable. Reality, though, is not forgiving in the face of such fantasy. We therefore need to get back to the reality of the world. One way to do this is to emphasize scientific facts. But the way that this is done in materialism is equally reductive, and so its solutions will be no better than dualism's are.

Materialism

Materialism is the belief that only material things exist. A majority of contemporary philosophers, under the influence of the scientific method, assume a materialist metaphysics. Applied to human beings, this theory concludes that a man is simply an aggregation of atoms and molecules, which functions mechanistically in accord with the scientific laws of nature.

Materialist theories of human nature become popular in reaction to the evident problems of dualism in conjunction with the obvious success of science. Dualism's most prominent failure is its inability to explain how an immaterial mind can interact with a material body. Because this interaction is perhaps the most obvious fact about human existence, we need to reject dualism. This (apparently) leaves two alternatives. On the one hand, we can argue that there is *only* mind, and no material bodies exist; this is a counterintuitive and even eccentric position that few philosophers embrace.[32] Or, we can argue that there is *only* body, and there is no mind independent of this material reality. When combined with the discoveries of modern science, materialism is a plausible way to know a man empirically (through

---

32 The most famous proponent of immaterialism is George Berkeley, who argues that our minds can only directly know our ideas, and so there is no reason to suppose the real existence of a material world as the cause of those ideas (see part 1 of *A Treatise Concerning the Principles of Human Knowledge*).

biology, neuroscience, and evolution), whereas the mind or spirit can be dismissed because it eludes all observation. Moreover, as atheism gets more ideologically entrenched in modern thought, there is an assumed need to repudiate anything hinting at the spiritual, a trend that reinforces materialism. This development is not surprising, for materialism, as part of a metaphysical naturalism (i.e., all being is natural, there is no supernatural reality), entails atheism, so they will stand or fall together.

It is obvious that the intricacy and sophistication of modern science has greatly increased our understanding of the material operations in the world. However, the philosophical principles of materialism, as well as their ramifications, remain largely the same as they have always been. For this reason, we can use as a model the thought of Thomas Hobbes (1588–1679), a contemporary of Descartes who developed his theory in part in response to Descartes's dualism. Hobbes forthrightly describes his materialistic premises: "The universe is corporeal; all that is real is material, and what is not material is not real."[33] The metaphysical implications of this position are clear: all entities are simply bodies in motion, and all phenomena must be explained by reference to matter.

Here materialism faces a problem as dire as that faced by dualism: how can matter alone explain everything we experience in the world? First, if everything is composed of matter, and matter is the essentially the same, why are there so many different kinds of things? Second, and more significantly, why are some things alive, and some of those conscious, while most things are not? It does not seem that matter alone can account for the obvious activities done by some material substances. Moreover, if materialism were true, the actions of bodies would be determined by the necessary laws of science; this would preclude the reality of free will and even free thought, making both ethics and creativity impossible. These are all problems for materialism, for, if it cannot explain the variety of things or activities like life, consciousness, and freedom, then it cannot be considered an adequate description of human nature as it really is.

Hobbes's own arguments, although rudimentary in comparison to contemporary science, stake out the logical strategy materialists use to answer these questions. He begins by describing consciousness as sensation resulting from purely material causes: sensation "is nothing else but . . . the

---

33 Hobbes, *Leviathan*, chap. 46.

motion of external things upon our eyes, ears, and other organs."[34] This physical motion then impacts the matter of the brain and creates an image, which allows for memory so long as that residual motion persists. Understanding is recalling that image through a verbal sign, but, since it is a wholly material operation, Hobbes concludes "understanding . . . is common to man and beast."[35] A consequence of materialism, then, is to collapse the distinction between mind and brain, intellect and sensation. There is no unique rational power in humans, and so we are not essentially different from an animal.[36]

Just as materialism reduces cognition to a merely mechanical process, human desires will be similarly mechanical.[37] Once a particle stirs the imagination in the brain, it will then incite an "endeavour, [which] when it is toward something which causes it, is called appetite, or desire." But as purely material beings, human appetites cannot be about anything transcendent; rather, they can only be about those bodily needs for survival that instinctively drive all animals. Satisfaction of these biological appetites is what we mean by happiness.[38] So, a human being acts in purely instinctive ways that are indistinguishable from those of other animals.

With these fundamental principles in place, we can discern the vision of human nature that materialism insinuates. First, there is no spiritual reality to lift people above animalistic sensation and instinctive desires.[39] The highest value is survival. Human life, therefore, is dominated by fear of harm and not, as both Greeks and Christians always held, a search for the greatest good, happiness.[40] Since there is no universal human nature, every person

---

34 Hobbes, *Leviathan*, chap. 1; he goes on to repudiate the "philosophy schools . . . grounded upon certain texts of Aristotle" that describe cognition as reception of an immaterial form, as opposed to this brute physical interaction. For Hobbes's wholesale rejection of Aristotle's "vain philosophy," see chap. 46.

35 Hobbes, *Leviathan*, chap. 2.

36 Reducing reason to sensation also implies nominalism, for sensation can only know individuals and universals are merely imposed names; see *Leviathan*, chap. 4.

37 Hobbes, *Leviathan*, chap. 6.

38 Hobbes, *Leviathan*, chap. 6 and chap. 11; Hobbes uses the term *felicity*.

39 In fact, Hobbes defines religion (in chap. 6) as "fear of power invisible, feigned by the mind, or imagined from tales publicly allowed." Religion, then, is based on fear of an imagined judge and not love for a benevolent Creator.

40 Hobbes bluntly says there is "no such *finis ultimus* (utmost aim) nor *summum bonum* (greatest good) as is spoken of in the books of the old moral philosophers" (chap. 11). As mentioned in chapter 2, framing life in terms of doubt and fear, as opposed to wonder and happiness, is a characteristic mark of modern thought.

pursues his own private ends. But since each person aims to satisfy his own desires, this inevitably leads to "a war as is of every man against every man." Hobbes speculates about this primal condition of human life:

> In such condition there is no place for industry, because the fruit thereof is uncertain: and consequently no culture of the earth; no navigation, nor use of the commodities that may be imported by sea; . . . no account of time; no arts; no letters; no society; and which is worst of all, continual fear, and danger of violent death; and the life of man, solitary, poor, nasty, brutish, and short.[41]

One might object that this bleak vision ignores our moral nature, that we are compassionate and naturally find common cause with others. But Hobbes perspicuously sees that materialism has no room for morality: "To this war of every man against every man, this also is consequent; that nothing can be unjust. The notions of right and wrong, justice and injustice, have there no place."[42] If a person is merely material, the only motives are pleasure and survival, and so an action is good if I want it, and evil if I am opposed to it.

In light of Hobbes's example, we can isolate three problems that bedevil all materialists, regardless of how scientifically developed those theories have become (today, employing insights from neuroscience, evolutionary psychology, and organic chemistry but adhering to the same logic as Hobbes).

First, there is the problem of explaining the fact of consciousness and cognition. Contemporary materialists explain consciousness in terms of the complex neurochemical changes in the brain (at bottom, identical to Hobbes). However, consciousness is an awareness of something other than that neurochemical change—it is a spiritual act of attention pointing to something other than the self. (This mental pointing is known as *intentionality*.) The perennial philosophy recognized the need to distinguish the physical change in the organ from the spiritual change that is sensation. Materialism cannot do this and so identifies awareness with the biological act. But to say this change in the brain makes us aware of an external object is begging the question, because we want to know *how* that physical change can, unlike any other physical change, cause an awareness of something other than—and completely unlike—that material event in the brain.

41 Hobbes, *Leviathan*, chap. 13.

42 Hobbes, *Leviathan*, chap. 13. In chapter 7, I consider the political implications of this.

Intentionality is not just a problem in what it does but also in how it functions. Consciousness is a subjective awareness of qualities, like blue or cold, that are qualitatively unlike what is happening in the material brain.[43] A neural firing makes me smell cookies: but this neural firing is utterly unlike the aroma of cookies. Moreover, unlike all purely physical reactions, this awareness is not subject to strict temporal limitations of the here and now. That is, consciousness flows freely from the past to imagined (not-yet-existent) futures, defying the strict temporality of a physical act. The unbounded nature of consciousness is also evidenced in our ability to grasp abstract universal concepts, such as justice or beauty, which cannot be reduced to material actions in the brain.[44]

The second problem arising from the materialist idea of human nature is determinism. Determinism is the belief that every event is necessitated by the scientific laws of nature. If a human being is simply a chunk of matter, then everything about him—including every thought and action—is completely determined by the laws of physics and chemistry.[45] Consequently, no one can ever be responsible for his actions, since he could not help but do them.[46] In fact, we cannot control even what we think, since the brain merely reacts to physical stimuli. This position elicits one of the great paradoxes for materialists. The philosophers who defend determinism do so by writing arguments to persuade others of the truth of their position; but if there is no freedom, then I can never be persuaded at all, since thought itself is outside of my control. It would appear that materialists fall into a performative contradiction here, since the very act of creative reasoning should be impossible if determinism were true.

---

43 For a critique of materialism on this problem, see David Bentley Hart, *The Experience of God: Being, Consciousness, Bliss* (New Haven: Yale University Press, 2013), 152–237.

44 This point is well established in Mortimer Adler, *The Difference of Man and the Difference It Makes* (New York: Holt, Rinehart, and Winston, 1967; reprint, New York: Fordham University Press, 1993).

45 Scientific determinism can take different guises: It can be based on purely physico-chemical laws, but it can also be a genetic determinism as argued in evolutionary biology. Sigmund Freud argued for a somewhat similar psychological determinism.

46 This is pointedly admitted in the determinism of behaviorist psychologist B. F. Skinner, whose attempt to outline a utopian society is entitled *Beyond Freedom and Dignity* (New York: Alfred A. Knopf, 1971). He argues that a human being is simply an animal and so ought to be trained, like a dog, according to the principles of operant conditioning. The only impediments to this utopia are the hoary myths of free will and human dignity, which mislead us (in his view) into thinking humans are somehow different than beasts and so deserving of respect.

The inability of materialism to account for consciousness and free will leads to the third problem. This is the overall image of human life that results from their premises. By reducing human beings to matter, materialists deny any higher reality that motivates human action. If materialism is true, there is no transcendence, and so there can be no reason to pursue ethics, religion, or art. Yet it must be admitted that these are essential aspects of our existence and that they distinguish human nature from that of other animals. A theory of human nature that tries to diminish these or explain them away as being side effects of brain chemistry or evolution is simply an inadequate account of the reality as we experience it.

A Note on Marxism

A special case of material determinism is found in Marxism, which remains quite influential in Western conceptions of human nature, not only within philosophy, but especially in other disciplines. Karl Marx (1818–1883) assumes that reality is wholly material and that human consciousness is determined by material forces. The difference is that for Marx these forces are not the laws of physics and chemistry but the *economic* circumstances of society.[47] A human is an animal who is distinguished from other animals by the fact that he *produces* his means of subsistence, instead of just taking from nature. In other words, our distinctive essence is not our rationality but the fact we are makers in economic activity. This productive activity requires social relations by which labor is coordinated to best exploit nature. This coordinated group labor, then, is what defines the essence of human nature. More significantly, it thereby also *determines* how those people think about the world. Thinking, for Marx, can be seen as just another form of making; it is the making of ideas: "Conceiving, thinking, the mental intercourse of men, appear at this stage as the direct efflux of their material behavior." Marx thus breaks from Western philosophy by claiming that it is not our ideas that determine the nature of our society, but rather it is our social and economic relations that determines our ideas and, indeed, our very consciousness. As a result, all ideological structures—culture and politics, religion and art—arise deterministically out of our economic activity. However, since the division of labor entails that there are different classes

---

47 Marx's economic and political works, such as *The Communist Manifesto* (1848), necessarily assume his philosophical idea of human nature found in *The German Ideology* (1846), which I quote here along with ideas from his preface to *A Contribution to the Critique of Political Economy* (1859).

with distinct economic activities, the worldviews of these classes are necessarily going to conflict. This is what fuels Marx's political polemics, since he believes that all history is the history of class conflict and the only way to eliminate conflict in society is by eliminating the class divisions that give rise to conflicting worldviews. This elimination of classes can happen only when there are no longer owners in opposition to workers, and all property (the means of economic production) is held in common. This is why communism, for Marx, is the end of history.

Marx's communism is therefore a utopian ideal. But this dream has two serious weaknesses. First, he assumes thought is determined by economic activity, and so there is no free will by which people determine themselves. Second, because people exist only as a member of class, it is those classes, not individual persons, that are the main actors in society. In other words, the basic unit of being is not the individual person, but the class, which is made up of persons like a body is made of cells. Both these points conspire to deprive the individual person of value, which has led to great atrocities, since entire groups can be summarily proscribed as enemies of history's inevitable victors.[48] This devaluation of the person also is incompatible with experience, and so now we turn from materialism to a more adequate approach to human nature.

HYLOMORPHISM AND THE UNITY OF MAN

Given the problems of dualism and materialism, we need to discover an approach to human nature that accepts our materiality but can also account for the reality of our spiritual nature. This is found in Thomas's hylomorphic theory, which is largely built on Aristotle's principles.

Our consideration of hylomorphism recalls the importance of the transcendentals once again. We have discussed that every being is *one*; that is, it is a united whole, for otherwise it would be two things, distinct beings. It

---

48 Marxian ideology has been extended (often in conjunction with a rejection of objective truth derived from Nietzsche's nihilism) to include many academic theories that divide the world into two opposed classes, oppressor and oppressed. These analyses are grounded on the dialectical logic of Marxist determinism, and so their assertions appear insupportable from most other perspectives. Moreover, they are often buttressed with tendentious vocabularies that serve merely to suppress opposition in defense of a supposed victimhood, and so intellectual debate becomes impossible. For a contemporary assessment, see Helen Pluckrose and James Lindsay, *Cynical Theories: How Activist Scholarship Made Everything about Race, Gender, and Identity—and Why This Harms Everybody* (Durham, N.C.: Pitchstone Publishing, 2020).

is particularly with respect to living things—human beings included—that the transcendental property of unity is important. Reductive approaches to human nature end up denying unity, dissolving a man into disunited parts. Indeed, as we have seen, this disintegration triggers something of a chain reaction: first we separate mind from body, then mind is separated from person, and then person from history and society, leaving only the barest point, a thin slice of space and time with no necessary connections to anything; for its part, body is reduced to evolutionary instinct, or genes, or chemicals, or atoms, or strings, all of which are seen to be the real subject of activity, utterly obscuring the agency of the person. The perennial tradition's argument hinges on integrating all these parts, appreciating the true unity of living beings as agents, for only this does justice to the reality and experience of living organisms.

A United Substance

When considering human nature, the primary fact that must be accounted for is that a human being is a united organism with many parts and many activities—chemical, biological, emotional, intellectual, spiritual—all of which are ordered to the flourishing of the organism as a whole. A typical body is composed of seven octillion atoms; these constitute the basic living unit, the cell, of which the typical body has thirty trillion. Cells themselves are miracles of biological activity on their own, with DNA, RNA, mitochondria, ribosomes, and so on, but, in the body, cells are all differentiated into diverse systems (nervous, skeletal, endocrine, digestive, respiratory, and six more to boot) that function in concert for the good of the individual substance. These facts should direct us away from reductionist theories that separate the soul and disintegrate the body, for the most obvious fact about a person is that there is an integral unity of many parts. There must be something other than the parts to explain the unity of the whole. The problem is how to explain this many-leveled unity? The answer is hylomorphism, the theory that material substances are a composition of form and matter.

In hylomorphism, form, as the principle of actuality, gives to the matter its "shape" taken in a broad sense, its intelligible structure and ordering of parts (this manifests the essential nature defining what it is), existence (its first act, its reality as a substance), and its powers to act (tendencies to second act, or final cause, as determined by the nature of the substance). The form then unites all the constituent material parts and gives the substance its diverse powers to act.[49] Moreover, since all these powers arise from the same form, they will act in a united way to attain the end of the substance. Thus, even in complex substances, activity is orderly and not chaotic.

Aristotle applies these principles of hylomorphism to living substances and concludes that the form of a living thing is a special kind of form because it gives a particular activity, life. He calls this form of living beings the *soul* (in Latin, *anima*, as in animate or animal). Thus, the soul is the form of a living body; soul is the first act that gives the intelligible structure to a living thing so that it might perform the activities characteristic of living things in order to flourish as an organism of that species (that is, attain the end for which it exists).[50]

It is important that we approach the idea of soul philosophically, without too many theological assumptions. (Theology augments, or perfects, this purely philosophical notion of the soul.) Philosophically, the soul is the principle of life, for life is the *being* of living things. Living things exist only because the soul gives them the powers of life that are dynamically coordinated so as to preserve the organism.[51] To understand a soul as a kind of form, then, we need to clearly distinguish living things from those without

---

49 We should note the conspicuous difference between *intrinsic unity* and *extrinsic unity*. Intrinsic unity describes those organic beings whose existence and activity are more than the sum of their parts. This is discernible where there is one center of activity ordered to a single final cause with a body such that parts cannot be interchanged at will. For example, a water molecule has a unity and acts differently from when the three atoms were not bound together. Similarly, a plant or animal is more than the sum of its chemical parts, and its activity goes well beyond mere chemical reactions. Extrinsic unity is an accidental condition describing groups of ontologically independent beings. Examples of extrinsic or artificial unity are things that share a common purpose or a common place, such as a basketball team or a puddle of water. A team is not really one being, but five substances whose "unity" is arises from their acting more or less together for the same goal. In the same way, a puddle is not one real thing since it is made up of many water molecules that will evaporate on their own; we call it by one name only because those water molecules share one location (at least for now). The most important application of this distinction is to artifacts: as constructed by humans, they have no intrinsic unity and so are not properly called substances. In other words, they have no single essence by nature; rather, the maker imposes an "imputed" essence on the artifact, because the maker determines what that artifact is and what it is to be used for. While philosophers frequently use artifacts as examples as substances, it should be understood that they are only analogically substances, since they lack the true intrinsic unity that characterizes a single being. On the distinction between intrinsic and extrinsic unity, see W. Norris Clarke, *The One and the Many*, 64–68.

50 Aristotle, *De Anima*, II.1 (412a12–412b7). Since the Greek for soul is *psyche*, the study of human nature is also known as *philosophical psychology*. Modern psychology, in its attempt to be scientific, often neglects the soul in considering only observable behavior—stimulus and response—that can be empirically studied.

51 *De Anima* II.4 (415b13).

life. Nonliving things only change when acted upon by something else: a raindrop falls due to gravity or evaporates due to heat. Living things, in contrast, have the power to change themselves: a plant will grow and a bird will fly. Thomas refers to this as the power of self-movement, the ability to grow or develop that arises from within the substance and not simply in reaction to another.[52] A soul is simply a form that causes this sort of intrinsic activity. Since accomplishing these life activities requires that the organism have a certain material structure, the soul is also responsible for constituting and maintaining that structure of the body. Thus, again we see how first act and second act, intelligible structure and activity, are coordinated: unless a plant had a specific structure, it would not be able to grow; unless a fish had a certain bodily structure, it would not be able to swim. The soul, then, gives the body the structure of a living thing and the powers of life to act as a living thing. And in both the body and the acts, the fact of unity—of parts and of operations—testifies to the presence of a soul. This is obvious in death, for without a soul the activities cease and the body decomposes.

But how do we know there is a soul when we cannot see it or scientifically test it? The soul is rationally necessary in order to account for a readily observable fact that requires *some* explanation: of all the things in the material universe, very few are alive. In other words, we perceive an evident effect—life—and realize that there has to be some rational explanation and cause for it. Since both living and nonliving things share the property of being made of matter, the explanation for why only some material things are living has to lie in *something other* than matter.[53] If matter explained life, then all material things would be living, which is clearly not true. The soul is the causal principle that is introduced to explain the difference between living and nonliving things that is evident in our experience.

Let us illustrate this with an example: A human being and a compost heap are both material beings; moreover, they are remarkable similar in terms of their material composition (similar proportions of carbon, oxygen, nitrogen, and so on). Despite this material similarity, the human being can do things that a compost heap cannot. Humans can read and create art, reason, and love. Humans can be aware of the world through sensation. Most fundamentally, though, humans are alive—their cells go through mitosis, a spontaneous change by which the person grows and actively

52 *ST* I.18.1.
53 *ST* I.75.1.

maintains himself in existence. Moreover, all of these acts are done in an orderly way so that the whole organism—the person—can flourish. The compost heap, in contrast, is controlled by changes in its environment: it grows only if something is added to it, and it suffers continual decomposition into its constituent elements. It does not maintain its bodily integrity in any way. It is obvious that there is no order or unity there. Nonliving things are subject to entropy, while living things resist it.

How can we explain the fact that a human being is able to do all these things the materially similar compost heap cannot? We can demonstrate again the necessity of the soul if we consider that there are only three ways of explaining life activity in relation to matter.

First, we could assume that since a man is living and conscious, and he is made up of atoms, then the atomic elements that comprise his body must also be alive and conscious. This argument assumes that, since we are made of atoms, the aggregate of atoms (the human being) can only have the powers that each atom has. This theory asserts that the mysterious powers that a person has actually belong to everything that exists. This notion, known as *panpsychism*, insists that everything has a soul. However, it has had few defenders, primarily because there is simply no evidence that atoms are alive and conscious. To assume otherwise violates Ockham's razor.

A second alternative is to assume that, since atoms are *not* alive or conscious, then the aggregate of atoms does not have these powers either. This is the position of materialism. The problem here is that it denies that life and consciousness are *real* powers of human beings. If they are not real, materialist philosophers need to explain away the appearance of their reality. An extreme version of this is *eliminative materialism*, which disregards anything other than atoms as unreal illusions. A related position is *epiphenomenalism*, which argues that life and consciousness are merely an aftereffect of the physico-chemical processes of the body. To understand this claim, consider this analogy: when we stare at a bright light we then "see" a blue dot when we close our eyes. The dot is not real but is simply an aftereffect of the reaction of the rods and cones to the light. Materialists suggest that life and consciousness are like the blue dot: the bodily events alone are real, everything else is an "aura" of the body and its chemical processes. But to reduce consciousness—and all it entails like love, art, culture, religion—to an unreal aftereffect seems to be an utterly inadequate explanation. (It also, as we have seen, entails denying free will and creativity, which intrinsically contradicts the very process of the philosophizing which produces materialist theories.)

The third option, then, it that, while a human being is made up of atoms that lack life and consciousness, there must be another causal principle in addition to matter that gives us the powers of life and consciousness. For the perennial philosophy, that causal principle is the form, for when that form is a soul it gives the body the powers of life and consciousness. These activities cannot be explained by matter alone, and so they must be explained by the soul that gives matter its intelligible structure, existence, and powers. Some might object that these life activities can be explained by the *order* of matter—it is the way matter has come together (e.g., in the brain) that is the origin of the powers of life and consciousness. But this begs the question about *why* some material beings have that order—how it arose, in giving coherent unity to trillions of operating cells and endowing them with life—while others do not. Thus, the soul as the form of the body is the only adequate explanation for the fact of an ordered and unified body doing things that most material substances cannot.

Nevertheless, this might seem like an unwarranted philosophical speculation just to explain the oddity of living things. But the fact that a higher-level form can change the activities of matter can be seen even in nonliving things. Oxygen behaves in one way on its own; for example, it boils at −297°. However, when it is combined with hydrogen and forms a new substance—water—its activities and properties utterly change; now it boils at 212°. Even more drastic changes occur in complex protein chains. Thus, forms that unite matter into complex substances can endow matter with new potential for activity. Life activities are the most notable example of this, for they represent a complete break with the mere reactions of non-living things.

Powers of the Soul

The soul endows matter with the powers of life, and life activities are remarkably diverse. This is easily seen in the differences between plants, animals, and human beings. Accordingly, to account for these differences, it must be the case that there are different kinds of souls, giving bodies distinct physical structures (including internal arrangement of parts) with distinct kinds of life powers. Therefore, following the principle that faculties are distinguished by their object, we distinguish souls into three general categories based on how broadly those powers can act.[54]

54 *ST* I.78.1 and *DQDA* 13.

First, all living things must be able to grow and maintain the integrity of their body—keep it healthy and whole. This requires the ability to take in nutrition from the environment, which converts the matter and energy of some other substance into one's own substance. For example, when I eat chocolate, the nature of that chocolate is changed and absorbed into my own being and I get a burst of energy and grow fat. This assimilative ability also extends to hydration (taking in water) and breathing (taking in air). Life's power to sustain itself also includes the ability to reproduce, since an individual can exist only if the species keeps itself alive. (This reproduction can be either asexual, as an amoeba splitting, or sexual, as with most animals or even plants that require pollination. Twinning is simply a form of asexual reproduction.) This first level of life is called *vegetative*, since it is identified with plant life. It is characterized by nutrition, growth, and reproduction. These are the lowest powers associated with the soul since these activities concern only the substance's own body, which changes through the processes of nutrition (taking in food) and growth.

Animals, in addition to being alive, have the power of sensation through which they become aware of and adapt to their environment. The way in which they respond to things in their environment is determined by the power of appetite, an instinctive tendency to react to things as beneficial or harmful. Since these reactions require that animals move themselves toward desirable things and away from detrimental things, this level of life also includes a power of moving location (called *locomotion*). Collectively, these powers belong to the *sensitive soul* and are common to all animals. This is a higher soul, since its powers act not only on its own body but by a conscious awareness of the bodies of things around it.

Finally, among animals, humans have the added power of intellectual cognition. As argued in the previous chapter, the mind is an immaterial power that grasps an immaterial, universal form. But just as sensitive awareness elicits appetitive reactions, corresponding to rational knowledge is another type of appetite. This rational appetite is not an instinctive response to any particular good appealing to our bodily desires; rather, it is a desire for the universal good—that which is good in all circumstances. In other words, just as the intellect can see a chihuahua, a golden retriever, and a Great Dane, and abstract a general notion of "dog" that is the common causal form to all, the universal good is that intelligible essence of goodness under which all things are desirable. In desiring the essence of good, the will is capable of seeking that which is good in itself, the highest good, that orders all other desires. Our desire for this highest good enables us to transcend our instinctive sensitive reactions and so endows us with free choice. This rational appetite is *the will*. (We discuss the will more fully below.) These powers belong to the *rational soul* and are proper to human beings. These are the highest powers, since their object is not merely another body but immaterial universal forms by which we can know an entire class of things.

The self-movement associated with life, then, involves the spontaneous growth of living bodies, the instinctive reactions of based on sense perceptions, and the acts of free will by which a man orders himself to the highest good. Thus, it becomes clear that life is an analogical term: all living things have the power of self-movement, but the way in which it is exercised varies by the nature of the soul in question.

Therefore, there are a panoply of powers given to the body from the soul, each of which distinguishes living things from nonliving. These powers also separate living things into different types, such as plants, animals, and humans.[55] At each level of life, there is a kind of spontaneity of action that goes beyond what matter can account for. This spontaneity nullifies determinism, since it is impossible to predict how living things will develop. The growth of a plant cannot be utterly controlled and even less the movement of an animal or the decisions of a person. While we are made of atoms, and atoms are determined by physics and chemistry, the soul makes living things something more than agglomerations of atoms, and so their activity eludes scientific reductionism and determinism.

A common objection is to ask how one soul can be the source of such diverse powers. If action follows from being, should there not be one form or soul for each kind of activity? Indeed, this apparent difficulty drove most medieval thinkers (for example, Saint Bonaventure and Duns Scotus) to say that there are a plurality of forms in any living substance to account for each

---

55 Many Christians today are surprised to discover that plants and animals have souls. But if they are living, it is obvious they must. The idea that only humans have souls is a legacy from Descartes, who thought plant and animal bodies are simply machines and so not really living at all. This was necessary for him to reduce the material universe to a purely mechanistic activity that could be known with scientific certainty. This is also why Descartes talks about mind and body, instead of soul and body. Since bodies are machines for him, there are no vegetative or sensitive powers and so no need of a soul to give the body these life powers. This Cartesian identification of life with mind alone is still a source of great moral confusion; for example, defining human death as "brain death" and not true bodily death is purely Cartesian and actually ignores the reality of the soul in traditional Catholic teaching. On the problem of defining death, see Robert Spaemann, "Is Brain Death the Death of a Human Person?" in *Love and the Dignity of Human Life: On Nature and Natural Law* (Grand Rapids, Mich.: Eerdmans, 2012), 45–69.

of these powers. More complex beings are that way simply because they have more souls acting within them. According to this theory, one form gave shape to the matter; plants add a vegetative soul; animals add a sensitive soul; and human beings have all three plus a rational soul. The advantage of this is that it makes the argument for immortality very easy: the other souls are tied to the body and die with the body, but the rational soul is not tied to the body and so it can just go on after death.

Thomas, however, sees that this solution causes more problems than it solves. The primary job of a form is to give unity—oneness in being and activity—to a substance. If there were a multiplicity of souls, they would not act in a united fashion since there would not really be one substance. It is obvious, though, that in a human being the diverse parts—cells, organs, systems—do not function independently but instead are coordinated like a masterful symphony ordered to the good of the whole organism. This can be explained only if there is one substantial form, which causes all these activities at once.[56] Thus, Thomas argues for the *unicity of substantial form*.

The substantial form determines the essence of the substance. Since the human essence is to be a rational animal—rationality is the action that defines human beings—the substantial form must be the rational soul.[57] But how can the rational soul cause the vegetative and sensitive powers? The answer can be found in Thomas's idea that essence is that which limits existence as a mode of being. Essences with very little existence have little activity, while higher essences are naturally endowed with more active powers because their existence is less restricted. These higher essences are qualitatively "bigger," so to speak—they have more existence and so more powers, but this will always be inclusive of the powers of the lower essences. Like a series of progressively larger concentric circles, the powers of the higher essences subsume all the modes of being and powers of the lower ones. Thus, a hydrogen atom can do very little because its essence limits existence very greatly; but water can do more because its essence includes the powers of hydrogen and oxygen, as well as its own unique powers as

---

56 Some contemporary philosophers have suggested that the brain is responsible for the united operations of the body. But this is impossible. The brain is itself an amalgam of parts functioning unitedly—so what accounts for the brain's unity? Moreover, the brain does not come to exist until well after the ordered unity of the organism has been manifested in the development of the embryo and then the fetus, and it is this developmental unity that allows for the differentiation and functioning of the brain.

57 *ST* I.76.1.

water; plants include not only those lower elemental powers but also the vegetative power of life; similarly, for animals, larger essences include life as well as the elemental powers of their constitutive atoms. Thus, Thomas can conclude that the rational soul, as the highest essence, the least restricted in being and activity, includes all the powers of the "smaller" more restricted essences:

> We must therefore conclude that in man the sensitive soul, the intellectual soul, and the nutritive soul are numerically one soul. . . . For we observe that . . . in the order of things, the animate are more perfect than the inanimate, and animals more perfect than plants, and man than brute animals; and in each of these genera there are various degrees. . . . Thus the intellectual soul contains virtually whatever belongs to the sensitive soul of brute animals, and to the nutritive souls of plants.[58]

The rational soul, then, contains virtually all inferior forms. This usage of *virtually* arises from the Latin *virtus*, power. Thus, to contain it virtually is to have the power of the lower form. While the rational soul is an immaterial power, since it virtually contains the powers of lower forms, it can exercise both vegetative and sensitive activities in the organism.

This is an important principle, for it answers a common objection that materialists raise. It is an indisputable fact that the human body is roughly 70 percent water. It is an indisputable truth that the cells on my arm contain carbon atoms. From a Thomistic perspective, this is troubling. If it is simply true that water is in me, then that water is not me—it is water, not human. Similarly, I would have to admit that the carbon is carbon and not simply *my* skin—it is not me. It would seem that in fact I am an aggregate of many different things. But we have seen that there can only be one substantial form. In that case, all the matter in my body must be attributed to that substantial form: my body is me, it is human. Nevertheless, it is irrational to deny these scientific facts—I *am* made of water and there *are* carbon atoms in my arm.

To resolve this apparent dilemma, we must say the lower forms— carbon and water—are *virtually* present in me.[59] The element's *power to act* is present in me, but those actions are subordinated to the goal of the substance constituted by the highest form. Thus, the water is me because, while

58 *ST* I.76.3; cf. article 4.

59 *ST* I.76.4.ad 4 and especially the short treatise *On the Mixing of the Elements*.

it is in my body, it is *me* and acts for my good. If I should spit, that expectorated water ceases to be me and now operates according to its own nature, evaporating or mixing with other elements.

This solves the problem of materialism. I am indeed made up of elements and molecules, but since the substantial form is the soul, all these parts are united as one being, a human person. The elements are only virtually present, which means that, while they can revert to existing on their own—as happens at death—so long as their activity is controlled by the higher form, they are really the body of the higher organism. In this way, the metaphysical idea of essences virtually including the powers of essences lower in the ladder of being allows us to accept the discoveries of modern science without surrendering souls as the substantial forms that explain the activities of living things.

An Active Substance

The soul, as the form of the body, gives the person a unity that begins at conception and ceases only upon death. The soul and the body, then, are constitutive principles, not separable things. Consequently, Thomas emphatically says, my soul is not *me*; rather, I am the union of soul and body.[60] This interdependence is manifested in that fact that the soul, as form, gives the living body the following: (1) its shape, the physical structure and internal arrangement of material parts—so an oak is different than a palm tree, a dog is different from a cat, and all are different from a human;[61] (2) its existence, since life is the being of living things, and the thing ceases to exist at death; and (3) its diverse powers to act, vegetative, and sensitive, and rational (where the higher powers are inclusive of the lower), which can only be done because the organism has the appropriately ordered body to carry out those functions.

The activities of an organism are, therefore, a second mode of unity given by the soul to living substances. Not only are the parts of the body united, but the diverse activities of a living being are united so as to be ordered to the perfection of the being's nature. Since action follows from being, these actions of a soul express the nature of the organism. Each plant

60 *ST* I.75.4.

61 Today, we might consider this physical pattern of an organism in terms of its genome, whose structure determines the overall development of the living body. But that genome is itself already an ordered body with certain activities, and so it too must be an effect of the soul as the form of the body.

and animal species has its own unique mode of acting such that it can be identified by the activity: apple trees grow apples and lions hunt antelopes. Since the soul is the source of these diverse powers, the first conclusion we can draw is that the soul is not identical to those powers to act.[62] There is a generative order: the soul causes the existence of the organism (first act), and so the organism has specific active powers (second act). These activities are manifested in the accidental changes—in quantity, quality, action—that reveal the nature of the substance as it develops and matures through life.

This distinction between existing (first act) and acting (second act) is of great consequence. In contrast to God, who is pure act, creatures are defined by potency. Thus, while creatures are given the act of existence in creation, that act is not perfect but is limited by potential; accordingly, it endows them with a dynamism to express their essence in activity and so to attain their final cause or perfection. In other words, created substances exist to engage in the activity characteristic of that particular nature.[63] Thus, there is a difference between the existence of a substance and its activity. Moreover, creatures have a multiplicity of powers—in human beings they include to grow, to eat, to run, to see, to think, to love[64]—all of which come from the soul, and so no one power can be identified with the entire potency of the soul. Thus, the soul makes the being what it is *and* it is the source of the actions. This may seem like an arcane point, but it is at the root of many controversies today, for there is a widespread tendency to identify the existence of a human being with one kind of *activity*. For example, many claim that a fetus is not human until it has brain waves or comatose persons are not truly human if they do not respond to stimuli. But this is confusing some arbitrarily chosen second act—rational or sensitive activity—for the presence of the soul by which a human being exists with those powers as *possibilities* to act. Since all the powers arise from the presence of the soul in a body, the only relevant criterion for determining whether someone is a human being is life, the reproduction of cells, or the ability to take in hydration and nutrition. When that is occurring, you know there must be

---

62 *ST* I.77.1.

63 *ST* I.105.5: "As the matter is for the sake of the form, so the form which is the first act, is for the sake of its operation, which is the second act; and thus operation is the end of the creature."

64 Since a human being is a complex union of body and rational soul, he has a greater diversity of powers than any other creature, including angels who, as pure spirits, lack the vegetative and sensitive powers of the body (*ST* I.77.2).

a soul present. Moreover, since there is only one soul, a living person must possess all the powers, including reason, even if he is not exercising them, or even able to exercise them, at a particular moment. The unicity of substantial form, where all the powers "flow from the essence of the soul, as from their principle,"[65] persuades us that a fetus and a comatose person are fully human because they *exist as* a human being. A substance is defined by its form as first act.

The powers of human nature follow from the human form, the rational soul. This includes the bodily powers of life, the vegetative powers to take in nutrition, grow, and reproduce; the sensitive powers; and the rational powers.[66] But because a human being is an integrated being, these lower activities are not for their own sake, but are ordered to a person's flourishing in terms of his intellectual powers.[67] In other words, eating and feeling are good for us as animals; but a human being exists to grow in wisdom and love, which (as we will see) fulfill the mind's capacity to know the highest truth and the will's capacity to love the highest good. For this reason, the lower powers—eating, reproduction, pleasure—should be controlled for the sake of our drive to grow in reason and love. Thus, we need to lead a disciplined life, restraining indulgence in sensual diversions in order to open ourselves to the fullness of being in all its exuberance.

Appetites That Motivate Action

Because these life activities are natural, organisms have an inherent inclination to perform them. Creatures do not need to force themselves to act; rather, they naturally tend to act for the sake of their flourishing. This natural tendency to act is referred to as the *appetite*. Thus, appetite—the inborn inclinations or tendencies to act—reflect the nature of the substance in question.[68] (This, again, simply restates the truth that action follows from being.)

Inclinations are of three kinds: natural, sensitive, and rational.[69] In substances lacking consciousness, there is a natural appetite, a tendency to act as

---

65 *ST* I.77.6.

66 *ST* I.78.2 and 3.

67 *ST* I-II.3.5. Aristotle argues that because reason is what sets us apart from other animals, it must be the purpose for our existence: *Nicomachean Ethics* I.7 (1097b23–1098a18) and X.7 (1177a12–19).

68 While the Latin word here is *appetitus*, I prefer to use *inclination*, since the English cognate *appetite* can be misleading if we restrict it to conscious desires alone.

69 *ST* I.80.1.

determined by the nature of the substance. Fire, by its nature, will always consume available fuel; this natural inclination is a universal activity of fire, and so it is one of its identifying properties. Similarly, a plant's foliage will grow toward sunlight naturally, so that it may flourish. Natural appetites are present in humans in a number of automatic biological activities, such as digestion or mitosis, which keep the body well and preserve life. As natural, though, these activities are normally subconscious and outside of our control.

More important tendencies to act arise from sensitive and rational powers. These are higher appetitive inclinations because they are elicited by awareness of an object as good or bad. That is, our awareness of an object brings with it a judgment of potential benefit or harm. Thus, consciousness of things is accompanied by appetitive reactions that direct our activity in the world: if we perceive something as good for us, we are inclined toward it and seek to possess it so that we might flourish; or, if the object is perceived as bad, we are repulsed by its potential harmfulness and strive to avoid it. These elicited reactions, though, operate somewhat differently in the sensitive and rational powers.

Sensation knows objects in terms of their particularity. As a result, the appetites the follow from sensation concern the suitability of that particular object for a human being inasmuch as he is an animal.[70] These reflect our biological needs and so are instinctive reactions to that object as good or bad for my bodily flourishing. What any animal finds good or bad will vary according to the species, reflecting the nature of the animal. For example, carnivores will not find fruit attractive, while elephants would not find hawks threatening. This is important, since the good of every being is determined by its nature, and the appetitive inclinations reflect this. But these instinctive reactions are directed by biological imperatives such as food, drink, sex, play, and sleep.[71]

The rational appetite is different. In contrast to sensation, rational cognition, or the intellect, knows immaterial universals. Thus, we know not just individual good things but the universal essence all good things have in common. Because a person is able to understand the nature of goodness, he can recognize all the different ways things are good. Consequently, the rational appetite is a desire elicited in response to the goodness of any being

70 *ST* I.78.1.

71 Plato explains that our sensitive appetites are primarily for food, drink, sex, and money, because money buys us food, drink, and sex (*Republic* IX 580e1–581a1). Human nature does not change.

whatsoever. This appreciation of the essence of goodness is very different from the instinctive judgment of the senses, for we are now able to grasp that which is *objectively good in itself* (good in being) as that which is most suitable to human nature, and not merely what is pleasing for us on the sensitive level (good in appearance).[72] Consequently, as rational, we must evaluate all perceived goods in light of this absolute notion of goodness to determine if something is really good for us as human beings. For example, when I see a cookie, I have an animal inclination to eat it *now* because it is sweet and my body craves sugars. However, the intellect considers goodness not just in terms of sweetness but also health. In this context, the attractiveness of the cookie is greatly reduced. This inclination to a universal good frees us from slavishly following instinctive reactions because we are able to judge the relative value of particular things.

This rational inclination to the universal good is known as the will.[73] There are two important points about the will that follow from its being the rational appetite. First, not only are we able to appreciate the goodness of all individuals, but we have an overriding inclination to a universal good. That is, we always act on a desire for a good that completely satisfies our desires as perfecting human nature in general. The name of this universal good is *happiness*. Thus, we always desire happiness in everything we do; all acts are done for the ultimate goal of happiness. But happiness, as the universal good most suitable for humans, must reflect our highest powers, the rational powers. Happiness, then, will not be found in satisfying the particular desires of our sense appetites but in perfecting the intellect and the will. That is, happiness will only be found in knowing all truths and loving the complete good.

The second important point about the will follows from this. Since the world is made up of finite creatures, no one thing in this world can fully satisfy the intellect's inclination for complete truth and the will's desire for universal goodness. (In the next chapter I argue that only God can do that.) Therefore, in this life, we have to compare the goods available to us and choose which one best leads me to that goal.[74] In other words, concomitant

---

72 *SCG* II.47 and 48.

73 *ST* I.82.1.

74 For example, if I am given too much change after a purchase, I am faced with two possible but contradictory goods: to keep the extra money, which is good for my survival, or to return the money in the interest of justice. While keeping the money is tempting, justice is a standard of objective good that fulfills rational desires.

with this inclination to the universal good is the fact of *free will*. While animal instincts determine a specific course of action, the inclination to happiness allows for many different actions and so entails freedom of choice.[75] This freedom follows from our knowledge of universals. Because animals only know particulars, they can only act in particular ways: when a bird builds a nest, it will do so based on instinct and so build a very particular kind of nest. By contrast, humans know universals and so can conceive of shelter in terms of the universal concept. We immediately grasp all the possibilities under that universal: an igloo, a tepee, a mansion, a houseboat, and everything in between. Because our actions arise not just with a particular sense perception but with a universal concept, we naturally are faced with choices as to which particular instance of a universal concept ought to be pursued. In other words, as a rational appetite about the universal good, the will is attracted to all these goods indifferently: they are all possible, and all are all partial goods that may contribute to happiness. But since my goal is happiness, I need to thoughtfully analyze these options to determine which is most fruitful for me. All choices bear significance.

Moreover, with free choice comes responsibility, for it is up to us to choose those particular acts that will be the best means to attain happiness. (This is, in fact, precisely what ethics is about, as we see in chapter 6.) While there are always little battles between the various appetites—wanting this and that simultaneously—the will, as the highest appetite, can override the lower appetites and direct us to act.[76] There is a unity of appetitive desire that follows from the unity of the soul. For this reason, a person is responsible for all his actions; no one is exonerated by claiming he could not control a desire.

We must, however, add a nuance to this idea of free will. Technically, the will is not free: the will *has to* desire the universal good, happiness. Appetites have a natural inclination to the good. As an appetite, the will is naturally inclined to the good and is repulsed by evil. As the *rational* appetite, the will necessarily desires the universal good, happiness, and so always acts for that end.[77] The idea of an utterly free will—the idea that a human being is not inclined to any particular good at all—would contradict the

75 *ST* I.83.1.

76 *ST* I-II.10.1.

77 *ST* I.82.1. Not all Christian thinkers agree here. Duns Scotus argues that freedom implies that the will is not oriented to the good by nature. This idea influences modernity by way of Immanuel Kant's idea of the will; we consider Kant's argument in the next chapter.

principle that all natures have a final cause. Moreover, this would also place human nature outside the order of providence, where God directs all creatures to their perfection. Because human nature is indeed a *nature*, it is ordered to a final cause, happiness; therefore, it is *not up to us to decide what makes us happy.*[78] Happiness is the perfection of human nature, and so the facts of human nature will determine the content of happiness (as we see in the next chapter). However, humans do have freedom of choice in deciding which particular appetites to act on, which specific goods to pursue, in order to attain happiness. It is in this choice of means that persons can express their individuality.

This notion of limited or qualified freedom is alien to both extremes in contemporary culture. On the one hand, materialists deny free will completely, since they believe that all action is determined by the laws of science. On the other hand, dualists separate the person from human nature and embrace an idea of unlimited freedom where a person determines the very meaning of life for himself.[79] In other words, modern philosophers err about human freedom by extremes of complete determinism and utter indeterminism. The truth is a mean: human freedom is, in the words of Yves Simon, a *superdeterminism*. By this he means that although we are determined to seek happiness, freedom arises from reason's knowledge of universals and the will's control over other powers that allows a man to have mastery over his diverse possibilities to act.[80] We all desire happiness, but we can achieve happiness in many ways and so exercise free choice in pursuing that end. The contemporary world's misinterpretation of freedom has far reaching significance, for both ethics and politics have come to accept that notion of freedom.

---

[78] The notion that freedom includes the ability to decide for oneself the very meaning of life has been called "expressive individualism." See Charles Taylor, *A Secular Age* (Cambridge, Mass.: The Belknap Press of Harvard University Press, 2007), 299–321, for an analysis of this post–World War II phenomenon that puts personal authenticity above all objective notions of the good.

[79] In this, the will is transformed from being a final cause ordering humans to happiness as their goal to being a brute efficient cause by which humans strive after inscrutable desires. This nihilism is prophetically announced by Nietzsche in *Thus Spake Zarathustra* (I.2–4), where he begins by rejecting happiness as the goal of life, and then rejects reason, virtue, justice, and pity as irrelevant to his own personal desires. In rejecting human nature, he reduces human nature to the level of a beast.

[80] Yves Simon, *Freedom of Choice*, ed. Peter Wolff (New York: Fordham University Press, 1969), 106–23.

Love

Because appetites are a natural attraction to the good, they can also be called love.[81] Love is a very misunderstood notion today. For Thomas, the most general idea of love is an appreciation of the goodness of an object.[82] That is, since the good is the end toward which creatures are drawn for the sake of perfecting their potential, love is the appreciation of that good that moves them to act for that activity seeks to unite the lover with the object of love as a means of perfecting its being.[83] But, as should be evident, since there are different kinds of appetites, there are different kinds of love. This is the source of the misunderstanding of love today: we fail to appreciate that love is an *analogical* term.

Since love arises from the knowledge of good object, sensitive love is very different from rational love. Sensitive love is an instinctive, animalistic desire for that which is pleasing *to the lover*. This is love as a passion or emotion. By contrast, rational love is an appreciation of that which is objectively good in itself because it is a perfected instance of its nature. While all animals have the emotional desires of sensitive love, only humans can have rational love.[84] Moreover, given the unicity of the substantial form, humans are called to order and integrate their emotional love by the higher love of reason. Because a human is a rational animal, human love will always have an emotional component; the challenge is to elevate it so that it is truly human and so *more* than merely emotional.

To illustrate the difference, though, let us consider them in isolation. With respect to relations with other persons, emotional love is a reaction to the attractiveness of the opposite sex; but rational love is an appreciation for the moral goodness of the person. Emotional love desires to possess the other for the lover's own benefit; it is primarily self-serving. Rational love wishes happiness for others for their own sake due to admiration for their goodness.[85] This is the love of friendship, where we the lover seeks happi-

---

81 *ST* I-II.26.1. Thomas notes that even natural appetites can be called *love* since in things without awareness, the apprehension of the good is in the "Author of their nature," God.

82 *ST* I-II.27.1. Love is, in fact, the first of the appetite's three actions: love, desire and joy (as described in the following section). This applies to both sensitive and rational appetite, and so accounts for the complex nature of desire in different substances (*ST* I-II.26.2).

83 *ST* I-II.28.1.ad 2.

84 Angels and God also have rational love but in an analogical fashion; see *ST* I.60 for angels and *ST* I.20 for God.

85 *ST* I-II.26.4. Note that I still seek the possession of a good that is perfective, but in friendship I desire that the other possess it for himself.

ness not for himself but for another out of love of that person. It should be obvious that marriage cannot be based only on a self-serving emotional love; rather, to be lasting, it must be a union of persons dedicated to mutual growth in virtue and happiness.[86]

Above these, of course, is the love of charity, love on the supernatural order (that is, above what human nature can do on its own). This is the gift from God that empowers us to appreciate the goodness of all persons as children of God—whether they be virtuous or not, friend or enemy.[87] For God's sake, I can love the unlovable: this love elevates us all. This is the perfection of love, for in charity I give myself completely to other people for love of God.

When society obliterates these analogical distinctions—as in the motto behind the movement for homosexual marriage, "Love is love"—it does violence to human nature and sacrifices the elevating love of virtue for the pursuit of wholly egoistic desires for self-satisfaction.

The Passions or Emotions

While our analysis of the soul has followed Aristotle's three levels of life, we cannot neglect Plato's tripartition of the soul into the cognitive, the affective (passions), and the appetitive. Thomas synthesizes the Platonic and Aristotelian triads by explaining the passions or emotions as attendant to the cognitive and appetitive powers.

The passions illustrate the centrality of hylomorphism to human nature, for passions arise due to the profound interdependence of the soul and the body. Because the soul is the form of the body, influence can flow in both directions.[88] When a change in the body causes some awareness in the soul, the result is a *corporal (or bodily) passion*. For example, if you tickle my foot, I feel pleasure; and if you cut my arm, I feel pain. The corporal passions are primarily these experiences of pleasure and pain.

More significant are the *animal passions*. These arise when an awareness in the soul (*anima*) causes a change in the body. For example, the sound of footsteps in a dark alley will cause your heartbeat to quicken. Or the smell of cookies can cause your mouth to water. These physiological changes are brought about by the passions, or emotions, that arise in the soul once we are aware of an object as good or bad. Our sensitivity to emotions is so great

---

86 *ST* Suppl. 42.4 and 49.3.

87 *ST* II-II.23.1 and 25.1.

88 *DV* 26.2.

that the good or evil need not happen to us: we can be made sad by hearing a child crying or our body can exhibit the greatest tension merely by watching a scary movie.

Since these passions are rooted in the union of body and soul, they are primarily understood as acts of the sensitive powers. They are reactions to the awareness of a particular object: if the object is good, it elicits a positive emotion, and if the object is bad, a negative one. Emotions are a crucial aspect of sensitive life, for emotional reactions to objects as threatening or enticing dispose the animal to act in a certain way and so help it survive.[89] Emotions reinforce instinctive judgments in order to heighten attention to the environment. Because emotions are part of sensitive awareness of the world, it is clear that animals share in having emotions. My dog is truly joyful when I get home, since I feed her. A squirrel really is scared when it sees a cat, since it knows it could well become the cat's prey.

Since emotions reflect our appetitive inclination to objects as good, the most basic emotion is love—an appreciation of the good as beneficial. From this natural appreciation of good things, Thomas develops a taxonomy of eleven primal emotions divided into two classes.[90] There are six *concupiscible passions*, which arise in reaction to objects that are simply good or simply bad. There are also five *irascible passions*, which arise in reaction to "arduous" goods, that is, objects in which good can be achieved only by overcoming an evil and so elicit more complex passional states.[91]

The concupiscible emotions are based on the threefold structure of the appetite: love, desire, joy. A perceived good elicits *love*, an appreciation of the object; if that good is needed, it elicits *desire*, the active pursuit of the good; and the attainment of that good elicits *joy*. For example, a donut will be appreciated ("That looks good!"); if I am hungry, I will strive to get it; and if I do eat it, I enjoy the goodness of the snack. More significant goods ought to elicit more intense loves, more ardent desire, and more exuberant joy.

The converse of all this is true for bad things. If I sense something harmful to me, I first *hate* it because I perceive it as evil. Then I want to avoid it, so I feel *aversion* or disgust. If that evil should befall me, I feel *sadness*. Thus, I hate being sick; I act so as to avoid it; but if I get sick, I am sad. Note that this hatred of evil is perfectly natural since evil is an impediment to my

89 *ST* I-II.22.1 and 2.
90 *ST* I-II.23.1 and 2.
91 *ST* I.81.2.

flourishing and attaining happiness. Indeed, if someone did not hate evil, he would be morally obtuse.

The irascible emotions deal with circumstances where attaining the good entails overcoming an evil, and so the passions are grouped in pairs based on whether one focuses on the good or bad, respectively. If there is a good goal, with some impediment blocking its attainment, this gives rise to *hope* (emphasizing the possibility of attaining the good) or *despair* (emphasizing the impediment that thwarts one's effort). For example, a person starts college with the hope of graduating but can fall into despair if the coursework appears too hard. If there is an impending evil, though, with a chance to evade it, this gives rise to *fear* (if you focus on the evil) or *boldness* or daring (if you focus on the chance to evade it). An upcoming exam in college might paralyze some students with fear, while others will be motivated to attack the material with vigorous study. (This is the "fight or flight" response, a feeling common to all animals.) Finally, if an evil befalls a person, and he no longer has any chance to evade it, he feels *anger*. Unlike sadness, though, anger looks forward to a restoration of the good in the future. If a student fails the exam and has to take the class over, he will be angry but will try to do better in class the next time.

Our hylomorphic nature makes the passions essential for life. As part of our nature, they augment our experience of the world because they make us keenly aware of goods and evils around us. As a result, feelings should never be simply ignored (as the Stoics and some dualists suggest) but neither should they be indulged (as Rousseau thought). Rather, they must be interpreted in light of rational judgments of truth. This is why emotions are important for the moral life in particular. Since the passions accompany sensations, they are immediate and powerful influences on our decisions about what goods to pursue. On the one hand, a strong fear can prevent us from helping someone in need; a strong lust can incite us to sin. On the other hand, hatred of an injustice or desire to achieve greatness change the world for the better. In the end, though, we are responsible for our emotions because, given the unicity of the substantial form, emotions can be subject to the control of reason. It is for this reason that a person is perfected by making his feelings accord with the true value of the object.[92]

There is also an analogical set of emotions, ones associated with the rational appetite. These are affective reactions to transcendent values appre-

---

92 *ST* I.81.3. This is the basis of moral virtue; we return to this in the next chapter.

ciated by the will as universal goods. This higher level of emotion does not manifest itself bodily, but it is more profound for our humanity. If you are sad, you cry; but contrition, a deeper spiritual reaction to evil, is not manifested in the body. An attractive person provokes desire, but a true friendship will provoke loyalty, a spiritual desire to maintain friendship. These are not properly called passions, since they are not tied to the body, but as a higher expression of affection we might refer to them as spiritual emotions.[93]

SIGNIFICANT IMPLICATIONS OF HUMAN NATURE

Thomas's presentation of the complexity of human nature demonstrates that the human soul is unique. This point is epitomized in the fact that the soul is *both* a form of the body and a thing in itself.[94] As a form, the soul is a co-principle with matter. As such, it is intimately united to the body, giving the body its substantial existence as an individual human as well as its vegetative and sensitive powers. However, the human soul also has intellectual powers. Because these powers are immaterial, they are not dependent on the body; consequently, the soul can exist without the body.[95] This ability to exist on its own makes the soul a thing as well as a form (a principle in union with the body). While animal souls are only forms and angels exist always without a body, the human soul is unique in being both.

The first crucial consequence of this is that, since the soul can exist without the body, the soul is immortal. The vegetative and sensitive powers can only function in a body; this is why the souls of plants and animals are mortal and cease to exist at death. But the intellect is immaterial, so when the human body dies, there is nothing to impede the continued existence and operation of the intellect.[96] In other words, the human soul is *by nature* immortal; it is not subject to corruption like material substances. Immortality, then, is a philosophical truth and not just a religious doctrine. What is religious or *supernatural* about immortality is the belief that the soul will

---

93 Thomas only mentions this in relation to angels (see *ST* I.59.4 and I-II.22.3.ad 3), but we can certainly ascribe them to humans also. For an analysis of this difference between transcendent and mundane affectivity, see Dietrich von Hildebrand, *The Heart: An Analysis of Human and Divine Affectivity*, ed. John Henry Crosby (South Bend, Ind.: St. Augustine's Press, 2007).

94 *DQDA* 1.

95 *ST* I.75.2.

96 *ST* I.75.6. This fact is reinforced by the intellect's drive to know the cause of all truth, which can only be attained in the Beatific Vision and so implies that, for a person to attain his end, the soul must be immortal (*ST* I-II.3.8).

participate in the Beatific Vision—direct knowledge of God's essence—that transcends the capacity of finite human reason and so can be attained only by a gift of grace.[97]

Nonetheless, this idea of immortality must be qualified by the fact of hylomorphism. Since the soul is the form of the body, its natural state is to be united to the body. Even if the soul *can* exist apart from the body, because of its rational powers, it retains the vegetative and sensitive power, even if they cannot be exercised. So, the soul in this condition, separated from the body, is incomplete. Indeed, if a person (the union of body and soul) is to attain complete happiness in the afterlife, this must include perfection of the body and not just of the intellect. Therefore, Thomas argues that there must be a resurrection of the body, where the soul is united to the body.[98] Personal afterlife cannot be a Cartesian mind without the body; rather, it must be the whole person who enjoys it. There are many Christians who, under the influence of modern philosophy, simply ignore the Creed and accept the philosophically untenable idea that a human being remains a purely immaterial being—that is, becomes an angel—after death. This is wrong, because it is the human being who is saved and it is the human being who enjoys the Beatific Vision.

This eternal destiny has implications for how human beings come to be in the first place. Biological reproduction—the union of the sperm and ovum to conceive a child—can adequately account for the material existence and bodily powers of that child. But there is no way a biological union can explain the existence of the immaterial powers of an immortal soul. Therefore, the only possible source for an immaterial immortal soul is God.[99] As a result, while animals merely reproduce—a purely biological function— humans *procreate*: the conjugal union provides the occasion for God acting in the creation of a human being with both material and immaterial powers.

This direct activity of God in the creation of each person indicates another important truth. The soul is created by God directly for that particular body. For this reason, we can say that form and matter are commen-

---

97 *ST* I-II.5.3 and 5.

98 *CT* I.151–60. Resurrection is not resuscitation—revival of a body that had died. Rather, resurrection is a miraculous transformation of matter so that it is no longer a principle of potency and so no longer subject to corruption. As such, a resurrected body will not be subject to physical laws as we know them, as is evidenced by the appearances of Christ recorded in the New Testament.

99 *ST* I.90.2.

surated—perfectly appropriate—to each other, for it is the individual as a union of soul and body, with all the particular accidents, that God brings into being.[100] Since the soul is the principle of actuality for a body, it is incoherent to say that a soul does not belong in a certain body.

This has implications for our understanding of sexuality. Since men and women belong to the same species, sex must be seen as an accidental difference.[101] But, unlike things like color that arise simply from the material elements in the body, sex arises from the soul. This is obvious because the soul causes the physical structure and powers of a body, and the reproductive organs and powers of men and women are clearly different.[102] The soul, then, must be of a particular sex in order to cause this distinction of the sexes.[103] These accidental sexual differences between men and women are complementary, since reproduction is possible only in the union of the two. (Indeed, reproduction is the *only* biological act that requires union with another person to complete.) The complementarity of the sexes extends to emotional differences (which, as affected by hormones, also manifest the bodily differences caused by different souls) that enable the human race to experience reality, to know and love, more perfectly than if there were only one sex. This complementarity also demonstrates the undeniable fact that sex is binary; there can be no alternate genders.[104] It must be noted, too, that because the intellect is immaterial and not directly determined by the body, the sexes are fundamentally equal with respect to rationality; as a consequence, as persons they are fundamentally equal despite the obvious differences between them.[105]

This equality extends to all individuals who possess human nature. For this reason, all persons possess *human dignity*. This dignity arises from a person's rational form, the same first act which endows all humans with equal powers. Differences among humans are accidental—size, color, loca-

---

100 *SCG* II.80–81.7. See also *ST* I.45.4, *SCG* II.68.3, and *DQDA* 1.ad 1.

101 *OBE* c. 6.

102 The gendered nature of the human soul is so profound that persons will retain their sex even after the resurrection of the body when it is not needed for procreation (*ST* Suppl. 81.3).

103 On this, see Jacques Maritain, "Let Us Make for Him a Helpmate Like to Himself," in *Untrammeled Approaches*, trans. Bernard Doering (Notre Dame, Ind.: University of Notre Dame Press, 1997), 150–64; and John Finley, "The Metaphysics of Gender: A Thomistic Approach," *The Thomist* 79, no. 4 (2015): 585–614.

104 Thomas comments that as numbers are necessarily either odd or even, so animals are either male or female; there is no third possibility (*CM* X.11.2128).

105 *ST* I.92.3.

tion, action. Accidental differences are real, and some, like moral quality, are critical. Yet these accidental differences are secondary to the fundamental equality that unites all people; as the Roman poet Terence famously said, "I am human, and so nothing human is alien to me." The human condition is experienced by all people, so to focus on accidental identities (like sex, race, nationality, class) is to repudiate the primacy of human nature.

This fundamental unity and common dignity of human nature is recognized when we refer to human individuals as *persons*. Persons are worthy of dignity because of all substances they are the "most perfect in all nature— that is, a subsistent individual of a rational nature."[106] This perfection is manifested in the fact that persons have the capacity for *dominion* over their actions.[107] That is, while animals act merely by instinct, people do not. Our rational powers allow us to know reality as it is in itself and to direct our love to that which is most noble. We therefore can control our actions, and so we are responsible for them. Furthermore, this self-control means that each person has the ability to develop himself in a truly unique way. Persons are not simply acting out their nature; rather they have an active role in shaping their identity by the choices they make. For this reason, each person is unique and irreplaceable.

That irreplaceability is confirmed in the immortality of the soul. Animals attain a semblance of immortality by keeping the species alive, so no animal is an end in itself. Human persons, in contrast, as immortal can be said to each have an end in himself, giving people a greater significance than any other animal.

This emphasis on the uniqueness of persons brings us back to the crucial fact that personhood is grounded in human nature. Although persons are free and can exercise autonomy in shaping individuality, this freedom does not give people a blank check to do as they wish. On the contrary, actions should always reflect the good as determined by human nature. In light of this, we need to nuance our idea of human dignity. Dignity is due to us all by reason of our rational nature: our intellect and free will. Yet reason is a power that seeks realization in second act. Thus, the fullness of dignity lies not in mere the fact that humans have freedom but rather in disposing that freedom to the benefit of truth and goodness. Reason allows us to evaluate our actions in light of the objective standards of truth and

---

106 *ST* I.29.3.

107 *ST* I.29.1: persons are "not only made to act, like others; but . . . can act of themselves."

goodness.[108] Human dignity, therefore, is manifested when a person perfects himself in reason by evaluating feelings, desires, and actions in light of the truth. We each must exercise this this personal responsibility if we are to be fully human. As a consequence, a person can repudiate his human dignity when he fails to critically evaluate his desires and actions in light of the truth. As long as a person tries to fulfill the potential of human nature, he has dignity, no matter how others might treat him.[109]

PERSONALISM

The capacity of persons to direct their own development calls for further consideration. The ability to act not by instinct but by free choice means that each person is radically unique and unrepeatable.[110] But this uniqueness is hard to analyze in terms of traditional Thomistic metaphysics, which focuses on human nature as a universal species. In order to grasp the uniqueness of each person, Karol Wojtyła realized we need to augment metaphysics with a different method, that of *phenomenology*.

Phenomenology is a method developed by Edmund Husserl (1859–1938) to overcome the skepticism and reductionism of modern philosophy. The central insight of phenomenology is *intentionality*, or the fact that our consciousness is always consciousness *of* an object.[111] That is, because an object reveals itself to us in our consciousness, by examining our consciousness of the object we can uncover the reality of the thing itself.[112] Since we can pay attention to things in different ways, the way of attending is a crucial

108 *ST* I.87.1. Thomas emphasizes that knowledge of the self falls under the rule that something is knowable inasmuch as it is in act. That is, we come to know ourselves only after we act in the world and then reflect on those actions. In this way, our actions should always be assessed in terms of what we know as being truly good. Unlike Descartes's *cogito*, there is no immediate intuition of the mind before our interface with the world. It also follows that it is impossible to doubt the existence of the world, since acting in the world is a condition for knowing the self.

109 The fact that suffering evil does not imply a loss of dignity, while doing evil does, is argued by Socrates (*Gorgias* 469c1–2). Cf. Mt. 5:11.

110 *ST* I.30.4.

111 Phenomenology is difficult to summarize, but see Robert Sokolowski, *Introduction to Phenomenology* (Cambridge: Cambridge University Press, 2000).

112 Husserl, in *Ideas: General Introduction to Pure Phenomenology*, trans. W.R. Boyce Gibson (London: George Allen and Unwin, 1931), sec. 24, says: "No theory we can conceive can mislead us in regard to the principle of all principles: that every primordial given [*dator*] intuition is a source of authority for knowledge, that whatever presents itself in 'intuition' in primordial form is simply to be accepted as it gives itself out to be, though only within the limits in which it then presents itself."

constituent of our experience of the thing. For example, a rose is looked at in different ways by a botanist, an artist, and a young lover; each one's experience reveals something else about the rose. Thus, a methodical analysis of the ways in which an object appears to our consciousness can reveal the reality of the object in its fullness. The phenomenological method, then, is antiskeptical because it gets us to the things themselves, and it is antireductionist because it can help to reveal the world in all its complexity.[113] For this reason, phenomenology became—and remains to this day—a popular method for many Catholic thinkers eager to combat the tide of atheistic scientism.

Wojtyła realized that the phenomenological method is best used not in describing objects in the world (for that is best done by Thomistic metaphysics) but in revealing the unique reality of a person to himself. For this reason, it must be done by each person for himself; my first-person narration is meant to illustrate this. Correcting the excesses of dualism, I begin by realizing I am not simply my consciousness, but consciousness is only one part of the complex whole that makes up the totality of me as a person. Consciousness is important, though, because it is the mirror by which I am able to reflect on all my experiences to know my self-identity—the unique person I have chosen to become. Reflecting on my consciousness, I understand that some of my experiences are things that *happen to me*: my sensations and feelings are reactions to things in the world. These are the somatic and psychic elements of my being; they are the natural actions of a hylomorphic human being in a material world. Therefore, these reactions reflect the human nature we all share and so do not make me unique. However, I also recognize that there are other actions that are not merely reactions based on human nature; rather, these actions come to be solely because I have willed to do them. It is through these acts, things I freely choose to do, that I determine the kind of person I am going to be and make myself unique among all human persons.[114]

Personal actions, therefore, transcend biological and emotional reactions because in them I have control of myself and can dispose myself to

---

113 Writing from Germany in the 1930s, Husserl acidly quipped that "merely fact-minded sciences make for merely fact-minded people" (*The Crisis of European Sciences and Transcendental Phenomenology*, pt. 1, sec. 2).

114 Hence the title of his major, but difficult, work, *The Acting Person*, ed. Anna-Teresa Tymieniecka and trans. Andrzej Potocki (Dordrecht: D. Reidel, 1979). For a briefer recapitulation of its main themes, see "The Person: Subject and Community" in *Person and Community: Selected Essays*, trans. Theresa Sandok (New York: Peter Lang, 1993), 219–61.

act as I choose. Wojtyła argues that the goal of a person is to be consciously aware of all these things that happen to me and actions I will, and to exercise self-determination in order to integrate them into a coherent personality ordered to the transcendent goods of reason and love. (Failing to do this, to allow myself to be controlled by bodily or emotional reactions, is literally a disintegration of the self, since I am not in control of those human reactions, and so it undermines my personal unity.) This ability to transcend the natural in favor of a spiritual goal manifests its highest ability when I surrender self-determination to another to form a "we," a community by which a common good is pursued.[115] This spiritual union with other persons expands my personhood and frees me from being controlled by what happens to me by exposing me to the totality of truth and goodness as contained in the experience of others.

This last phenomenological reflection on human experience brings us back to Thomas's idea of human nature as a rational animal. Reason as a cognitive power (the intellect) seeks to know the truth; as an appetitive power (the will), it is inclined to love the highest good. A person, therefore, is perfected by attaining wisdom and love. This fact discloses a person's radical potentiality in the face of being. Truth is achieved when the mind receives the *essence* of things. The good is achieved by possessing the very *existence* of objects and actions that perfect human nature.[116] In both cases, people need to be open to reality, to being as essence and existence, if they are to realize the perfection for which they exist.

This orientation to wisdom and love brings out one last truth about human nature: people are social. Wisdom and love are possible only in communion with other people. Human freedom properly disposes us not to selfish actions but to cooperative activities by which persons are mutually perfected. Openness to being must first be an openness to other persons, where friendship lifts people out of their isolation into spiritual intercourse. This truth is foundational for both ethics and political philosophy.

---

115 This is a good example of how phenomenology augments metaphysics. From the third-person perspective of metaphysics, it is impossible to determine if a person has really surrendered their autonomy to another for the sake of a common good. Only in analyzing our own consciousness can this be revealed. Both a chain gang and a symphony work side-by-side, but only the symphony can be said to be working together for a common good. The significance of this for personal relations, especially marriage, is best illustrated in Wojtyła's *Love and Responsibility*, trans. H. T. Willetts (San Francisco: Ignatius Press, 1981).

116 *DV* 21.1. There is an order here, reflecting the transcendentals. First, other things exist (being); then we come to know them (truth); and then we desire them (good; *ST* 16.4.ad 2).

There is, however, one way in which love's pursuit of the good is different from the mind's openness to truth. The intellect *receives* the essences of existent things, so we cannot choose what is true. The will, though, seeks to possess the existence of things, and so it must *act* to attain them. But this decision to act always opens up possibilities: I am free to pursue one good or another but not both (simultaneously). Therefore, I have to judge which good is best. This choice of the good to be pursued is the subject of ethics, to which we now turn.

FURTHER READING

Adler, Mortimer. *The Difference of Man and the Difference It Makes*. New York: Holt, Rinehart, and Winston, 1967; reprint, New York: Fordham University Press, 1993.

Clarke, W. Norris. *Person and Being*. Milwaukee: Marquette University Press, 1993.

Klubertanz, George P. *The Philosophy of Human Nature*. New York: Appleton-Century-Crofts, 1953.

Kupczak, Jarosław. *Destined for Liberty: The Human Person in the Philosophy of Karol Wojtyła / Pope John Paul II*. Washington, D.C.: The Catholic University of America Press, 2000.

Lee, Patrick, and Robert P. George. *Body-Self Dualism in Contemporary Ethics and Politics*. Cambridge: Cambridge University Press, 2008.

Maritain, Jacques. *The Person and the Common Good*. Translated by John J. Fitzgerald. Notre Dame, Ind.: University of Notre Dame Press, 1966.

Miner, Robert. *Thomas Aquinas on the Passions*. Cambridge: Cambridge University Press, 2009.

Rist, John. *What Is a Person? Realities, Constructs, Illusions*. Cambridge: Cambridge University Press, 2020.

Spaemann, Robert. *Persons: The Difference between "Someone" and "Something."* Translated by Oliver O'Donovan. Oxford: Oxford University Press, 2007.

Taylor, Charles. *Sources of the Self: The Making of Modern Identity*. Cambridge, Mass.: Harvard University Press, 1989.

Part II

What Ought to Be

Chapter Six

That Which All Desire: Goodness as the Principle of Human Acts

THE PROBLEM: WHAT MUST I DO?

Human beings are moved to act by an appetite to possess some good. The object is seen as being good because in coming to possess the very existence of the object—in making its being part of our own being—we perfect the potentialities of human nature. If I smell cookies, my hunger is aroused and I will eat for the sake of the pleasure and the nutrition I gain by making the goodness of the cookie my own. If someone asks me to volunteer at the parish, I agree because in making the charitable action my own I become a more charitable person. Thus, *acts exist for the sake of the good*; all substances move into activity in order to attain some perfection. This is the most fundamental explanation for the dynamism of the universe: the good is the sufficient reason for why substances are active, why there is second act at all.[1] Here again, we see that the primary terms must be understood in terms of being.

The one problem we face, though, is that, since we cannot do all the good acts we desire to—I cannot eat and pray and read and exercise simultaneously—we need to *choose* which good we will pursue at particular moment. To do this, though, we must have some basis for assessing these actions; we need some criterion by which to determine which action would

---

1 For this reason, Thomas identifies truth primarily with the stability of first act, while good is identified primarily with the dynamism as substances move into second act. See *DV* 1.10.ad 3 (contrary difficulties): "There are two kinds of perfection, first and second. . . . The note of truth in things results from first perfection; for it is because a thing has a form that it imitates the art of the divine intellect and produces knowledge of itself in the soul. But the note of goodness in things results from its second perfection, for this goodness arises from the end." However, since both the true and the good are convertible with being, they are convertible with one another. Good is true, because second act completes first act; and true is good, since first act is always desirable; see *ST* I.82.4.ad 1.

be best for us as humans to pursue. This criterion for evaluating actions is our definition of the good.

The search for a universal definition of goodness as a standard for human action is the subject of ethics.[2] In order to appreciate the philosophical nature of ethics, it is helpful to contrast it with morality. Morality is a personal code of conduct that guides a person's behavior. Ethics is the rational study of those codes of conduct. The obvious question is this: if personal behavior is guided by morality, why do we even need ethics? Why isn't morality enough?

The answer is that people's codes of morality fundamentally differ. Some people know that abortion is intrinsically evil, while others believe it can be justified as a right. This disagreement is a problem, both speculatively and practically. Speculatively, it violates the principle of noncontradiction, since it would mean that the same act is good and bad simultaneously, which is metaphysically impossible. Therefore, if the ideas of "good" and "evil" are to be meaningful, we need to assess the claims of personal morality and to subject them to the tests of rational coherence. More importantly, the practical problems arising from moral disagreements can tear a society apart. To let each person follow his own morality is to allow society to degenerate into chaos. It is clear we need to correct inadequate personal moralities and convince people of the true concept of goodness. Personal morality alone will not suffice.

Ethics applies philosophical principles to resolve these problems. It rationally analyzes codes of conduct in order to determine which ones are speculatively coherent and practically adequate for human needs. The aim is to discover which moral code is the best. But this is not without controversy: if thinkers define the good—the ultimate criterion for evaluating actions—in different ways, disagreement will persist. In fact, if we fail to discover a shared definition of the good, it will appear that moral differences are utterly irresolvable, since people will be literally talking past one another.[3]

---

2 Ethics has two branches. *Meta-ethics* is the attempt to provide a definition for the good as a criterion for action; *normative ethics* then applies that criterion to specific acts to determine whether they are good or bad. To debate about particular actions in the absence of an agreed-upon definition of the good is utterly pointless—a fact illustrated by interminable moral debates in our own society. I therefore concentrate on meta-ethics in this chapter.

3 See Alasdair MacIntyre's striking parable "A Disquieting Suggestion," in *After Virtue*, 1–5. MacIntyre develops his incisive analysis of this problem throughout his career.

The reason the debate would become irresolvable is because the good is understood to be the first principle for practical reasoning.[4] This means that our notion of the good is the ultimate, self-evident justification for everything we do.[5] For example, while we might justify exercising because it leads to health, and health is justified because it leads to happiness, if someone asks why we want to be happy, all we can say it, "It is good!" This is a sort of trump card, since to ask why anyone would want the good is an irrational statement. Attaining the good, then, is the ultimate goal that motivates all intermediate actions; accordingly, the good is the criterion by which we assess those actions as worthy of pursuit or not.[6] Given this, it is obvious that the way in which one defines the good is crucial. Seen in this light, moral disagreement in our society is not so much about the particular actions as about the divergent ideas of the good that lead people to opposing conclusions about which particular actions are *worthy* of pursuit.

This pursuit of a universal definition for the good highlights the difference between the social sciences like cultural anthropology or sociology and ethics. Cultural anthropology describes how people behave; but it has no standard about how they ought to behave. Ethics, in contrast, in discerning standards of goodness, prescribes how people ought to behave, regardless of whether anyone actually does so. Therefore, the social sciences should never be thought of as establishing norms for acting. The best they can do is to state that people have behaved in certain ways; they are never justified in suggesting that we ought to act similarly.

A new problem arises, though. If we cannot define the good by observing what people do, how do we discover it? Here is a notable difference between speculative reason, which discovers the universal principles of being by induction, and practical reason, which cannot use induction from experience since the definition of the good is supposed to guide action and

---

4 *ST* I-II.90.2. Practical reason is knowledge used for the sake of doing or making; it is builds on speculative reason, which, as in science and metaphysics, is knowing simply for the sake of the knowledge itself. Because action follows from being, knowing what something is speculatively determines how action should follow. As Thomas succinctly notes, the "speculative intellect by extension becomes practical" (*ST* I.79.11.sc).

5 Just as our understanding of being informs how we view reality in speculative reason, so how we understand the good motivates all our actions. For this reason, goodness holds the same place in practical reason as being does in speculative reason (*ST* I-II.94.2). More succinctly put, in practical matters the first principle is the final end, since the ultimate goal—to attain the good—is what guides our analysis and choice (*ST* I.82.1 and I-II.90.2).

6 *ST* I-II.1.6.

so must precede our experience of the moral act.[7] Nevertheless, we know that if the good is real, it is a mode of being. Therefore, we can rely on the principles of being to help understand the good. We have seen that definitions reflect the necessary causes that give rise to the being; these causes inform the thing that exists. Since the reality analyzed in ethics is human action in pursuit of the good, we need to consider the specific causes that motivate that activity and cause the human action to come into being in the first place. These principles of human action will grasp the good in diverse ways and move us to act in pursuit of different ends.

Consequently, we observe that, in general, human action arises for two reasons: either we *want* to do something or we *think we should* do something. This common-sense reflection echoes what we have already seen: human nature has both appetites and reason. Some philosophers take appetite (desire, sentiment, feeling) as the basis for action, and so will define the good in terms of the satisfaction of appetite, which can be identified with pleasure or happiness. Other philosophers downplay appetite and emphasize the importance of reason in determining action, and so will define the good in terms of fulfilling rational duties, especially a duty to law. These, however, are reductive approaches, because they set what people want (happiness) in opposition to what people ought to do (fulfill the moral law). The truth, however, is that, since human acts arise out of both reason and appetite, the best definition of the good must lie in attaining happiness by fulfilling the law. This is the heart of Thomas's theory of natural law.

As is evident from the preceding argument, ethical theories, in defining the human good, always have an implicit reliance on a theory of human nature. As ideas of human nature vary—emphasizing animal desires or abstract reason—so will the idea of the good vary. Theories of human nature, in turn, depend on epistemological and metaphysical assumptions: the focus on desires reflects empiricism and materialism; the focus on reason reflects rationalism and dualism. Thus, assessing ethical theories often leads one to a consideration of other aspects of philosophy in light of their adequacy in explaining humankind's experience the fullness of life. While ethical debates are most prominent in our society, the more fundamental points of conflict will often be in those other areas of philosophy.

---

7 Philosophers representing the whole spectrum of ethical theory agree and explicitly note this fact early in their arguments. See Aristotle, *Nicomachean Ethics* I.4 (1095a30–b5); Aquinas, *ST* I.1.8; Kant, *Grounding for the Metaphysics of Morals*, preface, 390; and Mill, *Utilitarianism*, chap. 1.

Religious Ethics

Some Christians might believe that all this philosophical argument is unnecessary because the true principles of morality are revealed in the Bible. In one way this faith-based ethics is indeed the most adequate ethics; however, in another way, it is simultaneously the least adequate approach to ethics. It is the most adequate because it is based on God's own word and therefore infallible; yet it is the least adequate because that truth is accessible only to those who have faith. Because of this need for faith, biblical ethics is simply not persuasive to people who do not accept revelation. Yet it is often these people whom we most urgently need to engage in our society.

Nevertheless, we must remember that the truths of faith never contradict the truths of reason. The God who reveals himself in Scripture is the same God who creates human nature and the natural law. For this reason, the moral truths of the Bible can also be demonstrated according to a rational understanding of the good. Indeed, it is important to see that morality is a fact concerning all human beings, not only Christians. In fact, Thomas argues that, because moral truth is knowable by reason, it is included in revelation only to persuade those who have difficulty accepting the guidance of reason.[8]

An important fact about religious ethics follows from this. Many people believe the moral law as stated in the Ten Commandments to be a set of arbitrary rules that God imposes on believers to test their fidelity. This position is known as *divine voluntarism*, since it asserts that the moral law arises from the arbitrary will (*voluntas*) of God. But this is a highly problematic theory, since it ignores the fact that natures have a final cause—the goal of their existence, or the good—that follows from their forms. For a metaphysical realist, the moral laws cannot be added to creation by God, because from the moment of creation there is already a final cause that is the standard of goodness for each nature built into nature itself.

A deeper problem is that voluntarism would vitiate the good as a philosophical concept. Plato first pointed this out in the *Euthyphro*. He poses the problem this way: Is something good because it is loved by the gods or is it loved by the gods because it is good?[9] The former would condemn goodness to being based on arbitrary desire and make all moral theories

---

8 *ST* I.1.1.

9 *Euthyphro* 5d–10e; I paraphrase, since Plato's specific topic is piety.

relativistic (even when based on the arbitrary will of God, for God could always change his mind).[10] The latter, though, sees the good as a standard grounded in nature that elicits desire because it is good. In that case, good is an objective reality whose truth can be used to judge the correctness of our desires and actions.

Plato's logic can be applied to the Ten Commandments: murder is not wrong because God prohibited it; rather, God prohibited it because it is wrong in itself. There is a moral order built into creation; that order is the natural law. God's commandments are simply reminders of what we ought to have learned from reason about what is good and evil.[11] This is why Christians should not hesitate to engage in moral debates, but they ought to do so on the basis of reason. While secularists are sometimes quick to dismiss points of view they deem to be "religious," they have to accept the force of reason when they are faced with rational arguments for human goodness.[12]

The Challenge of Relativism

Divine voluntarism is not the only form of relativism. In fact, relativism is a widely accepted approach to moral questions, in spite of the fact that it is utterly inadequate. Moral relativism (parallel to epistemological relativism's notion of truth) holds that each person defines the good for himself, so that the good is relative to one's perspective on the issue. Moral relativism is most evident in those people who reduce ethics to a matter of opinion and who try to shut down an argument by saying, "That's your definition of the good, not mine." Under the guise of the need for "tolerance," relativism has gotten a foothold in our society. The truth of the matter, though, is that to prohibit the recognition of objective good leads

10 This is evidenced in the moral theory of William Ockham, who argued that God could make it morally good to murder and even to hate God. This position, though, is a consequence of his nominalism, since, if there is no order in nature, then anything can be made good or bad by God's command.

11 The Bible itself attests to this, for Cain is punished for murder long before the Decalogue is revealed. This only makes sense if the moral rules are in force already.

12 The extent to which some secularists will go to avoid engaging reason in ethics is surprising. For example, Steven Pinker has argued in "The Stupidity of Dignity," *The New Republic,* May 28, 2008, that bioethics should repudiate the concept of human dignity because it is a religious idea, in proof of which he cites the fact that the word appears more than a hundred times in the Catechism!

13 In his last homily before being elected Pope Benedict XVI (April 18, 2005).

us, in the words of Joseph Ratzinger, into a "dictatorship of relativism."[13] Relativism prevents people from enforcing a common good and so enslaves everyone to the capricious urges that will frustrate the community's search for excellence.

It can be argued that Western philosophy reached maturity in the endeavor to refute moral relativism, for it is precisely this that roused Socrates to oppose the sophists. The sophists, presented with the fact of moral disagreement between peoples, conclude that moral beliefs are simply a matter of custom (*nomos*).[14] As customary, these value judgments are ultimately an arbitrary assertion of the will of the people, reflecting whatever they desire at the time. Since they are arbitrary, moral values are susceptible to continual revision in order to accord with mercurial public opinion.[15] Such relativism would be destructive of every significant human endeavor, for what is noble and worthy in one generation could become the object of disdain in the next. Collective wisdom becomes impossible.

In response to this, Socrates argues that moral truths are not mere conventions but are a matter of nature (*physis*). Because moral truths are grounded in nature, they are objective, unchanging realities that can be discovered by reason. This gives moral values true significance, since now they are the standards that guide our will in decision making instead of reflecting the will's arbitrary tastes.[16]

Despite the cogency of Socrates's position, relativism has reemerged in the past two centuries. The most notable example is the thought of Friedrich Nietzsche (1844–1900). Nietzsche's philosophy is motivated by his antagonism toward Plato and Christ, both of whom subordinate human desires

---

14 See, for example, Thrasymachos's position that the good is determined by those in power in order to maintain themselves in power (*Republic* I, 338c).

15 Here is the significance of the Tree of Knowledge in the Garden of Eden (Gn 3:5): the primary temptation for us is always to make ourselves into God by believing we have the power to determine what is good and what is bad, instead of accepting reality as God created it.

16 This distinction between custom and nature is the best framework for understanding the debate about so-called homosexual marriage. Realists understand that marriage is grounded on the natural distinction of the sexes as ordered to the procreation of children. Relativists argue that the definition of marriage is arbitrary and can be changed by the will of the people. But if this is true, marriage can be redefined in any way whatsoever and so cannot be a meaningful institution in itself. Thus, homosexual marriage is possible only if we first make marriage itself meaningless. This objection to homosexual marriage is not primarily religious; marriage is a natural institution before it is a sacrament (*ST* Suppl. 41.1). The sacramentalization of it reflects both its natural importance and the need for grace to elevate the participants of marriage to a higher state of unity based on charity (*ST* Suppl. 42.1 and 49.2).

to a transcendent world of value. Nietzsche rejects this with his proclamation of the "Death of God."[17] His intention is not simply atheistic; rather, his goal is to "erase the horizon" of all values, eliminating all moral frameworks, thereby freeing people to create values for themselves. In contrast to the traditional morality of "slaves" who obey moral laws, Nietzsche's morality encourages the noble person—the Overman—to create values, resulting in a transvaluation of values.[18] Nietzsche's influence on both philosophy and culture has been enormous. In particular, he is recognized by supporters and critics alike for the prophetic nature of his moral relativism: the twentieth century's rejection of God and morality led to death and destruction on an unprecedented scale.

Incredibly, even after the Nietzschean inspired horrors of the World Wars, many philosophers espoused another form of relativism called "emotivism."[19] Inspired by a scientism derived from Hume's fork, emotivism assumes that statements are meaningful only if they are empirically provable. While terms like *blue* or *tall* or *hot* can be empirically verified the word *good* does not appear to indicate anything real. They conclude that *good* and *bad* are merely expressions of the speaker's emotional reaction to something. To call something *good* is to say, "That pleases me, I like that;" to call something *bad* is to say, "I do not like that." As purely emotional reactions, these moral judgments are subjective and unarguable. Whatever is good or bad remains private and relative to one's inscrutable feelings.

The problems with relativism—in any of these, or other, incarnations—are abundant. First, relativism cannot accomplish the goal of ethics as a science. Ethics is the study of morality in order to determine the definition of the good; but relativism refuses to define the good. It is therefore simply incoherent as a theory, for it refuses to do what the science itself demands.

Relativism is also counterintuitive, for it refuses to acknowledge our natural use of the concept of goodness. The notion of the good is necessarily used as a standard, a measure by which we evaluate our actions and the actions of our society. If relativism were true, the good would always simply conform to the desires of the one measuring and so could not act as a measure for evaluating those desires. For ethics to be meaningful, there must be

---

17 Most famously in *The Gay Science*, section 125, and *Thus Spake Zarathustra*, I.2.

18 Friedrich Nietzsche, *The Genealogy of Morals*, I.4–13.

19 The most noted exponents of this were C. L. Stevenson and A. J. Ayer. A powerful response is offered by C. S. Lewis in the first chapter of *The Abolition of Man*.

a discernible distinction between what one does and what one ought to do. Without this independence of the good as the standard of what one ought to do, ethics as a branch of philosophy cannot exist.

Even more obvious are the practical problems with relativism, which shows that it runs contrary to the universal experience of human beings. If there are no objective moral standards, relativists can never criticize another's behavior nor can they blame another for doing wrong, nor can they ever act to make a situation better.[20] Relativism would force us to accept even the greatest evils, since there would be no "evil" to object to. In the end, this makes human action unintelligible since there is no way to distinguish good and evil actions: every action is equally appropriate for human beings and so there is no reason to choose one as opposed to its opposite. Relativism must be rejected as an inadequate philosophy, because denying the reality of truth and goodness is not a philosophical position at all.

REDUCTIVE EXTREMES
David Hume and the Fact-Value Dichotomy

The greatest challenge to ethics apart from relativism is the presumption that the good is not a part of being, that it is not an objective aspect of reality. If our idea of good does not reflect being, it must instead be derived entirely from human value judgments. In other words, if the good is not a part of the metaphysical order of nature, then it is in some way constructed by people in order to make sense of human experience. The methods adopted for constructing an anthropocentric idea of good will tend to be reductive and so obscure the fullness of the reality of goodness. While these ethical theories will grasp one aspect of the good, they will fail to be adequate theories because of their reductive and limited idea of goodness.

This antimetaphysical assumption, common to most modern moral theories, finds its origin in David Hume's fact-value dichotomy. Because later ethical theories often assume this as the only viable starting point for practical reasoning, Hume's argument is enormously influential. His point is outlined in this famous paragraph:

> In every system of morality, which I have hitherto met with, I have always remarked, that the author proceeds for some time in the ordinary way of

---

20 For a critique of relativism, see Francis Beckwith and Gregory Koukl, *Relativism: Feet Firmly Planted in Mid-air* (Grand Rapids, Mich.: Baker Books, 1998).

reasoning, and establishes the being of a God, or makes observations concerning human affairs; when of a sudden I am surprised to find, that instead of the usual copulations of propositions *is*, and *is not*, I meet with no proposition that is not connected with an *ought*, or an *ought not*. This change is imperceptible; but is, however, of the last consequence. For as this *ought*, or *ought not*, expresses some new relation or affirmation, it is necessary that it should be observed and explained; and at the same time that a reason should be given, for what seems altogether inconceivable, how this new relation can be a deduction from others, which are entirely different from it.[21]

The logical point of the argument is that if there is no "ought" statement in a premise, you cannot have an "ought" statement in the conclusion. This has implications for ethics, for Hume argues that factual statements about what something is in no way inform what actions ought to follow. For Hume, ought statements arise not from a rational understanding of nature, but instead arise solely from desire which drives us to act.

Let us say, for example, that there is a donut on a table. Four people enter the room, and all agree with the fact that there is a donut on a table. But what should we do? The actions will vary by what each person desires. One person is hungry, so he is apt to eat it; another person is altruistic and says it should be evenly divided; a third person is a fitness freak, and he wants to safely dispose of it; a fourth person is a conspiracy enthusiast, and he wants to report it as a suspicious trap. All four affirm the same fact; the difference arises because their desires suggest different actions.

If desire alone determines action, the good will be defined wholly in terms of the satisfaction of desire. Since desire is satisfied in pleasure, Hume identifies ethical goodness with pleasure: "All morality depends upon our sentiments; and when any action, or quality of the mind, pleases us after a certain manner, we say it is virtuous."[22] Because the good is defined by desire, reason is relegated to a purely instrumental role; as he famously argues, "Reason is, and ought only to be the slave of the passions, and can

---

21 David Hume, *Treatise of Human Nature*, bk. 3, pt. 1, sec. 1 (with some grammatical emendations).

22 *Treatise of Human Nature*, bk. 3, pt. 2, sec. 5. Identifying virtue with pleasure leads Hume to reject Christian morality: "Celibacy, fasting, penance, mortification, self-denial, humility, silence, solitude, and the whole train of monkish virtues . . . [do not] increase his power of self-enjoyment. . . . We justly, therefore . . . place them in the catalogue of vices" (*Enquiry Concerning the Principles of Morals*, sec. 9, pt. 1, para. 219).

23 *Treatise of Human Nature*, bk. 2, pt. 3, sec. 3.

never pretend to any other office than to serve and obey them."[23] In other words, we use reason simply to figure out how to get the things we desire.[24] But the desires themselves are inscrutable: one never has to justify the goodness of their desire.[25]

The widespread acceptance of Hume's argument in contemporary ethics is facilitated by the fact that it is grounded in other prevenient assumptions.

First, it assumes a nominalism in which there are no universal natures and no final causality to explain regularity in nature. For once we grasp that there are kinds of being, it is obvious that we do in fact derive what ought to be done from facts all the time: Bob is a policeman, therefore he ought to enforce the law. That is your pancreas, therefore it ought to secrete digestive enzymes. This is a tomato plant, therefore it ought to produce some fruit. In each of these, failing to fulfill the "ought" is a sign of something going wrong. Notice, though, what these all have in common: the first clause indicates a kind of being, or a nature; the second clause recognizes the final cause, or proper activity, of that kind of being. This clearly demonstrates that oughts are in fact factual claims for those people who recognize the existence of natures where action follows from being.

Hume's nominalism also led to his reduction of causal relations to a mere habit of belief based on a constant conjunction.[26] If there are no natures, then there are no final causes for which a substance acts. Therefore, *any* substance can act in *any* way whatsoever. There is no connection between being and activity. Hume concludes that the only explanation for action, then, is one's inscrutable desires. Accordingly, when Hume examines human action, he disregards being and sees only that a desire always precedes an action. This constant conjunction makes him believe that desire is not just one source of action but the only cause of action. Hume's metaphysical and epistemological ideas of causality, therefore, force him into a position where the fact-value dichotomy becomes necessary.

---

24 Hume turns traditional ethics upside down. From the time of Plato, the good person was one who uses reason to regulate his desires. That is, we ought to conform desire to reality. Hume liberates feelings from reality and makes them sovereign. But because feelings are irreducibly subjective, they cannot be argued about and so can never be "wrong." This is why compassion alone—unregulated by a rational analysis of what actions are worthy of compassion—can never be the basis for a just social order, since all actions would be equally deserving.

25 *Treatise of Human Nature*, bk. 2, pt. 3, sec. 3: "'Tis not contrary to reason to prefer the destruction of the whole world to the scratching of my finger."

26 See the discussion of Hume in chapter 4.

Accepting this separation of fact and value has significant implications for understanding the good. For the perennial philosophy, the good is part of nature, the result of the natural dynamism of essence and the act of existence. Thus, the good is, like truth, a state of being. Reductive metaphysics and epistemologies make it impossible for modern ethical theories to discover the good if being is considered to be atoms floating in space as known by science. If values cannot be grounded in the facts of nature, the only alternative is that the good must be determined—reductively—by human consciousness. As we have seen, this leaves two options: the good will be determined either by desire alone or by reason alone. The first is the road taken by Mill's utilitarianism; the second by Kant's deontology. These two theories dominate modern moral thought.

Good as an Object of Appetite Alone: Utilitarianism

Utilitarianism argues that, as desire for pleasure is the sole motivation for action, pleasure is the only criterion by which to assess those actions.[27] Although pleasure itself is a subjective experience, it can be an objective criterion for morality by insisting that it is not just an individual's pleasure that matters (that would be *hedonism*) but rather the cumulative pleasure of all people. The good according to this theory is that which brings the greatest amount of pleasure for the greatest number of people. This is utilitarianism's first principle for moral reasoning: we should act to maximize pleasure and assess actions on the basis of how much pleasure was attained. It has become the dominant public morality in much of the Anglosphere,[28] as evidenced in the common assertion that an act is good so long as it makes people happy and no one suffers.

Two aspects of utilitarianism make it an appealing ethical theory. First, it recognizes the truth that people are motivated by their appetites and that we naturally seek satisfaction of our desires. Second, it taps into the common-sense notion that ethical actions should benefit the majority of people and not just the one who is acting. Unfortunately, the way in which utilitarianism pursues these ends also reduces moral goodness to atomistic

---

27 Jeremy Bentham (1747–1832), the father of utilitarianism, begins his *Introduction to the Principles of Morals and Legislation* with the claim, "Nature has placed mankind under the governance of two sovereign masters, *pain* and *pleasure*. It is for them alone to point out what we ought to do, as well as to determine what we shall do."

28 A fact that led Nietzsche to sardonically comment, "Man does not live for pleasure, only the Englishman does" (*Twilight of the Idols*, Epigram 12).

experiences that make it difficult to frame a truly objective ethics. Let us consider why this is so in reference to the theory as articulated by John Stuart Mill (1806–1873).[29]

Mill clearly states the definition of the good for utilitarianism. An act is good if it produces happiness, but he adds this clarification: "By happiness is intended pleasure, and the absence of pain; by unhappiness, pain, and the privation of pleasure." Because pleasure and pain are the two "masters" dictating human action, the moral person is one whose acts maximize pleasure for as many people as possible. Mill immediately recognizes that many will question this identification of good with pleasure; he then defends the utilitarian theory by replying to a series of potential objections. Let us examine these replies sequentially to determine whether utilitarianism adequately articulates an intelligible theory of the human good.

The most obvious objection Mill addresses is that to identify the good with pleasure is to reduce the human being to merely an animal. Utilitarianism, the objection claims, is "a doctrine worthy only of swine." This is a serious objection, because humans obviously act for ends other than immediate physical pleasure. Mill replies that because a person is rational, he is attracted not only by the *quantity* of pleasure but also by its *quality*. Reason enjoins us to seek qualitatively higher pleasures, to experience pleasure in things that reflect human dignity, such as poetry and art, and not just sex and drugs. As Mill says, "It is better to be a human being dissatisfied than a pig satisfied." The problem with Mill's response is that it essentially changes the criterion for goodness: if we assess acts based on human dignity—a quality other than pleasure—then we are no longer basing it on pleasure alone. To introduce a consideration other than pleasure is to employ a theory other than utilitarianism. (In fact, to assess an act based on rational dignity is much closer to natural law.) It seems, then, that utilitarianism has no way to motivate people to act for these higher pleasures.

A second objection Mill addresses is the fact that most people simply will not be motivated to act for the happiness of the greatest number of people. People act for their *own* interests. Mill concedes this, but he dismisses the objection by claiming that what makes an act good is not the motive of the person but the consequences brought about by the action: "motive has nothing to do with the morality of the action." The pleasurable consequences are the only thing that matters in assessing the value

---

29 My presentation follows *Utilitarianism*, chap. 2.

of an action. For this reason, utilitarianism is often called a *consequentialist* theory.

But Mill's defense of the consequentialist nature of utilitarianism in fact opens it up to a number of serious criticisms. First, the good is determined by the maximization of pleasure; but there is no rational way to "count" pleasure and pain. In fact, since pleasure is a subjective feeling (as opposed to a universal rational concept) it is always private, and so it is simply impossible to judge the pleasure of the greatest number of people. Second, it seems counterintuitive to say that neither the motive nor the action itself are morally relevant. If someone explodes a radiation bomb with the intention of killing thousands of innocent people but accidentally cures all the cancer in the city instead, the utilitarian would have to say that his act was good because the consequences were conducive to pleasure. This seems absurd, since accidental effects cannot be the basis of morality. Nor can we discount the value of the act done in order to bring pleasure. If pleasure is all that matters, utilitarianism cannot object to *how* that pleasure is attained. For example, we might isolate people in laboratories and then stimulate the pleasure receptors in their brain with electrodes, reducing them to drooling, happy fools. This is maximally pleasurable, but would this be the ideal moral life?[30] It seems that regardless of the pleasure to be experienced, there are acts that are simply inappropriate for people to contemplate.

A related objection that Mill addresses is the claim that utilitarianism is expedient, that is, it will allow any act if it maximizes pleasure for the greatest number of people. This is the familiar position that the end justifies the means. Once again, Mill accepts the charge and admits that any act is moral so long as it brings about the greatest amount of pleasure. Here we see perhaps the greatest problem with consequentialism. Since there are no intrinsically evil acts, anything is permissible, so long as it has good consequences for the greatest number of people.[31] A couple of traditional examples illustrate the problematic nature of this. First, if I am visiting a friend in the hospital, and there are five patients awaiting organ transplants, would not the utilitarian be justified in killing me and giving my organs to the five

[30] This thought experiment was first suggested by American philosopher Robert Nozick, *Anarchy, State, and Utopia* (New York: Basic Books, 1974), 42–45.

[31] A troubling corollary is that neither are there intrinsically good acts: an act is good only if it leads to pleasure. Things like friendship, love, loyalty, and religion can be sacrificed in order to attain some maximal pleasure.

so that they might live?[32] Certainly the pleasure of five is greater than the pleasure of one. Similarly, would it be permissible to torture an innocent child for eternity if it would guarantee the eternal happiness of all other people? Again, the utilitarian would need to grant this, yet torturing a child is repugnant.[33] Nevertheless, utilitarianism appears to have no way to avoid these terrible conclusions.

This acceptance of expediency also undermines all traditional morality. Mill argues that moral traditions are valuable guides because they reflect many centuries of experience about what typically causes pleasure and pain. This should not prevent us, though, from breaking from traditional morality whenever the desires and attitudes of the people change. As a result, any traditional moral rule can be sacrificed whenever we discover new sources of pleasure. This reduces the calculation of pleasurable consequences to no more than a guess.

Although utilitarianism correctly identifies the importance of appetite for the moral life, in reducing human appetite to pleasure, it fails to do justice to human expectations for morality. Pleasure as a criterion can only be inherently subjective and fluctuating. So, even though utilitarianism is directed to a common good, this common good is merely the sum of individual pleasures (which are often divergent and even conflicting) and not really a shared moral vision for ordering society. This makes moral reasoning impossible. The good cannot guide moral actions, since it is a constantly moving target and one can never really be sure about what act will result in the greatest pleasure.

Good as an Object of Reason Alone: Deontology

Immanuel Kant takes Hume's fact-value dichotomy in the opposite direction. He begins with a forceful rejection of basing moral goodness on desire: ethics, he insists, is not about doing what you *want*, it is about doing what you *have to do*. This leads him to radically diminish the appetite's relevance for ethics and to argue instead that morality has to be based on reason alone. This is possible because desire is not the only motive for action. Reason can

32 This is not hypothetical. Some nations (e.g., Belgium, Canada, the Netherlands) have used legalized euthanasia as an excuse to harvest organs. This is often justified by the fact that the euthanized person had a "low quality of life," that is, limited experience of physical pleasure.

33 The logic of expediency would also nullify the assertion of human rights; Bentham famously rejected the idea of human rights as "nonsense, nonsense upon stilts." The example of torturing a child comes from Dostoevsky's *The Brothers Karamazov*.

act as a motive insofar as a person can recognize his duty to the moral law. When I recognize I ought to do something regardless of what I want to do, I am motivated by duty to the law. Moreover, since desire for pleasure is instinctive, people are not truly being free in acting on it. In contrast, when they act on reason, people are truly free and responsible for their actions.

We immediately see what makes Kant's approach to ethics attractive. He grasps the importance of moral duty even when it conflicts with desire. Also, since this duty is grounded in reason, and not subjective appetites, it offers a truly objective criterion for action that everyone can know. While this approach is certainly more rigorous than utilitarianism, it nevertheless goes too far in the opposite direction. By completely isolating reason from desire, he ignores the incarnational truth of human nature. His theory reduces the human being to something like a disembodied intellect, and so this theory can never reflect the complete human good.

Kant's reaction to the fact-value dichotomy must be understood within the context of his larger reaction to Hume's skepticism.[34] Hume's rejection of causal relations led to the conclusion that experience contained no necessary truths. Kant tries to save the laws of nature by arguing that necessity arises not from the objects of experience but rather from the structure of the mind, the a priori categories of judgment to which experience conforms. This is directly relevant for ethics because, if morality is about what you *have to* do, it is about *necessary* moral laws. For these laws to be necessary, they cannot be based on experience. Rather, for Kant, they have to be based solely on reason. Thus, whenever we come upon a law, whether in nature or in morality, we are seeing the work of the mind giving necessity to the content of our experience. This, in fact, is Kant's deepest philosophical inspiration: "Two things fill the mind with ever new and increasing admiration and reverence, the more often and more steadily one reflects on them: *the starry heavens above me and the moral law within me.*"[35]

This rationalist idea of the moral law means that we have to completely ignore any notion of goodness that might come to us from experience. This means that neither pleasure, nor happiness, nor human nature—all data from experience—can be used to ground morality. Indeed, Kant would insist that "insofar as [a moral rule] rests in the least part on empirical

---

34 See the discussion in chapter 4.

35 Kant, *Critique of Practical Reason*, conclusion, 161. This is also the epitaph on Kant's tombstone in Kaliningrad.

grounds, perhaps only in terms of motive, [it] can indeed be called a practical rule but never a moral law."[36] This metaphysical point about the nature of law as originating in reason is critical for understanding his ethical theory. However, this isolation of reason from experience, this abstractness, also presents some difficulties in making it a fully adequate ethical theory.

Where utilitarianism's initiating observation is the dominating role of pleasure, Kant begins by noting that "it is impossible to think of anything at all in the world . . . that could be considered good without limitation except a good will."[37] While there are many good things—money, power, fame, strength—they can all be used for evil purposes. In fact, all these things can be considered good only when they are used well. A good will, then, is good in itself because it is the condition for the good use of everything else.[38] In fact, a good will is good even if it never accomplishes anything at all, for it is the will to do good that matters. This illustrates how Kant's reaction to the fact-value dichotomy develops into the mirror opposite of Mill's consequentialism: for Kant, motive—a good will—is the only thing that counts, and consequences are irrelevant. All objects of desire, even happiness, are irrelevant to morality since they have to do with experience and not the moral law. In fact, reason exists not to find happiness but to produce a pure moral will.[39] This pure moral will must be completely isolated from experience if it is to be the source of the moral law.

The transition from a good will to moral law is made by recognizing that reason enables us to act on account of duty. There is a stark division between acts motivated by rational duty and those motivated by desires. Kant illustrates this with some striking examples by which he demonstrates that acting in accord with duty is not enough; we must be motivated by duty. For instance, if a shopkeeper gives correct change only for the sake of not losing business, his motive—a desire to keep business—means he is not motivated by the moral law, and so he is not truly honest and his act is

---

36 Kant, *Groundwork of the Metaphysics of Morals*, preface, 389. I follow this text, though the argument is laid out in greater detail in *The Critique of Practical Reason*.

37 Kant, *Groundwork*, sec. 1, 393.

38 Kant is here echoing an insight from Saint Augustine's *On Free Choice of the Will*. This idea is influentially developed in the Middle Ages by Duns Scotus in his assertion that the will has two distinct inclinations: the *affectio commodi*, which inclines us to happiness, and the *affectio iustitia*, which inclines us to morality by following the law.

39 Kant, *Groundwork*, sec. 1, 396. Note that Kant's usage of *will* is significantly different from the tradition. Instead of being an appetite, which Kant regards as empirical, it is a pure practical reason, or reason ordered to the moral law.

immoral. Similarly, if someone performs benevolent acts out of a charitable nature, that act has "no true moral worth," since the person was motivated by love and not a sense of duty. Moral worth, Kant insists, can emerge only when "all sympathy" with others has been extinguished.[40] Only this can guarantee that a person is acting on duty and not on desire or sentiment.

This recognition of duty is possible only if there is a moral law that stands independent of all desire. This law—what *has to be done*—must be based in a priori reason. This presents something of a puzzle, which also leads to Kant's great discovery. The puzzle is that the moral law he is looking for cannot consider any data from experience if it is to be necessary. But how can there be a law that is not *about anything*? Kant's ingenious insight is that the moral law can only be about acting in a law-like way: "Since I have deprived the will of every impulse that could arise for it from obeying some law, nothing is left but the conformity of action as such with universal law, which alone is to serve the will as its principle, that is, *I ought never to act except in such a way that I would also will that my maxim should become a universal law.*"[41]

This is Kant's "categorical imperative," his definition of the good that is the first principle for all moral decision making. To act in a law-like way means that the action can become universal and necessary for all people. Therefore, when considering an action, the agent should discern whether it could be willed as an action for everyone; if it can, it must be a law. As a law, I have a duty to obey it and would manifest a good will by following that duty.

We test the morality of an action, then, by trying to universalize it, that is, will it universally so that it does not lead to any contradiction. For example, if I want to steal someone's car, then I make all car theft universally allowable; but that leads to a contradiction, since as soon as I steal the car, someone can steal it from me. It is contradictory because, although I aim to possess a car, I end up depriving myself of it. We can apply the same reasoning to giving a false promise. A promise only works because people trust one another. If all promises were universally false, though, no one would ever believe them. Thus, this cannot be made into a law without contradiction. We therefore know that no one should ever give a false promise.

---

40 *Groundwork*, sec. 1, 398.

41 *Groundwork*, sec. 1, 402. This might be thought of as a rationalized version of the Golden Rule.

While the categorical imperative is an abstract formula for assessing actions, Kant insists that it implies one absolute moral rule that always obtains. This is the fact that we should "act that you use humanity . . . always as an end, never merely as a means."[42] This asserts that human beings deserve respect because it is their good will that is the source of the moral law. The very idea of moral goodness depends on persons willing the moral law; for that reason, to respect the moral law implies respecting those persons who are its source. This dignity should never be violated by using persons for our own purposes; rather, we ought to respect the autonomy of persons and never impose rules on them (for that would be to force them into submission to our own will).[43] This formulation of the categorical imperative is of great importance in the twentieth century, for it becomes (along with the natural law) the basis for much of the human rights legislation.[44]

Kant's respect for human dignity and the objectivity of moral law is laudable and clearly an improvement over utilitarianism. This, however, should not blind us to the many problems of his theory. These problems arise from his insistence that ethics must be derived from abstract reason alone, without consideration of the facts of human existence.

First, Kant is forced to view desire as necessarily opposed to morality, and so a person cannot *want* to be good. This results in a separation of the right—fulfilling the moral law—from the good—attaining moral perfection. We are thrown into an unending battle where our desire for happiness is an impediment to obeying the moral law.[45] This repudiation of the naturalness of the appetite also eliminates the relevance of love and virtue, for good acts arising from desire have no moral worth for Kant. A moral life that cannot take these into consideration, however, is blinding itself to the most important sources of human action. Kant's reduction of ethics to reason simply fails to reflect reality as we know it.

---

42 *Groundwork*, sec. 2, 429.

43 *Groundwork*, sec. 2, 426–28.

44 The context of Kant's philosophy, though, makes applying this doctrine a little tricky. Since morality cannot be based on anything empirical, Kant's idea of a person is not the phenomenal object of experience but the noumenal mind capable of free will. Only those capable of rational activity, then, are considered to have moral agency. Some philosophers have used to this to argue some humans do not count as persons: fetuses, comatose patients, people who have disabilities are all subject to depersonalization.

45 *Groundwork*, sec. 1, 405.

A second problem is that even these rational duties are ineffectual when taken too abstractly. Duties are always duties to someone or something in particular and not merely abstract rules. This is illustrated when we consider that moral dilemmas are often not merely a question of what my duty is but rather how to decide between competing duties. For example, say my wife is sick and needs to be taken to the hospital, but I need to go to work. Common sense tells us that this is easily resolved. But Kant's theory would insist that this is a no-win situation, since whatever you choose would entail a violation of duty at the other end. If we fail to see the personal nature of duty, we become paralyzed since it is impossible to be responsible to all people equally. The Kantian notion of duty—very much like utilitarian focus on consequences—has the odd effect of creating a depersonalized ethics: rules for acting that ignore that it is *persons* who are acting.

Related to this is another problem that arises from Kant's complete separation of reason and the law from appetitive inclinations. This is simply the problem of whether people would be motivated to follow the law merely to be rationally consistent. If the moral law also guaranteed happiness, as it does in the perennial tradition, people will be inclined to obey it. But if the moral law is completely isolated from happiness, or a sense of fulfillment, the promise of intellectual consistency is likely not enough to move people to obey.

This brings us to the main problem with the categorical imperative. Because of its abstractness, there is no reliable way to formulate a clear set of moral laws from it. The problem lies with how one generalizes the rule of action one is contemplating to generate a moral law.[46] Depending on how the agent describes his action, anything could be allowed or prohibited. For example, some cultures observe the tradition of "honor killing" a disgraced child. How is this act to be described? On the one hand, it can be said that a father is merely defending the honor of his family, and so this act would be permissible. On the other hand, it can be said that the father is killing his daughter, and so would be prohibited. The categorical imperative in itself is too abstract to determine which formulation of the action is better. Consequently, there is no way to specify the content of moral law with reliability.[47] Without some sense of the real conditions of human life, includ-

---

46 See the specific formulation of the categorical imperative in *Groundwork*, sec. 2, 421.

47 Indeed, Adolph Eichmann defended his actions in the Holocaust by invoking the categorical imperative. It is always wrong, he said, to disobey the orders of a superior, for if that were universalized then social order would collapse. Hence, he felt that he was right to follow Hitler's orders.

ing its ultimate goal, happiness, there is no way to meaningfully assess how actions ought to be framed in terms of their moral content.

More far-reaching consequences arise from Kant's argument that each person wills the moral law for himself. This is the modern notion of freedom as autonomy (*self-law*).[48] Kant's reason for asserting that persons are autonomous is that, if the law were taken from another (Kant calls this *heteronomy*), it would be empirical and so not a moral law at all. Thus, each person has to will the law for himself. This means that the moral law cannot be discovered in the order of being or even received from God. If, however, each person wills the moral law for himself, what prevents this from devolving into rampant relativism? As he argued with respect to our experience of scientific laws, Kant is able to secure the objectivity of the moral law because of his Enlightenment assumption that everyone's reason functions in the same way and so would arrive at the same law.[49] However, when that Enlightenment optimism evaporates later in the nineteenth century, there is nothing to prevent autonomy from evolving in a more problematic direction where people will utterly subjective values for themselves; this ultimately finds fruition in the thought of Nietzsche.

The weakness of both utilitarianism and deontology is that, in basing themselves on a reductive idea of human nature and human action, they fail to account for the fullness of human experience. In distancing themselves not only from human nature but also from the metaphysical principles of being, they define the good in terms of a calculus applied to actions and not in terms of a person being good by fulfilling his potential. (These modern theories are act centered, as opposed to the way traditional theories are agent centered. In other words, modern theories tend to be minimalist in the sense that we seek only to avoid evil acts, whereas traditional theories are aspirational where we seek to become the best person possible.) In fact, in the past few decades, there has emerged a combination of the two theories in which unlimited autonomy gives law-like authority to desires so that each person's desires have to be fulfilled (to the extent this is possible). Thus, ethics is reduced to what might be called a sentimental imperative.[50] In this context, the only limit to human behavior is no longer truth

---

48 *Groundwork*, sec. 2, 431.

49 Kant refers to this rational unanimity as "the kingdom of ends" in *Groundwork*, sec. 2, 433.

50 See Alasdair MacIntyre, "On Having Survived the Academic Moral Philosophy of the Twentieth Century" in *What Happened in and to Moral Philosophy in the Twentieth Century,* ed. Fran O'Rourke, 17–34, and esp. 19–25 (Notre Dame, Ind.: University of Notre Dame Press, 2013). See

or an objective good, but personal "consent." As Plato had seen, morality dissolves if the good is not different from the merely desired.

VIRTUE ETHICS: BEING A BETTER PERSON

The fact-value dichotomy undermines the hylomorphic unity of the human person. As such, it forces modern philosophers to evaluate the rightness of an act based on an abstract calculus reflecting pleasure or duty. What is lost in this is any concern with a *person* becoming good. In other words, modern thought tries make moral judgments about isolated acts. But acts exist only because a person desires to attain the good. Goodness, then, is not primarily about the act but about the desired state of being for the person who is acting; an act is good if it helps to attain that desired state of being. There is a wide agreement about what that desired state of being is: happiness. Happiness is the goal of morality for the Greeks as well as both Old and New Testaments.[51] It is seen to be the ultimate goal that motivates moral reasoning. This common idea was only overturned when the fact-value dichotomy insinuated that goodness had nothing to do with being and so reduced morality to subjective pleasure or abstract law as a rule for assessing actions.

To say that happiness is the goal of ethics leaves two important questions: What is happiness? And how is happiness attained? Aristotle's "virtue ethics" provides foundational answers for both of these questions. These ideas would be assimilated by the Christian tradition and become an integral part of the perennial tradition and natural law ethics.[52]

It is important to begin by recognizing the way in which happiness is the goal of our acting. As Aristotle notes, *every* action we do is only undertaken in order to attain some goal: "Every art and every inquiry, and similarly every action and pursuit, is thought to aim at some good; and for this reason the good has rightly been declared to be that at which all things aim."[53] The good is the desired end state for any undertaking. Built into this

---

also John Rist, *Real Ethics: Rethinking the Foundations of Morality* (Cambridge: Cambridge University Press, 2002), 178–88.

51 See, for example, Plato's *Republic*, bk. IX; Ps 1:1–2 (Happy are those who[se] ... delight is in the law of the Lord), and the Beatitudes in Mt 5:3 (Blessed [i.e., happy] are the poor in spirit, for theirs is the kingdom of heaven).

52 It is a testimony to the truth of Greek virtue ethics that the Church Fathers were able to absorb it into the Christian tradition with relatively minor modification, despite the great cultural differences between paganism and Christianity.

53 Aristotle, *Nicomachean Ethics* I.1 (1094a1–3).

is the idea that within the action itself is a standard of acceptability that is aimed at: medicine aims at restoring health and strategy aims at winning. That every action aims for some good is, importantly, not restricted to humans. His definition does not depend on what all human beings desire; rather, every action of every substance aims for the good. This is because there is an inherent tendency in every nature to an activity characteristic of it. This end at which things aim is the substance's final cause—the end state of development and activity for which the nature exists. This is important because it debunks the fact-value dichotomy: every agent has a state of being that is good for its nature, so knowing what something is implies we know what it ought to do. It does not take a profound philosopher to know that an apple tree is good if it grows lots of apples and bad if it does not.

Humans, however, do *many* different activities: they eat, sleep, play, work, read, build, fight, each of which can be done well for a specific good. In order to determine which of these things takes priority, there must be one supreme good, one end for which all other things are done. It is this supreme end that motivates all these other actions. Otherwise, these actions would be ultimately capricious and pointless—we would do them just to do them but for no reason beyond that. For example, we arise from bed, eat, exercise, pray, work, each aimed at some goal—but unless there is a goal beyond these acts, there is no way to justify *why* we did any of these things. In this case, life would be merely a random series of events, essentially pointless and resulting in a spiritless anomie.[54] Alternatively, someone might try to motivate himself by saying: I work to make money to pay rent so I can sleep comfortably, which refreshes me so I can work some more to make more money to pay rent again so I can sleep again and then go back to work. . . . This life is soul killing because it is pointless. For life to be meaningful, there has to be one supreme goal to which all these other actions are ordered. There has to be a goal for life itself.

This supreme good must have two characteristics.[55] First, it must be an end-in-itself: it is not chosen as a means to something else but rather everything else is chosen as a means to it. So, all our other actions, and the goods they aim at, are ordered to attaining this supreme good. Second, it must be self-sufficient: once this good is possessed, nothing else is needed or wanted

---

[54] *Nicomachean Ethics* I.2 (1094a19–24). For an amusing rendition of the same truth, see Dorothy Parker's poem, "Inscription for the Ceiling of a Bedroom" (1936).

[55] *Nicomachean Ethics* I.7 (1097a15–b20).

in addition to it. For this reason, popular ideas of the supreme good—money, wealth, power, fame—fail, for each of these is either a means or something to which other goods could be added to make life better. The only thing that is truly an end in itself and self-sufficient is happiness (or *eudaimonia*). We do all things to be happy, and happiness is self-sufficient, for if a person is happy, he is completely satisfied with his life. It is the state of being that is the goal of every person from the moment of conception and that motivates all growth and development the person experiences during the course of his lifetime.

As the supreme good, happiness is the first principle, or ultimate explanation, for moral reasoning. It is the final answer explaining why a person did something: because he wants to be happy. This principle is self-evident, for if someone were to question why he should want to be happy, it would be clear that he did not understand the word at all.

But what *is* happiness? Notoriously, there is great disagreement about what happiness consists of. Aristotle sees happiness as a person's final cause and so defines happiness by considering a person's nature and function.[56] A good flute player plays music well; a good doctor heals well. But simply as *human*, a person is defined by reason; hence, a good person is one who is rational. Happiness, then, lies in being rational in the most excellent way. In Aristotle's words, happiness is a rational activity of the soul in accord with virtue.[57] This is the first principle of virtue ethics, the definition of the good that acts as a standard for evaluating all our actions.

Three aspects of this definition of happiness are worthy of note. First, only the rational activities of a person can lead to happiness. While life entails vegetative and sensitive powers, mere survival or pleasure are not the goal of life. Second, happiness lies in the activity of reason and not merely its potential, since all people would then be happy. Third, because happiness is an activity of the soul, it is utterly within the power of each person to be happy; indeed, it is the responsibility each person to develop himself so as to be happy.

This definition of the good also reveals the answer to the question about how we may attain happiness. We attain happiness by living a life of virtue. Virtue signifies excellence; it is exercising a power in the best way possible. *Moral actions*, those for which we are responsible, are those that arise from

---

56 *Nicomachean Ethics* I.7 (1097b21–1098a18).

57 *Nicomachean Ethics* I.7 (1098a16–18) and I.13 (1102a5–6).

a choice that is the result of both desire and reason, for people have both appetitive and cognitive powers. As Aristotle puts it, "choice is either desiderative reason or ratiocinative desire, and such an origin of action is a man."[58] That is, to make good moral choices, appetite and reason cooperate in guiding our decision. We need to desire the right end, since, if we do not want the right thing, there is little chance we will do it; but what that right end is must be determined by reason. Thus, if moral choice is to reliably point us toward happiness, it has to be informed by virtues in both our desires (or appetites) and our reasoning.[59] This idea of choice unites what Mill and Kant had separated and puts the moral focus not on the action alone, but on the person who possesses virtue and acts to attain the state of being that is happiness. Let us now consider how virtue enables people to attain happiness.

First, we have sensitive appetites, our animal instincts for particular objects as beneficial for survival, like food, drink, and sex. Since people are rational, these appetites must be regulated according to reason so that we desire them in the right way. This is called *moral virtue*. This control of the appetites cannot be taught but is attained only by habituation—getting used to feeling a certain way. A smoker can change his habit only if he stops smoking long enough for the desire to smoke to go away. Once the desire is gone, the smoker is no longer tempted to do a bad—irrational—act. A habit of moral virtue is formed by repeating an action to inculcate a disposition, a state of character, to feel a certain way. In particular, this disposition is one that moderates the influence of pleasure and pain on choice, since those easily lead us astray.[60] A virtuous desire is one that is neither too much nor too little; it is a median between excess (feeling too much) and defect (feeling too little).[61] Thus, there is a virtuous feeling—a mean— associated with every act. Once we make this feeling habitual, it becomes, in a telling idiom, our second nature perfecting human nature's inborn tendencies by guiding us to choose in accord with reason.[62]

---

58 *Nicomachean Ethics* VI.2 (1139b3–5); cf. III.2.

59 *Nicomachean Ethics* I.13.

60 *Nicomachean Ethics*, II.3 (1104b8–11).

61 *Nicomachean Ethics* II.6 (1106a25–b3).

62 To gain this control of feelings is a long and difficult battle, for "to feel them at the right times, with reference to the right objects, towards the right people, with the right motive, and in the right way, is what is both intermediate and best" (*Nicomachean Ethics* II.6 (1106b20–23). In II.9 (1109a29), Aristotle says such judgment is "rare and laudable and noble."

Determining the mean between excess and defect is often not easy. In fact, it is something that can only be done by right reason, something possessed specifically by the "man of practical wisdom."[63] This excellence in thinking is called *intellectual virtue*. Intellectual virtue (in contrast to moral virtues) can be taught, for training the intellect to think well is the object of education. However, since reason considers two kinds of truth, there are two categories of intellect virtues.[64]

Some truths are universal and unchanging (such as math and metaphysics), knowledge of which is made possible by the *scientific intellect*. Three virtues help perfect this kind of thinking. *Understanding* is the ability to intuit the first principles or self-evident bases for arguments in a particular area. *Science* is the ability to make arguments from those principles to further conclusions. *Philosophical wisdom* is the ability to know the highest first principles, those of metaphysics.

Some truths are contingent or changeable. For example, if I ask a carpenter how to build a chair, the answer will depend on who it is for, what is the budget, what sort of room it will go in, and so on. Similarly, discerning the nature of courage depends on the person and situation at hand; a soldier and civilian are expected to act in different ways. This sort of reasoning about changeable truths is an activity of what is known as the *calculative intellect*, since it requires adapting the judgment to the concrete circumstances. There are two virtues to perfect this kind of thinking. *Art* is the virtue of knowing how to make things well; *practical wisdom* (or prudence) is knowing how to act in a given situation to attain the moral good. This is critical for ethics, since prudence is the "reasoned and true state of capacity to act with regard to human goods."[65] Prudence is the capacity to grasp the true good in a given circumstance, that which ought to be desired in order to attain happiness. For this reason, prudence is the foundation for the moral virtues, for it grasps the mean to be aimed at as the best way to feel and act.

Although prudence is fundamental, it is not sufficient for human happiness. For if happiness lies in reason, it must lie in the highest use of reason. This is philosophical wisdom, the contemplation of the highest truths. Prudence, though, is necessary as the means by which philosophical wisdom

63 *Nicomachean Ethics* II.6 (1106b36–1107a2).
64 *Nicomachean Ethics* VI.1 (1139a3–15). The intellectual virtues are dealt with in bk. VI.3–7.
65 *Nicomachean Ethics* VI.5 (1140b20–21).

can come into being.[66] A person cannot engage in philosophical contemplation so long as his desires are not controlled. If I am torn by gluttony or lust, my mind will not be able to concentrate to do the thinking required of metaphysics or of praying to God. Therefore, we first need prudence to create in us the habits of moral virtue; but, once these desires are controlled, the mind is free to pursue the highest goods. In this way, virtues are liberating; they free us to accomplish that which we could not have done without them. Just as running a marathon is only possible after disciplined training, so happiness is only possible after the moral discipline of virtue.

It is now clear how virtues are the necessary means to attain happiness. The prudent person will be able to assess which pleasures reflect human nature's true end.[67] This is important because pleasure is a by-product of a faculty operating well.[68] For example, I can run: if I am in shape and run a good race, pleasure results; if I have a torn muscle, I cannot run well and so have pain. But if pleasure is a by-product of a human faculty operating well, there are pleasures related to *everything* we do. The trick is to judge which pleasures we ought to pursue. Prudence allows us to judge that the best pleasure we can seek is that associated with our highest activity: philosophical contemplation. "For man, therefore, the life according to reason is best and pleasantest, since reason more than anything else is man. This life therefore is also the happiest."[69] This is especially true because the development of our rational powers requires friends who are wise and virtuous themselves, for only in communion with them is real wisdom attainable.[70] So the pleasure of friendship is an essential part of happiness.

Because this contemplation is an end in itself and is self-sufficient, everything else is done for its sake. This includes not only the development of personal moral virtue but also all political activities. Politics is relevant, because a person would not be able to develop the moral virtues that make contemplation possible unless he lived in a peaceful and moral society.[71]

---

66 *Nicomachean Ethics* VI.13 (1144b30–1145a10).

67 *Nicomachean Ethics* X.5 (1176a10–20).

68 *Nicomachean Ethics* X.4. Note how this corrects the error of utilitarianism: we seek to do an act, and pleasure is a by-product of the act; we do not seek pleasure itself as an end. It is human nature that makes certain activities meaningfully pleasant and other actions viciously pleasing.

69 *Nicomachean Ethics* X.7 (1178a6–8).

70 Aristotle devotes the whole of books 8 and 9 to the issue of friendship, in which friends are seen as "another self" (1166b1–2) whose happiness we wish for because of the virtue they possess.

71 *Nicomachean Ethics* X.9.

The goal of politics, then, is to create laws to make citizens moral, enabling them to attain happiness.

Aristotle's union of desire and reason presents a solid basis for moral reasoning. He recognizes that humans are motivated by both appetite and reason and discovers virtue as the way to integrate them into a life ordered to human nature's intended state of being. There is one notable problem, though. His dependence on the person of practical wisdom to decide what is the mean in each case seems to leave ethics without absolute rules—laws—that are known even by those without practical wisdom.[72] This leaves those without a person of practical wisdom, or those born into vicious societies, seemingly without a foundation to improve themselves. Moreover, Aristotle assumes the function of a person is to be happy, but he cannot explain why being happy is *obligatory*. If a person should choose to reject being virtuous and rational, there is no authority obliging him to do otherwise. Natural law theory builds on virtue ethics but is able to indicate specific obligatory laws, known by all, that are the necessary means for any person to attain happiness.

THE NATURAL LAW
The Good as the Perfection of Being

Because the metaphysics behind other ethical theories partially obscure the true nature of being, they end up with ideas of the good that are reductive and so only partially true. Utilitarianism is correct in saying that the good should bring happiness to the greatest number of people, yet in defining that common good in terms of individual pleasure they neglect our shared rationality. Kant is correct to insist that morality is adherence to law, but, in assuming law is derived from abstract reason, he makes it impossible to discover concrete laws reflecting the real needs of human nature.[73] Aristotle is right

---

72 Behind this problem is Aristotle's assumption that ethics is a matter of calculative reason: since its truths are all contingent, there are no necessary truths—no universal laws—to guide us. Though at times he does imply the reality of universal moral laws (*Nicomachean Ethics* II.6 [1107a9–16] and V.7 [1134b18–34]), he does not develop this and emphasizes instead the prudential judgment of contingent circumstances.

73 These ethical theories became a source for bad moral theology in the decades after Vatican II. Utilitarianism inspires proportionalism, which argues an act is morally licit if it maximizes the good, and so no act is intrinsically evil. Kantianism inspires interpretations of natural law based on an abstract order of reason, which is understood in opposition to the incarnational order of nature and implies that human bodily nature is morally indifferent. Both of these innovations reflect a desire to undermine traditional sexual ethics.

in arguing that a good person seeks to perfect himself in virtue, but Aristotle's focus on the contingency of good acts obscures the need for a transcendent source of reality as an obliging sanction to do the good. What is needed is a moral theory that can integrate the positive insights of all three traditions. We find this in the perennial tradition of natural law ethics.[74]

Thomas's idea of good can incorporate the other insights because it starts not from a person's faculties or even from a nature's final cause but from being itself. The first principles, or definitions of the good, for the three theories already considered picked out one particular quality: maximal pleasure (utilitarianism) or rationally universalizable duties (Kant's deontology) or contemplative happiness (virtue ethics). Thomas's first principle for moral reasoning, by contrast, is "The good is to be done and pursued, and evil is to be avoided."[75] This may appear tautological and vacuous. However, the key is how rich the idea of goodness is. As we have seen, good is convertible with being, and so his idea of moral goodness is tied to the foundations of reality itself. Moreover, because his idea of goodness encompasses all aspects of being, it can holistically integrate the partial truths of the other theories; namely, for Thomas moral goodness entails fulfilling a law to perfect a person's nature in happiness for the sake of the common good.[76]

The crux of this argument, then, is the convertibility of goodness with being. Recall that the transcendental good indicated being under the aspect of desirability. What aspect of being makes it desirable? It is the fact that being, as the *act of existence*—the act of all acts and the perfection of all perfections[77]—perfects things by drawing them out of potency to act. Being is desirable because it is a perfection. Thus, all being is good.

> Now it is clear that a thing is desirable only in so far as it is perfect; for all desire their own perfection. But everything is perfect so far as it is actual. Therefore it is clear that a thing is perfect so far as it exists; for it is existence

---

74 Even with respect to the tradition of natural law thought, Thomas's theory natural law is a remarkable synthesis of disparate strands: Cicero's identification of the natural law with human reason, Ulpian's identification with what people have in common with other animals, and Gratian's identification with the moral teaching of Scripture; see Michael Bertram Crowe, *The Changing Profile of the Natural Law* (The Hague: Martinus Nijhoff, 1977).

75 *ST* I-II.94.2. I sometimes reword this more concisely as "do good and avoid evil."

76 The argument of the remainder of this section may appear somewhat abstruse. However, grounding morality in the metaphysics of being is necessary to establish the objectivity of the good.

77 *DP* 7.2.ad 9; see the discussion in chapter 3.

that makes all things actual. . . . Hence it is clear that goodness and being are the same really. But goodness presents the aspect of desirableness.[78]

The good, for Thomas, is grounded firmly in reality, for the good is the desirability of the *perfection of being*.[79]

But, as we have seen, the perfection of being happens in two ways: the substantial existence of first act and the accidental activity of second act. As a result, the good as the perfection of being points in two directions, so to speak. It points "backward," so that everything that exists possesses some goodness; but it also points "forward," so that everything that exists desires the complete perfection that is attained only in actualizing all potential. The first way of possessing being is important because it provides a philosophical explanation for of the doctrine from Genesis that all things are good. Since God alone, as Creator, is the one who bestows that act of existence on all things, it is clear that things can be called good simply because they are created by God. The act of creation demonstrates that those creatures were desired by God first and so possess some perfection that makes them desirable in themselves as beings. (This is most evident in that all things desire their own being, since they strive to resist destruction.) Therefore, we can say that all things that exist are good.[80]

This claim, though, brings an immediate objection, tied to the second point: is it really true that everything that exists is good? Aren't there defective cars, bad hearts, and evil people? It is here that the distinction of being as first act and second act plays a critical role:

> A thing is . . . said simply to have being, accordingly as it is primarily distinguished from that which is only in potentiality; and this is precisely each thing's substantial being. Hence by its substantial being, everything is said to have being simply; but by any further actuality it is said to have being relatively. . . . But goodness signifies perfection which is desirable; and con-

---

78 *ST* I.5.1.

79 Conversely, with respect to Thomas's first principle, the "evil to be avoided" is the lack or privation of being, or not being able to act; in other words, death and disability are evils—bad things—in the most generic sense and so we naturally fight against these. This is addressed more fully in chapter 9.

80 This is why Manicheanism, which argues that the material world is evil, must be opposed by Christians. It ultimately undermines God's role as Creator since this world was caused by him and so must be good. Moreover, theologically, Manicheanism questions both the Incarnation and the Sacraments, since it considers the material realm to be incompatible with divine goodness.

sequently of ultimate perfection. Hence that which has ultimate perfection is said to be simply good; but that which has not the ultimate perfection it ought to have (although, in so far as it is at all actual, it has some perfection), is not said to be perfect simply nor good simply, but only relatively.[81]

The crucial insight here is that the two modes of being are correlated with two kinds of goodness. Substantial being, or first act, is the primary notion of being (being *simply*). Accidents, such as weight, color, and actions, are real, but they are dependent on the substance for their existence. They are being, but as second act they exist in a dependent and limited way. So, Thomas says they exist relatively, or in a certain respect (*secundum quid*).

This order is inverted for goodness. Since the good is *perfection* of being that is desired, only the full perfection of being is considered good *simply*. This, of course, is attained only when a substance fulfills its dynamic potential and performs the activity for which it exists. Thus, second act is the primary sense of good. Nevertheless, to exist is better than to not exist at all, since it is to possess *some* perfection. Thus, to exist as a substance is good but only relatively or in a certain limited way. The primary denotation of goodness, good simply, is realized in the second act by which a nature fulfills its potential to act.

The result is a characteristic both/and: everything is good, but some things are better than others.[82] This insight rests on a profound sensitivity to the act of existence that comes from God to make all things real, both in first act and in second act. And so the more being (second act) a substance has, the better it is; and the better it is, the closer it is to God, who is Being and Goodness itself.[83] Thus, all apple trees are good; but a fecund tree, full of the activity of bearing fruit, possesses ample accidental being that makes it qualitatively better as an apple tree. It is that perfection of its potential as an apple tree that makes it more desirable—because it has more goodness—than do other apple trees.

---

81 *ST* I.5.1.ad 1.

82 Thus, "good" is a transcendental property, for all first acts and second acts possess existence; yet good can also be considered only in terms of an accidental quality (second act) when evaluating the relative worth of two things of the same nature. Thomas argues (*DV* 21.2.ad 6): "A thing can be called good both from its act of existing and from some added property or state. Thus a person is said to be good both as existing and as being just and chaste or destined for beatitude. By reason of the first goodness being is interchanged with good, and conversely. But by reason of the second, good is a division of being."

83 *ST* I.6.1.

Understanding goodness in terms of the perfection brought by the act of existence also helps to demonstrate why there is an obligation to attain the good to which the nature is ordered. This can be shown both on the level of natural causality and of supernatural causality.

On the level of natural causality, the nature of the act of existence allows us to understand how perfective activity is necessary for any substance. Aristotle took it as a brute fact that natures act for an end. But, if the cause of being is the *act* of existence, there is a natural dynamism of being simply as act. But that dynamic activity is circumscribed by the nature of the being, that is, according to the form that determines what the substance is. For this reason, the formal cause is only fully comprehended in light of final cause. The final cause is the good or complete state of being that all things desire; but if the good is the perfection of the act of existence, we see that the activity of things is simply the fruition of their existence. Since "every agent, in so far as it is perfect and in act, produces its like,"[84] act desires to overflow into more act, because act is good per se. In fact, Thomas argues that existence is ordered to the perfection of activity: "All things created would seem, in a way, to be purposeless, if they lacked an operation proper to them; since the purpose of everything is its operation. For the less perfect is always for the sake of the more perfect . . . so the form which is the first act, is for the sake of its operation, which is the second act; and thus operation is the end of the creature."[85] Because all beings are caused by the act of existence, they are obliged to act: the goodness of their being causes them to desire the greater perfection of being by increasing their existence at all times.[86]

In addition to this purely natural explanation for the obligation to pursue the good, there is a more profound supernatural explanation. This is the fact that God as Creator not only gives existence to creatures, but also exercises divine providence over them. Thomas explains providence in this way: "In created things good is found not only as regards their substance, but also as regards their order towards an end. . . . Since, however, God is the cause of things by His intellect . . . it is necessary that the type of the

---

84 *ST* I.19.2; cf. I.5.4.ad 2. This Neoplatonic notion of the self-diffusiveness goodness became an important aspect of the tradition, especially through the influence of Pseudo-Dionysius; see chapter 4 of the *Divine Names*.

85 *ST* I.105.5. See also *SCG* III.113.1: "Each thing appears to exist for the sake of its operation."

86 *SCG* III.25.3: "Whatever is fittingly related to its proper operation is said to be virtuous and good."

order of things towards their end should pre-exist in the divine mind."[87] God endows creatures with the dynamism of the act of existence so that they might attain the end for which he created them.[88] More succinctly, creation is for the sake of the perfective activity of creatures seeking the good. The obligation of creatures to attain their end is therefore reaffirmed. This sense of obligation is brought out in the fact that the providential order is also called the *eternal law*—the rational order by which God directs activity in the universe for the sake of the universal good.[89] It is human knowledge of the eternal law's ordering of creation that is the basis for the natural law for in knowing the perfective end of human nature, we can also know what actions are necessary to attain it.[90]

The Goal of Human Life

All creatures, then, are ordered to the perfection of being; they naturally seek the good appropriate to their specific nature. This is important for the correct interpretation of the natural law. Recall that *nature* is an internal principle of development; it is this determinate pattern of development and change that reveals the nature of a being. In fact, this teleological orientation is so integral to natures that Thomas, following Aristotle, defines essence as *quod quid erat esse*, that which the thing was to be.[91] That is, from its inception, every essence is directed to the fullness of being as its goal. A substance is most truly what it is not at the beginning but at the end of its essential development.[92]

---

87 *ST* I.22.1.

88 There are two traditional objections to this notion of providence: the problems of evil and of free will. Evil is a problem since, if God orders all things to perfection, it seems evil should not exist at all. But providence is God's oversight of creation as a whole, and the perfection intended is the perfection of the universe. In order to attain that common perfection, some creatures will suffer evil (*ST* I.22.2.ad 2). Chapter 9 addresses this issue. Second, the reality of free will would seem to be incompatible with God's control of creation. But God's creative act does not deny the creatures really are active on their own (*ST* I.22.3). God creates the universe, but in the universe creatures act according to their natures, and so human beings are free (*ST* I.22.4). Chapter 8 deals with this distinction between the primary causality of God and the secondary causality of creatures.

89 *ST* I-II.91.1.

90 *ST* I-II.91.2.

91 *OBE* c. 1 and *CM* VII.2.1270.

92 This has important implications for how we understand the natural law. The natural law is not about static rules that are read off some fatalistic order of nature. This was the imperfect understanding of some ancient and Enlightenment era versions of the theory. If this were the

This has significance for us, since if we are naturally directed to an end, the meaning of life would lie in discovering what this end is and how to attain it. We desire our own perfection, and so this is what drives all we do. An obvious truth presents itself: since we are rational, our perfection is realized in being rational. The perfection of a rational being is known by the name *happiness*[93] (though what specifically happiness consists in will have to be established). A person's attaining happiness will necessarily coincide with what God wants, for he created us to be rational.[94] For this reason, we can only offend God if we fail to be happy.[95]

Yet, as we saw in the previous chapter, humans are not simply disembodied minds. Human nature is complex—we are rational animals—and so we need to consider the perfection of the human person as whole. As animals, we are living material beings with vegetative and sensitive powers that endow us with instinctive desire and emotional reactions for material goods that allow us to survive and have pleasure. As rational, though, the intellect grasps reality as it really is and the will judges those particular goods in light of the universal good, happiness, as an objective standard. The will's desire for this universal good motivates and orders all our choices to act on particular goods.[96] Thus, by reflecting on human nature, we can know which goods are necessary to pursue as constitutive aspects of our perfection and thereby order our activity so that we attain the end of the

---

case, natural law would be subject to Hume's critique in the fact-value dichotomy, where some random fact of nature is used to justify behavior. Against this, true natural law is about how people attain their connatural end, since essence is inherently dynamic. The natural dynamism of essences is why the fact-value dichotomy does not apply to natural law. For examples of a "static" reading of natural law, see Lloyd L. Weinreb, *Natural Law and Justice* (Cambridge, Mass: Harvard University Press, 1987), 1–42; and, Crowe, *The Changing Profile of the Natural Law*, 223–90.

93 *ST* I-II.1.4–7. Since only rational creatures can be happy, animals can be said to be happy only by analogy (*ST* I-II.1.8).

94 Thus, reason is the proximate rule for human goodness, since we have to be rational to be happy; yet the eternal law is the ultimate rule for human goodness, since God created us to be rational (*ST* I-II.19.4 and 21.1).

95 SCG III.122.2.

96 *ST* I-II.10.1: "Now this is good in general, to which the will tends naturally, as does each power to its object; and again it is the last end, which stands in the same relation to things appetible, as the first principles of demonstrations to things intelligible: and, speaking generally, it is all those things which belong to the willer according to his nature. For it is not only things pertaining to the will that the will desires, but also that which pertains to each power, and to the entire man. Wherefore man wills naturally not only the object of the will, but also other things that are appropriate to the other powers . . . all of which are included in the object of the will, as so many particular goods."

person as a whole. This directive authority of reason and will means that no person is ever controlled by his lower powers except when he freely refuses to act for the universal good.

Thomas's idea of happiness is similar to Aristotle's: it is the fulfillment of human nature's characteristic potential as rational, the ability to know universal truth. But Thomas integrates Aristotle with Augustine here: happiness is not only perfecting the intellect in possessing the highest truths in philosophical contemplation but also perfecting the will in loving the highest good. This absolute Truth and absolute Good cannot be found in any finite creature.[97] Thus, happiness is found only in union with God.[98] However, because we do not have direct access to God in this world, we have to exercise choice among the finite goods available to us so as to bring us as much truth and goodness as possible. For this reason, some acts are by nature more fulfilling than others: acts ordered to higher truths and greater goods are more noble; they fulfill our potential more fully and so ought to be chosen over other acts.

By reflecting on this, we can come to know the universal truths about what actions are conducive to human perfection. These truths comprise the precepts of the natural moral law: rules that must be followed in order to attain happiness.[99] We employ our knowledge of these truths in an act of conscience, which morally guides choice by judging an action in light of these necessary rules.[100] For this reason, a well-informed conscience, one based on

---

[97] Thomas makes a point of noting that no external good (such as wealth, power, or fame) or bodily good (such as beauty, strength, health, or pleasure) can lead to happiness, since they are not perfections of the soul's rational nature (*ST* I-II.2.4–5). In light of this, what should we make of the inordinate media concern with money, fame, health, and beauty?

[98] *ST* I-II.2.8. In *ST* I-II.3.8, Thomas specifies that this union with God is the Beatific Vision: "Consequently, for perfect happiness the intellect needs to reach the very Essence of the First Cause."

A corollary of this is that, although we cannot attain perfect happiness in this life, we can attain an imperfect happiness by moving closer to God in wisdom and love (*ST* I-II.5.3). Similarly, since union with God is not something we can attain on our own, perfect happiness requires the gift of grace; yet again, though, an imperfect happiness is available to those who perfect their natural powers in virtue (*ST* I.12.4 and I-II.5.5). In both cases, the supernatural builds on and perfects human nature, so there is a continuity between worldly happiness and eternal blessedness.

[99] Aquinas corrects Aristotle here, who assumed that practical reason only concerned particular circumstances (*CNE* VI.1.1123).

[100] I.79.13. Conscience is an act of *synderesis*, reason's habitual knowledge of the first principle of practical reason, which is "to incite to good, and to murmur at evil" (*ST* I.79.12). Note that conscience directs judgments prior to acting, as well as during and afterward. It is not simply a feeling of guilt after the fact (which would be of very limited value in moral decision making).

a profound understanding of human nature and the true characteristics of happiness, is the necessary condition for all moral action. As Saint John Henry Newman succinctly puts it, "Conscience has rights because it has duties."[101]

The Moral Act and Virtue

To recapitulate: Happiness is the goal of human life; yet happiness is not mere pleasure; therefore, we need to use reason's knowledge of the order of nature to inform our desires. Reason, then, grasps the moral law, which are concrete rules recognized as the necessary means to obtain happiness. This brings us to the critical aspect of our lived reality as moral beings: making a *choice* about what to do. Since choice involves the whole person's good, it can be reduced to neither following the appetites nor to obeying abstract rational laws. Rather, choice is a *deliberated desire*: reasoning about our inclinations to discern which is best.[102] In fact, only those actions that ensue from such deliberation (as opposed to unintentional or coerced actions) are relevant to the moral life.[103] Our moral actions, therefore, arise from a complex interplay of the desire for happiness, which is moderated by the particular goods available to us and informed by reason's deliberation to determine what the true good for us is.[104] Indeed, when the will refuses to follow reason and opts for a lesser good, this is really a rejection of human nature's inclination to happiness and so is evil.[105] It is also, by extension, a rejection of the providential order of creation since we are refusing the activity for which we were created by God, and so it is also a sin.

The act of choice is made difficult, though, since as complex beings we have multiple desires that naturally seek various kinds of goods that perfect us in different ways: food, sleep, sex, prayer, friendship. The lower, animal-

---

101 Cited in John Paul II, Encyclical Letter *Veritatis Splendor* (August 6, 1993), 34. The pope's discussion of conscience in this encyclical is a bracing corrective to many popular but flawed ideas of conscience; see especially 54–63.

102 *ST* I-II.13.1.

103 *ST* I-II.1.1. These acts, arising from knowledge and free will are called *human acts* and are distinguished from those not willfully done, that is, done unconsciously or accidentally, which are known as *acts of man*.

104 *ST* I-II. QQ. 6–17, where Thomas analyzes the act of choice into thirteen steps in which knowledge of the good moves the will to act to attain the good. The details of this decision process are beyond the scope of this book but for an overview see Josef Pieper, *Living the Truth: The Truth of All Things and Reality and the Good*, trans. Lothar Krauth and Stella Lange (San Francisco: Ignatius Press, 1989), 145–51 and 179.

105 *ST* I-II.71.2.

istic desires should always be controlled by our reason and directed by the will to happiness. Therefore, in choosing which act to undertake, we need to have some criteria for what makes one better than another. Additionally, in order to choose well consistently, we need help to overcome the lure of physical pleasure. Thus, let us now consider the nature of a good act and see how our act of choice is enlightened by virtue and law.

Since a person is defined by his rationality, to perfect our human nature we should choose acts that are fully rational. While we can say that every act, merely as existing, is good in a certain way,[106] an act is morally good only if it is as fully rational as it can be. An irrational act is a betrayal of human nature and so incoherent in itself: why would we use reason and free will to choose an act that lacks rationality and enslaves us to our animal desires? Since action follows from being, a rational action perfects our nature and an irrational one frustrates that nature and undermines our desire for happiness.

The primary aspect in determining whether an act is adequately rational is the moral object. The *moral object* is the act that we choose to do to bring about some desired goal.[107] For example, if someone chooses to steal, regardless of whether it is for personal gain or to give to the poor, one is choosing an irrational act, taking that which does not belong to them, which disrupts the social order and makes happiness impossible.[108]

Great care needs to be taken in evaluating the moral object. This is because two acts that appear similar can have different moral objects and two acts that appear different can have the same moral object. With respect to the former, fending off a mugger by swinging a bat can have one moral object if what the person wills is merely to stop the assault (which is licit) but another moral object if the person actually wills to kill the assailant (which is illicit, because it is willing murder). With respect to the latter, although the use of a condom and taking the pill appear to be very different acts, they in fact both have the same moral object because what is willed is the contraceptive effect.[109] Any object that is

---

106 *ST* I.18.1. This is why a morally bad act, such as adultery, can have good *ontological* consequences, such as the conception of a beautiful child (ad 3).

107 *ST* I-II.18.2.

108 Though there is much nuance about this: see *ST* II-II.66.7.

109 For clarification on this complicated issue, see Steven J. Jensen, *Good and Evil Actions: A Journey through Saint Thomas Aquinas* (Washington, D.C.: The Catholic University of America Press, 2010), 19–43, and Steven A. Long, *The Teleological Grammar of the Moral Act* (Naples, Fla.: Sapientia Press, 2007), 10–33.

inherently irrational is incompatible with happiness and so will always make an act morally wrong.

However, even good moral objects can be part of a morally bad action. This is because we also need to consider the circumstances and intention of the action.[110] The circumstances are like the accidents of the act: who, where, when. Practicing one's musical instrument is good, but, if done at the wrong time (2:00 a.m.) or the wrong place (in the library), the action becomes irrational and so is wrong. *Intention* signifies the ultimate goal of an act, what you hope to bring about by means of the object. If one does a good act for the wrong reason (for example, giving to charity only to become popular), the act is irrational and so wrong. On the other hand, no matter how good the consequences and intention are, they can never validate a bad moral object. (The end can never justify the means.) Notice that where Mill focused solely on consequences (a kind of circumstance of the action) and Kant solely on intention, Thomas includes both of those but centers his analysis on the act itself, what the person actually does. Because it is the object of the act— the thing willfully done—that matters most, some acts are intrinsically evil.

It is clear, though, that determining which act is most rational in all three aspects is difficult.[111] Therefore, there are certain aids, two intrinsic and two extrinsic, built into creation to assist us in making good moral choices. One intrinsic aid is our natural inclinations that order us to happiness; we are not neutrally positioned but inherently desire the perfection— happiness—that comes with being fully rational. Second, while we have subrational inclinations associated with our sensitive desires, we can control and perfect these inclinations by subordinating them to reason in the development of virtue.[112] Thus, we can form habits so that good moral choices come more easily. The external aids are law and grace, both of which are given to help people lacking virtue know what ought to be done.[113] Let us first consider virtue, then turn our attention to law.

---

110 *ST* I-II.18.3–9 and I-II.20.4–5.

111 This difficulty is exacerbated by the effects of concupiscence from original sin. See Saint Augustine's rhetorically powerful description of this darkening of the intellect and distortion of the will in *On Free Choice of the Will*, I.11. However, since original sin is properly a theological topic, with a properly theological answer (grace from the sacraments), I bracket consideration of those issues here. Moreover, Thomas's understanding of the effects of original sin is somewhat more benign, since he says it does not deprave human nature but affects only the operation of powers (*ST* I-II.85.1).

112 *ST* I-II.49. proem.

113 *ST* I-II.90. proem.

Thomas largely follows Aristotle's virtue theory, but he improves it in two ways. First, he more parsimoniously connects the virtues to the principles of human action. Since human acts, as deliberated desires, arise out of our powers of reason and appetite, each of these faculties can be perfected by a specific cardinal virtue.[114] The sensitive appetite is divided into the concupiscible desire for pleasure and the irascible aversion from pain;[115] these are perfected by temperance and fortitude, respectively. The rational appetite, the will, desires the universal or common good; the virtue regulating how to attain the good for all people is justice. Practical reason is perfected by prudence that Thomas, like Aristotle, sees as the key to all virtues since it determines the true good in a specific situation.[116] Since practical reason relies on speculative reason's knowledge of reality, we also need the intellectual virtues of understanding, science, and wisdom. Thus, each of the virtues plays an essential role in a well-made choice.

The second improvement reflects Thomas's idea that perfect happiness lies in the Beatific Vision. Since this is beyond our natural capacity, we need supernatural assistance to attain it. This is the role of the theological virtues of faith, hope, and love.[117] These enable us to do that which is not possible by human nature alone: to love the naturally unlovable (e.g., an enemy), to hope for the naturally impossible (that I should be saved), to believe in the incomprehensible (the Word became flesh). The natural virtues, then, are necessary for the imperfect happiness available in this life, but eternal happiness can never be earned and is possible only because of these gifts from God.

One obvious problem is that we can develop virtue only if we know the objective standards for human goodness, the standard that will specify what acts are rational and so to be sought. This standard of rationality is found in the precepts of the natural law, and so virtue is possible only if we know the natural law. As Thomas notes, the natural law is the foundation for virtue since "all acts of virtue are prescribed by the natural law."[118] We attain virtue

---

114 *ST* I-II.58.2–3 and 61.2.

115 *ST* I.81.2.

116 *ST* I-II.57.5.

117 *ST* I-II.62.1–4.

118 *ST* I-II.94.3; cf. *ST* I-II. 92.1.ad 1. Aristotle argues that one of the functions of the polis is to educate the young in virtue (*Nicomachean Ethics*, X.9). However, this assumes that the legislators are themselves people of practical wisdom, which assumes they were raised well, and so on. To avoid an infinite regress, people need access to a natural law.

when obeying the natural law becomes habitual, an internal disposition to act in the most rational way. So, we are now brought to the natural law as the ultimate foundation for the moral life, for its precepts indicate what a person must do to be virtuous and attain happiness.

Law

That law is an aspect of moral philosophy is not obvious today, since law often contradicts morality, and morality (it is believed) cannot be legislated regardless. However, these are two profound errors. Both positions assume that the law is wholly man-made and so arbitrary. In contrast, the essence of law is to direct action so that it conforms with reality: to make human action follow truly from the being of human nature. This point is epitomized in Thomas's definition of law: law is an ordinance of reason for the common good promulgated by the proper authority.[119] We need to examine each of the characteristics in this definition in order to demonstrate how law can only be good and so inextricably bound to morality.

First, to claim that law is an ordinance of reason means that it must follow from reason's grasp of truth. Because people seek to be fully rational, law is a rational guide that will lead to their moral perfection, or happiness.[120] Laws are needed to point us to the rational truth because our appetites and free will tend to fall into error; as an ordinance of reason, law shows how *in fact—in truth—*a person ought to act.

Insisting on the rational nature of law is of great consequence, for the alternative theory is that law arises from the will of the legislator (which is known as *voluntarism* or *legal positivism*). Voluntarism is a perennial challenge for civilization, from ancient tyrants to modern democracies, for it exalts the will of the legislator as the sole criterion for law. The problem with this theory is that, if law is based on will alone, no law can ever be wrong or unjust: what has been willed has been willed. The recognition of unjust laws leads to the primordial insight that there *must be* some standard of justice other than the law itself. There must be a law, known by reason, by which to evaluate the laws people have willed for themselves. This truth is the common heritage of natural law thinking from Sophocles's *Antigone* to Martin Luther King's *Letter from Birmingham Jail*. Recognizing that unjust laws ought to be changed ineluctably points us to an order of justice above

119 *ST* I.90.4.
120 *ST* I.90.1.

human society. This is the natural law, a rational order that should direct all our legislations.[121]

As an ordinance of reason, law directs us to the *universal* good, that which is good for all people. The common good, then, is happiness, but happiness that can be participated in by everyone.[122] These common ends are found in the human desires to perfect our intellect in knowledge and to perfect our will in love. (This common good differs markedly from the sum total of individual pleasure aimed for in utilitarianism.) Law, then, provides the conditions necessary so that people can grow together in wisdom and love.

Law must be also promulgated by the proper authority.[123] Laws can only be made by those who have care of the community. In accord with the principle of subsidiarity, we all belong to many communities, each of which has its own proper authorities and orders of law. The school, the city, the corporation, the club, the state, and nation are distinct, overlapping communities, each with denominated authority empowered to make laws for the common good of that specific community (principal, mayor, CEO, governor, and president). For this reason, it is important that all authority be respected, for without it we cannot attain happiness.

Since law orders a community, the distinction of communities allows us to discern four general kinds of law that order human life in different ways.[124] The largest community we belong to is that of creation. God, by his providential reason, orders the universe to the common good of all creation. This is the eternal law that directs the activities of all creatures by inclining all natures to act for a final cause. The totality of all those actions leads to the perfection of the universe, as intended by God. Second is the community of man. While people are subject to the eternal law's direction to the good—we are naturally inclined to happiness—we can also know this order by reason. This rational grasp of the order of nature allows a person to be "provident both for itself and for others."[125] This is the natural law.

---

121 Augustine, *On Free Choice of the Will*, I.5 and *ST* I-II.93.3 and 95.2. This is developed in the next chapter.

122 *ST* I-II.90.2.

123 *ST* I-II.90.3–4.

124 *ST* I-II.91.

125 *ST* I-II.91.2. The fact that people can act on behalf of the providential order to others includes our stewardship of creation. This understanding of natural law that includes the environment is the surest grounding for an ecological ethics. On this, see my essay, "The Rational Order of Nature and the Environmental Implications of Natural Law," *Lex Naturalis* 2 (2016): 65–86.

Third are particular human communities—nations, cities, schools, clubs, corporations—which need to make rules to order a group's behavior for the common good. These are human laws (or *positive laws*, put in place by man).[126] Finally, there is the community of the Church, the people called by God and covenanted to him. This is reflected in the revealed laws given by the authority of Scripture to Jews and Christians for the sake of salvation.[127] These are the divine law. While these are theologically essential, the moral rules to attain happiness are contained in the natural law.

The Precepts of the Natural Law

The natural law encapsulates the essence of human existence. All being has within itself in inclination to perfection. For this reason, people have a natural inclination to happiness. People also have reason, which is inclined to know truth. Included in this truth is an understanding of human nature itself and what it necessary for us to attain our end.[128] This understanding of what people must do to be happy is the natural law.[129] Given the facts of human nature, this law provides detailed rules that direct people to the fullness of rational flourishing. That is, the natural law indicates what is necessary for us to grow in knowledge of truth (wisdom) and appreciation of the good (love). It also, therefore, is the foundation for virtue as the necessary conditions for correctly judging the true and the good. Just as one cannot prepare for a marathon by eating Doritos and watching television, so one cannot prepare for happiness by violating the natural law. This law is not added to human nature; rather, it is inherent in a person's dynamic inclination to fulfill himself by perfecting the intellect in wisdom and perfecting the will in love.

These laws, or precepts, fall into three levels of increasing specificity that range from very general laws to highly detailed prescriptions; the nat-

---

126 Chapter 7 discusses this more fully.

127 The Old Law (i.e., the Old Testament) includes three kinds of rules: ceremonial (regulating worship in the Temple); judicial (indicating punishments, like stoning); and moral (*ST* I-II.99). When the New Law of love superseded the Old Law, it only affected the ceremonial and judicial precepts (like dietary laws). The moral law remains unaffected, because it is based on human nature. So, while attitudes to eating pork and stoning have changed, the moral status of adultery or homosexuality has not changed. This refutes the common calumny made by secularists who blur these distinctions in order to subvert biblical morality.

128 Because the natural law is understanding our place in the order of creation, Thomas defines the natural law as the participation of a rational creature in the eternal law (*ST* I-II.91.2; cf. I-II.93.6).

129 Note how concisely this integrates the insights of Mill, Kant, and Aristotle.

ural law is this entire integrated body of precepts, all of which are relevant for attaining happiness.

These levels of precepts are known as the primary precepts, which are self-evident and so known by all people; the secondary precepts, or immediate conclusions from the primary precepts, which are general rules known to most people (though passion or vice may obscure knowledge of them); and the tertiary precepts, or applications of the secondary precepts to a concrete instance, which can be tricky and so require prudence.[130] Since the more detailed precepts are derived logically from the primary precepts, they should not be understood as a multitude of discrete rules that must be obeyed legalistically; rather, the more detailed precepts only specify what is already contained in the general ones, providing in more precise detail what is necessary to attain happiness. We therefore have to begin with the most general precept that will illuminate all the other precepts that follow.

In order to know what to do, practical reason needs a self-evident first principle, a parallel to speculative reason's principle of noncontradiction.[131] This self-evident principle, then, directs all practical reasoning because it points out the goal of our acting. We have already seen that all action, as directed to fulfilling a tendency to perfection, aims at a good that is desired. The first precept of the natural law reflects this as the most general rule about acting: "good is to be done and pursued and evil is to be avoided." This is nearly a tautology, though, since it merely states the fact that actions exist for the sake of attaining perfection.[132] Nevertheless, as the first principle of demonstration, it is impossible for someone to be ignorant of this.[133] It is therefore the basis for all reasoning about what ought to be done.

We can then apply this to human beings in particular to determine what the human good is. These precepts are self-evident so long as one knows

---

130 See *ST* I-II.100.1: "(1) Every judgment of practical reason proceeds from principles known naturally . . . (2) For some matters connected with human actions are so evident, that after very little consideration one is able at once to approve or disapprove of them by means of these general first principles: (3) while some matters cannot be the subject of judgment without much consideration of the various circumstances, which all are not competent to do carefully, but only those who are wise." Cf. *ST* I-II.100.11.

131 This summary follows *ST* I-II.94.2.

132 Indeed, Thomas points out that this is the equivalent of the principle of noncontradiction: just as the most general truth of all being is that is cannot be and not be in the same respect simultaneously, the most general truth of good, applying to all action necessarily, is that it is sought as the end of action. This is a universal truth that encompasses the dynamic reality of action in creation.

133 *ST* I.2.1.

what human nature is,[134] for we can see that the natural human inclinations indicate what is good for us. The inclinations of human nature, though, reflect the dynamism of existence as directed by our essence. Thus, inclinations will arise from the act of existence, our genus as animal, and our species as rational.

First, simply as existent, we have an inclination (shared with all being) to preserve the good of our existence. For this reason, ending one's own existence is a primordial evil since it rejects the goodness of creation. Second, as an animal, we have inclinations to preserve the species by reproducing and raising offspring. Third, as rational, our specifically human good is to perfect rationality in wisdom and love. But learning and loving is only possible in communion with other people, in conversation and friendship; thus, the precept specifically declares that we must form society with other people and know God as the highest object of knowledge and love.[135] These ends are intrinsically related, though: social intercourse is necessary to grow in wisdom and love, and as we grow in wisdom and love we are oriented to the True and the Good, God. These precepts are all self-evident and universally known, for as soon as you know that a person is a rational animal these precepts immediately follow as necessary for his perfection as a being, an animal, and rational.

Crucially, though, these precepts are not all equal. People have one ultimate end: union with God in the Beatific Vision. The other ends must be subordinated to achieving the final end, and so the lower ends can be sacrificed for the sake of a higher end. Suicide is prohibited, but one can give one's life for children (as even animals do), for country (as in a just war), or for God (as martyrs do). Similarly, reproduction is good; but where lower animals mate indiscriminately, children require the virtuous social order of a family and so procreation is restricted to stable monogamous marriages. Others forsake procreation completely and are celibate for the sake of union with God. Finally, the call of God can even lead some people to withdraw from society and live monastic lives.

---

134 While "do good and avoid evil" is *self-evident to all*, because it belongs to all being (as a transcendental), the good of human nature is *self-evident in itself but not to all* because we need to first understand what it means to be human, and it is possible to be ignorant of this. This distinction also plays a crucial role in the question of whether God's existence is self-evident (*ST* I.2.1).

135 Note that these self-evident precepts, the two highest ends of man, are simply the two great commandments: love your neighbor and love God. This Scriptural doctrine is known by reason in the natural law.

Yet these precepts—"live in society" and "love God"—are terribly vague. For true moral direction, we need more concrete rules telling us *how* to love God and *how* to live in society. This is the role of the secondary precepts, which, as "immediate conclusions" from the primary precepts, are easily inferred as necessary conditions to realizing social order and love of God. Even though these rules are not self-evident, as the most general moral precepts they are fairly obvious and broadly known. These precepts are often identified with the Decalogue.[136] The first tablet indicates what is necessary to do for our relationship with God, and the second tablet provides details for how to live justly with our neighbor.[137] Following these rules enables a person to form proper relationships with other people and with God thereby satisfying our inherent human desire for truth and love.

What actions do these precepts command? God can be known (imperfectly) by reason even without revelation;[138] since all can acknowledge the Supreme Being this obliges that he be put before any creature, that time be set aside to worship the Creator, and to speak respectfully of him. Similarly, in order to live in society, we must first respect authority, for it makes laws for the common good. Then we must protect the life of persons, for attainment of happiness—or any act—is impossible without life. Then we must protect the integrity of the family, the building block of society, by prohibiting adultery. Private property must be respected, for without a reliable system of propagating sufficient material wealth, we will not have the leisure to pursue friendship and religion. We also must protect the communal search for truth by insisting on honesty in speech. Finally, we must accept the order of justice by not desiring things that are not ours. These principles, then, indicate what actions are inherently rational and so what we must do the attain happiness in communion with others.

Nevertheless, these precepts still need to be applied to concrete situations. These applications constitute the tertiary precepts of the natural law. We know we should not steal, but what counts as stealing is not always obvious: I can put ten packets of sugar into a coffee I buy, but I cannot just walk off with that sugar in my pocket. Similarly, not all killing is murder; self-defense and just war are instances of licit killing. But, since is not always

---

136 *ST* I-II.100.1, 3, and 11. Although these precepts are easily known, they were also revealed to allow all people to know them with certainty (*ST* I.1.1).

137 *ST* II-II.122.

138 *ST* I.2.3 and I.13.10.ad 5. This is developed in chapter 8.

easy to make these judgments, the virtue of prudence is required to know how a law applies in a particular instance, especially when there appear to be conflicting duties. The more specific the situation, the more prudence is needed, for there will be more exceptions and a greater likelihood that vice or passion will distort one's judgment.[139] It is at this level that there can be legitimate disagreement among virtuous people about what the true good is. This contingency in applying the law explains why there is moral diversity among humans, even though all are guided by the natural law.

In fact, since the natural law is the foundation for all the virtues, living a virtuous life is an essential element of the promulgation of the natural law. Not only is the natural law made known by reason's participation in the eternal law; more concretely, it is manifested in people who can practically distinguish what needs to be done from what they want or the customs of their society. The virtuous person is himself a rule and measure of what ought to be done because he concretely lives according to the natural law, a fact that other people recognize because it is attuned to what people naturally see as necessary for happiness. Being able to make these judgments, which is possible only with the possession of virtue grounded in the natural law, is itself a manifestation of what needs to be done in order to fulfill human nature.[140]

If people know the natural law, one might wonder how it is possible that so many people violate it. There are many answers to this. The main answer is free will, for people can always freely refuse to pay attention to the natural law, even though they know it.[141] It is this act of the will ignoring reason's grasp of truth that is the primary source for why people act irrationally. This is especially the case when people lack virtue and so are more inclined to follow sensitive appetites against the rule of reason.[142]

We should also acknowledge that the use of reason is not static in history. Societies will embody unequal use of reason based on many contingencies. This is important, for it explains how, while the natural law remains the same, humanity's knowledge of it can progress over the eras of history.

---

139 ST I-II.94.4–6.

140 This issue of promulgation is a neglected aspect of the philosophy of natural law, but see Scott Jude Roniger, "Do Friends Need Justice or Do the Just Need Friendship? Natural Law as the Foundations for Justice and Friendship," *Lex Naturalis* 3 (2018): 57–84, esp. at 72–76.

141 ST I-II.77.2.

142 ST I-II.71.2.ad 3: "Now the presence of vices and sins in man is owing to the fact that he follows the inclination of his sensitive nature against the order of his reason."

Many things once thought acceptable (slavery and child labor) are now understood to be contrary to the natural law. Similarly, when a society regresses and enters a moral dark age, things once known to be evil may once again become socially acceptable (abortion and homosexual activity).

The natural law, in short, simply acknowledges that the world is composed of different kinds of being, each of which has an activity that characterizes its flourishing. Humans, too, have a determinate goal for their existence. But this flourishing cannot be achieved in just any way; on the contrary, there are things that must be done in order to flourish. The necessary steps are articulated in the precepts of the natural law that enable people to be happy, to grow together in wisdom and love and eventually to know God in heaven. And because humans are all the same, this ethic applies to all people at all times, regardless of the state of the society in which they live.[143]

Final Thoughts on Natural Law

We see, then, that natural law combines the best parts of the other moral theories with none of their limitations because it defines the good as the perfection of being. Being is naturally dynamic and oriented to the good. People, for their part, are motivated by both appetite and reason. Utilitarianism and deontology, choosing one or the other, reduce ethics to pleasure or abstract duty. But natural law realizes that our perfection, happiness, can be attained only by following specific laws based on human nature. Moreover, as Aristotle observes, this makes us excellent as persons, for the natural law dictates what it is to be rational and in what virtue lies. This perfection of our rational nature is realized in wisdom and love and so flows over into the common good of society and, indeed, all of creation in providential stewardship of the world.[144] Thus, the perfection of human beings contributes to the perfection of the being of the universe. Being as good is consummated in the goodness of being as perfected.

However, we have also seen that attaining happiness requires living in society; for this reason, we must turn to the constitution of the social order in political philosophy in the next chapter. Before that, though, let us consider another kind of good: beauty.

---

143 The most ubiquitous challenge to natural law is nominalism. If there is no human nature, nothing can be obligatory for humans. But nominalism then has to face the problem of explaining the regularity of nature; this regularity includes the fact that humans all desire happiness, friendship, and truth.

144 *SCG* III.77–78.

THE GOOD OF MAKING: BEAUTY AND ART

Epistemology analyzes knowing the truth as a perfection of human potential; ethics analyzes the doing the good as a perfection of human activity. In addition to knowing and doing, however, human beings have a third fundamental activity that is necessary for flourishing: making things.[145] Thus, there are three ways people bring perfection to the world by increasing the amount of being in it. Knowing and loving (as well as life activities in general) are activities through which we increase our own being in terms of the accidental qualities of wisdom and love. Since the perfection of this activity remains in the one who is acting, it is called *immanent activity*. But we can also act to perfect the material world around us by making things from the potency of nature. This activity, where the perfection is in the object that is produced, is called *transitive*.[146] While the former activities are the truest perfections of human nature, we cannot neglect the importance of transitive activity.

People make things for two very different reasons. Some things are made because they are useful; these are tools, which even other animals can use in order to survive. Yet there is another kind of making that has no practical usefulness: we make these things simply to express our creativity as something that is good in itself. These objects are works of art: they aim not at usefulness but at beauty; in that way, they are simply good in themselves. Of course, many useful things also aim for beauty, which shows that making has a purpose beyond mere utility. In this sense, the beautiful is similar to the true and the good, as being something sought for its own sake. This is why art is so important; it is one of the activities that make human existence integrally meaningful.

The beauty sought for by art is a sort of good. But, as with the true and the good, beauty is reduced when it is separated from the fullness of being. We can see this with respect to beauty in a couple of contemporary clichés. On the one hand, the notion that "beauty is in the eye of the beholder" disregards that, if beauty is to be valued—if it is to have the significance, we think it does[147]—it must be grounded in objective reality. On the other hand,

---

145 Aristotle, *Metaphysics* VI.1 (1025b22–28).

146 *DV* 8.6, *SCG* II.1.2, and *ST* I.18.3.ad 1. Typically, because immanent acts change the agent, they are an accident of quality, while transitive acts, in changing other things, are an accident of action.

147 The existential significance of beauty has been a commonplace in Western thought since Plato. For example, Plato identifies it with the Good as the source of all intelligibility (*Symposium* 210e5–211c6; this is interestingly recapitulated by Plotinus in *Ennead* I.6); Augustine, at the

art is often discussed as primarily being a vehicle for "messages" in a way that makes beauty irrelevant. But this reduces the reality of art, since it ignores the distinction between beauty and truth. To properly appreciate both beauty and the place of art, then, we have to show how it is a special kind of good that manifests a distinctive property of being.

Nevertheless, it is also obvious the people's judgments about beauty vary tremendously, not just among individuals but especially among cultures. While it is true that some things—discordant sounds and repugnant sights—can never be seen to be beautiful, the music, dance, and sculpture of Western, African, and Asian peoples clearly show that there is something to the claim that beauty has to appeal to the person who is experiencing it. The resolution to this apparent conflict is, once again, that the truth is both/and: beauty is both an objective reality and an element of subjective experience. As rooted in being, beauty is a transcendental property, but that reality must be apprehended by an individual in such a way as draw him to a sort of higher experience that is not simply about "facts."[148]

In order to clarify the place of beauty in the perennial philosophy, let us first distinguish the act of *making* from *doing* that is the object of ethics. The goal of making, beauty, must then be defined, showing how it is grounded in the principles of being. Finally, we can explore how our subjective ability to appreciate beauty shapes our experience of this property of being.

Art and the Creation of Beauty

Making, the urge for people to be creative, is an essential aspect of human nature. While the immanent activities of knowing the truth and doing the good perfect human nature directly, making things is an act by which a person imitates the productive activity of God. In creation, God acts gratuitously by making things, not only by creating them ex nihilo but also by imposing order by giving form to matter.[149] This is the creation of natural

---

point of his conversion, invokes God as "Beauty so ancient and so new" (*Confessions* X.27); and Fyodor Dostoevsky's Christ figure from *The Idiot*, Prince Myshkin, famously claims that "beauty will save the world." For an insightful history of the idea of beauty, see Piotr Jaroszynski, *Beauty and Being: Thomistic Perspectives*, trans. Hugh McDonald, Étienne Gilson Series 33 (Toronto: Pontifical Institute of Medieval Studies, 2011).

148 In fact, Plato argues that this sort of experience can only be caused by some sort of divine inspiration (*Phaedrus*, 248a1–257b6). This notion that beauty is tied to the divine remains with us in the fact that works of art are housed in a museum, or a building dedicated to the Muses.

149 *ST* I.44.2 and 3.

beauty.[150] As we are in the image of God, we too aim to make gratuitous beauty by giving form to matter in the creation of works of art. To gratuitously bring about beauty is a paradigmatic act of spiritual transcendence: beauty serves no biological purpose; it is not something that is needed to survive. Yet all human societies create and value beauty because it is an expression of our appreciation of the goodness of creation. Thus, like philosophical contemplation, the creation of art is one of those acts of leisure that is done simply as an end in itself. As Thomas notes, "The reason why the philosopher is compared to the poet is that both are concerned with wonders."[151]

The ability to produce objects well is *art*, the virtue of practical reason ordered to making things. This making can be divided into two main types. All those things people produce to help themselves survive, things that serve a utilitarian purpose, are the servile arts. This would include everything from how to build a wheel to computer science. Those arts that directed to making things simply to be enjoyed for their own sake are the liberal arts, since they reflect our transcendent freedom.[152] Both of these types of art require the maker to possess two gifts: creativity and skill.

First, the artist must have a sensitivity to the beauty in the world that allows him to see into its metaphysical depth and express it in a new and provocative way. The artist desires not to merely copy the world but to present the wonderful nature of reality in an attractive and compelling fashion.[153] This creative insight of the artist's spiritual imagination endows the materials

---

150 Augustine, *Sermon 241* (available at http://www.vatican.va/spirit/documents/spirit_20000721_agostino_en.html): "Question the beauty of the earth, question the beauty of the sea, question the beauty of the air . . . question all these things. They all answer you, 'Here we are, look; we're beautiful.' Their beauty is their confession. Who made these beautiful changeable things, if not one who is beautiful and unchangeable?" This sentiment is wonderfully communicated in Gerard Manley Hopkins's poem, *Pied Beauty*, in which he writes: "Glory be to God for dappled things."

151 *CM* I.3.55.

152 Indeed, there is more freedom in making than in either knowing or doing. In knowing, truth is obtained in adhering to reality as it is; in doing, good is attained only by following the natural law as the necessary means to happiness. But in making, the artist's ability to express beauty is limited only by his personal creativity and skill.

153 In *On the Teacher* 14, Augustine makes the acerbic but obvious point that no one pays a teacher to find out the teacher's opinion; we pay teachers to find out the truth. In the same way, we might say that no one pays an artist to find out what the world looks like; we can discover that on our own. Rather, we pay an artist to see how his transformative vision can reveal the beauty of creation that would not be evident apart from his artistry.

of nature with even greater beauty.[154] We can say that "art imitates nature" not in being a slavish representation of it but rather in having an awe for its splendid creativity, for being able to impose form on the potency of matter. In this way, the artist continues the creative activity of God. A fine illustration of this is the way in which trees are pictured by van Gogh: his artistry takes something from nature and endows it with new meaning, magnifying our experience of nature and filling it with new affective significance.

But even with this creative intuition, the one who makes art must have the skill to bring the idea to fruition. This is where the tradition recognized a virtue, parallel to prudence's ability to know what the morally correct act is, which empowers people to make things well.[155] This is, for Thomas, the proper meaning of art: it is the virtue concerned with right reason about how things are to be made.[156] Art, then, is a virtue of practical reason. The key difference between prudence and art is that while acts of prudence perfect the agent—the one who is acting becomes a good person—acts of the virtue of art perfect the object being worked on. Consequently, the measure of whether someone possesses this virtue is in the work of art itself.[157] (For this reason, the name *art* is eventually transferred to the works themselves.)

Like all the intellectual virtues, art is an excellence of reason. If art is imposing form on matter, it is imposing intelligibility onto the potency of the materials. Sculpture, painting, music, dance: all take the raw material of the world and impose new order on it, giving it a new intelligibility. We might observe, as a corollary, that to the extent a work of art lacks rationality, it is bad art; it might reflect the baser animal impulses, but it cannot be considered a fully human production.[158]

---

154 Just as God creates the universe by means of the divine ideas (*ST* I.14.8 and I.15.2), and so God's mind is the rule for the truth of things in the world, artists' ideas are creative of a new reality and so they are the rule of the truth of the artifact produced (*ST* I.14.8.ad 3).

155 See Aristotle, *Nicomachean Ethics* VI.4–5.

156 *ST* I-II.57.4.

157 Art is good if it is beautiful; art is bad if it is ugly. Since good is distinguished from beauty, art, in itself, has no moral responsibility (*ST* I-II.57.4: "Art does not presuppose rectitude of the appetite"). A well-made piece of art can lack a morally redemptive message. However, since every artist is a human being, he has a primary duty to morality and so should refrain from creating art that is not morally edifying. Prudence, then, is superior to art. For that reason, particularly vile examples of art ought to be censored for the sake of the common good, especially if they are well made and so enticing (*ST* II-II.169.2.ad 4).

158 This might be the easiest way to distinguish art from pornography. While both often portray nudes, the former does so in way in which appeals to the intellect and the latter appeals to the

Yet because art is the virtue that perfects *practical* reason, it must also be distinguished from the virtues of speculative reason. Because art is different from science, beauty is different from truth. Art is about making beautiful things—it is not primarily meant to convey information. This is why politicized art—art whose main goal is to make a point—essentially fails as art and is better seen as propaganda. This reduction of art to messaging fundamentally repudiates the fact that beauty ought to be redemptive: it pulls us out of the quotidian material world and points us to the transcendent realm.

Beauty as a Property of Being

We now need to consider the object of the virtue of art: beauty. Thomas recapitulates much of the tradition in defining beauty as *that which gives joy when seen*.[159] Since this definition's invocation of the sense of sight might seem to restrict beauty to material objects alone, we can make room for spiritual beauty by rephrasing it as *that which gives joy when contemplated*. This definition makes two points about beauty: it arises from an act of contemplation and that contemplation elicits joy. This definition reveals the significance of beauty: it combines a cognitive act (contemplation) with an appetitive act (the feeling of joy).

Beauty, then, is not reducible to truth or goodness alone. Both truth and beauty are known in contemplation, but, since the contemplation of beauty gives rise to joy or is pleasurable, it is different from the contemplation of truth that perfects the intellect with knowledge. Yet neither is beauty reducible to the good. The good elicits in the appetites a desire to *possess* the object. Beauty departs from this because we are satisfied merely with the sight, or contemplation, of beauty. Where an apple incites a hunger to eat it, to possess its very being, music elicits a desire simply to listen; contemplation alone gives joy.

Beauty, then, relies on both the cognitive and the appetitive faculties. Recognition of beauty occurs when we consider an object of perception not in terms of its truth, nor in our desire to possess the thing, but rather when we rest in the vision itself for the sake of the joy.

There are three important consequences of this definition of beauty. First, this explains the uniquely compelling nature of beauty. Because beauty

---

sensual libido. In fact, Thomas argues that it is good for women to adorn themselves—with cosmetics, clothing, and jewelry, say—just so long as it does not incite lust (*ST* II-II.169.2).

159 *ST* I.5.4.ad 1.

appeals to both the intellect and will—contemplation and joy—it can exercise a stronger influence than truth or goodness alone. Beauty, because it appeals to intellect and will simultaneously, can speak to us in a voice that is more direct, more profound than the other properties of being.

Second, the fact that beauty is rooted in cognition—and not appetite alone—means that beauty must have some relation to the truth. That is, it has to have an objective ontological grounding. This attention to the cognitive dimension is necessary, for if we focus solely on the experience of pleasure, we are liable to fall into relativism because different observers might gain pleasure from different things.

Third, since beauty is related to both truth and goodness, we can conclude that like the true and the good, beauty is a transcendental property.[160] That is, like all transcendentals, beauty is an inherent property of all being. It is this objective foundation in reality that enables us to be cognitively aware of beauty to begin with; yet it also guarantees that there are objective principles governing what is beautiful. Let us explore the transcendental nature of beauty more fully.

Recall that the transcendental properties belong to all things just because they are beings. In contrast to the ten Aristotelian categories that mark out some division or kind of being, transcendental properties are convertible with being, since they apply to all entities in all categories of being.[161] One consequence of this is that, while we can define specific kinds of being (e.g., blue, tall, living, or human), we cannot define (i.e., make finite) the transcendentals, since they cannot be limited to some kind of thing.[162] In contrast, as notional additions to being, the transcendentals represent being—every being—considered under a certain aspect. As a result, the transcendental properties can be differentiated from one another insofar as each one focuses our attention on a particular aspect of being (even though that that aspect belongs to every existing entity).

---

160 Because beauty elicits joy, which is an act of the will, Thomas himself sees beauty merely as a species of the good, which is the object of the will (*Summa Theologica* I-II.27.1.ad 3); see the discussion in Jan Aertsen, *Medieval Philosophy and the Transcendentals: The Case of Thomas Aquinas*, Studien und Texte zur Geistesgeschichte des Mittelalters 52 (Leiden, New York, and Cologne: E. J. Brill, 1996), 335–59. However, others argue for beauty as a transcendental property distinct from the good; see Francis J. Kovach, *Philosophy of Beauty* (Norman, Okla.: University of Oklahoma Press, 1974), 236–50.

161 *DV* 1.1. This paragraph is a summary of the argument in chapter 3.

162 This is what Aristotle means when he says that being is not a genus, or subdivision of being. *Metaphysics* III.3 (998b21–25).

Being is able to be considered under these diverse aspects because being, as act, presents itself to us in a variety of ways and so has a variety of effects on us. First, being can present itself to the mind's potential for grasping forms, and this correlation of being and thought is the true. Second, being can present itself as the act of perfection and so elicit desire from the will, and this is the good. Third, being can present itself with characteristics that call for joyful or pleasurable contemplation, and this is the transcendental beauty.[163] Since all of these are grounded in being—in the act of existence—the threat of relativism in all areas (epistemology, ethics, and aesthetics) is eliminated.[164] Thus, truth is grounded in the intelligibility of act, for a thing is knowable inasmuch as it is in act and obscure or unknowable to the degree it remains in potency.[165] The activity of a being reveals what it is, and so the intelligibility of act allows for the adequation of the thing and mind as receptive to being. In addition, it is a metaphysical principle that being actualizes potency, for it is "the act of all acts and the perfection of all perfections."[166] The good reflects this, since the good is the perfection of being that is desired by all things.[167]

In similar fashion, then, beauty must be based on an objective property of being caused by the act of existence. Thomas specifies three characteristics that make a being beautiful because they will elicit joy in the one who contemplates: proportion (or harmony), integrity (or wholeness), and clarity (or radiance).[168] Instead of arising directly from the act of existence, as truth and goodness, the characteristics of beauty arise from the form, which communicates actuality to matter. First, the formal cause structures matter so as to make it identifiable—a formless blob causes confusion until we

---

163 See Jacques Maritain, *Art and Scholasticism*, 30: "Like the one, the true and the good, the beautiful is *being* itself considered from a certain aspect; it is a property of being: it is not an accident superadded to being, it adds to being merely a relation of reason, it is being considered as delighting, by the mere intuition of it, an intellectual nature. So everything is beautiful just as everything is good, at least in a certain relation."

164 *ST* I.4.1.ad 3.

165 *ST* I.5.2 and I.87.1.

166 *DP* 7.2.ad 9; see also *OBE* c. 4.

167 *ST* I.5.1.

168 *ST* I.39.8. Proportion is the oldest of these criteria, arising first with Pythagoras, whose notion of mathematical order informs both Plato and Aristotle. Clarity was first proposed by Plotinus (*Ennead* VI.7) in order to account for beauty in simple objects without parts, like color or light. Integrity as a criterion for beauty was original to Thomas, possibly under the influence of the idea of moral beauty as articulated by Hugh of St. Victor. See Christopher Scott Sevier, *Aquinas on Beauty* (Lanham, Md.: Lexington Books, 2015), 103–45.

figure out what it is. This structuring of matter gives the thing integrity and proportion, since it will have all the parts appropriate for that particular form and they will be internally harmonious in accord with the nature of the form. Form not only gives order to matter, but in communicating act it pulls matter from the obscurity of potency to the intelligibility of actuality; the form makes the thing what it is. This is what is intended by radiance or clarity, where the being of the thing shines forth due to the presence of the form. These three qualities give objects an immediate sensuous appeal we call beauty.

As with all the transcendentals, we recognize that beauty is an analogical property. There is purely physical beauty in material objects, with a material sense of proportion and integrity.[169] But there is intellectual beauty associated with mathematics, especially in the abstractions of geometry and scientific equations where there is proportion, harmony, and an intelligible clarity.[170] There is also moral beauty, the proportion of human behavior to human nature, the integrity of all the love and wisdom one would expect, and the radiance associated with the holy life that makes saints the most attractive of people. (In fact, the halo represents the radiance of this beauty.) Finally, there is the Beauty that is God, an infinite refulgence of glory to be seen in the Beatific Vision.

The criterion of clarity helps us appreciate the contemplative nature of beauty as well as how that contemplation differs from cognition of truth. In giving order to matter, the form of the thing can be made luminously present. On the one hand, in contemplating the thing, we intuitively grasp the reality of the thing at the level of its particularity. Truth, on the other hand, is a contemplation directed to grasping the nature of the substance, which, as we have seen, is attained through the process of abstraction in which the universal form is separated from matter. This abstraction lets us understand the individual in terms of universal properties, giving knowledge the necessity needed to ground certainty.

---

169 Even in the arts, beauty is realized in a highly analogical fashion due to the nature of their materiality. Architecture needs to be useful, so its beauty has to be integrated with its usefulness; literature has to present some meaning, and so beauty is conditioned by that. Music might be the purest of the arts because it is pure form and so its beauty need not be conditioned by meaning or usefulness. (An exception, of course, is religious music—in fact, religious art in general—that must be beautiful as well as meaningful and useful, a fact which indicates why it is such a difficult art. See Maritain, *Art and Scholasticism*, chap. 8.)

170 Paul Dirac, one of the great physicists of the twentieth century, argued that discovering a beautiful equation is most important, for then it will certainly be true.

With beauty, contemplation always remains at the level of the particular. That is, instead of abstracting a universal form from the matter, we contemplate the individual in the matter, and in so doing let the form become present to us in that radical uniqueness. In this contemplation of beauty, the power of the form to structure matter, to make it what it is, to express itself through the potency of the matter impresses us. This is clarity: the radiance of existence at the level of the particular existent.

This also explains one of the curious aspects about our experience of beauty. If someone asks us why something is beautiful, we can give some vague descriptions, but in the end we have to simply exhort "Look at that sunset" or "Listen to this music." The problem here is that language works at the level of universals and abstractions; words are ideal for communicating truth in terms of universal categories or kinds. The particularity of beauty—the direct contact with the thing itself—can never be fully conveyed by means of these universal words. It can only be experienced. Oscar Wilde is on to this fact when he sardonically observes that there are two ways to dislike art: to dislike it or to like it rationally. This is the case because in rationalizing art we are abstracting some meaning from the work itself, which suppresses the particularity of the experience of beauty.

Grasping art in this way means that there is a way of knowing other than the abstractive processes leading to truth. This other way of knowing is called *connaturality*. Connatural knowledge is the nonconceptual receptivity to being that enables us to know a truth even in the absence of conceptual (or abstract) knowledge. Thomas introduces the idea by noting: "Now rectitude of judgment is twofold: first, on account of perfect use of reason, secondly, on account of a certain connaturality with the matter about which one has to judge."[171] The most common example of connatural knowledge is how a virtuous person can intuitively know what the good thing to do is even if they have never studied moral philosophy.[172] In connatural knowledge, there is a direct intuition of the reality present without abstracting to the nature of the cause as a universal principle.[173]

For our purposes here, we note that the experience of beauty is similarly connatural: people can recognize the orderliness of form not only by

171 *ST* II-II.45.2.

172 *ST* I.1.6.ad 3. In fact, studying philosophy has been known to prevent one from knowing the good.

173 See Jacques Maritain, "On Knowledge through Connaturality," in *The Range of Reason* (New York: Scribner's, 1952), 22–29.

abstract cognition of essences but also in the immediacy of sense-experience. Because sense-experience is tied to the emotions,[174] that sensitive experience will be accompanied with an affective reaction, the feeling of joy. There is a union of cognition of particular form with the emotional reaction to it.[175] It is the refulgence of the form, shown forth by the harmony of the parts of the thing and the completeness of the substance, that is connaturally perceived as good in itself and that gives rise to joy, a quiescent resting in the good of creation itself.[176] Beauty is the intelligibility of existence and form as actual, perceivable in the sensible, in matter as particular. This is an aspect of every being whatsoever, and so the world should always be attended to with an awe-filled appreciation.

Aesthetics: The Subjective Experience of Beauty

Beauty is a transcendental property, for all beings have a form that orders the matter and gives it (at least some) proportion, integrity, and radiance. If the matter fails to express these qualities, the object is ugly.[177] As one philosopher puts it, "The feeling of displeasure, revulsion, or even fright that accompanies our perception of an ugly thing is owing to our awareness that something has gone wrong in it: it is not all it should be."[178] We recognize beauty by a connatural intuition, a vision by which we grasp the clarity of the thing and so react with joy. Let us now turn to that subjective element in this experience of beauty.[179]

While beauty is an objective reality, it is nevertheless true that it is in our reaction to that reality that beauty is fully realized. The response of joy arising from our awareness of the object is what distinguishes beauty from the other

---

174 *ST* I-II.22–23.

175 *ST* I.5.4.ad 1. Just as moral knowledge requires a virtuous disposition, so aesthetic receptivity requires a sensitivity to the presence of beauty in the world.

176 *ST* I-II.23.4.

177 In the same way, we can say that a barren fig tree lacks something of the truth and goodness of a fecund tree.

178 Armand Maurer, *About Beauty: A Thomistic Interpretation* (Houston: Center for Thomistic Studies, 1983), 13.

179 Modern thought's emphasis on the individual subject has made this experience their primary philosophical concern about beauty. In fact, the study of aesthetics was given that name only in the eighteenth century by Alexander Baumgarten (1714–1762), and it implies the subjective sensitive experience as opposed to investigating the metaphysical nature of beauty. This parallels the developments for truth and goodness: the *cogito* puts the human mind at the center of truth, as does the fact-value dichotomy in ethics.

transcendentals. Thus, beauty can only be grasped in the active experience of the object; it is not a judgment after the fact, as might happen with truth, it is an immediate awareness coincident with the vision or hearing itself. We take a natural pleasure in the beauty of sensible things;[180] we do not need to cogitate and argue ourselves into believing something is beautiful.

Yet it is clear that many in our world have become inured to the joys of beauty. Why has our world largely gone blind to it? There are two aspects to this subjective experience that we need to consider: the demeanor of the viewer or listener and the culture-bound nature of artistic expression.

In order to experience the joy that is characteristic of beauty, the perceiver must be attentive to beauty and ready to appreciate it. More philosophically, we can say he must be in a state of equilibrium to properly receive the radiance of the form. We need to be open to the experience. If we look at the object only in terms of its usefulness, we miss the gratuitousness that is beauty. An attitude of pragmatic exploitation of the world would preclude the possibility of aesthetic experience. Similarly, an emotional hardness, an inability to be moved to joy at the goodness of the universe, also blinds us to the reality of beauty. (This modern condition is best seen as the sin of acedia, the spiritual blindness to the good that the world has to offer.) The first step to enjoying beauty, then, is to have a mind that is open to seeing the beauty of the world. This is a kind of moral virtue: we refrain from imposing our needs on the world and instead let truth, goodness, and beauty shape our spiritual reception of reality.

The second consideration about our appreciation of beauty is the fact that our vision is always mediated by cultural contexts. Although beauty is not in the eye of the perceiver, it is nevertheless true that our ability to appreciate beauty requires knowledge of the cultural idiom in which the object is presented. The way a specific society or tradition understands the world shapes how they create and consume works of art. Additionally, even within one society, the development of the cultural milieu informs aesthetics, so that over time different periods will have different criteria for beauty. Our musical and artistic tastes differ from those of fifty, a hundred, and three hundred years ago, because the styles and media have changed. Such changes are sometimes evident in a single society over a fairly short time: King David is represented in radically different way by Donatello (1440), Michelangelo (1504), and Bernini (1624). All are masterpieces, yet each

180 *ST* I.91.3.ad 3.

speaks in a particular cultural voice. The techniques and materials change; the grammar of symbolism changes. To fully appreciate any work of art, one needs to be familiar with these rules. A lack of familiarity will obviously impede the ability to perceive beauty. A person unfamiliar with opera or jazz is not in a position to judge the beauty of a performance.

What is true of changing tastes during the Italian Renaissance is magnified when we consider the difference between world cultures. We need to exercise restraint in criticizing works we do not understand; we need, rather, to be open to appreciating the new modes of beauty culturally foreign works can reveal to us. In other words, we need to distinguish our personal taste—that with which we are comfortable and conversant—from objective judgments of beauty. Since beauty is always in a particular object that resists universal abstraction, we cannot make universal rules that narrowly define integrity, harmony, and clarity. We need therefore to take each new object with an eye open to the spiritual fecundity of human creativity and natural sublimity. This is the only way to do justice to the creative genius of humankind.

Final Thoughts on Beauty

Art and beauty are significant for human life, since they call us out from the mundane and utilitarian aspects of the world.[181] By combining the intellect and the will in appreciating the depth of being, beautiful objects reveal that there is a reality that goes beyond what can be grasped by the sciences. In this way, as Goethe comments, "Beauty is not so much a fulfillment as rather a promise."[182] Beauty whets our spirit for something greater.[183] In fact, even Joseph Ratzinger argued that "[t]he only really effective apologia for Christianity comes down to two arguments, namely, the saints the Church has produced and the art which has grown in her womb. Better witness is borne to the Lord by the splendor of holiness and art which have

---

181 In fact, Pseudo-Dionysius suggests that the Greek word for beauty, *kalon*, is derived from the verb *kaleo*, meaning to call or beckon; see *The Divine Names*, IV.7.

182 Cited in Josef Pieper, *"Divine Madness": Plato's Case against Secular Humanism*, trans. Lothar Krauth (San Francisco: Ignatius Press, 1995), 48.

183 This desire is well articulated by David Bentley Hart, *The Experience of God: Being, Consciousness, Bliss* (New Haven: Yale University Press, 2013), 283: "[Beauty] is the movement of a gracious disclosure of something otherwise hidden, which need not reveal itself or give itself. . . . The beautiful affords us our most perfect experience of that existential wonder that is the beginning of all speculative wisdom. This state of amazement, once again, lies always just below the surface of our quotidian consciousness; but beauty stirs us from our habitual forgetfulness of the wonder of being."

arisen in the community of believers than by the clever excuses [of] apologetics."[184] This must always be kept in mind in considering what Jacques Maritain refers to as the "majesty and poverty" of philosophy: philosophy leads us to grasp the highest truths of which we are naturally capable; but there is always something greater beyond that nature. Beauty is the arrow pointing us that way.[185]

FURTHER READING
Ethics and Morality

D'Entreves, A. P. *Natural Law*. London: Hutchison, 1951.

Jensen, Steven J. *Good and Evil Actions: A Journey through Saint Thomas Aquinas*. Washington, D.C.: The Catholic University of America Press, 2010.

_____. *Knowing the Natural Law: Precepts, Inclinations, and Deriving Oughts*. Washington, D.C.: The Catholic University of America Press, 2015.

_____. *Sin: A Thomistic Psychology*. Washington, D.C.: The Catholic University of America Press, 2018.

MacInerny, Ralph. *Ethica Thomistica: The Moral Philosophy of Thomas Aquinas*. Rev. ed. Washington, D.C.: The Catholic University of America Press, 1997.

MacIntyre, Alasdair. *A Short History of Ethics*. New York: Touchstone, 1966.

_____. *After Virtue*. 3rd ed. Notre Dame, Ind.: University of Notre Dame Press, 2007.

_____. *Ethics in the Conflicts of Modernity: An Essay on Desire, Practical Reasoning, and Narrative*. Cambridge: Cambridge University Press, 2016.

Pieper, Josef. *The Four Cardinal Virtues*. Translated by Lawrence E. Lynch. Notre Dame, Ind.: University of Notre Dame Press, 1966.

Rist, John M. *Real Ethics: Rethinking the Foundations of Morality*. Cambridge: Cambridge University Press, 2002.

Rommen, Heinrich. *The Natural Law: A Study in Legal and Social History and Philosophy*. Indianapolis: Liberty Fund, 1998.

Rziha, John. *Perfecting Human Actions: St. Thomas Aquinas on Human Participation in Eternal Law*. Washington, D.C.: The Catholic University of America Press, 2009.

Simon, Yves R. *The Tradition of Natural Law: A Philosopher's Reflections*. Edited by Vukan Kuic. New York: Fordham University Press, 1965.

Veatch, Henry B. *Rational Man: A Modern Interpretation of Aristotelian Ethics*. Bloomington, Ind.: Indiana University Press, 1962.

184 Joseph Ratzinger with Vittorio Messori, *The Ratzinger Report*, trans. Salvator Attanasio and Graham Harrison (San Francisco: Ignatius Press, 1985), 129–30. That the holiness of saints is, ontologically speaking, a mode of beauty is compellingly demonstrated in Ramos, *Dynamic Transcendentals*, 147–225.

185 In the striking phrase of Orthodox theologian Nicholas Cabasilas, beauty is an "arrow that wounds." This idea is analyzed by Joseph Ratzinger in *On the Way to Jesus Christ*, trans. Michael J. Miller (San Francisco: Ignatius Press, 2004), 32–41.

Aesthetics and Beauty

Eco, Umberto. *The Aesthetics of Thomas Aquinas*. Translated by Hugh Bredin. Cambridge, Mass.: Harvard University Press, 1988.

Gilson, Étienne. *The Arts of the Beautiful*. New York: Charles Scribner's Sons, 1965.

_____. *Forms and Substances in the Arts*. New York: Charles Scribner's Sons, 1966.

Jaroszynski, Piotr. *Beauty and Being: Thomistic Perspectives*. Translated by Hugh McDonald. Étienne Gilson Series 33. Toronto: Pontifical Institute of Medieval Studies, 2011.

Maritain, Jacques. *Art and Scholasticism*. Translated by J. F. Scanlan. New York: Charles Scribner's Sons, 1930.

_____. *Creative Intuition in Art and Poetry*. New York: Meridian Books, 1954.

Maurer, Armand A., CSB. *About Beauty: A Thomistic Interpretation*. Houston: Center for Thomistic Studies, 1983.

Pieper, Josef. *Only the Lover Sings: Art and Contemplation*. Translated by Lothar Krauth. San Francisco: Ignatius Press, 1990.

Sevier, Christopher Scott. *Aquinas on Beauty*. Lanham, Md.: Lexington Books, 2015.

Trapani, John G. *Poetry, Beauty, and Contemplation: The Complete Aesthetics of Jacques Maritain*. Washington, D.C.: The Catholic University of America Press, 2011.

Chapter 7

The Person and the Common Good: Political Philosophy

THE PROBLEM: RENDERING UNTO CAESAR WHAT IS CAESAR'S

The hyperpoliticization of American society might seem to vindicate Aristotle's observation that "man is by nature a political animal."[1] But I think the Greek philosopher would say today's acrimonious climate fundamentally misses his point. Aristotle was not advocating for partisan divisions but rather recognizing what we have already noted: that in order for people to attain happiness, they must live in society. Human rational faculties—both the intellect's search for truth and the will's inclination to love—require intensive human interaction to come to full fruition. Aristotle himself recognizes this uniquely social aspect of human happiness when he proclaims that to live outside of society makes one "either a beast or a god."[2]

Politics, then, arises from the fact that *a person exists for something beyond himself*. The natural human inclination for the good, the perfection of human nature in terms of wisdom and love, necessarily involves the individual forming relations with others. We have seen, though, that these inclinations point to two different kinds of relations. First, there are necessary temporal relations in human society: communities in which humans interact for the sake of a mutual material benefit and safety but also for spiritual communion in virtue and friendship. Politics, therefore, exists for the sake of guiding people to happiness in community. Because its goal is the perfection of human nature, politics must be seen as continuous with ethics. However, since complete happiness is not found in finite, temporal ends, a person longs to form a higher relation, that of being in eternal union with God. Aristotle notes that, if there were nothing beyond this world—if God

---

1 Aristotle, *Politics* I.2 (1253a3).

2 Aristotle, *Politics* I.2 (1253a29).

did not exist—then politics would be the highest science;[3] but because people have a superior end, politics must pursue its own goals as a contribution toward that ultimate end. Thus, people can find happiness only in recognizing they exist for life in society and, ultimately, for God. When politics fails to attend to these realities of human nature as known in the natural law, when it degenerates to an exercise of power for its own sake, it perverts itself for it destroys the people it was meant to serve.[4]

Living in society, though, requires that there be peace and order. Political philosophy explores the principles for attaining these conditions so that that flourishing becomes possible. While we naturally get along with friends, we need some intelligible principle to guarantee that we treat even strangers well. The principle ordering social relations is justice,[5] which establishes the objective standard to guarantee that everyone is given what is owed to him. This is foundational for society for, as Augustine notes, when everyone respects the rules of justice, a society has peace, the "tranquility of order."[6] Thus, justice secures peaceful order as the necessary precondition for forming relations conducive to human flourishing in terms of wisdom and love. However, because some people will not adhere to these rules of justice, political theory also acknowledges the need for a public authority—the state—to make and enforce just laws for the sake of the common good. So, in addition to treating others well, a good political order means that people must grant unto Caesar what is owed him for the sake of that common good. Conversely, though, since Caesar exists for the sake of the common good and not for his own ends, there are clear limits on what Caesar may legitimately ask for. A well-ordered society, then, has a threefold set of relations: (1) the multifarious relations of citizens to one another that are (2) overseen by a state mechanism

---

3 Aristotle, *Nicomachean Ethics* VI.7 (1141a20–22). This explains the uncompromising nature of purely secular politics where power is seen to be the highest end. For an incisive analysis of this point, see Charles N. R. McCoy, *The Structure of Political Thought: A Study in the History of Political Ideas* (New York: McGraw-Hill, 1963), 46-51.

4 For the ancients it was obvious that, because politics was concerned with the good, it was a branch of ethics (Plato, *Republic* VIII–IX and Aristotle, *Nicomachean Ethics* X.9). The modern idea that politics concerns how to use power stems from Niccolò Machiavelli (1469–1527), who defines "virtue" in terms of strength and the retention of power (*The Prince*, chapters XIV-XVIII.). One effect of this change is our tendency to reduce *politics* to being merely about governmental activity, as opposed to being about personal flourishing in a complete human community; see the analysis in Pierre Manent, *Natural Law and Human Rights: Toward a Recovery of Practical Reason*, trans. Ralph C. Hancock (Notre Dame, Ind: University of Notre Dame Press, 2020), esp. 19–41.

5 Aristotle, *Politics* I.2 (1253a39); *ST* I-II.100.2.

6 Augustine, *City of God* XIX.13.

acting for the common good of those citizens who are then (3) guided to act for that common good themselves. We might call these three aspects civil society, law, and happiness.

As with other parts of philosophy, reducing the complexity of these relations will produce inadequate political philosophies. Justice is the first principle for forming relations. But, since one's idea of justice is dependent on one's conceptions of human nature and its good, distortions about any of these will lead to distortions about the nature and function of the state. The interminable nature of much political debate points to these deeper philosophical disagreements, for, if people cannot agree on the first principles of society—if there is no common understanding of justice—they will never agree on concrete policies. Even worse, though, is that a lack of agreement on first principles can prevent us from even engaging one another intelligently about the foundational principles of society at all.[7] In this case, society will inevitably disintegrate.

Defining justice is difficult because there are two undeniable facts about human nature that pull political philosophy in opposite directions. These are that each person is an individual with goals of his own, yet he nevertheless *must* live in society. In the perennial philosophy, these divergent facts can be reconciled as a both/and because persons are understood to share a common human nature with a common teleology. That is, all people seek happiness, and happiness is the same for all people. However, in philosophies without a robust theory of human nature to explain how individuals unite in a common good, these two facts remain discordant. (This is typical of modern thought characterized by nominalist metaphysics.) Unable to reconcile individuality and society, modern political theory will

---

7 In *We Hold These Truths* (New York: Sheed and Ward, 1960), 6–14, John Courtney Murray recognizes the urgent need for continued dialogue about the first principles and what happens when we fail to engage in that debate. It is worth quoting at length:

> The specifying note of political association is its rational deliberative quality, its dependence for its permanent cohesiveness on argument among men. In this it differs from all other forms of association found on earth. . . . [As] a heritage and as a public philosophy, the American consensus needs to be constantly argued. If the public argument dies from disinterest, or subsides into the angry mutterings of polemic, or rises to the shrillness of hysteria, or trails off into positivistic triviality, or gets lost in a morass of semantics, you may be sure that the barbarian is at the gates of the City. . . . Today the barbarian is the man who makes open and explicit rejection of the traditional role of reason and logic in human affairs. He is the man who reduces all spiritual and moral questions to the test of practical results or to an analysis of language or to decision in terms of individual subjective feeling. . . . When things like this happen, men cannot be locked together in argument. Conversation becomes merely quarrelsome or querulous. Civility dies with the death of the dialogue.

typically privilege one aspect against the other. On the one hand, some will emphasize human nature as social, elevating the importance of the state and disregarding the value of the unique individual; on the other hand, some will place importance on the individual and downplay social relations as merely artificial constructs. The former position is known as *statism* or *collectivism* and finds expression in the ideologies of communism and fascism. In these philosophies, the state is the primary unit of reality and so the good of persons is subordinated to the ends of the state. This failure to respect the value of the individual often results in moral atrocities. The latter position is the liberal tradition,[8] whose nominalist assumptions dissolve objective human nature, thereby defining a person in terms of his natural freedom, and so the good is seen to be the maximization of individual freedom. The state exists to protect this freedom, which is understood to extend to every aspect of life, even the nature of the good life itself. In this context, the state serves the individual and can restrict freedom only if it becomes harmful to others.[9] The only "common" good, then, is this radically individual pursuit of personal expression.

In short, nominalism's elimination of a common human nature leads to a stark dichotomy: either society exists for the sake of the individual or the individual exists for the sake of society. This dichotomy disregards the fact that the human person is both individual and naturally social. Once again, the truth lies in recognizing the both/and nature of reality. The individual needs to live in society and in that sense is only a part of that larger whole, but the goal of social relations is to enable each person's spiritual perfection, so the society exists for the good of the person. We owe a deference to the state for the sake of the common goods of peace and justice; but

8 Note that this is classical liberalism, a position common to most modern democracies, and should not be confused with the popular use in contemporary America of *liberal* as opposed to *conservative*. In fact, later in the chapter I show that this contemporary division is in fact simply a schism within liberalism itself.

9 This is famously articulated in John Stuart Mill's harm principle (*On Liberty*, chap. 1): "That the only purpose for which power can be rightfully exercised over any member of a civilized community, against his will, is to prevent harm to others." The radicalness of this individual determination of the good in opposition to communal interests is made clear at the start of chapter 2: "If all mankind minus one were of one opinion, and only one person were of the contrary opinion, mankind would be no more justified in silencing that one person, than he, if he had the power, would be justified in silencing mankind." This philosophy presumes that happiness is found in each person's unique individuality and not in any common good. We should note, however, that without some ontological grounding as what counts as harm, this principle is impossible to apply, for each person is at liberty to claim harm when anything at all contrary to his interests happens to him.

the state is constrained by the fact that it exists to facilitate our spiritual goals, ordering persons to the mutually enrichment of wisdom and love. Political thought, then, must be saved from these extremes if it is to fulfill the good for which it exists.

REDUCTIVE EXTREMES
Collectivism: The Individual Exists for Society

The more obvious errors of collectivism have become the stuff of history. On one level, fascism and communism appear to be polar opposites. On the one hand, fascism sees the state as the highest product of human history, and so the person becomes identified with the state as the manifestation of his essence.[10] As such, the person defers in all things to the interests of the state. On the other hand, Marxist communism envisions the withering away of the state, for it believes that, once classes are eliminated, there will be no class conflict and the state will have no need to exist. Nevertheless, in communism the individual person has no value or identity on his own. Although Marxism identifies human essence with active labor, human agency is severely restricted by the historical and economic conditions in which a person lives. As a result, one's class determines a person's identity, his ideas, and his actions. Therefore, the group, the class, has an ontological priority over the individual.[11] What these have in common is the idea that the good of the individual is possible only when society as a whole acts with a single will. The will of the state, then, determines what is to happen, and so an individual's aims and purposes are simply of no consequence.

Both forms of collectivism nullify personal dignity because they both deny human transcendence. Since they believe that human existence is purely earthly, the good of the whole—the state or class—is obviously more important than the good of any individual who is merely a part. This moral judgment is grounded in a metaphysical error about substance: they assume the state or society is itself a *thing*, a substance, thereby making an individual merely a part, like a cell in a body. (In reality, since persons are substances, the state must be understood to be an accidental unity constituted by relations

10 The origin of this lies in Hegel's philosophy of history, epitomized in his assertion that the state is the march of God through history; an accessible summary of his position is in G. W. F. Hegel, *Reason in History*, trans. Robert S. Hartman, Library of Liberal Arts (New York: Pearson, 1995).

11 Not coincidentally, Marx's reduction of the person to class consciousness was also inspired by Hegel.

and common actions.[12]) If the state were a substance, it would have a teleology of its own, independent of the goods of the persons who compose its populace. Thus, the good is that of the state or group, and the individual has no freedom to controvert that collective good. This is why collectivist societies require complete conformity into which individual interests are dissolved.

The ontological error of collectivism explains the moral error that makes it so heinous. Because it has a distorted view of human nature, it fails to recognize the moral imperative of happiness. A person is viewed only as a part, and his need for wisdom and love is sacrificed for the manufactured goals of the state.

These errors invite two rebuttals, one theoretical, the other practical. First, since human beings are the primary substances, society must be recognized only as a complex accident resulting from the activity among them. Society is not a thing; it is the activity uniting individual persons in pursuit of a good that transcends each individual's end. The state (which exists to facilitate that common good) can have no legitimate interests apart from those of the people. The practical rebuttal arises from the obvious moral violence done against human dignity by collectivism. Human nature is not infinitely plastic, a clay to be reshaped by the powers of the government. On the contrary, the human need for truth and love cannot be extinguished. The oppression of statism will engender its own destruction, for people cannot live where there is no love.[13] The idea that the person exists for the sake of the state, then, is self-defeating from the start.

Individualism: Society Exists for the Individual

The liberal tradition is apparently more humane.[14] Where collectivism denies human freedom and so makes itself intolerable, liberalism sees the exercise of individual freedom as the primary good. However, this becomes a reductive

---

12 *CNE* I.1.5.

13 National Socialism's thousand-year Reich lasted only twelve and in Russia Marxist Communism had a tempestuous history of seventy-five years, leaving over a hundred million corpses along the way, as determined by Stéphane Courtois, Nicolas Werth, et al., *The Black Book of Communism: Crimes, Terror, Repression*, trans. Jonathan Murphy (Cambridge, Mass.: Harvard University Press, 1999). In contrast, the ascetic spiritual communism of Christian monks like the Benedictines has lasted unperturbed for two millennia because it is leavened by a true idea of the human good in service to God.

14 I say "apparently" because, as Jacques Maritain comments, "Of the three [i.e., fascism, communism, and liberalism], the most irreligious is bourgeois liberalism. Christian in appearance, it has been atheistic in fact." *The Person and the Common Good*, trans. John J. Fitzgerald (Notre Dame, Ind.: University of Notre Dame Press, 1966), 97.

extreme when liberalism embraces a metaphysical nominalism in which human nature has no predetermined good, or final cause. Lacking a meta-physical grounding, this understanding of freedom entails that every person is able to determine the goal of human life for himself. In light of this pre-sumption, the primary purpose of the state is to protect and facilitate the indi-vidual's exercise of freedom. Thus, the state exists in service to the individual.

Concomitant with freedom is another good valued by the liberal state: equality. For, if people are defined by freedom, the state must ensure the equal opportunity of people to exercise freedom. The goal of liberalism, then, is to defend freedom and equality by balancing the two goods so that every person is as free as possible.[15] Balancing these two claims is inherently problematic, however: the more you grant freedom, the less equal people will be; conversely, the more you enforce equality, the less freedom people will have. Since there is no ontological standard for determining how these goods are to be proportioned—there is no human nature or common good to inform what *ought* to be done—the liberal tradition will argue that it is up to the people themselves to decide the correct balance. This idea is epit-omized in the theory of the *social contract*, where the rules of a society are willed into being by the consent of the people. This is a radical extension of freedom: freedom not only characterizes the action of individuals but also society in its free determination of the purpose of society itself.

The philosophical origins of this positions are in John Locke (1632–1704), whose defense of the Glorious Revolution recognizes the prerogatives of the people over the authority of the monarch. To justify his argument, Locke proposes a "state of nature" in which a person exists apart from soci-ety as an atomistic individual with unconditional freedom. In this state, a person is "absolute lord of his own person and possession equal to the great-est and subject to nobody."[16] This condition has one drawback: people can suffer when others refuse to respect their lives or their property. In order to gain protection for themselves, people form a society by leaving the state

---

15 The centrality of this problem for liberalism is well illustrated by the fact that John Rawls—the premier philosopher of liberalism in the twentieth century—begins his *Political Liberalism* (New York: Columbia University Press, 1993) with a clear statement of the problem (3–7). This is seen also in his seminal *A Theory of Justice* (Cambridge, Mass.: Harvard University Press, 1971) where the two main principles—the veil of ignorance and the difference principle—reflect the primacy of freedom and equality.

16 John Locke, *Second Treatise of Government*, IX.123. John Courtney Murray nicely captures the real effect: a person is "a hard little atom in the midst of atoms equally hard, all solitary and self-enclosed" (*We Hold These Truths*, 303).

of nature and freely surrendering some of their liberty to a government. Thus, a group of equals consents to a social contract that stipulates how the state will protect the person and his property.[17] This property includes all those things necessary for the exercise of self-determination, both a person's rights to freedom as well as the material goods needed to exercise them. The government, then, exists only to protect the freedom of the individuals; it must be completely agnostic about how that freedom should be used in pursuit of the good. Since there is no natural good for people, decisions about what ought to be protected are decided by a majority vote. When the government fails to respect the rights or opinions of the people, the citizens are entitled to withdraw their consent and constitute a new government.[18]

Locke's understanding of an amoral state of nature transformed by the social contract guaranteeing equal freedom becomes the basis for classical liberalism.[19] In this theory, it is the social contract that dictates what is just, since the people are bound only by what they agree to. Since government is inherently limited by the will of the people, rights tend to be seen as negative liberties, that is, *freedom from* government interference. The individual should be able to conduct his life as he pleases. However, in the twentieth century, the goal of equality begins to assert itself, for the government cannot be said to protect freedom unless it first guarantees the right of *all persons* to exercise that freedom. Thus, one branch of classical liberalism mutates into progressivism, which emphasizes positive rights of citizens to a variety of desirable goods as a precondition for free action.[20] This innovation authorizes government to become activist in redistributing goods to ensure equal opportunity. But again, since there is no ontological or moral

---

17 John Locke, *Second Treatise of Government*, VIII.95 and IX.124. Locke is inheriting the ideas of state of nature and social contract from Thomas Hobbes; see *Leviathan*, chaps. 14 and 17. Rawls offers a very sophisticated and influential version of the social contract in *A Theory of Justice*, 11–17.

18 John Locke, *Second Treatise of Government*, XIII.155. In this, Locke is seen to be a primary influence on the argument of *The Declaration of Independence*.

19 This political vision is often merged with the economic liberalism of capitalism, since they both give preeminence to the freedom of the individual. However, it is important not to conflate the two: liberal political systems can espouse socialist economies (as in postwar Scandinavia) and capitalist economies can be employed by despotic totalitarian governments (as in China in recent decades). The question of economic systems is important for the temporal common good, but it is beyond the scope of this book.

20 Historian Jacques Barzun characterizes this as "the Great Switch" in *From Dawn to Decadence: 500 Years of Western Cultural Life 1500 to the Present* (New York: HarperCollins, 2000), 688–89.

basis for evaluating rights, progressivism tends to the lowest common denominator and so to give precedence to material resources desired by popular opinion; spiritual concerns about transcendent values come to be disdained as expressions of personal taste.[21]

Thus, modern liberalism, in its attempt to balance freedom and equality, exists in two very different forms. On the one hand, libertarianism[22]—or what might be called right liberalism—gives precedence to unencumbered freedom as the sole good for humankind and so minimizes public life. On the other hand, progressivism—or left liberalism—gives precedence to *equality* of freedom and so expands government to bring about that end. The differences should not distract us from the fact that both reflect the same elementary premise: *that freedom (and/or equality) is paramount and so precedes the moral order.* If we assume freedom precedes morality, then the good is itself an object of free choice and so can only be subjective and arbitrary. Happiness is no longer defined as fulfilling objective human needs but only as pursuing one's own interests. This anthropology, then, distorts our understanding of the duty of government: instead of acting to assure the common good of justice, it must now conform to the arbitrary will of the people. This throws the entire political realm into incoherence, since the acts of the state change with public opinion and there are no objective standards to evaluate them. This lack of common objective principles is bound to lead to never-ending acrimony as people—whose interests must all be taken as equal—assert incompatible claims as to what deserves government recognition as necessary for happiness. Without a standard of justice, peace, the tranquility of order, can never be attained.

This incoherence manifests itself differently in the two branches of liberalism. Libertarianism's apotheosis of individual freedom against a common good tends to isolate people from one another and subvert the social order. The material goods it values, unlike spiritual goods like wisdom

---

21 This attitude is implicit in liberalism's emphasis on personal freedom. For example, in his *Letter Concerning Toleration,* John Locke lists the interests of a citizen as being "life, liberty, health, and indolency of body; and the possession of outward things, such as money, lands, houses, furniture, and the like." This denigration of spiritual interests is also clear in his definition of a church as "a voluntary society of men, joining themselves together of their own accord in order to the public worshipping of God in such manner as they judge acceptable to Him." *Political Philosophy: The Essential Texts,* 3rd ed, ed. Steven M. Cahn (Oxford: Oxford University Press, 2015), 395–96. Note that as a *voluntary* association, religion is no longer essential to human happiness and, moreover, as a question of subjective taste, is not considered to be a claim to metaphysical truth.

22 A representative defense of this position is in Nozick, *Anarchy, State, and Utopia.*

and love that can be shared without diminution, can only be shared by dividing them among the claimants. This inculcates a self-interested conception of happiness, in opposition to true communal flourishing, and so will undermine virtue, wisdom, and love. Even cooperation is predicated on private benefit, so that cooperation itself—paradoxically—becomes adversarial. This sense that freedom begets competition tends to make all things subject to the calculations of the market: all goods can be bought, but they will be bought by those who can pay the most for them.

Progressivism, for its part, debases the human good in a different way. In idealizing equality, with no human nature to act as a standard, all behaviors are deemed equally worthy. Citizens are not encouraged to excellence. Worse, though, this emphasis on equality leads progressivism in certain ways to mimic the overbearing paternalism of statism that, in the end, actually diminishes freedom. Since the government cannot be morally judgmental about how people behave, social problems tend to be seen as issues of material distribution and so the solutions proffered will always involve more government bureaucracy and more efficient technology.[23] For example, illegitimacy is dealt with not by teaching chastity but rather with access to welfare, contraception, and abortion. Even as the state maximizes individual freedom, it further undermines traditional norms and destroys a common morality; the state, then, must step in to police all social relations, since personal morality has been sacrificed to freedom.[24] Indeed, if everyone is seen to be absolutely free and equal, then *all* social ties (including family and church) are weakened since they become purely voluntary and can be rejected if they are seen to limit one's freedom. This returns us to the state of nature. Furthermore, since there can be no social attachments other than the individual to the government, that government is endowed with disproportionate powers to control an unruly populace.[25]

---

23 One manifestation of this is the fact political science has largely displaced political philosophy in university education. If politics is a science, then it is not concerned with moral values and instead investigates only what is effective for gaining legislative victories. The source of this change can be traced to the famous lecture by Max Weber, "Politics as a Vocation" (1919).

24 Eric Voegelin diagnosed this situation: "As long as virtue and the desire for justice are considered 'right-wing extremist,' while disregarding the structure of reality and opining based solely on sincere conviction, philosophical illiteracy, and spiritual dullness are seen as virtues, there is always a chance that progressivism will slide into Communism." *New Science of Politics* (Chicago: University of Chicago Press, 1952), 178.

25 This argument has been made by Patrick J. Deneen, *Why Liberalism Failed* (New Haven: Yale University Press, 2018). This dependence on government is epitomized in the meretricious misconception that, if something ought to be done, it ought to be done by the government; this is

Liberalism's commitment to freedom points to a deeper metaphysical problem: metaphysical agnosticism. Liberal society maximizes individual freedom only by abjuring any common beliefs about human nature or "comprehensive" worldviews about the nature of the good life. Government must be neutral with regard to transcendent values. But this is a performative contradiction, for without shared metaphysical principles, there can be no philosophical foundation for asserting that all people are free and equal. These philosophical foundations are critically necessary, for from a purely empirical point of view the one obvious truth is that human beings are neither free nor equal: we are animals who act on instinctive desires and who are endowed with utterly unequal gifts. Thus, the only way to justify liberalism's premises (freedom and equality) would require metaphysical commitments that would in fact limit freedom and define equality in ways incompatible with liberal practice.

This metaphysical problem also has practical implications. Most importantly, without a metaphysical understanding of human nature and the moral good, there is no firm foundation for human rights. We can believe that rights are recognized through democratic processes, but this is in fact to deny the existence of rights. For, if rights exist only because they are desired by the people, as desires change, government will accordingly redefine rights. But, if rights are inalienable moral certainties that cannot change, then there cannot be true rights at all.

In sum, the problem with liberalism is that in privileging the individual over community, it destroys the natural moral significance of relations. In privileging freedom and equality, it displaces the primacy of justice. Justice alone, not the social contract, can define right relations, since it shows how those communal relations must be ordered for the moral perfection of the individual. In other words, we must let justice determine what freedoms we have and how equality is to be respected. This alone respects both a person's social nature and the dignity of the person in society.

---

exacerbated by the insistence that it ought to be done by the federal government. People deprived of virtue and community are deprived of true agency and so must depend on the state.

COMMUNITY: THE TEMPORAL AND THE ETERNAL ENDS OF A PERSON

The Foundation of Society: Right and Rights

Human nature makes social relations both natural and necessary. We cannot reduce a person in such a way as to ignore either his sociability or his unique dignity. The complex reality is that the individual exists for society *because* society exists for the individual person. This is profoundly rooted in human nature: to be happy, I must grow in wisdom and love; but to grow in wisdom and love, I need to form social relations. Yet, society can only flourish if there are rules. For that reason, true human freedom—flourishing in wisdom and love—can be attained only by following the principles of justice in the law. Therefore, I owe deference to society because a well-ordered society is the only way to attain personal happiness. Both society and the individual person have to be seen as equally important in constructing a political philosophy.

Political philosophy, consequently, has to begin with justice as the principle of these well-ordered relations. Freedom and equality are important, for they reflect objective realities of human nature. But they must be defined in terms of the principles of justice as the objective standard for social relations. Every political philosophy must account for these three primary notions: justice, freedom, and equality. However, starting with the wrong one will distort the vision of society. Liberalism depreciates justice by beginning instead with either freedom or equality. The ineluctable result is that there are no truly objective standards for justice: freedom and equality both metastasize, becoming ends in themselves, thereby becoming enemies of amicable social relations instead of being realized in them. In contrast to this, the perennial tradition prioritizes justice: the natural law determines the right relations of individuals in justice, from which peace and happiness will follow.

One starting point that immediately illuminates the differences between the tradition and liberalism is the meaning of the word *right*. For the tradition, the right (*ius*) is the object of justice.[26] When used in this sense, *right* denotes a correct relation between persons, an objective sense that each person is getting what is appropriate to him or owed to him.[27] (In this same

---

26 *ST* II-II.57.1.

27 *ST* II-II.58.1. This is the classic definition of justice: the habitual will to give to each what is his due.

sense, someone might say that "2 + 2 = 4" is right because it is an objectively correct relation between the two sides of the equation.) This measure is not merely a conventional agreement; rather, it is objective because it is metaphysically rooted in human nature.[28] A society is just to the extent it reflects this objective order.[29] It follows, then, that the rules of justice can never be "decided" by a social contract, for these right relations are normative for society whether people consent to them or not. (One obvious problem with the social contract is that it is possible that people will give consent to unjust laws so as to gain personal benefit. This intuitive truth points out the primary problem with voluntarism: a law based on will has no standard by which it might be judged to be unjust.)

In modern political thought, *right* typically indicates something quite different.[30] Now it refers to an individual's claim to some prerogative that must be respected by others (as in "I have a right to do this"). Traditional natural law recognizes such claims but only as derived from our duties to justice. According to natural law, the overriding duty of each person is to perfect human nature by attaining happiness, which is strictly defined in terms of virtue, wisdom, and love. Because all people have a natural relation of duty to that end, they will have rights to those things necessary for attaining that end. Because rights are derived from moral duties, there can never be a right that stands in contradiction to the moral order of justice; in other words, there cannot be a right to abortion or so-called homosexual marriage or harmful narcotics.

In liberalism, however, the moral grounding of rights in the natural law is annihilated by the privileging of freedom. All that remains is the subjective claim an atomistic individual holds against other atomistic individuals. In this context, *right* is no longer about relations between people; instead, it is something belonging to an individual prior to all social relations.[31] Thus, *right* is no longer a norm but is now simply a power that can be exercised.

---

28 This is not to deny that in every society there are some laws that are merely conventional; see *Nichomachean Ethics* V.7 (1134b18–1135a14) and *ST* II-II.57.2.

29 *ST* I-II.95.2.

30 The scholarship explaining this transformation in the meaning of right is vast, offering diverse theories; for a brief overview, see Riccardo Saccenti, *Debating Medieval Natural Law: A Survey* (Notre Dame, Ind.: University of Notre Dame Press, 2016).

31 This is in fact another consequence of Ockham's nominalism. In his insistence that only individuals really exist, Ockham reduces Aristotle's categories from ten to two: substance and quality. There are no real relations anymore; so, rights can only be qualities possessed by the individual as a claim against other people.

In Locke's imaginary state of nature, people possess rights reflecting their interests. Thus, these claims arise not from the objective needs of human nature as social but simply from the inscrutable desires of the person making the claim. However, if personal desire is enough to justify a right, then the idea of rights will evolve to include positive entitlements: if I have an interest in something, it must be supplied to me by the state. Thus, "the new rhetoric of rights is less about human dignity and freedom than about insistent, unending desires."[32] And, since these desires are not grounded in a common human nature, conflicting claims about rights end up causing division in society instead of ordering us amicably to the common good.

There is, then, a great distance between the perennial tradition's notion of what is just and that of contemporary philosophy. The capricious nature of modern rights makes it hard to define the meaning of justice today; people with diametrically opposed views invoke the justice of their position, and there is no way to adjudicate the debate (other than popular opinion). The perennial tradition, in contrast, has a clear notion of justice: to make sure each person gets what is objectively owed to him in light of the natural law's ordering people to happiness. This is founded not on arbitrary desire but on human morality, for a just society will encourage the development of virtue for the sake of growing in wisdom and love.

Justice

As we saw in the previous chapter, we can use *justice* to refer to a personal moral virtue: a habit regulating the will wherein each person is given what is owed to him. However, because this notion of what is owed is an objective condition of *equality* in which persons in a relation get neither too much nor too little, justice refers first to this objective standard for correct relations. It is this standard that is the basis for the virtue.[33] Thus, in order for social relations to be fair, they must be subject to this condition of equality.[34]

---

32 From former ambassador to the Vatican Mary Ann Glendon, *Rights Talk: The Impoverishment of Political Discourse* (New York: Free Press, 1991), 171. David Wootton, in *Power, Pleasure, and Profit: Insatiable Appetites from Machiavelli to Madison* (Cambridge, Mass.: The Belknap Press of Harvard University Press, 2018), argues that the modern world is created by this focus on desires for power, pleasure, and profit that are unending because there is no natural satisfaction of them.

33 *ST* II-II.58.10.

34 This condition of equality, in fact, morally regulates all our relations by recognizing duties of what is owed. First, I have duties to God, which are the demands of religion as a kind of justice (*ST* II-II.81); second, I have a duty to myself to develop virtue if I am to establish "equality" with

There are three kinds of social relations that are ordered by distinct kinds of justice.[35] First, one can consider the relation of the individual to society as a whole, to determine what the individual owes society. This is called *legal justice*. Second, one can consider the relation of society to the individual or what society as a whole owes the individual person. This is known as *distributive justice*. Finally, one can consider the relation between two individuals in order to determine what each owes the other in a particular transaction.[36] This is *commutative justice*. Let us look at these more closely.

Legal justice is, in some sense, the most important. As rational, humans are inclined to the universal good. This, though, is not just *my* happiness; as universal; it is the condition for the happiness of all people. Thus, legal justice recognizes what I owe to all people for the sake of this common good.[37] It regulates social interactions because I owe it to my fellow citizens (or coworkers or teammates) to respect those conditions that catalyze everyone's happiness. Since this means, in effect, that I should be as virtuous, wise, and loving as possible, legal justice can be seen as a general virtue, including all the other virtues and all moral actions as necessary for promoting happiness.[38] A just person, then, sees that people are always owed the fulfillment of their nature that God gave them and that this can be accomplished when all people obey the natural law.

Reversing this relationship, the community owes individuals fair treatment. What this "fair treatment" consists of is the goal of distributive justice. This kind of justice regulates how the community distributes benefits or assigns burdens to those who make up that community. The community is obliged to do this because it *exists* to facilitate the individual's happiness.

---

my own human nature (*ST* II-II.58.3); third, I have duties to other people because we are social animals (*ST* II-II.122). For this reason, when a person is unjust—when he sins—he does not just violate his relation with his neighbor but he also offends his own nature and God as his Creator. Punishment is, accordingly, threefold: temporal penalty from society, lack of personal happiness, and eternal purgation (*ST* I-II.87.1).

35 Thomas's discussion of justice builds upon Aristotle, *Nicomachean Ethics*, bk. 5. For a lucid commentary, see Josef Pieper, "Justice" in *The Four Cardinal Virtues*, trans. Richard and Clara Winston, Lawrence E. Lynch, and Daniel F. Coogan (Notre Dame, Ind.: University of Notre Dame Press, 1966), 41–113.

36 *ST* II-II.61.1.

37 *ST* I-II.113.1: "Since justice, by its nature, implies a certain rectitude of order, it may be taken . . . as legal justice, which directs a man's acts by regulating them in their relation to the common good of society."

38 *ST* II-II.58.5. It is called "legal justice" because laws are meant to direct people to the common good (*ST* II-II.58.7).

Accordingly, the community must make judgments about how certain activities further that goal and structure rewards and duties to encourage the common good. (*Community* here primarily means the state, but it is important to see that it applies to all communities—corporations, schools, clubs, and so on—since a person belongs to multiple communities at any given time.) Distributive justice guarantees that this distribution is fair—that those who merit more reward be given more reward and that those who can carry a greater burden be given a greater burden.[39] Crucially, in order to accomplish distributive justice, a community needs a responsible authority to judge what is fair in a given instance; we consider that issue later in this chapter.

As an example of distributive justice, we can point to a pay scale in a business. Entry level workers make less than the company president because their contribution to the company is less significant. As one works his way up the ladder, pay and responsibility increase in proportion to each other. Greater merit is recognized with greater burdens (more work and responsibility) but also greater rewards (pay). In a different way, distributive justice is also the principle behind the graduated income tax: those who make the least pay the least taxes—not just absolutely but as a proportion of their overall income. Those who make more money, in contrast, have a greater responsibility to the common good and so bear a greater burden. (We see below how these must be regulated by legal justice.)

Finally, there are the interactions between private individuals that are regulated by commutative justice, which seeks to assure that each person gets what he is owed. Most commonly, this involves all those voluntary interactions that make up commerce: trades, sales, loans, and so forth. Since justice is a state of equality, in a fair transaction neither person gets too much nor too little. This is evident in a primitive barter system that aims for equality in trades. The introduction of money, though, establishes a standardized value for estimating fairness: a loaf of bread is worth three dollars and a cell phone is worth $500. In transactions of this sort, the merit of the people is irrelevant, for equality is determined by the value of the goods involved.[40]

---

[39] For this reason, Aristotle says this kind of equality is geometric, so that the equality is proportional to merit—A/B::C/D—and not simply absolute equality (*Nicomachean Ethics* V.3, 1131a30–1131b16).

[40] The value of the goods should reflect not just the cost of the materials but also the time and talent of the persons who produce the good, so price includes room for a fair profit (*ST* II-II.71.4 and II-II.77.1 and 4); nevertheless, the state may regulate the market to make sure this profit is not excessive (*ST* II-II.77.2.ad 2). Cf. John Paul II, Encyclical Letter *Centisimus Annus* (May 1, 1991), 35.

Thus, whether I or the pope buy a loaf of bread, we should both be treated the same and be charged the same fair amount.[41]

A special case of commutative justice involves involuntary transactions, or crimes. The victim is owed restitution equivalent to his loss. However, in order to avoid cycles of personal vengeance, the state protects peace by intervening and administering punishments. In retributive justice, if a person takes a life, the state exacts a punishment to equal that loss; if a person steals a car, the punishment is less severe. Whatever the penalty, it must be neither too harsh nor too lenient, else the order of justice and peace will be disrupted.[42]

The primacy of legal justice is now clear, for in establishing the rule of the common good, it puts limits on distributive and commutative justice. Relations must be for the sake of the common good, so distribution of wealth and duties cannot exclude anyone, nor can the burdens or rewards be disproportionate. Similarly, commutative transactions must be fair, but no transaction can ever violate the natural law since it is necessary for the common good. This is again why the liberal political order is problematic, for in privileging freedom, these objective limits of the natural law are effaced.[43] Without legal justice to define what constitutes a fair distribution or a fair exchange, "fairness" is determined solely by the will of the participants. Let us consider some examples of how legal justice can regulate distributive and commutative justice.

With respect to distributive justice, without legal justice the rewards and burdens become unhinged from the true needs of the common good. This is seen in controversies concerning the just wage. The natural law insists that, whatever the wage is, it must be at least sufficient to support workers and their families in a way to enable happiness. For this reason, the market alone cannot determine what the wage ought to be, yet too often this is the sole criterion for determining wages, leaving the needs of the worker unmet. This applies, too, in the other direction: without a sense of the common good as defined by the natural law, there is nothing to rein in the exorbitant pay of corporate executives; instead, it will be determined by whatever companies freely agree to pay. Thus, wages at both ends need to reflect the real needs of both the individual and the community. Equally obtuse, though, is the claim

---

41 For this reason, Aristotle says this kind of equality is arithmetic, an absolute equality of 1:1 (*Nicomachean Ethics* V.4, 1132a1–1132b9).

42 *SCG* III.142.

43 In the collectivist political order, the individual has no moral standing to begin with and the state unilaterally dictates what is "fair."

that income inequality is inherently unjust. Rather, pay ought to be proportionate to merit in order to encourage personal qualities necessary for the common good, such as ambition and creativity.[44] This same reasoning applies to taxes: everyone should pay what is most fruitful for the common good, but the tax burden should never be so heavy as to deprive people of an ability to dispose of their property according to the precepts of charity. (For this reason, true socialism is incompatible with charity, since, if society owns all wealth, the citizen can never give a gift.[45])

The effects of ignoring legal justice are even more perilous in the area of commutative justice. If relations between people are determined by freedom instead of by moral commitments, there is no way to regulate what sorts of contracts are made. The only limit to what is acceptable is the consent of the people involved. As a result, everything becomes subject to the market mentality.[46] Thus, there is no reason to prohibit trafficking in prostitution or narcotics so long as the participants are consenting adults. There is no limit to what a merchant might sell or charge, provided someone agrees to pay for it. Absent objective moral standards, commutative justice will redefine the fundamental structures of society to accommodate the people's most brute desires.

Thus, in order to give intelligible limits to distributive and commutative justice, legal justice, the natural law's orientation to the common good of happiness, has to be the foundation for all determinations of justice.

The Rule of Law

In order to regulate society, this order of justice must be formulated into laws; that is, it is promulgated to be a guide for the people in society so that all might develop virtue and strive for the common good.[47] Because these

---

44 Note that this contemporary debate about income inequality is actually between freedom (for the corporate executive) and equality (for the employees as a whole) and not really about justice at all.

45 Aristotle, *Politics* II.5 (1263b5–12).

46 This is the fallacious notion of freedom that Saint John Paul II criticizes in the Encyclical Letter *Evangelium Vitae* (March 25, 1995), 19–20:

> When freedom, out of a desire to emancipate itself from all forms of tradition and authority, shuts out even the most obvious evidence of an objective and universal truth, which is the foundation of personal and social life, then the person ends up by no longer taking as the sole and indisputable point of reference for his own choices the truth about good and evil, but only his subjective and changeable opinion or, indeed, his selfish interest and whim. This view of freedom leads to a serious distortion of life in society.

47 *ST* I-II.92.1.ad 1 and 94.3.

laws must be for the common good, they must of course be grounded in the natural law.[48] But, because the concrete conditions of societies differ, they also need to be prudently adapted to meet the circumstances of the particular society. This middle course calls us to avoid two errors. One error is the position that assumes that there is no rational grounding for the law, so law is simply what is commanded by the arbitrary will of the legislator; this is *voluntarism* (or *positivism*). The other error assumes that the entire body of law can be known by reason without any adaptation to the real conditions of our society; this is known as *rationalism*.[49] Mediating these errors, natural law accommodates both an objective grounding and prudential legislation. This is made clear when we consider how the three levels of precepts in the natural law can be applied in political society to include both the necessary universal principles as well as the detailed applications.

Recall that the precepts of the natural law specify those actions that are required to attain happiness in terms of wisdom and love in community with other people. Since law is, by definition, an ordinance of reason for the common good, positive (or civil) law must reflect the needs of human nature. The most general, primary precepts of the natural law simply indicate the universal goals of humankind as the most basic conditions for happiness: live in society and know the truth (especially about God as first cause and final end). However, since these are the self-evident foundation of all moral precepts, there is no need to formally legislate laws reflecting them. Indeed, we obey these precepts naturally in acting on our natural drive for friendship and curiosity for truth.

The secondary and tertiary precepts, in contrast, are not self-evident and so need to be promulgated as laws for the community. The secondary precepts (i.e., the Decalogue) are the most basic rules for justice within a society, for society cannot function without respect for authority, life, family, property, and communicative discourse. Even though these rules are common to all known societies,[50] under the influence of passion or vice, people may violate these laws. Therefore, in order to protect the peace,

---

48 *ST* I-II.93.3.

49 Modern democracies tend toward voluntarism, since the will of the people is sovereign. Enlightenment strains of natural law tend to rationalism, since they blithely assert certain goods to be "self-evident" and so not needing any metaphysical grounding. Ralph Barton Perry described such theories as "credulous intuitionism." *Puritanism and Democracy* (New York: Vanguard Press, 1944), 417.

50 An illuminating compendium of examples of this is collected by C. S. Lewis in "Illustrations of the Tao," the appendix to *The Abolition of Man*.

society must enforce these rules by making laws with punishments. These man-made laws, which simply enforce the basic rules of the natural law, are called *derivations* from the natural law since they merely restate the content of the precept. They include things like the prohibitions on murder and theft.[51]

The tertiary precepts are more specific, for they prudentially adapt the general laws to the specific circumstances of a given society. This means that the laws of any two communities may vary greatly, yet both can be equally just. This diversification arises because there are plenty of actions beyond the Decalogue that we need to regulate in order to guarantee peace and order. (Hence, these are called *determinations* from the natural law, since we need to specify the precept's application.[52]) For instance, the natural law says nothing about what side of the road cars should drive on, yet such a law is critical for a society to function well. Again, the natural law insists that citizens support the state financially, but the specific details of taxation—whether it is on sales, or income, or property, or trade, as well as the rates—need to be determined in light of the economic conditions of the specific society. Therefore, laws at this level of particularity must prudentially consider many contingent factors of the nation—size, economy, education, environment—in order to be both just and efficient.

The principles of the natural law are the universal standards for just laws, even though the implementation in the tertiary precepts will vary. This is why a good nation needs sagacious governmental officials and ample political debate in order to discern the best policies for the people here and now. This is also why laws must be able to change if the conditions of the nation alter their usefulness.[53]

---

51 *ST* I-II.95.2.

52 *ST* I-II.95.2.

53 *ST* I-II.97.1–3; although Thomas also insists that because laws habituate people and create a customary order in society, the state should only change laws when necessary, for willy-nilly changes undermine the people's faith in government.

However, to insist a specific policy as the only right one, for all peoples and at all times, is *ideology*—the blind adherence to one answer that impedes reason's prudential assessment of reality as it is. Since many political philosophies come to be articulated in reaction to specific historical events (e.g., Hobbes and the English Civil War, Locke and the Glorious Revolution, Marx and the industrial revolution), as opposed to being grounded on the objective principles of being as in the perennial tradition, they can easily take the form of ideologies.

The Content of Law

Although the details of a society's laws should reflect its specific nature, the secondary precepts provide the principles for legislating the kinds of laws required for people to attain happiness.

We first must recognize the limits of what the law can do. Although law exists to inculcate virtue, government should try neither to legislate *all* virtues nor prohibit *all* vices.[54] Laws should prescribe only those virtues that are fundamental to the common good, such as are needed to protect peace and ensure just relations. Similarly, laws should prohibit only those "more grievous vices" that would directly interfere with the maintenance of society.[55] These restrictions on law reflect the necessarily limited role of government. We cannot expect government to substitute for personal conscience and morality; more importantly, government cannot substitute for family, friends, and Church in the formation of conscience. Government's job is the most general protection of peace and justice, and so its law concern only those relations; it does not extend to personal virtues like fortitude or temperance.[56] This explains why prohibition of alcohol, which is normally used in moderation and so not an impediment to wisdom and love, was unwise, while prohibition of narcotics, which by nature have intoxication as their end and so impede the use of reason, is wise.

Because the goal of law is the common good, it is necessary that law inculcate virtue. Yet the common good, as we have seen, is understood in two ways. The ultimate, eternal common good of man is the Beatific Vision; attaining this end is the province of the Church, and so the state only aims at this indirectly, by protecting the free operations of the Church as a crucial mediating institution. More directly, though, the state must provide those conditions where virtue, wisdom, and love can flourish for the sake of our temporal common good. It does this in three ways.[57] First, it secures peace, protecting a person from harm and ensuring rights, thereby enabling a life of secure freedom. Second, the government promotes justice by legislating laws that encourage acting together to achieve

---

54 *ST* I-II.96.2 and 3.

55 *ST* I-II.96.2.

56 In other words, government can criminalize only actions, not thoughts or attitudes. Only God can punish sins of the heart (Augustine, *On Free Choice of the Will*, I.15–16).

57 *De Reg* I.15–16.

objectives that contribute to furthering the common good. Finally, the government aims to assure a sufficiency of material wealth, for true flourishing is possible only if there is enough wealth to allow time for leisure. A virtuous society will use the leisure time to develop wisdom and friendship and religion; however, a vicious society will abuse leisure and wallow in mindless recreation and bestial entertainments. Hence, this third goal of government is beneficial only if it properly executes its first two so that people grow in virtue.

We can now specify the sort of rights that should be enshrined under legal protection. As argued above, these are derived from the basic human needs epitomized in the Decalogue as preconditions for happiness.[58] Hence, since our goal is the Beatific Vision, the most important right is the freedom of religion, by which each can develop the knowledge of God necessary for eternal happiness. Second, everyone has a right to a society ordered by peace and justice, and so authorities must be obeyed (on all levels, not just government but also parents, teachers, and designated persons in all fields of life). Third is the right to life, for unless we protect existence, or first act, happiness, or second act, is metaphysically impossible. This right to life must extend to all humans regardless of their state of development or health. Following the right to life is the right to the integrity of the family as the foundation for a person's existence in the development of virtue and religion. Accordingly, all irrational expressions of sexuality are prohibited since they deprive a child of the right to a stable family necessary for happiness. Since wisdom requires access to the truth, there is also the right not to be deceived. This includes laws prohibiting false advertising and libel and protecting the integrity of education as the pursuit of truth. Finally, reflecting the need to develop enough wealth for the sake of leisure, there are laws protecting the right to private property. Private property best secures this wealth for three reasons: it encourages hard work; society is more orderly when people know who is responsible for what; and it encourages peace and justice, since each learns to be content with what is rightfully owed to him and not to unjustly covet what he has not earned. Therefore, having stewardship over property not only contributes to the common good by increasing the wealth of society, but, more importantly, it allows each person

58 *ST* I-II.122.1. Heinrich Rommen argues in *The State in Catholic Thought: A Treatise in Political Philosophy* (St. Louis and London: B. Herder Book Co., 1945), 249n2, that these rights accrue not primarily to the individual, but to the family, since that is the primarily building block of society and the school of virtue.

to develop virtue by enabling him to meet his personal duties to the family and the community.[59]

Therefore, while the prudential application of these laws needs to be adapted to the circumstances of each society, these basic rights must be respected for without them life in society—and the chance to attain happiness in wisdom and love—becomes impossible.

Obligation to Law

Since just laws are a necessary part of the common good, we can also affirm that people have a *moral obligation* to obey them.[60] This follows from the priority of legal justice: if I am dedicated to the common good, I will follow laws that have been legislated for the sake of that common good. To refuse to obey the law is to implicitly reject the relevance of the common good. Thus, running a red light is not only a traffic infraction, but it is also a sin, because you are acting against reason and against the authority's determination for the common good.

The obligatory nature of the law is often denigrated by referring to it as coercive—something we follow only because we are forced to.[61] In fact, the law is only coercive to those who lack virtue and disdain the common good. If one is virtuous, there is already an inclination to accept an ordinance of reason for the common good. This stands in stark contrast to the liberal vision, which gives priority to personal freedom over justice and so views all law as a coercive limitation on individual freedom of expression. This betrays divergent conceptions of freedom's relation to law. Since a liberal values freedom above all else, he will obey the law out primarily out of fear of punishment. In the natural law, by contrast, a virtuous person obeys the law out of a desire to possess the highest good, for true freedom comes with the communal development of wisdom and love.

There are two exceptions to this moral obligation to obey the law. First, as we have noted before, an unjust law is not a true law and so is not binding.[62] In fact, since such decrees are often opposed to the common

---

59 *ST* II-II.66.2. This is consistently echoed in the Catholic Social Teaching, from Leo XIII's Encyclical Letter *Rerum Novarum* (May 15, 1891), 8–9, to John Paul II's *Centisimus Annus*, 30–48.

60 *ST* I-II.96.4.

61 This perspective is tied to voluntarism where the only ground for a law is the arbitrary will of the legislator. Voluntarist political philosophies tend to supplant natural law starting with Marsilius of Padua (ca. 1275–ca. 1342).

62 *ST* I-II.95.2 and 96.4.

good, there is a moral imperative to oppose them by civil disobedience. For example, even though *Dred Scot* had the force of the Constitution, its inhuman treatment of people demonstrated that it never had moral legitimacy and so Lincoln was correct to ignore that decision. Again, a law can be unjust if it is not an ordinance of reason, even if it is for the common good; for example, the arbitrary prohibitions that typify tyrannical societies are unjust simply because they are not rational. In light of the teleological orientation of human nature, we can say broadly that any law is unjust if it interferes with the development of love and wisdom leading to friendship with other people and with God.

The other exception is the case of *epikeia*, or equity.[63] This is the idea that citizens are morally bound not by the letter of the law but rather by the intention or spirit of the legislator who made the law. We need to recognize this because laws are universal statements—"It is always prohibited to do X"—that are written to address the normal case. But such universal statements cannot anticipate all circumstances. Sometimes following the law will actually harm the common good. In these cases, we are called to pursue what the legislator intended to accomplish—peace and happiness—in making the law. For example, if there is a law saying a certain door should remain locked, but a fire breaks out and that door is the only viable escape route, then obeying the law would be irrational and so wrong. The wise person would open the door to save lives. Equity is in fact a *higher* form of justice in correcting the limitations of the written law.[64]

The Legislator as Authority

The existence of laws necessarily raises the need for a lawgiver, or legislator. This legislator is some person (or group of persons) who is empowered to make decisions on behalf of everyone else. In other words, the legislator is the proper authority for making laws in a given society. In political society, this is the state or government; other social organizations—clubs, schools, corporations—have their own structures for leadership. With respect to political theory, the modern presupposition of radical individualism and a concomitant legal positivism (that law is merely the will of the legislator)—both reflecting an absence of a natural common good—has led to misconceptions about the nature of legislative authority. To clarify these points, we

63 *ST* I-II.96.6.
64 *Nicomachean Ethics* V.10 (1137b27–28).

first consider the nature of the state; then, we consider the nature of the authority exercised by the state.

Since people are ordered to wisdom and love as the perfection of their nature, society is formed naturally and necessarily simply as a result of fulfilling these faculties. Contrary to the claims of modern thinkers, society need not be constituted by a social contract of atomistic individuals; rather, human existence is unthinkable without society. But human society takes two primary forms: the family and the *polis* or community.[65] Family is fundamental. We are born into it with the natural relations that form our personhood: it shapes our personality, inculcates social skills and virtues, is the basic economic reality, and is our primary identity throughout our lives. But the family is not a perfect society,[66] since it cannot provide everything needed for human flourishing. This need is most obviously economic, where people need access to the great variety of material goods that make civilized life possible. More importantly, this also includes cultural, scientific, and religious goods, all of which enable full maturation in reason and love. So, beyond the family, people exist in the *polis*, the political community of people united for a common good. This civil society includes all the cultural institutions that communicate the fullness of human excellence. This is, in reality, the meaning of *civilization*: the rational perfection of the natural human tendency to form community in order to inculcate excellence in human life and to pass it on to future generations through established customs and structures.[67]

This political life of a person, civil society, must not be conflated with the state. Thriving civil society antecedes the state in fulfilling human needs. However, because all these families, economic structures, and cultural institutions need to be harmoniously ordered, authority to make laws for the common good of all must be granted to a small segment of society. The state or government, then, is constituted with delimited responsibilities to legislate for the common good.[68] The state is inherently a servant of civil society;

---

65 As Rommen notes in *The State in Catholic Thought*, 376, Catholic political philosophy has three overlapping and symbiotic subjects: the person, the family, and the community, each of which has its own ends, rights, and duties.

66 *ST* I-II.90.3.ad 3; cf. Aristotle, *Politics* I.1–2.

67 This is why Jean-Jacques Rousseau's argument that civilization corrupts people—and that they are best when they are "noble savages" who eschew virtue and tradition—has had such deleterious influence on the West.

68 There are instances where everyone participates directly in governance and not through delegated representatives. However, this can occur only in very small communities, like ancient

consequently, it must recognize the limits to its authority. It can never inter-fere with the good of the family; nor can it interfere with the healthy func-tioning of all the other institutions of civil society, such as schools, clubs, corporations, and churches (unless they are harming the common good by their activity).[69] More positively, because laws are for the common good, the goal of the state is to legislate in order to encourage the flourishing of these institutions, for it is primarily through them that the person develops virtue, grows in wisdom and love, and so attains happiness.[70]

These institutions of civil society are often called "mediating institu-tions," because the mediate the relations of the person to the state. The absence of such mediating institutions means the person is directly subject to the state, which is a characteristic of totalitarianism. However, when there is no recognized common good uniting all people, these mediating institu-tions can degenerate into antagonistic interest groups that undermine social cohesion and cause a hypertrophy of partisan political activity. Therefore, it is important to defend the health of these institutions in service of the common good, for they are the primary forums of human sociability.

It is because the state is a mechanism of the whole of civil society that democratic processes are the most prudent way to pass authority from the people to the state. Because the state acts on behalf of the people, authority

---

Greek cities (where citizenship was highly restricted) or the traditional New England town meet-ings. Since the structure of the government is the result of deliberation by the citizens, the ques-tion of the best regime must be prudentially determined in light of the specific circumstance of those citizens, as Aristotle argues in *Politics* III.4. However, it is interesting to note how proposed best regimes reflect a philosopher's metaphysical principle: for instance, Plato's Forms and the Philosopher-King (*Republic* V, 473d–e), Aristotle's pluralism and the polity (*Politics* IV.11), and Hobbes's materialism and the Sovereign (*Leviathan*, chap. 18). For Thomas's proposal—which looks similar to the U.S. Constitution—see *ST* I-II.105.1; this reflects his notion of creation as an ordered hierarchy (*De Reg* I.3 and I.13).

69 This is the principle of subsidiarity, which argues that authority should rest on the most local level possible, since they are in the best position to evaluate the situation and implement actions to resolve any problems. This notion is explicitly introduced by Pius XI's Encyclical Letter *Quad-rigesimo Anno* (May 15, 1931), 79–81.

70 This distinction between the state and civil society provides an answer to the oddly contro-versial claim that America is a Christian nature. Secularists cite the 1797 Treaty with Tripoli—"The government of the United States of America is not, in any sense, founded on the Christian religion"—to argue that America is not a Christian nation. But it is an historical fact that the huge majority of Americans were Christian. Thus, America is a Christian nation in terms of its civil society and inescapably so. However, the state is religiously neutral in order to secure the peace and freedom of various churches, as affirmed in the First Amendment. The only way to deny that America is a Christian nation is to identify the nation with the government, which is the premise of fascism, as we have seen.

rises up from the people to the state.[71] Democratic processes keep government functionaries accountable to the needs and wisdom of the people. In fact, whenever the state separates its interests from the people, when the government and the political class act for their own good rather than the good of the people, the state becomes despotic.

But this emphasis on democratic processes should not be exaggerated, for that can lead to pernicious results. Democratic processes are always only a means and are never an end in themselves. The end is always, and must be, the common good as defined in terms of the natural law. Democratic processes enable a state to draw on the collective wisdom of the people in order to attain that end. Thus, when justly implemented, democratic processes keep the authority of the state in check with a real sense of the common good. However, if democratic processes themselves become an end, if democracy is itself seen to be *the good*, then we succumb to a moral relativism where the will of the many determines the good. This rejection of an objective good uniting society and motivating its leaders can only tend to exacerbate class divisions and lead to the dissolution of society as a whole.

This brings us to our second point: the nature of the state's authority. If the authority given by the people to the state is exercised justly, the state serves, not as an impediment to freedom but rather as a necessary condition for freedom. Let us examine how the essence of a citizen's freedom is discovered in obedience to the state.

Since the state should exercise its legal authority with prudence and for the common good, we should not expect it simply to implement the majority opinion of the people. Rather, political representation always filters those desires through an objective moral lens of what is truly best for the people. The state has a responsibility to direct people to what is needed for the common good. In order to fulfill this duty, the government exercises authority in two distinct ways: a *substitutional* function and an *essential* (or perfective) function.[72] The substitutional function is one by which the government secures peace in society by punishing people when they break the

---

71 This is not the case for the Church. While the state is rooted in the natural order of human sociability, the Church is constituted by Christ for the sake of salvation. Thus, authority was passed from Jesus to Saint Peter and to the other apostles as bishops, who then share that authority with duly ordained priests. In the Church, authority flows from God down, not from the people up. For this reason, cries for "democratic reform" in the Church fundamentally misconstrue the nature of the Church as a social order.

72 This terminology follows Yves R. Simon, *A General Theory of Authority* (Notre Dame, Ind.: University of Notre Dame Press, 1962).

law. This is necessary, for without orderly respect for law, society would descend into chaos. It is considered *substitutional* because a person should know that he ought to obey the law; the government intervenes to force the person to respect the law and to act for the common good only until he develops virtue for himself. This exercise of authority is not meant to be permanent; like a parent who disciplines a child, it will persist only until that person gains the commitment to legal justice required of all citizens.

This exercise of authority is given priority in modern political theory. Since it assumes that maximal individual freedom is the goal of law, the primary function of the state is seen to be protection of that freedom. Because such freedom can easily run amok, the authority of the state is most evident in punishing violations of the social contract. But note how this idea of authority fundamentally inverts the basis of the natural law tradition. Where the *polis* in the natural law is ordered by a love for a communal highest good (*summum bonum*), the liberal tradition is motivated by an individual's fear of the greatest evil (*summum malum*). This fear of harm is at the heart of the social contract for both Hobbes (fear of death or physical injury) and Locke (fear of loss of property).[73] It is obvious that societies with such divergent starting points will come to embody very different ideas of how government should operate.

This is clear when we consider that, in addition to handing out punishments, the natural law tradition sees something else as the essential function of authority. That essential function is helping people attain a shared happiness in wisdom and love. This requires authority, since that shared good can only be attained when people are united in intention and action for mutual enrichment. Just as a good coach not only disciplines his team but instills in them the desire to work together to make the most of their individual talents, a government acts to bring out the best in its citizens by ordering cooperative action for the good.

Where the substitutional function of authority is necessary because some people turn from reason and behave like beasts, the essential function of authority is necessary because a person's rationality gives him freedom, and so happiness can be pursued in a multitude of different ways. But if each person follows his own judgment—even if all are perfectly rational— it is likely that society would be chaotic. Thus, to harmonize the activity of

---

73 For Hobbes, see *Leviathan*, chaps. 13 and 14; for Locke, see *Second Treatise of Government*, secs. 57 and 124.

reasonable people, an authority is needed to decide what particular actions a society will undertake. For example, in a monastery comprised of the holiest of monks, all utterly dedicated to the common good of prayer, there is still a need for an abbot to decide when to ring the bell for vespers. In society, even among virtuous adults, there is still a need for some authority to determine the specific actions by which the group will achieve the common good. What will be taxed, where will the road be built, how should welfare be distributed? Intelligent people will disagree, since these are very specific applications; but to make sure people work together, one policy must be agreed upon. Indeed, because this cooperative activity among virtuous people can only foster greater wisdom and love, this obedience to authority increases our freedom to act in the future. That is, as society helps perfect its citizens, its citizens are able to do things they could not in the past. This new freedom of operation then calls on authority once again.[74] The wise guidance of law, then, becomes indispensable for a person realizing all the potential he has. This is why there is a true moral obligation to obey the law, and there is no conflict between following the law and freely attaining happiness.

Individuals, Persons, and the Common Good

The state, then, has authority to make laws to allow for the common good. This is first directed to more basic needs, like the protection of peace and the acquisition of material goods needed for civilized life. More crucially, though, it is directed to uniting the people in action toward the development of wisdom and love. So, while the state assures a temporal common good aimed at peace and prosperity, and so demands the fidelity and deference from the people, it does this for the sake of the dignity of those same people. This is the critical both/and of a person's existence as a political animal.

One obvious truth jumps out from this: the notion of the common good we have defended is at odds with common modern political conceptions. The collectivist assumes that the individual exists for the good of the state, and so the common good is defined by the success of the state. History has shown in the regimes of Hitler, Stalin, and Castro that this actually frustrates growth in wisdom and love. The liberal imposture is both more tantalizing

---

74 Yves R. Simon epitomizes this point: "Thus autonomy renders authority necessary and authority renders autonomy possible—this is what we find at the core of the most essential function of government," *Philosophy of Democratic Government* (Chicago: University of Chicago Press, 1951), 71.

as well as more common and for that reason it is a greater threat to democracies.[75] The liberal conception of the common good is to maximize the freedom of the individual. But, lacking a common teleology, each person essentially becomes a little god dictating what is required for his individual happiness, especially in terms of material wealth and sensual pleasure. This, however, is clearly not a *common* good at all, since each person pursues his own particular desires in defiance of human nature and moral norms.[76]

Both these interpretations fail to see that the common goods of the human persons are especially those spiritual goods that only exist and thrive when people grow in community with one another: virtue, wisdom, love. Since these are truly personal, the state cannot provide these goods. Rather, the state ensures a peaceful and just order, as well as the material sufficiency, which provides the occasion for persons to grow in this more profound way. The limits of justice and the state now become evident: the laws of the state regulate behavior between strangers; but, if we never grow beyond being strangers, we can never attain happiness. Thus, in the end, the state's justice exists as a propaedeutic for friendship.

The fundamental error of the modern framing of the issue is now exposed. Liberalism is based on a nominalist metaphysics that sees people as radically individual. Since there is no natural community in a shared human nature, the individual is viewed in opposition to society: either the state is for the individual or the individual is for the state. The reality is a balanced both/and: in one way, the individual is at the service of society, for he has to work to secure the temporal common good of a peaceful and just society; but in a more significant way, society is at the service of these persons, for it is only through social intercourse that they grow in wisdom and love and so order themselves to God as their common eternal end. The common good has to be understood in two complementary ways: one temporal and political, the other eternal and personal.

---

75 John Paul II's encyclical *Centisimus Annus* (1991) recognizes that the Western civilization, having overcome collectivism of fascism (1945) and communism (1989), now faces the most daunting task of rejecting the bourgeois liberalism that sacrifices moral excellence for the sake of material consumption.

76 This lack of unity, as argued earlier, necessitates the growth of the state as an artificial source of unity. As Jacques Maritain comments, "Bourgeois liberalism, whose pretension is to base everything on the individual considered as a little god . . . inevitably ends in *étatisme* [statism], the hypertrophy and absolute primacy of the State. The rule of numbers produces the omnipotence of the State." *Scholasticism and Politics*, trans. Mortimer J. Adler (Garden City, N.Y.: Image Books, 1960), 80.

This dual notion of the common good is a corollary of human nature's hylomorphic foundation.[77] Matter, as the metaphysical principle of individuation, causes us to be true *individuals*, distinct from everyone else; form, as the principle of our universal nature, constitutes a common essence in all humans. Matter, as individuating, separates us; yet form, as common, unites us. The human essence is form and matter taken together, so both principles are essential for us. Nevertheless, this hylomorphic constitution of human nature pulls us in opposite directions. Our material individuality focuses on the material needs of human beings. This leads us to a self-centeredness, because we are concerned solely with our own benefit, and material goods can only be shared by dividing them and giving some to others.

But these material desires alone do not define us, nor can material goods satisfy us. The rational soul creates in us a natural thirst for knowledge and a natural demand for love. Reason lifts us above our animalistic selfishness to see reality according to its true value in terms of objective truth and absolute goodness. These rational powers are nurtured by joining with other people in inquiry and friendship. In this way, our spiritual nature pulls us away from our egotistic opinions and selfish desires. As spiritual persons, we overcome our individualistic tendencies to unite with others in the transcendent realities of being, truth, goodness, and beauty. Here we discover the full meaning of human existence: friends united in virtuous activity.[78]

In light of this complex set of needs, people are related to society in two distinct but complementary ways.[79] On the one hand, as material individuals, we need society to make up for our material defects; that is, our needs for food, clothing, and shelter that we cannot supply for ourselves. Since these can only be attained in a political community, that community also needs to protect the peace. These goods are worldly goods, which satisfy our temporal needs on earth. Thus, as a material individual, justice requires that I seek the common good of my society by subordinating my own

---

77 This argument, with its foundations in Thomas's texts, is clearly presented in Jacques Maritain, *The Person and the Common Good*, trans. John J. Fitzgerald (Notre Dame, Ind.: University of Notre Dame Press, 1966).

78 *CNE* IX.10.1894–1899.

79 As Maritain notes in *The Person and the Common Good*, 70, Thomas recognizes this fact, though we need to piece together comments from different places: (1) "Each individual person is relates to the entire community as the part to the whole" (*ST* II-II.64.2); (2) "He that seeks the good of the many, seeks in consequence his own good . . . because the individual good is impossible without the common good of the family, state, or kingdom" (*ST* II-II.47.10. ad 2) and (3) "Man is not ordained to the body politic according to all that he is and has" (*ST* I-II.21.4.ad 3).

desires to the good of society. This is done by being just, by obeying the laws of the state and contributing to the polis as I am asked. My participation in this temporal common good means that I sacrifice my own goals for the sake of the public good. I accept the decisions of authority and offer to society my time, treasure, sweat, and blood so that there is peace and prosperity for all in this society. Of course, this subordination to society can never nullify my rights; the state can only ask of me what will not countermand human dignity.

On the other hand, as spiritual persons, society is just only when it nourishes our transcendent spiritual needs. Society exists to guarantee happiness, the spiritual flourishing characterized by virtue, wisdom, and love. This second sense of the common good indicates the spiritual union of persons in friendship,[80] which prepares the way for union with God in the Beatific Vision. The state, then, must not only protect justice as its proper province but must also encourage mediating institutions, especially families and churches, who are directly responsible for this eternal happiness.[81] In short, the state's role is to protect peace and justice in order to inculcate virtue as the prerequisite for personal flourishing.

This twofold notion of the common good has myriad implications for political philosophy. Let us note three.

First, this accentuates why social contract theory is inadequate. The social contract assumes that people are radically atomistic individuals whose social relations are all freely entered into and so characterized by a thin notion of commutative justice: I give this and you get that. But it is clear that this is not how friendship—especially that paradigmatic friendship, marriage, and the family—operates, since one gives to the other not

---

80 There can be friendships of pleasure and utility but only those based on mutual appreciation of virtue are true friendships, since friendship is to wish happiness for another, and only virtue leads to happiness (*Nicomachean Ethics* VIII.2–4). Friendships based on utility or pleasure will have an element of mutual exploitation.

81 In other words, our temporal common good in a flourishing society exists for the sake of our eternal common good in heaven. Thomas has a helpful metaphor he frequently invokes to illustrate this relation between an intrinsic common good and an extrinsic common good: an army (*DV* 5.3, but see also *SCG* III.64, *ST* I-II.100.6, *ST* II-II.39.2.ad 2, *CNE* I.1.5). The units of the army are well-ordered to one another in order to attain the good of the commander, which is victory. The good of the parts, then, is for the sake of the good of the whole, which is extrinsic to those parts. There are two other significant applications of this principle. In marriage, the intrinsic common good of the spouses—to grow in wisdom and love by a life of virtue together—is ordered to the extrinsic good of children as the natural fruition of the overflowing of that love (*CNE* VIII.12.1724). And, in creation, all the creatures are ordered to one another for the sake of the glory of God (*ST* I.22.2 and *ST* I.103.3).

out of contractual debt,[82] but one does so simply for the sake of the other's happiness.[83] Viewing society as contractual makes this impossible, since people remain selfishly concerned with what they are owed in their transactional relations with others. (Marriage itself has suffered from this idea, since if it is viewed merely as a contract, the threat of divorce encourages people to put their own interests first.) Proper human society needs the rules of justice to enforce the natural law; but the natural law orders people to go beyond justice to love.[84] As Thomas comments, "Justice without charity is cruelty; charity without justice, weakness."[85]

Second, this ideal of friendship informs the necessary social virtue of tolerance. If I recognize the dignity of others and view them with charity, I can respect them despite differences of opinion.[86] The social contract, in contrast, bases tolerance not in a respect for dignity but in a skepticism about our ability to know what is truly good. Since it is based in skepticism, this version of tolerance discourages argument in pursuit of truth since there is no hope of reaching consensus. Under these conditions, tolerance is grudgingly accepted for the maintenance of order; but it is a very brittle tolerance, for public opinion can be whipped up so as to peremptorily rule out opinions if they appear incompatible with the order desired by the majority. This intolerance, in turn, suppresses the search for truth, and so a valueless tolerance will evolve into despotism.

---

82 Aristotle, *Nicomachean Ethics* VIII.1 (1155a25–28): "When men are friends they have no need of justice, while when they are just they need friendship as well, and the truest form of justice is found in friendship." Here, again, reason can discover the wisdom revealed in the Golden Rule (Mt.7:9–12), but Christian charity extends friendship to all children of God (*ST* II-II.25.1).

83 Indeed, Thomas sees charity—a perfect relation to others—in terms of friendship (*ST* II-II.23.1).

84 The idea that friendship and religion are goals beyond the political is rejected in philosophies that totalize the political. For example, when Marx begins the *Communist Manifesto* with the claim "The history of all hitherto existing society is the history of class struggles," he reduces all human activity to political conflict. Thus, there is nothing beyond the political: not art, not religion, not philosophy, not even family. Accordingly, there can be no friendship that transcends politics. This follows from Marx's materialistic assumptions (see chapter 5), but it also terribly disfigures all human relations.

85 *Catena Aurea*, Mt. 5:7 (cited in Pieper, *Four Cardinal Virtues*, 112, slightly modified). Cf. *ST* I-II.99.1.ad 2: "Every law aims at establishing friendship, either between man and man, or between man and God."

86 John Paul II, *Fides et Ratio* (92): "To believe it possible to know a universally valid truth is in no way to encourage intolerance; on the contrary, it is the essential condition for sincere and authentic dialogue between persons. On this basis alone is it possible to overcome divisions and to journey together towards full truth."

Finally, this clarifies the true nature of the relation between Church and state. In any society, the Church must have a preeminent role as the institution that is directly concerned with directing the person to his eternal end, the Beatific Vision. But the Beatific Vision is possible only through the gift of charity, the supernatural lifting of a person from the temporal to the eternal. Just as justice is perfected in friendship, so friendship is perfected in charity. Thus, participation in the sacramental order of the Church perfects our worldly activities by directing them to our eternal goal. For this reason, the Church must remain independent of the state. Church and state have distinct, but parallel, ends: the state advances justice to guarantee the temporal common good of a well-ordered society; the Church offers charity to ameliorate the human condition but ultimately to lift persons to their eternal common good.[87] When the Church is not allowed to leaven society to the good of persons, the state will inevitably treat those persons as mere individuals.[88]

Conclusion: Freedom and Equality Revisited

The problems with modern political philosophy arise because it misconceives the relation of the person to society and the state, thus subordinating justice to desire instead recognizing it as a rule for evaluating desire. Starting from the position of a hypothetical state of nature in which all people are free and equal atoms, they attempt to derive a society in which that freedom and equality are protected as absolute values of the individual. But this dissociates freedom and equality from both human nature and the common good that these traits should serve. We cannot start with claims to absolute individual rights, for that will always put people into opposition with one another since their own desires will never be moderated by reason. The alternative is that we start with justice—objective

---

87 This is why Christians, *when acting on behalf of the state as officials*, can do things for the sake of justice—for example, apply capital punishment and wage war—even if as private citizens they would do otherwise for the sake of charity. However, a Christian society will always allow justice to be moderated with mercy for the sake of the spiritual good of the person.

88 This superiority of the Church's mission is obscured in liberalism's giving primacy to freedom over objective goods; this has driven the courts to see religion not as a right to be protected as required for happiness but as something contrary to the individual good of unfettered liberty; see Russell Hittinger, "The Supreme Court v. Religion" in *First Grace: Rediscovering the Natural Law in a Post-Christian World* (Wilmington, Del.: ISI Books, 2003), 163–82; see also Steven D. Smith, *The Rise and Decline of American Religious Freedom* (Cambridge, Mass.: Harvard University Press, 2014).

rules for attaining human excellence in the context of communal relations and activities—and understand the rights associated with freedom and equality based on that. Understanding that people are naturally social, that we have to rely on one another for the happiness of each and of all, is how the natural law corrects the reductive tendencies of modern political philosophy.

We can see this by considering the ontological foundation for freedom and equality. We have already observed how freedom and equality are inversely related: the more you emphasize freedom, the less equality there can be; the more you emphasize equality, the less freedom there can be. This, in itself, shows the futility of the attempt to build society on balancing these two, as is the goal of liberalism. Only by seeing what reality demands, and subordinating freedom and equality to reality, can the true good of human relations be protected.

We start by recognizing that human nature, like all being, is inherently dynamic. Human nature exists (first act) with a natural inclination to perfect itself in activity (second act). In the previous chapter, we saw how Thomas saw being and goodness as inversely related in this: First act is being simply and good in a certain respect; second act is good simply and being in a certain respect. This same analysis explains the relation between freedom and equality.

In our first act, we all share human nature. In this, all people are equal and are deserving of protections of those basic rights we have outlined above: life, family, property, honesty. In general, we can affirm that in this sense, all people are equal before the law. Justice demands equality of opportunity to exercise the capacities of their human nature. Part of this endowment of human nature is the fact of free will: all people have to make choices to determine the direction of their lives. Thus, in society we need to respect the freedom of people to exercise the self-determination that characterizes human life. Nevertheless, while freedom is rooted in first act, it exists for the sake of human perfection in second act: we are free so that we can perfect our intellect and will. But this means that it is only in virtue that true freedom is discovered: an assiduous student will have more freedom in a choice of college; a person who controls his desires will be freer in deciding what he will do. Abusing drugs, leading a slothful life, rejecting friendship may all be freely chosen, but they are incompatible with happiness and a flourishing society. Thus, freedom of choice is only freedom in a certain respect; freedom simpliciter is the ability to order one's life by virtue, truth, and goodness for the sake of happiness.[89] As Saint John Paul II succinctly put it, "Freedom consists not in doing what we like but in having the right to do what we ought."[90]

Yet the difference between first act and second act means that in their free activity people are not equal at all. Rather, people differentiate themselves into a hierarchy of merit based on how well they have used freedom of choice. Thomas sees hierarchical distinction as a necessary element of a well-ordered society.[91] So, while justice demands that we treat all people equally with regard to first act—which is shared absolutely by all humans—that same justice requires that we discriminate between good people and bad people, between worthy actions and unworthy actions.[92] This difference is due to the inverse relation each principle has to attaining happiness: although all people have to be given the opportunity to exercise free choice to direct their lives to happiness, not all choices are equally deserving of respect because only some of those choices perfect the agent by leading him to the higher freedom that comes with virtue. Further, since people are naturally social, an individual's choice always has implications for the happiness of society as a whole, and so we ought to encourage those choices that make society as a whole more free—that is, more virtuous, wiser, and more loving.

Thus, it is justice—what is demanded by human nature, as individuals who necessarily act socially for a common good—that determines the very meaning of freedom and equality. Freedom and equality, as inverse relations, cannot be made coherent as atomistic claims; rather, they are coherent only when understood as aspects of our naturally dynamic social relations by which all are ordered to the common good.

---

89 Servais Pinckaers profoundly develops this distinction between freedom of indifference and freedom for excellence in *Sources of Christian Ethics*, trans. Mary Thomas Noble (Washington, D.C.: The Catholic University of America Press, 1995). A similar distinction between free choice and freedom of autonomy (or spontaneity) is an important theme in the work of Jacques Maritain; see *Freedom in the Modern World*, trans. Richard O'Sullivan (London: Sheed and Ward, 1935), 29–54; and "The Conquest of Freedom," in *The Education of Man: The Educational Philosophy of Jacques Maritain*, ed. Donald and Idella Gallagher (Garden City, N.Y.: Doubleday, 1962), 159–79.

90 John Paul II, *Homily at Camden Yard, Baltimore, Maryland*, October 8, 1995. He is quoting a formulation originally from Lord Acton.

91 *De Reg* I.1 and I.13; *ST* I.96.3–4; *SCG* III.97. To ignore this natural hierarchy and impose an artificial equality is inherently totalitarian, for it forces people to ignore the truth of reality.

92 But remember, justice moderates relations between strangers, and all hierarchical differences can be erased by the equality of friendship (*CNE* VIII.7.1632), which is the ultimate goal of just social relations.

This analysis of freedom and equality also sheds more light on the question of human dignity we introduced at the end of the previous chapter. A just society will necessarily protect the dignity of its citizens as the basis of their rights. But we need to understand precisely what this means. The problem is that dignity is attached to human nature in an absolute fashion, like equality, but needs to be perfected and so varies from person to person, like freedom. Dignity is a universal fact of human nature arising from the rational capacity to attain happiness by transcending sensory opinions and desires in attaining truth and love. All men are equal in having this capacity. We should, therefore, never deprive people of the opportunity to exercise that capacity; indeed, as we have seen, we should do all we can to facilitate their growth. However, dignity is fully manifested in those who exercise those capacities to realize what a rational being is capable of. True dignity cannot be found in submitting to ignorance or immoral desires. Dignity, then, is both a fact of human nature and also something that must be fully attained by acting in accord with the natural law.[93] Dignity inherently reflects the dynamism of human nature; only in moral perfection is dignity realized.

As one last thought: understanding freedom and equality in terms of this metaphysical framework might help us interpret this familiar claim from the Declaration of Independence: "All men are created equal, that they are endowed by their Creator with certain unalienable Rights, that among these are Life, Liberty and the pursuit of Happiness." In light of the natural law, we see that this structures our rights on the difference between a person's existence (first act) and his perfection (second act). The right to life affirms the sanctity of personal existence, our first act; liberty affirms the potential for characteristically human activity, especially for the development of virtue; and happiness is the teleological goal of second act, the perfection of human nature as indicated by the natural law. The founders certainly knew—even if some today have forgotten—that this perfection is possible only when a person's political nature is nurtured by a government that protects peace and justice, inculcating virtue for the sake of the dignity of persons united in civic friendship.

---

93 J. Brian Benestad, *Church, State, and Society: An Introduction to Catholic Social Doctrine* (Washington, D.C.: The Catholic University of America Press, 2011), 35–52.

FURTHER READING

Deneen, Patrick J. *Why Liberalism Failed*. New Haven: Yale University Press, 2018.

Gilby, Thomas. *The Political Thought of Thomas Aquinas*. Chicago: University of Chicago Press, 1963.

Manent, Pierre. *An Intellectual History of Liberalism*. Translated by Rebecca Balinski. Princeton: Princeton University Press, 1995.

Maritain, Jacques. *Man and the State*. Washington, D.C.: The Catholic University of America Press, 1998.

McCoy, Charles N. R. *The Structure of Political Thought: A Study in the History of Political Ideas*. New York: McGraw-Hill, 1963.

Murray, John Courtney. *We Hold These Truths*. New York: Sheed and Ward, 1960.

Rommen, Heinrich. *The State in Catholic Thought: A Treatise in Political Philosophy*. St. Louis and London: B. Herder Book Co., 1945.

Schall, James. *Roman Catholic Political Philosophy*. Lanham, Md.: Lexington Books, 2004.

Simon, Yves R. *Philosophy of Democratic Government*. Chicago: University of Chicago Press, 1951.

Voegelin, Eric. *The New Science of Politics*. Chicago: University of Chicago Press, 1952.

Part III

Ever Shall Be

Chapter 8

God: The Alpha and the Omega

THE PROBLEM: THE HIDDEN GOD

In the first chapter, we said that philosophy seeks to discover self-evident first principles that enable us to make sense of the world. We have argued that being, understood as the act of existence, provides the explanation for why things exist at all; that truth as the intelligibility of being provides the explanation for how we know reality; that good as the perfection of being provides the explanation for why these beings are dynamically and intelligibly oriented to action; and that beauty as the radiance of being provides the explanation for why contemplating creation brings joy. Being, in its many faces, makes life worth living. Humans form community and develop culture to facilitate immersion in being in all these ways.

Now we must address a more profound question: what is the source of this being? It is clear that none of the things in the natural world *has to* exist. The universe existed without them at one time in the past and will exist without them at some time in the future. Indeed, the universe itself is contingent, coming into being almost fourteen billion years ago. There must be some causal explanation for how all these things come to participate in existence.

Because of the convertibility of the transcendental properties, this source of being would also explain why things in nature are comprehensible, desirable, and delightful (i.e., true, good, and beautiful). For this reason, we immerse ourselves in reality in thought and through love, realizing our potential to be open to the highest Truth and the universal Good. Attaining this end can only result in a contemplative joy. This joyful contemplation is truly sacred, set apart from the rest of our actions; let us call it *worship*.[1] The source of the universe, of truth and goodness, is the goal we seek in pursuing human fulfillment in worship.

Here, though, we are faced with a puzzle. The cause of being, truth, goodness, and beauty must be ever-present, for these are part of every

---

1 *ST* II-II.84.1.

human experience. It seems, then, that we ought to be able to know this cause as well as we know its myriad effects in the world. Nevertheless, it also seems that this great discovery eludes us, for many people are unaware of this cause completely or conceive of it only vaguely and in disparate ways. This obscurity is understandable, for the cause of the world cannot be part of the world itself. Just as an artist must stand outside the painting in order to create it, in the same way the creator of being, truth, and goodness must stand outside the universe he creates.

This is the great puzzle that faces philosophers when they come to address the ultimate cause of being, which they will refer to as "God."[2] On the one hand, cause and effect cannot be utterly separated; God must be present in the world to function as a cause of the things we experience. In other words, God must be *immanent*. The presence of being, truth, goodness, and beauty are the evidence from which we reason to know God as the cause of the universe. On the other hand, God cannot act as creator if he is part of creation itself. In other words, God must be *transcendent*; he must exist above all of creation that he makes and holds in existence. But if God is transcendent, if there is an ontological abyss separating God and this world, he would appear to be unknowable by reason.

Historically, those who emphasize the transcendence of God have suggested that God can be known by two distinct religious methods. One is a super-rational mysticism by which people lift themselves up to God (as exemplified in Buddhism and Plotinus). But this mystical ascent is a rare talent that is not shared by most people. The alternative is that God reaches down and reveals himself to people in the world (as believed by Judaism and Christianity). But this requires that we have faith in revelation. The problem is that both of these exclude the use of reason, the only approach that is universally available to all people. Moreover, reason *must* be able to grasp the ultimate cause: if knowledge is knowledge of causes, being ignorant of the ultimate cause would plunge us into skepticism and despair because finite and partial causes would lack grounding. If there were no principle guaranteeing the universal intelligibility of being, whatever facts

---

2 Note, though, that this philosophical idea of God is minimal, for it considers God only in terms of his creative activity and not in terms of the saving acts that reveal his being more completely. However, this minimal idea of God is ideal for philosophers, since it can be accepted by people of all monotheistic religious traditions and even by serious intellects outside of any religious tradition.

we can grasp would never add up to anything more significant. If we do not know the highest cause, life itself would be meaningless.

Therefore, there must be a rational approach to God. Once again, though, problems arise when philosophers approach this as an either-or problem, since this will reduce God to one aspect of his being. As God must be both immanent and transcendent, the most logical solution is to have a philosophy that affirms both and reconciles the apparent contradiction. This solution, as we will see, draws on the idea of the act of existence that analogically unites the infinite Creator with finite creation; because God is being, he will be knowable, lovable, and delightful, for he is the Truth, the Good, and the Beautiful. But philosophical approaches that do not start with the act of existence will inevitably end up with a distorted notion of the cause of being.

REDUCTIVE EXTREMES

If we accept that God is only immanent—present in the world—he cannot really be God. He would be just another being *in* the universe—maybe more powerful, but he would be different only in degree and not in kind from all other beings. This, however, is not God. On the other hand, if we accept that God is only transcendent—apart from this world—he might possess the difference in kind characteristic of God, but then he would be inherently unknowable. There would be no way to bridge the abyss separating creature from creator. Ironically, both of these reductive approaches lead to atheism. In neither instance can we know God as he truly is, and so we end up believing in nothing. Let us consider these points more closely.

God as Immanent

The tendency to see God as immanent, to the exclusion of transcendent, is characteristic of paganism and pantheism, which place the gods firmly in nature. Consequently, it is best exemplified by ancient Greek thought. This is evident in the very first Greek philosopher, Thales. As we noted in chapter 2, Thales claimed that all things are made of water.[3] What was not mentioned at the time was that this famous assertion is accompanied by a more puzzling one: Thales believed that all things were full of gods.[4] To modern,

---

3 As reported in Aristotle, *Metaphysics* I.3 (983b20–27).

4 As reported in Aristotle, *De Anima* I.5 (411a8–9). My presentation of the development ancient and modern thought is highly informed by Étienne Gilson, *God and Philosophy*, 2nd ed. (New Haven: Yale University Press, 2002).

scientific-minded philosophers, this is paradoxical: if water is the first principle of being that explains all of reality, there is simply no need to posit the existence of gods. But Thales had a serious reason to insist on both. He sees that in order to account for all the changes we observe, we need two causal principles at work in the world. Therefore, Thales makes one philosophical claim—that all things are made of water—that explains things that happen with a scientific necessity; and he makes a parallel religious claim—that all things are full of gods—that explains things that happen spontaneously and contingently. While Thales thought reason could understand how water, due to its ubiquity and fluidity, is the basis for the laws of nature, it is also clear that not *all* changes exhibit such rational necessity. There are spontaneous changes—like the free acts of people—that cannot be traced to the laws of nature. These spontaneous actions of living things are evidence of the causal activity of the gods. Thus, there are gods attached to every kind of natural being to account for spontaneity in the universe. This division of the world into a pair of ultimate causes becomes characteristic of most Greek philosophers. It also exemplifies their tendency to view the gods as wholly immanent causes in the world.

The rationality of the Greek philosophers also latches onto another principle that cements this understanding of gods as worldly causes. This is the inescapable logic of the principle *ex nihilo, nihil fit*: from nothing, nothing can be made. The Greeks thought it was impossible to get something out of nothing: it violates reason since it is, quite literally, magic—like pulling a rabbit from a hat. Philosophy was meant to get past that sort of superstitious thinking. Therefore, the universe itself could not have come from nothing; whatever composes the nature of the world must always have been that way. The gods, then, could not have *created* the world. Since the gods cannot be creators, the only thing they could do is to cause changes in the world (which existed from eternity). Thus, purely immanent gods are not creators; they exercise a more limited power as explanations of change. This is precisely how Thales saw the gods.

These parallel philosophical and religious causes tend to show up in later Greek philosophers as paired principles: a passive material principle that constitutes the nature of beings, and an active principle that causes those beings to change. For example, in Empedocles the four elements constitute being, but changes are caused by the active forces of Love and Strife; in Anaxagoras, being is made of "infinite seeds" that are stirred into motion by a Mind.[5] More influentially, this dualistic system of causes plays a central role in the thought of Plato and Aristotle.

Plato identifies being with the Forms, the unchanging immaterial objects of knowledge.[6] But the Forms are nevertheless many, and so Plato realizes there has to be one principle of intelligibility common to all the Forms, one principle to explain *why* the Forms are the way they are. This is the Form of the Good, the source of the being of Forms as well as our knowledge of truth.[7] As the Form of Forms, Plato does not see the Good in the same way Christians view God. The Good does not create the world, since the Forms, as Being, are eternal and uncreated. The Good is a *philosophical* principle explaining intelligibility, like a law of nature; it is not a personal being acting with a mind and will.

Nevertheless, Plato does make room for a god. One persistent problem with Plato's theory of Forms is how an unchanging realm of Forms could cause change in this world. Plato attempts to solve this problem by introducing a Demiurge—a god-like "creator" who causes change in this world by making things in this world as copies of the Forms: "Now everything that becomes or is created must of necessity be created by some cause, for without a cause nothing can be created. The work of the creator, whenever he looks to the unchangeable and fashions the form and nature of his work after an unchangeable pattern, must necessarily be made fair and perfect."[8] Note that this "creator" creates neither the Forms nor the material reality of this world. Rather, Plato, like Thales, has recourse to the god(s) only to explain the spontaneity of change—why things change from participating in one Form to participating in another. We can be assured these changes are orderly and good because the Demiurge looks to the Forms and so instills order into this world. Clearly, Plato's god is not the creator of the Christian tradition.[9]

---

5 As noted in chapter 2, the exception to this are the atomists, who say reality is made up of atoms moving through a void and so try to explain change without reference to the gods. However, to account for the fact of spontaneous change, later atomists introduce an uncaused "swerve" of atoms—a solution that destroys the intelligibility of the world because now change is utterly random (see Lucretius, *De rerum naturae* II.216–25).

6 For a very brief statement, see *Republic* VI (507b): "We speak of a self-beautiful and of a good that is only and merely good, and so, in the case of all the things that we then posited as many, we turn about and posit each as a single idea or aspect, assuming it to be a unity and call it that which each really is."

7 *Republic* VI (508e1–3).

8 *Timaeus* 28a3–28b1.

9 In fact, inasmuch as Plato sees human souls as immaterial and immortal sources of spontaneous change, we can consider the human soul as a kind of god (see *Phaedo* 80a–b). This is a polytheism.

For Aristotle, the basic unit of being is not the Form but rather substance. In this world, this is manifested in the hylomorphic composition of form and matter. Because these worldly substances contain within them principles of both act (form) and potency (matter), the fact of change (or becoming) is explicable in terms of their formal and material causes. However, to explain *why* change happens, Aristotle introduces two extrinsic causes—the efficient cause to bring substances into existence and the final cause as the end that elicits accidental change. Therefore, when Aristotle comes to think about God, he naturally associates it with these causes of change: God, then, would be interpreted as the first efficient cause or final cause of change.[10]

Aristotle's arguments for the existence of a first mover would be very influential for Christians, Jews, and Muslims alike. His essential insight, which would be adopted by later philosophers, is that in a chain of causes, an infinite regress of causes is impossible. That is, we cannot explain a change in A by saying it was caused by B, which was caused by C, which was caused by D, with this chain going on forever. If this were the case, you would never come to the start this whole series of changes, and so there would be no *explanation* of the change at all. There must be something at the beginning of the series of changes that did not need to be caused by anything else. Because this first cause of motion is not caused by anything else, it is understood to be without potency to change. Lacking potency, it is both an *immaterial* substance and pure actuality. This fully actual being that causes all change is God.

Like other Greek philosophers, Aristotle thinks that creation is impossible, and so he assumes the material world (with both intrinsic principles of form and matter) must always have been. Further, that material world must always have been changing, because time is a measure of change and time must always have existed.[11] These premises, however, make it difficult to argue for God as an efficient cause. An efficient cause acts by beginning the motion of things; if God were an efficient cause, there would have been some point at which he, as the first mover, began the motion of the universe. But this is impossible for two reasons: first, it would mean there was a beginning to time; second, it would imply that, prior to acting, the first mover

---

10 *Physics* VIII.4–6 (254b7–258b9); *Metaphysics* XII.6–9 (1071b3–1075a12).

11 *Metaphysics* XII.6 (1071b6–10). The problem is that time is a measure of before and after—that is, of changing things—but one cannot say "before time existed" since that itself would imply before and after, which is to be in time.

was in potency to causing that motion, which implies that it changed in initiating action.

Given the problems with the argument from efficient cause, Aristotle turns to final causality as a better explanation for the first mover. He gets to it by examining the structure of our changing universe. Our terrestrial world is composed of the four elements, which constitute the matter in terrestrial substances. These elements are constantly being moved to change by the motion of the planets, which exerts a causal influence on material substances on the earth. The planets, in turn, are always in motion, since their motion is the measure of time. The cause of the motion of the planets, then, is the first cause of motion, an unmoved mover, which must be always in act and so be an immaterial substance without any potency to change.[12]

The fact that the first mover must be pure act and without potency explains why it can be understood to be a final cause. As purely actual, the first mover is perfect, and as perfect, it is desired by all substances that seek perfection. As a final cause, it can "move without being moved" because it causes action not by acting but by being an object of desire for other things. All things seek the good, and so all things are moved by their desire for perfection embodied by the first mover.[13] All other movements in the universe, then, arise from this desire for perfection as a final cause. So, unlike an efficient cause, a final cause can cause eternal motion since it does not have to do anything to initiate movement.

The nature of the first mover's perfection has significant implications for Aristotle's conception of God. The first mover is an immaterial being, so it must be a mind (a being whose activity is immaterial). As mind, the pure actuality of the first mover must be thinking, which is the most perfect kind of activity. However, in order to remain unchanging, this pure act of thinking must think only about itself, for if it thought of other things its thoughts would change as those things do. Thus, God for Aristotle is a self-thinking thought.[14]

While this perfect Thinker might bear similarity with the Christian God, we need to note its limitations. First, as self-thinking thought, Aris-

---

12 Aristotle, *Metaphysics* XII.6 (1071b18–23).

13 Aristotle, *Metaphysics* XII.7 (1072a20–30).

14 Aristotle, *Metaphysics* XII.7 (1072b15–20); this idea of God as self-thinking thought is developed in XII.7 (1073a3–13) and XII.9 (1274b15–34); this last passage concludes, "Therefore it must be of itself that the divine thought thinks (since it is the most excellent of things), and its thinking is a thinking on thinking."

totle's first mover God does not know things other than itself, and so it is unable to exercise providence over the world.[15] Indeed, where the Christian God moves all things by *loving* them, Aristotle's God, as final cause, moves by *being loved*, so it remains indifferent to the fate of substances. Second, it is clear that this God, as the final cause of planetary motion, is *in* the universe. It is not transcendent; it is simply the highest cause in the order of natural causes. For this reason, Aristotle's God is not a creator. Form and matter—the intrinsic causes of substances—are eternal, and God is simply the cause of change in substances. Finally, Aristotle argues that, as God is the unmoved mover of the planets, each "planetary sphere" will need its own mover; Aristotle concludes that there must be forty-seven unmoved movers—clearly a polytheism![16]

However, Aristotle's identification of God with philosophical causal principles does tend to collapse the dual questions about causes into one that is purely philosophical. While this is in some ways an improvement, it is done is only at the cost of reinforcing the presumption that God is not a transcendent being worthy of worship. For if God is nothing but a final cause, a purely philosophical principle, then he is simply an operative force in the universe that functions with necessity. This logic influences later Hellenistic philosophies.

We see this exemplified in Stoicism. The Stoics agree with Aristotle that nature has determinate causes, but, where Aristotle believed in a plurality of natures, the Stoics associated nature with the cosmos as a whole, so that Nature is one reality. Because there is a one deterministic cause for this Nature as a whole, everything in the cosmos happens with necessity.[17] The Stoics, then, identify this philosophical causal necessity with the religious source of spontaneous movement, God's mind. As an immanent cause in the universe, God is eventually identified with the universe itself in a pantheism.

---

15 Bonaventure (*Collationes in Hexaemeron* VI.2–5) brilliantly exposes how this point, if carried out, erodes almost all essentials of Christian doctrine about God.

16 Aristotle, *Metaphysics* XII.8 (1073a13–1074a16). Nevertheless, Aristotle humbly recognizes the limits of his own reasoning: "Let this, then, be taken as the number of the spheres, so that the unmovable substances and principles also may probably be taken as just so many; the assertion of *necessity* must be left to more powerful thinkers." For a good explanation of the Aristotelian-Ptolemaic idea of planetary spheres, see C. S. Lewis, *The Discarded Image: An Introduction to Medieval and Renaissance Literature* (Cambridge: Cambridge University Press, 1964), 92–121.

17 Our use of *stoic* as one unmoved by emotion reflects this idea that the wise person can only resign himself to this cosmic fate.

Cicero summarizes their position: "It is certain that nothing at all is superior or more beautiful than the cosmos. . . . And if nothing is better than reason and wisdom, it is necessary that these be present in that which we have granted to be the best. . . . Therefore, the cosmos is rational."[18] God is the cause of change because God is identical with nature. But this immanent, deterministic cause cannot be loved or worshipped; it is merely abided.[19]

This attempt to completely capture God in philosophy as an immanent rational principle naturally engenders a religious reaction in the opposite direction. The transcendence of God would be reasserted by emphasizing an experiential, often irrational, idea of religion. This dialectical pattern repeats itself in the history of philosophy. The Stoics' cosmic God of Nature is answered by the rise of the mystery religions; similarly, Enlightenment deism and Kantian scientism both deflate the idea of God and so give rise to the fideistic responses of Pascal and Kierkegaard, respectively; finally, Darwinism and dehellenized liberal Christianity of the nineteenth century would spawn the antirationalism of Pentecostalism and fundamentalism in the twentieth century.[20] The lesson here is that any acceptable philosophy of God will have to balance God's immanence with a respectful sense of transcendence.

God as Transcendent

While it is clear that to conceive of God as wholly immanent reduces his reality to a cause within the universe, the apparent alternative—affirming God's transcendence—can also become problematic. Affirming God's transcendence allows us to respect his role as a creator separate from creation; however, this approach can reduce God by removing him completely from the world of experience. The problem is that an absent God is one who is inherently impossible to know, and so he is easily neglected and then for-

---

18 Cicero, *On the Nature of the Gods* II.18–21.

19 See Epictetus, *Enchiridion* 31: "The most important aspect of piety toward the gods is certainly both to have correct beliefs about them, as beings that arrange the universe well and justly, and to set yourself to obey them and acquiesce in everything that happens and to follow it willingly, as something brought to completion by the best judgment. For in this way you will never blame the gods or accuse them of neglecting you." Very similar premises and conclusions can be found in the modern pantheism of Baruch Spinoza.

20 The term *liberal* here has nothing to do with political liberalism. Rather, this is the traditional label for that post-Enlightenment Christianity that tended to be skeptical of the supernatural and to downplay the objective significance of dogmas. The term is used by Benedict XVI in his Regensburg speech and, as we will see, by John Henry Newman.

gotten. In modern thought, we witness this incremental removal of God from experience and the scope of speculative reason; beginning in deism, it ends in fideism or atheism. This trajectory is nicely epitomized by John Rist, "From an unknowable God we move fast to an irrelevant God, and eventually to his elimination as superfluous."[21]

An important reason for this reductive approach to God lies in the choice of philosophical methodologies. In general, there is a deference to the scientific method in a way that minimizes metaphysical reasoning. But if God is the creator *behind* the world of experience, this weakening of metaphysics would tend to make God appear to be unknowable. This is exacerbated by the widespread assumptions of nominalism (that only individual things exist) and a univocal idea of being (all beings exist in the same way, which questions the analogical dependence of creature on Creator), which conspire to "flatten" being by depriving reality of layered causal principles. This position suggests that our reasoning concerning God's existence cannot be notably different from that for any other substance. If God is creator, though, he must be unlike any creature and would be known only indirectly as the analogical cause of being, truth, and goodness. Thus, one's idea of being and theory of knowledge will in many ways foreordain the conclusions one reaches about God.

Yet many (but not all) of these thinkers did not intend to marginalize God. Ironically, some believers hoped to respond to the growing skepticism and atheism of modernity by placing belief in God on more secure philosophical foundations. This is true, for example, of Descartes. His motive, as we have seen, is to make knowledge more certain. This included, at the invitation of the great spiritual teacher Cardinal Pierre de Bérulle (1575–1629), an attempt to fend off atheism by showing that knowledge of God is as certain as scientific knowledge. Descartes fulfills his pledge by applying his mathematical method and making God's existence indispensable for science itself. Descartes, then, shows that science and religion are both reasonable.[22]

Recall that Descartes answers skepticism by basing knowledge on an indubitable principle: the fact that as long as he thinks, he must exist (the *cogito*). As a thinking thing, Descartes is aware of many ideas, but because of the Evil Genius, he cannot be sure that they are reliable. However, one of

---

21 John Rist, *Real Ethics*, 157.

22 See Descartes's Letter of Dedication in the *Meditations* to the Faculty of Theology at the University of Paris. For the story of Bérulle's invitation, see Michael J. Buckley, *At the Origins of Modern Atheism* (New Haven: Yale University Press, 1987), 71–72.

his ideas is that of an infinite, perfect being: God.[23] While his other ideas can be subject to doubt, Descartes argues that this idea of God *must* be true. As infinite, it could not have been conceived of by a person's finite mind, since it has more reality than a person's mind possesses; moreover, as perfect, this God *must* exist, for if he did not, he would lack the perfection of existence. Thus, Descartes concludes that his idea of an infinite and perfect being shows that God must exist.[24] Further, since no human mind could have conceived of this idea of God, the only way that Descartes can come to possess that idea is if it is *innate*, placed in the mind by God at the time of the mind's creation. But if God is the source of *all* the innate ideas, then we can know that there is no Evil Genius and that at least these clear and distinct, innate ideas are reliable. This includes the mathematical ideas that are the basis for infallible knowledge of the material world. In this way, Descartes shows that the mathematical results of modern science are a reliable description of the world. Descartes is clear, however, that the certitude of science, and of all knowledge, hinges on the existence of an infinite and perfect God to justify our confidence in innate ideas.[25]

It is important to note the function of God in this argument. He is not the creator who explains the existence of the universe (though Descartes does not deny this). On the contrary, since Descartes's main interest is to refute skepticism, the existence of God functions primarily to underwrite the discoveries of science. This epistemological concern, and Descartes's rationalist method relying on innate ideas, causes Descartes to invert the traditional approach. Traditionally, philosophy examines the natural world and discovers evidence in it for a God who is the creator. Descartes's method, in contrast, was to doubt the existence of the universe; as a consequence, it is the discovery of God that certifies the universe as knowable. While accomplishing the goal of fighting skepticism, this approach ends up diminishing God. For God is discovered only as a means to prove that science works. However, in this approach, all we can really know of God is that he guarantees the regularity of mathematical laws of science; he becomes an impersonal lawmaker for a world that is known by the principles of scientific materialism.

---

23 This idea of God as infinitely perfect shows the influence of Christianity, since it is foreign to the ancient pagans, even Plato and Aristotle. Thus, it is not a purely philosophical idea of God but implicitly relies on revelation.

24 These arguments are in the *Third* and *Fifth Meditations*.

25 See *Discourse on Method* IV, 38–39, and *Fifth Meditation*, 71.

This method, then, has a number of consequences (which go beyond Descartes's intention) about how God is understood in terms of philosophy. First, since God is conceived as underwriting science, it depreciates anything mysterious about God's action in the universe. For example, a scientifically minded God would not allow for miracles, since a rational lawmaker would not violate his own laws. Similarly, the notion of providence is domesticated, since a rational creator would create a world that would exclude all harm to humans. Indeed, this leads to a denial of sin, since a rational lawmaker would not make a world subject to the Fall and in need of redemption. Finally, although God is the Lawmaker for the universe, he is otherwise not actively present in the world because scientific laws account for all that happens. As a consequence, though, it is impossible to form a *personal* relationship with this absent God. Ironically, the more one emphasizes God as a lawmaker who underwrites scientific truths, the more the universe itself become purely mechanistic and so inherently godless because God is simply no longer needed.[26]

This vision of God as the creator of laws underlying the scientific order of the universe is known as *deism*. While accepting that God must exist, it otherwise minimizes his relevance to human existence. God is not actively present in the world because science alone is adequate to explain the work of nature. This philosophy is perhaps best epitomized in the epitaph Alexander Pope wrote for Isaac Newton: "Nature and Nature's laws lay hid in night: God said, 'Let Newton be!' and all was light." The reliability of science is the sole evidence for this lawmaking God. All other evidence—the metaphysical, the supernatural, the redemptive, the mystical—is repudiated, since it would undermine the sovereignty of science. This scientific basis for knowing God is inherently unstable, though, for as soon as science can explain those laws without having to invoke God—as it inevitably will—people will abandon the lawmaker in favor of atheism. The natural world is able to explain its own operations, and so God is relegated to irrelevance.

---

26 The most striking response to Descartes is that of his contemporary Blaise Pascal (1623–1662): "I cannot forgive Descartes. In all his philosophy he would have been quite willing to dispense with God. But he had to make Him give a fillip to set the world in motion; beyond this, he has no further need of God" (*Pensées* 77). Pascal himself would emphasize the unavoidable need for faith in his famous Wager (233), where opposing possibilities of heavenly reward versus eternal damnation should lead one to embrace faith. This faith is not subject to argument, since it necessarily goes beyond reason, for "[t]he heart has its reasons, which reason does not know" (277). In fact, Pascal concludes that, because deism does not lead to a true love of God, it is as bad as atheism (556).

That a causally irrelevant God is unknowable and so functionally the same as atheism is asserted boldly by David Hume, whose arguments have greatly influenced many contemporary philosophers. As with Descartes, this conclusion follows from his reductive philosophical method. Hume's method is a radical empiricism: if God cannot be known by direct sense experience, we are not justified in believing God exists. However, Hume acknowledges that arguments for God's existence rely not on direct sense-experience but on cause-and-effect reasoning about God as creator. Therefore, Hume's significance lies in how he applies his critique of cause-and-effect reasoning to arguments for the existence of God. We have seen in chapter 4 that Hume rejects the validity of all such reasoning, reducing it to merely a habitual belief about customarily conjoined events. For this reason, Hume's arguments about God are best seen as a reflection of his broader skepticism.

Hume begins by granting that causal reasoning is the basis for arguments concerning the existence of God. "The chief or sole argument for a divine existence . . . is derived from the order of nature; where there appear such marks of intelligence and design, that you think it extravagant to assign for its cause, either chance, or the blind and unguided force of matter."[27] In other words, because we witness an orderly design in nature, we conclude that there must be a *designer* as its cause. Hume finds two problems with this type of causal argument. First, in causal reasoning, we can attribute to the cause only those qualities that are seen in the effect, and we are never justified in going beyond that evidence. Applying this to God and the world, we see that this world is finite, imperfect, and violent; consequently, we are not warranted in concluding that the creator is infinite, perfect, and just. Given this limitation, though, since we can never attribute to God anything beyond what is perceived in the world, the idea of God in reality *adds nothing* to what we already know about the world itself. Religion is a superfluous hypothesis, since it reveals no truths beyond what we know from experience. The second problem with using causal reasoning to establish God's existence is that this reasoning is impossible anyway. Cause and effect relations are, for Hume, based on habits of repeated experience: we see builders make houses and so get used to relating one to the other. Forming such an idea of God is impossible since, even if he did act as creator, this only happened once at the beginning of time, depriving us of the repeated experi-

---

27 David Hume, *An Enquiry Concerning Human Understanding*, sec. 11.

ences needed to form a habit relating cause to effect. As it is, though, we have no habit concerning God's causal activity, and so we can draw no conclusion at all about God.

Many have found Hume's argument persuasive; however, we should note how it reflects the reductive nature of his empirical method. First, Hume's empiricism rules out truly metaphysical arguments that get to causes *of the existence* of the universe. As a result, the only argument for God's existence Hume recognizes is based on the orderly design of the world, which demonstrates a benevolent deity. But, for those who accept metaphysical reasoning about being, this argument from design is understood to be a weak argument to begin with. The problem with it lies in the fact that it ignores the primary evidence for God: the fact that the universe exists. Instead of focusing on the existence of the entire universe, the argument from design focuses on one finite property of the universe—that it is ordered.[28] However, any finite property can be explained by a finite cause. It is possible that the order in the universe is the result of the fundamental forces of physics that make the laws of the universe. Existence, in contrast, requires a truly transcendent cause, one who is not in the universe but brings it to be from nothing. Second, Hume's assumption that we cannot attribute perfection or infinitude to God arises from this same neglect of the question of existence. For, if we appreciate that creation is not about order but about bringing being *out of nothing*, it does imply infinite power. Third, his assumption that creation happened only once in the past is again due to his overlooking the fact that the *continued existence* of contingent beings requires a cause here and now. Thus, creation—the giving of being to things that do not have to exist—is experienced in every moment of consciousness and is certainly data for rational inference. Hume's empirical method, focusing on a determinate property of the world rather than its existence, prevents him from asking the questions necessary to get to the existence of God.

Similar issues mark Hume's other famous foray into theology, his critique of miracles.[29] His argument, again, depends wholly on his tendentious interpretation of cause-and-effect reasoning based on nominalism where there

---

28 The argument from design suppresses the most important issue about the universe. The argument frames the question of God in terms of this question: "*Given that the universe exists, why does it have property X?*" But that first clause is really the one that theistic metaphysics aims to explain and so should not be taken as a mere "given."

29 David Hume, *An Enquiry Concerning Human Understanding*, sec. 10.

are no necessary relations in nature. Since causal relations are mere habits of experience, he begins by asserting, "A wise man . . . proportions his belief to the evidence." That is, if something happens all the time, you can have near certainty about your belief. If something only happens half the time, you have a cautious level of probability. Accordingly, though, if your experience shows that something rarely or never happens, you are entitled to be skeptical about the event. He then applies this to miracles. Hume defines a miracle as "a violation of the laws of nature." But Hume's idiosyncratic idea of law of nature—based on his nominalist critique of cause-and-effect relations—is simply something that is expected based on habitual experience. A miracle, then, is something that goes against the strongest habits of experience. But, if it goes against your expectations, you should be skeptical about the event. This is especially true if the miracle is known through the testimony of other people—that is, if other people tell you it happened. Proportioning belief to evidence, when someone tells you a story of an event that contradicts your strongest habitual expectations, you should always reject that story. Belief in miracles, Hume concludes, is never justified.

Notice that this argument does not show that miracles do not occur; it only shows that, based on his empiricism and his nominalist idea of causal reasoning, they ought not to be believed. For Hume, if a miracle contradicts habit, I should not believe it. This rule of reasoning, though, proves both too much and too little. On the one hand, it proves too much because this reasoning does not just rule out miracles; it makes it impossible to believe *anything* new. For example, just because there has never been a fire in my office does not justify my doubting someone who tells me there is one.

It proves too little, on the other hand, because it assumes reductive principles that fail to grasp how belief in miracles operates. First, he fails to understand belief. Hume's skeptical epistemology conflates opinion with faith. Opinion is what we have when we proportion belief to evidence; faith is the state of certainty based on the reliability of the person giving the testimony. Hume turns all belief into opinion and so rules out all beliefs that are not based on a calculus of probability concerning the event. Second, and more important, his empiricism reduces cause and effect to a habit of customary experience, instead of being a metaphysical state of being, an ontological dependence of the effect on the cause. In other words, from a metaphysical perspective, the effect *cannot exist* without the cause. This is why miracles are believed: because there appears to be no natural cause to explain the existence of the effect. Indeed, this same ontological dependence underlies our arguments for the existence of God as creator of a contingent universe. Thus, while the conclusions of Hume's arguments follow from his principles, those principles themselves are reductive and, as a result, they make God's evident activity invisible. We can conclude that a purely empirical approach to the question of God is not capable of capturing the breadth of human experience.

Once again, the most profound reaction to Hume's skepticism comes from Immanuel Kant. As with epistemology and ethics, his innovative approach attempts to save knowledge of God by fundamentally reframing how the issue is to be approached. Kant thought he could resolve the inconclusiveness of traditional metaphysical speculation by restricting knowledge of God to the realm of practical reason, or morality. Although this approach is a valiant response to Hume's outright skepticism, while also tapping into some profound intuitions about the nature of ethics, by removing God from the purview of theoretical reason Kant pushes God a little further from man's experience of the world.

The key to Kant's argument against Hume's skepticism is his second Copernican Revolution: the mind does not conform to reality but rather reality conforms to the mind.[30] Metaphysics, for Kant, is not about objects in the world per se. It is about the necessary structure of cognition so as to make knowledge certain. Thus, the logical judgments the mind makes about objects of experience determine the limits of legitimate human knowledge. So, for example, the logical judgment of cause-and-effect relations can be applied to objects of sense-experience to give us scientific knowledge of the world. However, that logical judgment cannot be applied to what is *not given* in experience. For this reason, speculative knowledge of the traditional objects of metaphysics—including immortality, free will, and God—are simply beyond the capacity of human knowledge.

Nevertheless, it is clear that we have *ideas* of these metaphysical objects. This is because reason naturally seeks for ultimate causes beyond our experience. It looks for a logically necessary being even though it cannot be given in experience. For example, if we know that in experience every event has a cause, reason naturally tries to extend that judgment by abstract reasoning to try to discover the cause of the universe as a whole. Obviously, though, the universe as a whole is never an object of experience for us. Nevertheless, there is a natural tendency to *think* there is such a cause, even

---

30 *Critique of Pure Reason*, Preface B, xvi–xvii.

though it can never be proved in terms of scientific experience. Similarly, every experience of the world has a cause that is characterized by deterministic laws of phenomena; it appears, then, that there can be no free actions. But, since no chain of natural causes can go on to infinity (think Aristotle's infinite regress), that chain of causes must have started with a free act. Again, though, while I have to logically *think* this is necessary, it is not properly known since it is impossible to have experience of that act.[31] Importantly, these ideas arise from reason's logical speculation, and not the judgment of the understanding, because there is nothing in our experience to correspond to them. Though not given in experience, and so not knowable by the judgments of the understanding, these ideas are nevertheless thinkable due to the natural inquisitiveness of reason. This means that, whatever value they have, they cannot be the genuine speculative knowledge.

This is where Kant's reframing of metaphysics bears ingenious fruit. Kant's insight here is that these ideas that reason naturally conceives serve not as a speculative truth but rather as practical postulates. That is, even though we cannot have determinate knowledge of these ideas, we believe them as the necessary conditions for the moral life. Recall that in ethics, Kant argued that a good will is the only thing that is unconditionally good; but a good will is one that freely wills that moral law according to reason. Thus, in spite of our experience of the deterministic laws of the scientific universe, we can know that the human person is free. This is necessary because freedom is the indispensable ground for moral responsibility. In the same way, we can be convinced by these practical postulates that the person has an immortal soul that will be judged by God. This practical knowledge—of freedom, immortality, and God—is the basis for the moral life. Although Kant's reframing of metaphysics takes these topics out of the realm of speculative argumentation, he nevertheless makes them necessary in the realm of practical philosophy. As he famously puts it, his philosophy has "found it necessary to deny *knowledge*, in order to make room for *faith*."[32] Thus, religious notions serve the important purpose of motivating the moral life.

Let us consider how this approach applies specifically to God. The idea of God is of a Supreme Being, that is, one who possesses all possible attributes. As such, God is the source of everything else, of all the discrete prop-

---

31 Kant takes the contradictory results of these arguments as proof that the topic is truly beyond the proper limits of knowledge; see the Antinomies of Pure Reason in *Critique of Pure Reason*, A406/B433–A460/B488.

32 Immanuel Kant, *Critique of Pure Reason*, Preface B, xxx.

erties given in experience. But obviously, this most perfect being is never given to us in experience, since everything we experience is limited according to the particular conditions of sensation and judgment. For this reason, Kant argues that all proofs for the existence of God ultimately reduce to a fallacious "ontological argument" such as that employed by Descartes. This argument moves from the idea that there is a most perfect being to the fact of its existence: God, as a perfect being, necessarily exists, for, if he lacked the property of existing, he would not be perfect and so would not be God. The error here, for Kant, is that you cannot use an idea of something to prove the existence of that thing. As he puts it, "*Being* is obviously not a real predicate."[33] A real predicate is something that adds to the notion of the thing, a sensible quality like *green* or *big*, that can be predicated of *hat* to increase my knowledge of it. However, you cannot use the idea of being (as in God is the *perfect being*) to prove the existence of anything, since we only know things exist because they are given in sense-experience. While the idea of God as a perfect being is thinkable, knowledge of the existence of things must be *a posteriori*. Being is not a meaningful property of things and does not add anything to at all to our concept of a thing. Although there is no way to know the existence of the most perfect being, we must nevertheless believe in him as an ideal that regulates our moral life.

We can see how Kant's reframing of metaphysics has both benefits and drawbacks. On the one hand, a notion of a truly transcendent God beyond human experience is secured. This certainly protects the dignity of God, and it makes faith in him critical for the moral life of the person, which is more meaningful than a seemingly cold metaphysical fact. (This reflects Kant's Lutheran background.)

On the other hand, this reframing of metaphysics away from being to the structure of cognition does remove God from the fabric of being in the world. This is exemplified in Kant's understanding of being in his critique of the ontological argument. For Kant, being is reduced to a grammatical function connecting two terms; it has no *ontological* significance in itself.[34] This is because existence, for Kant, is a judgment made about that which is given in experience and so serves as a determination of our experiences. By contrast, in traditional metaphysics, being is a causal principle that serves

---

33 Kant, *Critique of Pure Reason*, A598/B626.

34 Indeed, Kant concludes his argument with this point: "A hundred real thalers [i.e., dollars] do not contain the least coin more than a hundred possible thalers." Thus, existence is an accident accruing to a concept or not.

a necessary ontological role of explaining why a contingent being exists. As a causal principle, it can be isolated and known in itself, and this would be evidence of God's activity in the world. Kant is correct in doubting that being is a *thing*, a simple quality that can be predicated, because being is not some sort of definable essence in one of the categories like *green* or *big*. But being is not so negligible as to be nothing in itself. Being is, rather, the act of existence, not a thing but a constitutive principle. As the universal cause of all existent things, being cannot be grasped as a concept of an essence attained by abstraction; rather, it is attained by the metaphysical judgment concerning the cause of existence. This is why the question of being—when properly defined—is the critical path of inquiry that leads to God's existence. But, since Kant's metaphysics focus on the conditions for knowledge and not being, this is not a valid object of inquiry for him.

Further, as we have seen in other areas of philosophy, Kant's scrupulous rationality guarantees an objectivity to these regulative ideals so that he can assert them as knowable by all. However, in the absence of that scrupulous rationality, his conclusions become seeds for more problematic positions. For example, Kant's limitation of speculative knowledge pushed knowledge of God to practical reason; however, some take this rejection of speculative certainty about God to imply that ideas of God ought to be relegated to the sphere of purely subjective faith. In the aftermath of the Enlightenment, a chasm emerges in some thinkers between knowledge, which comes to be restricted to science, and religious belief, which is based on faith alone. As a result, God comes to be seen as a mere fiction of personal belief.[35]

Again, even if knowledge of God is necessary for ethics, the doctrinal nature of religion—the Creed and Catechism—are seen as having have no truth value. Religion is seen as being more about personal emotions than objective reality. This idea is one source of what John Henry Newman called "liberalism" in religion: "the doctrine that there is no positive truth in religion, but that one creed is as good as another. . . . It teaches that all [creeds]

---

[35] For example, Ludwig Feuerbach, in *The Essence of Christianity* (1841), especially chapter 1, argues that as people we have ideals, such as love, wisdom, power, and beauty, which we are unable to attain, and so we create a fictional God as a projection of our deepest hopes. However, this only deprives us of the opportunity of attaining those ideals and so belief in God leads to self-alienation. This argument exercises a great influence on Karl Marx's idea (in *A Contribution to the Critique of Hegel's "Philosophy of Right"*) that religion is "sigh of the oppressed creature, the heart of a heartless world. . . . It is the opium of the people." For an incisive overview of the development of atheism in the wake of Kant, see Cornelio Fabro, *God in Exile: Modern Atheism from Its Roots in the Cartesian* Cogito *to the Present Day*, trans. Arthur Gibson (Westminster, Md.: Newman Press, 1968), 491–745.

are to be tolerated, for all are matters of opinion. Revealed religion is not a truth, but a sentiment and a taste."[36] Going into the twentieth century, this leads opponents of faith to deride religion as sheer subjective feelings, something that one might glom onto if it is needed to make one behave ethically but irrelevant to the search for truth.[37] Thus, once God's transcendence is seen to remove him from the fabric of being, he can become so distant from experience that we cannot know him by reason at all.[38]

In reaction to Kant's subtle distinction between the objects of faith and of knowledge, philosophers tend to pursue two reductive approaches that erect a wall between the two. Ironically, though, both approaches share an exulted notion of God's transcendence that makes him completely invisible to reason. On the one hand, some exult the nature of faith as irrational and privilege it over scientific knowledge. On the other hand, some stress the limits of knowledge by elevating the sovereignty of science and eliminating religious faith as irrelevant. These two trends dominated Western approaches to religion in the twentieth century.

The first reaction, a fideism that privileges faith and downplays the importance of science, was put forth by Søren Kierkegaard (1813–1855) in his claim that "truth is subjectivity."[39] Kierkegaard responds to Kant by introducing a distinction between objective truth and subjective truth. The former are scientific facts—rationally certain but existentially irrelevant since they do not really affect the way I live. Subjective truths, things like ethics and religion, are by contrast uncertain since they can never be proved, but they are existentially crucial since they shape the way I live. But this means that these uncertain truths are more important to me than is any objective fact known by reason. Since these subjective truths cannot be reached by reason, they have to be accepted by means of a leap of faith. The

---

36 John Henry Newman, *The Biglietto Speech* of May 12, 1879, upon his appointment as cardinal. Another important source of liberalism in religion is the rise of "higher criticism," which reads Scripture in terms of its human history without regard to the supernatural. This ultimately has its source in Benedict Spinoza, *Tractatus Theologico-Politicus* (1670), which assumes Spinoza's identification of God with nature and so rejects all claims of divine revelation.

37 This is the perspective behind the case that began the elimination of religion from the public square, *Everson v. Board of Education* (1947). A corollary of this rejection of the speculative truth of religious doctrine is that people assume that "all religions are the same because they all teach us to be good." This is a claim that is questionable at any level of investigation, yet it is widely held by those who misunderstand the true nature of theism.

38 In fact, Kant acknowledges, in *Religion within the Limits of Reason Alone* (bk. 4, pt. 2, sec. 1), that "it is in no way reprehensible to say that every man *creates a God* for himself."

39 *Concluding Unscientific Postscript*, pt. 2, sec. 2, chap. 2.

model for such a leap is Abraham, who was willing to go against all reason in sacrificing Isaac.[40] Since these nonrational subjective beliefs inform me of what really matters, the leap of faith is the most important thing I can do. In fact, *that* I believe is more important than *what* I believe. As Kierkegaard observes:

> If someone who lives in the midst of Christianity enters, with a knowledge of the true idea of God, the house of the true God, and prays, but prays in untruth, and if someone lives in an idolatrous land but prays with all the passion of infinity, although his eyes are resting upon the image of an idol—where, then, is there more truth? The one prays in truth to God although he is worshipping an idol; the other prays in untruth to the true God and is therefore in truth worshipping an idol.[41]

While the call to authenticity in Kierkegaard is edifying, his fideism can be seen as allowing for forms of religious relativism. If faith is isolated from rational truth, religious belief will be as capricious as any act of taste.[42] We have seen this in the history of the Protestant denominations. Prioritizing subjective faith has resulted in thousands of sects. Worse, if faith is unhinged from reason, this opens the door for atheists to equate God with an absurdity like the Flying Spaghetti Monster.[43] From this we can conclude that God cannot be defended by fideism, no matter how impassioned it may be. Fideism exaggerates God's transcendence to the point where the issue of rational truth is neglected.

The other response to Kant is to reduce all knowledge to science and so to eliminate religion. This assumes that, even if there is a God, he is so transcendent so as to be utterly irrelevant. This philosophy, known as *positivism*, since it accepts only what can be positively proven by science, originates with Auguste Comte (1798–1857) and is still prevalent in the form of contemporary scientism. Positivism sees human understanding of the causal principles of reality as evolving from a theological stage (gods are causes), to a metaphysical stage (abstract principles are causes), finally culminating in a scientific stage (empirically demonstrable physical

---

40 Søren Kierkegaard, *Fear and Trembling*, Problema II.

41 *Concluding Unscientific Postscript*, pt. 2, sec. 2, chap. 2.

42 The Catholic faith has always been scrupulous about uniting the person's act of faith (*fides qua*) with the objective truths to be believed in that act of faith (*fides quae*); see *ST* II-II.2.2; cf. *CCC* 170.

43 This is the mocking belief of the "Pastafarians," a sham religion invented in 2005.

causes).[44] As science progresses, any remaining theological or metaphysical causes will simply evaporate since they are no longer meaningful.[45] This is the familiar position of many of the so-called New Atheists who claim that evolution and the Big Bang obviate the need to invoke God as a cause (either philosophically or religiously).[46] Since science explains everything, holding on to other causes is simply superstition.

The great irony of positivism is that, in reducing all knowledge to science, it illicitly limits the scope of human rationality. In repudiating both metaphysics and religion, it denies the human ability to grasp any transcendent cause. This, then, leaves only immanent causes of nature to explain the world. Science's empiricism and mechanistic laws are very good at revealing *how* things happen; they can discover the immanent natural causes of change. But, if there is nothing other than immanent, mechanistic causes, then there is no explanation for *why* anything happens.[47] This means that we can know facts, but we cannot discern the purpose of anything in the universe. For example, if all actions are explicable by mechanistic natural laws, then all things happen of necessity. If this were true, then we would have no control over either our actions or our thoughts. In that case, life would be pointless, since there would be no reason to try to do anything, and, even if we did act, there would be no point to it. To put this problem another way, science cannot ask, let alone answer, a *why* question providing a meaningful explanation of the purpose of existence and action.[48] Scientific

---

44 Auguste Comte, *Introduction to the Positive Philosophy*, chap. 1. Comte does not deny the existence of metaphysical causes; rather, he only asserts that they are scientifically irrelevant: "We do not pretend to explain the real causes of phenomena, . . . we try only to analyze correctly the circumstances of their production, and to connect them by normal relations of succession and similarity."

45 For example, the logical positivist philosopher Rudolph Carnap advocated "The Elimination of Metaphysics" (1932) because it was not knowledge at all but only soothing noise with empty words; he wryly commented, "Metaphysicians are musicians without any musical talent."

46 This group includes most notably Richard Dawkins, Daniel Dennett, and Sam Harris; see the critique of their argument in David Bentley Hart, *Atheist Delusions: The Christian Revolution and Its Fashionable Enemies* (New Haven: Yale University Press, 2009), esp. 3–18.

47 This is famously illustrated in Newton's *"Hypotheses non fingo."* That is, he uses mathematics to describe what happens, but about why it is happening, he makes no hypothesis. Benjamin Franklin reiterates this pragmatic perspective: "Nor is it of much importance to us to know the manner in which nature executes her laws; it is enough if we know the laws themselves," cited in *American Thought before 1900*, ed. Paul Kurtz (New York: Macmillan, 1966), 127.

48 Max Weber, in his famous lecture "Science as a Vocation" (1917), specifically notes that science eschews all value judgments, so it cannot say whether the universe deserves to exist, whether human life has value, or whether a work of art ought to be made.

facts, of themselves, do not provide meaning to life; there has to be some overarching principle by which we interpret those facts to discover meaning in terms of truth, goodness, and beauty. We attend to reality through the filters of these values. But to know these values requires that we be able to know the ultimate cause, the first principle: of being. This is the job of metaphysics and theology. To simply deny that transcendent causes can be an object of knowledge is to block the natural path of human inquiry.

The choice we face, then, is clear. On the one hand, we can agree with the positivists and assume the most important questions cannot be asked, let alone answered, by reason, a position that entails the ultimate pointlessness of existence. On the other hand, following the perennial tradition, we can assert that reason is not limited to scientific inquiry of immanent causes. Rather, philosophy and theology—faith and reason—can go beyond the facts of science and discover the transcendent causes that provide *purpose* to existence, why things are the way they are. In light of these alternatives, positivism—insisting on the unknowability of certain truths—ironically appears to be a blind dogmatism. A more rational perspective on reality, and a more realistic assessment of the powers of reason, accepts the human capacity to know ultimate causes in metaphysics.

The Greeks recognized this. They knew that there had to be something other than natural causes, so they theorized about both natural and divine causality in the world. However, the Greeks lacked a proper understanding of the nature of that divine cause. This is what Thomas has, and because of it he can show how God is both transcendent and immanent with respect to creation.

"I AM WHO AM" (EX 3:14)

Approaches to God

If we are to know God, we have to affirm that he is immanent, that there is reliable evidence in this world from which we can argue God's existence. Nevertheless, to avoid the errors of paganism and pantheism, we also need to affirm that God is transcendent, so this inferential knowledge of God can never capture his essence, and so some truths will only be known by revelation.

This argument, then, requires that we find a principle that is common to both God and creation. But because of the distance between God and creation, this principle must respect the radical difference between God and creature. In other words, it must be an analogical concept. Here we once again discover the crucial centrality of being—the act of existence—as the principle of actuality uniting all that is.

It is interesting to note that the significance of being necessarily implies that the other transcendental properties, as convertible with being, may also be used to prove the existence of God.[49] There is ample evidence for this in the tradition of Catholic philosophy. For example, Saint Augustine argued that the reality of Truth proved the existence of God.[50] Truth, as opposed to opinion, must be unchanging. However, all creatures are in time and so are changing. God alone is eternal and unchanging. Thus, knowledge of unchanging truths, such as those of mathematics, point to the existence of an eternal mind, and so prove the existence of God. Others, such as Saint Bonaventure, have invoked the metaphysics of the good, the diffusiveness of being that is the source for the goodness of all creation, as a proof for God's existence.[51] Still others have argued God's existence on the basis of goodness as a moral quality. For example, Saint John Henry Newman argues that the obligation of conscience is really binding only if it is based in a moral authority higher than humankind.[52] Beauty, the gratuitous order of the world, has also been seen as an indication of God's creative activity radiantly present in the world;[53] indeed, just as evil is a stumbling block for theists that demands an explanation, atheists have to acknowledge that the pervasive beauty of the universe is prima facie evidence against their denial of a creator.

Since these properties are grounded on being, though, it is being that provides the primary pathway to God.

One way to make this argument is from the *idea of being* itself: if something is defined as being, it must exist. This is the strategy employed by Saint Anselm.[54] God is defined as That-than-which-nothing-greater-can-be-

---

49 It partially is for this reason that postmodern atheists are so adamant about disputing the objectivity of truth and goodness, and even beauty, since they recognize that order in the universe eventually points to God. As Nietzsche comments, we will not have gotten rid of God so long as we still believe in grammar (*Twilight of the Idols*, "Reason in Philosophy" 5).

50 Augustine, *On Free Choice of the Will* II.3–13; see also the dialogue, *On the Teacher*.

51 In *Journey of the Mind to God*, Bonaventure's argument evinces not just the existence of God, but also his trinitarian nature, since we find a plethora of trinities in creation.

52 John Henry Newman, *An Essay in Aid of Grammar of Assent*, pt. 1, chap. 5.

53 Augustine employs this inference in *Confessions* XI.4. See also the "theological aesthetics" of Hans urs von Balthasar.

54 Anselm, *Proslogion*, chaps. 2–5. This argument inspires a family of roughly similar arguments in a great variety of thinkers: Bonaventure, Scotus, Descartes, Spinoza, Leibniz, and others up to the present (e.g., Charles Hartshorne and Alvin Plantinga). Kant labels the modern version of

thought. In so conceiving God, it is clear I have an idea of him. Now, either God exists *only* as an idea or he exists in my idea *and* in reality. But, if God existed only in my idea, he would not be That-than-which-nothing-greater-can-thought, because I would be able to think of something greater: that which exists as an idea *and* in reality. Anselm concludes that God, as the Supreme Being, necessarily exists. Indeed, in contrast to all contingent being, he cannot even be thought of as not existing.

This short argument has been as controversial as any in the history of philosophy. The problem is that, while the logic is perfectly clear, many find the argument unpersuasive. There appears to be a sleight of hand, since a mere definition of God cannot be used to prove his existence. Thomas rejects the argument because in order to know the definition of anything, we need to experience it.[55] (In fact, Anselm seems to anticipate this objection, since in the first line he asks God to help him "to understand that thou art as we believe." Anselm's argument is based on faith, a theological reflection of a monk writing for other monks, not a proof for modern atheists.)

Since we cannot start with the idea of being, we need to examine the nature of being itself. Accordingly, Thomas argues that we can find evidence for God's existence in creatures inasmuch as they are the effects of his causal activity. This approach uses the existence of nature as evidence to prove the existence of God.[56] This purely rational analysis grants that God as cause must be *present to* the effects in creation (i.e., immanent) and yet must be simultaneously *outside of* creation in order to be its cause (transcendent). Not only will this show us *that* God exists but it also gives us some idea (albeit limited) of what he is like. Coming to knowledge of God through the reality of created beings involves three argumentative steps. First, we know that God *exists* from the fact of creation; second, we know what God *is not* by showing how he must be different from creatures; and, third, we know what God *is like* in light of the perfections he has made in

---

this argument the "Ontological Argument," which is often applied, anachronistically, to Anselm. However, despite superficial similarities, Anselm's version relies on very different, Platonic premises. See Anton C. Pegis, "St. Anselm and the Argument of the 'Proslogion,'" *Mediaeval Studies* 28 (1966): 228–67.

55 *ST* I.2.1.ad 2. More specifically, Thomas argues that God's existence is self-evident in itself (since he is Being itself), but it is not evident *to us* because we do not experience God in this world. We therefore know God only by rational inference or through faith. Direct knowledge of God is possible only in the Beatific Vision (*ST* I.12.1 and 7).

56 Anselm's argument from being is *a priori*, based on the concept of being; Thomas's argument is *a posteriori*, based on our experience of the world.

creatures.[57] Let us now explore these arguments about the ultimate cause of being, truth, goodness, and beauty.

That God Is: The Fact of Creation

The notion of *being* is the most obvious way to approach God, because it is the most fundamental principle of reality and the source of intelligibility, goodness, and beauty. It is, moreover, the property that most clearly ties God as Supreme Being with contingent creatures who possess existence. While being is at the heart of all of Thomas's arguments for the existence of God, perhaps the clearest statement is in this argument:

> If things that differ agree in some point, there must be some cause for that agreement, since things diverse in nature cannot be united of themselves. Hence whenever in different things some one thing common to all is found, it must be that these different things receive that one thing from some one cause, as different bodies that are hot receive their heat from fire. But being is found to be common to all things, however otherwise different. There must, therefore, be one principle of being from which all things in whatever way existing have their being.[58]

The one property all beings have in common is the fact that they *exist* (otherwise they would lack existence and so be nothing). Since things in this world are contingent—they come into existence and can cease to existence—none of them *have to* exist; it is not part of their essence. But, if existence is not part of their essence and essence determines what something can do (that is, action follows from being), then they cannot cause existence in other beings. Indeed, determinate essences account for the determinate properties that are characteristic of natures—a human can make human-like things, a dog can make dog-like things, apple trees grow apples—but they cannot account for the very existence of the thing that comes into being.[59] Being, as a universal effect extending to all things,

---

57 *ST* I.12.12. This threefold approach is a development of Pseudo-Dionysius's "super-eminent predication" in *Mystical Theology*.

58 *ST* I.65.1.

59 *DP* 7.2: "The reason for this is that since a proper effect is produced by a particular cause in respect of its proper nature or form, different causes having different natures and forms must needs have their respective different proper effects: so that if they have one effect in common, this is not the proper effect of any one of them, but of some higher cause by whose virtue they act. . . . Now all created causes have one common effect which is *being*, although each one has its peculiar effect whereby they are differentiated: thus heat makes a thing *to be* hot, and a

requires a cause that is similarly universal in extent and power. Therefore, there has to be a cause, infinite in its own actuality, that is the source of the existence of all the contingent substances, for all things characterized by potency in any way. One consequence of this is that being has to be analogical: there is an intrinsic difference between dependent, contingent beings and the necessary being by which other things exist. Thomas would use this insight in his more specific arguments for the existence of God, as we see later in this chapter.

The fact of creation, therefore, provides abundant evidence for God's existence. But we need to understand what this means: creation is not a one-time historical event of the past; rather, creation is the metaphysical dependence of a continent being on a necessary being.[60] Every time we encounter something that does not *have to* exist, we are encountering God's creative activity, sustaining it in existence. Recognizing this requires no elaborate argument, for it is an intuitive and immediate recognition that *something* has to be causing these things to exist. If we reflect on the radical contingency of our own existence—I do not have to exist, even now, I have done nothing to merit it or even account for it—we can get a sense of the inexplicable giftedness that is this act of creation holding me in existence.[61]

Even when formulated as an argument, however, there is nothing occult about this knowledge of God. It follows the same principle that guides our knowledge of natural causes: action follows from being. This is how our reasoning about substances in this world works: we perceive the activities of a substance and infer the formal cause that determines its nature. It is similar with God: we perceive an activity—the giving of existence to things that need not exist—and infer the necessary cause. Because causal activity of an agent flows from its essence—an apple tree grows apples—an agent whose activity is the giving of existence must have an essence that is *existence itself*. For this reason, Thomas calls God *ipsum esse subsistens*—subsistent Being Itself.[62] Since God is the cause of being, he exists *necessarily*

---

builder gives *being* to a house. . . . There must therefore be some cause higher than all other by virtue of which they all cause being and whose proper cause is *being*: and this cause is God."

60 *ST* I.46.1 and 2.

61 Reflections of this sort are the heart of the work of Gabriel Marcel; see, for example *Mystery of Being*, trans. G. S. Fraser (South Bend, Ind.: St. Augustine's Press, 2001), vol. 1, chap. 9.

62 *ST* I.4.2; see also *DP* 7.2 and *OBE* c. 4–5. Note the significant difference between Aristotle and Thomas here. Both see God as pure act; but Aristotle's God is the pure *act of thought* and so cannot give existence; Thomas's God is the pure *act of existence* and so can give existence.

and *essentially*, and so we can attribute to him greater perfection of being than is known in creatures, who as contingent and finite are imperfect.

Basing our knowledge of God on the fact of creation has two salutary consequences. First, it is the foundation for affirming that God is both transcendent and immanent. The Creator cannot logically be part of creation, so he must be transcendent; yet creation cannot exist unless the Creator were actively present holding it in existence, so he must be immanent. Both truths are necessary if we are to explain the existence of the world we experience. Second, this doctrine of creation unites our philosophical and religious ideas about God. Philosophically, because God is the cause of the existence of creatures, we can affirm he is Being Itself, the Supreme Being. Religiously, we recognize that, because creation did not have to happen, it must have been an act of free will. As such, God is a personal God, one who loves us into being and so one who can be loved and worshipped in return. In other words, creation is itself a revelation of God to the people he created, one accessible to all rational humans. This presence of God in creation is simultaneously the most quotidian fact and the most astonishing truth in human experience: I exist only because God puts me here.

Thomas expounds this insight in more detail in his Five Ways to prove the existence of God. Thomas prefaces the argument by noting an important limitation of these proofs, all of which argue from creation-as-an-effect to God-as-cause. Finite creation can never *fully* manifest the infinite glory of God; therefore, arguing from creation to God can prove *that* God exists, but it can never comprehend *what* he is.[63] This differs from our knowledge of creatures, in which the effect can fully reveal the cause. For example, a scientific argument might begin by investigating an effect (an illness) in order to discover the cause (a virus). Eventually, the totality of symptoms will reveal to the doctor the nature of the cause, since only virus X can cause symptoms X. Thus, in finite creatures, the effects fully reveal the cause allowing us to know *what* the cause is. But because God is infinite, he can never be fully revealed in nature, no matter how much we investigate.[64] Thus, while we can be certain *that he exists*, we can never grasp *what he is*. Know-

---

63 *ST* I.2.2.

64 It is this disproportion between infinite cause and finite creation that led Hume to atheistic skepticism and Kierkegaard to a fideistic leap of faith. Both fall into extreme positions because they fail to see that reason grasps existence as a principle based on the fact that action follows from being (*ST* I.2.2.ad 3), but existence is analogical so we have true knowledge that is incomplete.

ing that God exists, though, will also ensure that we know some aspects of his nature.[65] Brian Davies suggests an illuminating metaphor: if the SETI project detected alien radio waves, we would know that someone was out there and that that being was rational; but details of what the aliens were like—are they little green men or squid people, are they many or few— would remain unknown to us because of the limited evidence.

Each of the Five Ways is predicated on some obvious element of human experience that necessarily points to the existence of a cause who is pure act.[66] The first deals with the fact of change (or motion). It is obvious that all things in the world are in a constant process of change. Philosophically, change is understood to be the movement from potency to act; that is, it is going from lacking a certain property (*potency*) to having that property (*act*). Since the changing thing is in potency to this property, it cannot change itself (because it lacks that property that it is in the process of attaining). Thus, the change must be caused by something that actually has the property—one that is in act. For example, a stick can catch fire, but it is only ignited by something that is actually hot enough to ignite it. However, that hot object had to be ignited or heated by something else, and so there must be something in act prior to it. But this cannot go on forever; there has to be something that is not changed by another, and this is the ultimate cause of all the changes, for it is the ultimate source of the actuality of that property. In other words, there has to be an unmoved mover, which, as Thomas says, "everyone understands to be God."

Let us understand this properly. Since potency of itself causes nothing, act must absolutely precede any change. But, since the entire universe is changing in some way, there must be something outside the entirety of the universe that is the principle of actuality moving things from potency to act. There must be a first cause or else there would be no effect. This is true both "horizontally," or chronologically, and "vertically," or hierarchically.[67]

---

65 *BDT* 6.3. For a brief listing of Thomas's view of what we can know about God, see Appendix II.

66 *ST* I.2.3. More detailed versions are presented in *SCG* I.13. None of these arguments are original to Thomas. They are based on Aristotle's arguments against an infinite regress of causes and were developed by various Christian, Jewish, and Muslim thinkers. The presentation in *ST* is notable because Thomas states them succinctly and orders them so as to better expound the consequences of the logic.

67 For technical reasons beyond the scope of this book, the argument is best understood in the hierarchical fashion; see *ST* I.45.5 and 46.2.ad 7. See also Edward Feser, *Five Proofs of the Existence of God* (San Francisco: Ignatius Press, 2017), 17–68.

Chronologically, there must be a pure act at the start of the changing universe: if I eat a piece of cake, it is because someone made the cake, out of wheat that was grown, from seeds that were planted, from an earlier generation of wheat, and so on back to the Big Bang. But the Big Bang itself did not have to happen, since it is a contingent event in time. Thus, there has to be something that was already in perfect act, that did not need to be changed by something earlier, at the origin of this. This reasoning is also true when taken vertically. In this sense, there must be a pure act at the source of every concatenation of changes that constitutes reality now. For example, I eat a piece of cake because my muscles move my jaw, and my nerve signals move my muscles, and atoms move my nerve signals, and atoms move because of vibrating strings of energy, which themselves vibrate because, ultimately, there has to be something that is purely actual in order to cause the entire chain of changes. Because all the principles of being in this universe are changing at every moment, there has to be an unchanging cause outside this universe at every moment. In both cases, since change or movement is coming into existence, it must be the case that something with pure actuality is the source of this movement coming to be. Thus, there is a *first mover*.

The second argument, from efficient cause, is similar but focuses on the existence of substances. No substance can cause itself to exist; it must be caused to exist by something prior to it. But, if everything needed to be brought into existence by something prior, there would be no first cause of being, and so there would be no substances coming into existence subsequently. Since we know substances exist, there must be a *first efficient cause* of being, which we call God.[68] God not only causes change; he also causes the substances that are changing.

The third argument arises from the existence of contingent beings. A contingent being is one that does not have to exist, and so there needs to be an explanation for its existence. If that cause is any finite thing in the universe, no matter how fundamental—such as atoms or gravity or the forms, or even the universe itself—we see that these too are contingent, since they did not have to exist. But if *everything* were contingent, there would be nothing at all. Therefore, there must be a necessary being, a being whose existence is impossible to question. Therefore, the efficient cause of being and

---

68 We "understand" or "call" this God because we cannot know what God is in himself; yet we can name him from his effects.

of change is one that *must* exist, since the existence of other things is unthinkable without this *necessary being*.

The fourth way, the degrees of perfection, notes that this necessary being must itself embody all possible perfections of being. It is obvious that perfections in the world are variable and changing; that is, they are contingent. As such, the existence of these perfections must lie in the source of being, which as source is the exemplar of all perfections possessed by creatures. God, then, as pure act and *exemplar cause*, possesses all perfections of being.[69]

The fifth way recognizes the teleological orientation of beings to second act. The action of natures in the world is not random; it is orderly and regular. This regularity can either be caused by some intelligent being directing natures or it can be a random accident. This second option is impossible, since order cannot be the result of a random accident; if it were, that order would be only apparent, not real, since it would be liable to change at any time. Universal human experience, however, is built upon regularity in nature, for otherwise the world would not be intelligible at all. The regularity in nature, then, must be the result of intelligent direction. Thus, God not only possesses all perfections, but he also causes all creatures to reliably strive for perfection by the ordering natures to final causes.[70]

Thomas acknowledges two possible objections to the existence of God that, remarkably, remain the most common reasons for disbelief even today: scientism and evil. First, if science explains everything in nature, we do not need to suppose God exists. Second, if God is a perfect creator, there should be no evil. Since these are perennial problems, we address them separately

---

69 This inverts the logic of modern versions of the ontological argument. Where that argument says because God is perfect, he must exist, Thomas claims that because there are degrees of being in creation, there must be a Supreme Being who—as Supreme Being—must be perfect.

70 This argument is not an argument from design. Design arguments are common in modern thinkers, because their nominalism and concomitant rejection of final causes leads them to assume order is imposed on the whole mechanical universe by an extrinsic cause. If the universe is a machine, there must be a builder who puts all the parts together in order. Design arguments are weak because the extrinsically imposed order *could be* the result of purely natural principles like the laws of science or even intelligent aliens. Because those alternate causal explanations are possible, design arguments can only show that God is probable but they can never establish God as a necessary cause. The argument in the fifth way, by contrast, sees order as intrinsic to specific natures because of final causality; it is about the created beings as they exist in themselves. The fact that natures—all natures, from atoms to human beings—are teleologically oriented cannot be explained by any natural principle, since even that nature would itself already be teleologically oriented. Thus, there has to be something outside of nature to account for this teleological orientation of natures to their ends, and so this argument can establish God as a necessary cause. See *SCG* I.50.4.

in the last section of this chapter (on the distinction between God and scientific causes) and in the last chapter of this book (addressing the problem of evil).

What God Is Not: The Way of Remotion

From these obvious factors of human experience—change, efficient cause, contingency, degrees of perfection, and order in nature—we can conclude that there must be a first cause of being who is pure act. If God were to have potency in any way, he would need to be caused and so could not be the first cause. The fact that God is pure actuality allows us to discern aspects of his nature, especially insofar as he is different from creatures that are characterized by potency and finitude. This difference manifests God's transcendence: as cause, he is apart from and unlike the world. Nevertheless, because God is the abiding cause of perfections in the world, we must also recognize his immanence (as we see in the subsequent section).

Investigating God's nature insofar as he is different from creatures is traditionally referred to as the "way of remotion," that is, *removing* from God any limitation characteristic of creatures. Because of God's transcendence, this must be the primary way to approach God; as Thomas says, "because we cannot know what God is, but rather what He is not, we have no means for considering how God is, but rather how He is not."[71] Ultimately, God remains mysterious to us, and philosophers should never presume to have complete understanding of his nature. The most fundamental way God is different from creatures is that God is simple (that is, noncomposite). Creatures, as we have seen, are composed of various parts and principles that limit them to a *kind* of being. God's simplicity means that he is just existence itself. This makes God ineradicably distant from the way creatures exist, and it will inform how we understand all the other properties that we attribute to the Divine nature.

The metaphysical principle governing the assertion that God is simple is the idea that act is, of itself, infinite, and it can only be limited by principles of potency into which it is received. We have seen that differences in creatures are the result of the act of existence being limited by potency in three ways: when existence is received into essences to make species, when form is received into matter to constitute individuals, and when individuals manifest diversified accidents by which a substance changes over time.

71 *ST* I.3.proem.

Creatures, then, are composite in various ways: essence and existence, form and matter, and substance and accident.

Because God is simple, he is composite in none of these ways. As noted in chapter 3, any composition is a composition of act and potency. This would imply a limitation of being because of the potency of the thing receiving it.[72] Since God is pure act, he is simply Existence itself. Divine nature is not a kind of being or a species of a finite essence; rather, it is identical with existence itself. Thus, God is infinite being not limited in any way.[73] God is not a form received into matter, and so is not one individual of a species, like Socrates is an individual human; rather, God is the Divine nature itself. He possesses all that there is of divinity. Again, as pure act, God cannot change, and so he has no accidental properties that contingently come and go. For example, where people *have* knowledge and love, God *is* knowledge and love; as such, they are identical with his Being.

This notion of divine simplicity is most concisely articulated in the idea that *his essence is existence.* This explains how he is the source of all being in the universe, since he can communicate existence to other beings. But it is also why we can never fully comprehend the Divine nature. We can know that God exists because the intellect is ordered to know being as its proper object.[74] The human intellect, though, is ordered to knowing to finite material essences. Therefore, God's nature remains beyond our comprehension. For this reason, the best way to refer to God is by recognizing the infinity of his being with the name revealed to Moses: God is YHWH, "I am Who Am."[75]

The infinite existence implied by divine simplicity will immediately entail other properties that can be ascribed to the divine nature. These include other ways in which a simple being is necessarily unlike creatures who are composite. First, we can conclude that God is perfect, since there is no aspect of being he lacks.[76] Indeed, all created perfections, as finite and

---

72 *ST* I.3.1–8, esp. article 4.

73 This crucial point is missed by many atheists, who present God as if he were a powerful but finite *kind* of being, another thing in the universe like atoms or gravity. This is essentially the pagan idea of the gods, who were not the Supreme Being. This error makes their critiques of theism straw men.

74 *ST* I.12.1.

75 Ex.3:14; Thomas argues for this philosophically in *ST* I.13.11.

76 *ST* I.4.1. This idea again depends on the idea of being as the act of existence which is "compared to all things as that by which they are made actual" (ad 3). This is lost in the modern nominalist idea of being, where perfection would flow not from an essence that is being itself, but from an accidental amalgamation of all possible properties.

contingent, can only be a very distant likeness of God's own perfection.[77] If God is perfect, it follows that he is good, for the good is simply the perfection of being that is desired by all.[78] As pure act, though, God is infinite Goodness itself; for this reason, whenever any creature desires a good of any kind, it is actually desiring some likeness of God who embodies all perfections due to his simplicity.[79]

God's simplicity—that he is existence itself—also means that he is unlimited. Finite creatures are limited in *what* they are and *where* they exist; that is the nature of finitude. God, in contrast, is infinite, encompassing all possible forms or ways of being.[80] He is also omnipresent, existing everywhere where being is present, because there is no being independent of him.[81] These truths again carefully balance the demands of immanence and transcendence, avoiding deism and pantheism. God must be everywhere, since he alone causes existence; indeed, if God were not causally in a place, it would fall into nothingness.[82] Thus, Thomas can argue, "Being is innermost in each thing and most fundamentally inherent in all things. . . . God is in all things, and innermostly."[83] This abiding presence of God in causing the existence of things is the basis for God's continuing activity in providence, grace, and miracles. Nevertheless, creation is distinct from God—it is finite, with finite natures distinct from God's divinity, and so this transcendence makes pantheism is impossible.

Since God is pure act, we can also conclude that he is immutable.[84] God lacks the potential needed for change to happen. Moreover, if he were to change, it could only mean a *loss* of perfection, which is impossible. However, God's immutability must not be seen as some sort of limitation on him. In creatures, immutability implies a resistance to a change needed to bring that being to perfection. Since God already is perfect, his immutability is not this kind of inertness. Rather, as perfect, his being is utterly

---

77 *ST* I.4.3.

78 *ST* I.5.1.

79 *ST* I.6.1.ad 2 and 6.3. Note that God's goodness is not a moral goodness defined by a potency to second act. This is important for the problem of evil, as we see in chapter 9.

80 *ST* I.7.

81 *ST* I.8.

82 *ST* I.104.3.

83 *ST* I.8.1. Thomas is here echoing Augustine: "You were more inward than the most inward place of my heart" (*Confessions* III.6).

84 *ST* I.9.1.

active, never lapsing into dormancy. God's immutability means his perfect activity is unchanging: his knowledge never lapses and his love never wanes.

This immutability implies, in turn, that God is eternal.[85] Time is a measure of before and after; but before and after point to some change (whether it be the location of the sun or moon, or a microwave emission). Time, then, is a characteristic of creatures, who experience their existence through a process of becoming, spread out over successive moments. God is unchanging, and so he is outside of time. As a result, God possesses all being simultaneously and not in terms of successive historical moments.

Finally, from all this, Thomas concludes that there can only be one God.[86] There are many creatures, since the act of existence is received into diverse essences and forms into matter. But simplicity implies that existence is not diversified by any finite essence in God. Moreover, since God is perfect, a being can differentiate itself from God only by being different from him, which is to be imperfect; but such a being is not God. There cannot be two Gods; the Five Ways point to a single being who is the cause of all actuality in the universe.

This is the way of remotion; it is helpful to remind ourselves how these properties are really just negations of creaturely limitations, showing how God must be different from creatures. Thus, we can rephrase these points by saying: God is not composite, not imperfect, not finite, not changing, not temporal, and not many. Although these express how God is not, they nevertheless inform us about God's nature, for with each denial our idea of God becomes less vague.[87] Nevertheless, given the absolute nature of God's transcendence, Thomas insists that "man reaches the highest point of his knowledge about God when he knows that he knows him not."[88] But we cannot rest here, for if we only knew what God was *not*, he would remain wholly transcendent, something alien who could not be loved on a personal level. We therefore have to turn to how God is present with us and understand how we are like him in some way. This is discovered in considering the perfections in creation.

85 *ST* I.10.1–2.

86 *ST* I.11.3.

87 *BDT* 6.3.

88 *DP* 7.5.ad 14.

What God Is Like:
Analogy and the Knowledge of God's Nature

The Bible describes God in a variety of ways: God is good, love, merciful, just; he is our shepherd, our Father, a warrior, and a judge; he is a rock, and life, and light. The problem is that each of these words, though meaningful, also points to some finite reality. If God is infinite, it would seem to be impossible to use *any words at all* to positively describe God. From this fact, some philosophers conclude that God is simply ineffable, that we cannot speak meaningfully about him, and that he is therefore unintelligible to us. This answer cannot stand, for an unknown God cannot be loved.

To resolve this dilemma—our need to talk about God and the apparent incapacity to do so—we must recognize that when we talk about God, we use language *analogically*. Sometimes words are used *univocally*, so that the word means exactly the same thing in different contexts. This is how most words are used. At other times, words are used *equivocally*, when the same word happens to mean two different things (as *bat* can be a piece of baseball equipment or a flying mammal). But we can also use words analogically, where the word indicates the same reality but that reality has to be understood differently in light of what it refers to. For example, both humans and other animals know and love, but rational knowledge and willed love are notably different from merely sensitive awareness and instinctive desire.

This analogical use of language is how we talk about perfections of being shared by God and creatures. We must use analogy because God, as infinite being, possesses all perfections of necessity and in an infinite way, while creatures possess those perfections contingently and in a limited way.[89] But because these creaturely perfections only exist because they were created by God, we can use that perfection to "signify the divine substance" even though "they fall short of a full representation of Him."[90] Because God is the source of all these perfections, the terms themselves apply primarily to God because he possesses those perfections absolutely. God, then, is the exemplar of goodness, and justice, and power, and mercy, and love. However, we come to know about these perfections through our experience of creatures. Therefore, our knowledge of the perfection always reflects some creaturely limitation.[91] So, despite the fact that we only know

89 *ST* I.13.5.
90 *ST* I.13.2.
91 *ST* I.13.6.

finite perfections, we can grasp something of their infinite connotation in God.

We should note that much of the Bible's talk about God is not analogical. There are many terms, like "rock" or "shepherd" that are based on our material existence. Since God is necessarily immaterial, these sorts of words have to be seen as metaphors. You can distinguish metaphor from analogy by asking yourself if a certain perfection can be literally true of an immaterial God. If it cannot, then you know it is merely a metaphor, a literary device, and not analogy, a philosophical assertion of truth. For this reason, purely material perfections—such as tall, or strong, or fast—while common in creatures, are not applied to God.

What perfections that are literally true of an immaterial being can we know? Although all human knowledge begins in sense-experience, we can know immaterial perfections by reflecting on the immaterial powers of the human soul: our intellect and our will. Consequently, we can affirm the truths about God's knowledge and love as analogical to ours. For both God and humankind, knowing and loving are immanent activities that characterize a nature. The difference is that, because human nature is finite, these activities are limited and contingent: we have some truth and some love. Because God is the infinite act of existence, the activity of his knowledge and love are unlike ours: God *is* Truth and God *is* Love. Nevertheless, these spiritual perfections reveal that God is not merely a philosophical principle of being but rather a personal being with whom relationships are formed. Thus, creation is the fruit of his Wisdom and Love. Let us consider what we can know about these.

God's knowledge follows from his simplicity. We can show this by invoking some general metaphysical principles. First, action follows from being. But, because the activity of any creature is determined by its essence, more limited essences have fewer powers and less activity, while higher essences are less limited in being and so have greater powers to act. For example, atoms exist but are not alive, plants have life but not sensation, animals have sensation but not intellect. The greater the essence, the less constricted its abilities to act. This same principle applies to knowledge. Recall that knowledge is the possession of a form in the mind (that is, intentionally, as opposed to existentially). So, cognition is more limited according to how an essence limits the capacity of a mind to possess forms intentionally. People can only know essences of material things through sensation; angels are higher beings, and so they have intuitive knowledge of their own essence. But God's essence is existence itself, and so there is no constriction to his abilities to possess forms intentionally. It follows that there is no limit to his knowledge.[92] Indeed, since this infinite knowledge is of God's own essence, we can say that God is Truth. It follows that he knows all creatures, since in knowing himself as the infinite act of existence, he has ideas of every possible being.[93] This is why we call God *omniscient*: He knows everything that can possibly exist. This omniscience is possible because, unlike people who know by learning from the world, God knows by creating the world (his intellect is practical, not speculative). He determines the truth of being and so need not wait to discover anything. This omniscience extends to every detail of creation, for he creates both form and matter from nothing. Thus, he determines not just the nature of the substances he creates but also the individuating material details that distinguishes one blade of grass from another. These individuating details include every accident and every activity the substance will realize.[94] Thus, God's knowledge is utterly exhaustive of all reality: any fact that comes into existence has its foundation in God's eternal wisdom.

Since the will is the appetite that accompanies cognition of a universal good, we can affirm that God has a will because in knowing himself he knows the universal Good itself. Unlike the human will, which reacts to goods as they come to be known, God's will is eternal and unchanging because he cannot discover any new or greater good. And since the primary act of the will is to love the good, it is clear that he loves himself always and infinitely. In other words, God is Love since love is inseparable from his existence.[95] This eternal possession of the infinite good also makes God blessed, or perfectly happy.[96]

The essential nature of God's love is manifested in his love for creatures, for "in so far as they exist, they are good, since the existence of a thing is itself a good."[97] In fact, God's love for his own infinite goodness is so intense that it diffuses itself, or overflows, into the gratuitous act of creating creatures, who did not have to exist, simply to share in that goodness.[98] It is

92 *ST* I.14.1.

93 *ST* I.14.2, 14.5, 15.2, and *SCG* I.53.

94 *ST* I.14.8, 11, and 13.

95 *ST* I.19.1, 19.5, and 20.1. Of course, this philosophical doctrine that God is love is somewhat bloodless and in need of augmentation from revelation, as in 1 Jn 4:7–12.

96 *ST* I.26.1 and 4. Note that Thomas's argument about God's will includes only two of the three acts of appetite—love, desire, and joy. Desire is excluded because God, as perfect, lacks no good, so there is nothing for him to desire. It follows that God does not need to be worshipped to make him happy; rather, we need to worship him as an act of justice required for us to attain happiness.

97 *ST* I.20.2.

98 *ST* I.19.2 and I.47.1.

clear, then, that I exist *because* God loves me (an important correction to the oft-invoked idea the God loves me because I exist). This is the uncon- ditional nature of God's love: that out of nothing he extended to me the incomprehensible gift of sharing in existence, loving my goodness into being.[99] It is the recognition of this great gift of being that is the common inspiration for religious holy days and sabbaths. Religion arises out of cele- bration of this greatest good, the incomprehensible gift of being, and not out of fear of great evils like death or punishment.

The created universe, then, reflects both God's knowledge and will. He knows all possible being, but, because creatures are constituted by the causal principles of form and matter (which are necessary principles for the diver- sification of the act of existence into species and individuals), God's utterly free act results in a predictable and intelligible activity, as known in the laws ordering creatures to their end.[100] God could have created any universe to manifest his goodness, so his choice to create this particular universe is a free act of love.[101] We can know God's act is radically free because he is the sole cause of the entire universe. God constitutes creatures out of nothing by making essences—form and matter—participate in the act of existence.[102] As the creator of essences, God is also the efficient cause of the universe. Further, because all creatures are naturally dynamic, they are oriented to perfection in second act, which is nothing other than a similitude of God's own perfect being. Accordingly, God is also the final cause of this free act of creation.[103] God could have created another universe, which might have been better, but this universe contains the perfection that God has willed for it as one expres- sion of his infinite love.[104] God's creative act, then, determines all that comes to be in the universe. He is the Supreme Being and source of all that is.

We can conclude that this power to create from nothing means that God is omnipotent.[105] God is infinite in being, and, since action follows from being, his active power is unlimited. Importantly, though, this means

99 *ST* I.20.3 and I.21.4.

100 *ST* I.21.1 and I.22.1.

101 *ST* I.19.3 and 5, and I.47.1. Thus, God is omniscient but not omnivolent (*DP* 1.7.ad 5), that is, he does not will all things but only what comes to be.

102 *ST* I.44.1–3 and 45.1.

103 *ST* I.44.4. Note that because God's creative activity accounts for all four causes, he is ulti- mately the only cause; see *DP* 3.5 and 6.

104 *ST* I.25.6.ad 3.

105 *ST* I.25 and *DP* 1.7.

not that God can do *anything*; rather, he can do anything that might possibly be done.[106] That is, while the activity of creatures is limited by their form or their individual matter, God can act without any of these limitations. As infinite being, he can bring about any effect of any being. He can make a bush burn without being consumed; he can make a donkey talk or a pig fly; he can stop the sun in the sky; he can raise a man from the dead; he can turn bread and wine into the Body and Blood of Christ.

However, this means that omnipotence does not include the ability to do things that imply a contradiction of being, since these are logically impossible. For example, God cannot make a square circle, since a thing cannot be A and not-A simultaneously. Similarly, he cannot make a rational donkey, since a donkey is by definition a nonrational animal. (God could make a different intelligent species that looks like a donkey, though.) God cannot change the past, for he has already willed the past to be and he cannot contradict his own perfect will. God cannot create a homosexual marriage, for marriage is by nature for man and woman. God cannot sin, since evil is a lack of goodness and God is essentially good. Finally, he cannot create another God, for every creature, as created, *must be* defined by potency.[107] For this reason, we are careful to say that the Word of God is begotten, not made.

Two Objections

Creation is the action of an omnipotent God sharing his infinite goodness and love. This raises two perennial objections. First, if God only creates out of a desire to share his goodness, why is there evil? Second, if God's knowledge and will determines what happens in creation, how can people have free will? It would seem that God's will makes my own will irrelevant.

In answer to the first, we must distinguish the antecedent and consequent will of God.[108] This distinction is necessitated by the fact that while God wills that all people be saved, some will nevertheless end up in hell. God's antecedent will, on the one hand, is what God wills simply; that is, the good he intends for all creation, ignoring the concrete circumstances of what will happen in reality. The consequent will, on the other hand, is what God wills in view of factual conditions of creation, that is, in light of the reality of creatures interacting with one another. Although antecedently

---

106 *ST* I.25.3 and *SCG* II.22.

107 *SCG* II.25.17.

108 *ST* I.19.6.ad 1.

God wills that all creatures flourish, in the factual order of creation, some creatures can flourish only when others suffer: a lion survives only by eating antelopes.[109] Similarly, antecedently God wills that all people be saved, but in fact some people will use free will to reject God and consign themselves to perdition. God's antecedent will reflects his infinite love by which all things are brought into existence; God's consequent will reflects the unavoidable limitations of imperfect creatures. We return to this point more fully in our discussion of the problem of evil in the final chapter.

The second problem, the problem of divine foreknowledge, is one of the stickiest problems in philosophy. Thomas is eminently aware of this difficulty, because he offers the same argument in reply to it three times in the space of eight questions: with respect to God's knowledge, God's will, and providence.[110] The basic problem is similar in each: God necessarily knows the truth, so this implies that events must happen; God wills creation into being, so events must occur as he wills; and God providentially orders creation, so events are caused by God and not by creatures. In all three cases, free will would appear to be impossible. The resolution of this dilemma involves two elements. First, we note that God's knowledge is eternal. It is outside of time, and so he does not know what happens *before* creatures act. Rather, God knows creation as the totality of being, and so his knowledge simply corresponds to what creatures do. This, however, is an imperfect answer, since God's knowledge and will are still creative, causing things to happen. The second element, then, is to distinguish the primary causality of God and secondary causality of created natures. God's knowledge and power are perfect; they concern not just what happens but *the way by which* they come to be. Therefore, while the ultimate cause is God's knowledge and will, the proximate cause—a natural agent acting in the world—determines *the way by which* the effect came to be. Some natural causes are necessity (fire is always hot, so it will necessarily make things hot); some natural causes are contingent (which of three squirrels a dog will chase is highly contingent); and human acts are free (we can choose to sin). It is the nature of the proximate cause that protects the contingency and freedom in creation. God nevertheless still acts as the cause of the existence of the universe in which these natural beings act. God, then, is the primary cause because

---

109 *ST* I.22.2 ad 2.

110 *ST* I.14.13, 19.8, and 22.4. Thomas's solution builds on the arguments of Augustine, *On Free Choice of the Will*, and Boethius, *The Consolation of Philosophy*, bk. 5.

he makes things exist; creatures are all secondary causes, since they act according to their nature, causing the determinate effects observed in the world. Thus, when a person acts freely, his act is free because God created him to act in this way.

This truth, that God and creatures are both causally active in the world, is in fact the most important both/and in this book.

THE MASTER BOTH–AND: PRIMARY AND SECONDARY CAUSE

We can now weave together all the causal principles we have been tracing since the second chapter. We know the world by investigating the principles of nature, but we have argued, these principles also lead us to knowledge of God. Recognizing God's creative act, however, does not negate the fact that these creatures, while dependent on God for their existence, are active principles in their own right, acting according to their nature. The act of existence *makes* creatures dynamic causes. Thus, the natural world is always intelligible in its own right, as science insists; that same natural world is nevertheless always revelatory of the creative act of God, as shown in metaphysics.

This is our most important both/and solution for it is the one that provides the perspective required to make sense of everything else. Events in this world are always the effect of God; for this reason, they are characterized by being, truth, goodness, and beauty, traces of their divine origin. Yet, events in this world are also always the effect of nature; because of this science can frame laws based on the principle that action follows from being. Human knowledge of causes, then, is always bivalent. God is the *primary cause*, for he is always the cause of the *existence* of the effect; the natural substance is a *secondary cause*, for it always causes the *specific nature* of the effect.[111] Therefore, God can exercise a loving providence without denying the real significance of our experience of the world.[112]

---

111 *DP* 3.7 and 8. Stephen Barr, in "Chance, by Design," *First Things*, December 2012, offers a nice metaphor for this: an author and his characters. We might ask who kills Polonius, Hamlet or Shakespeare? Clearly Hamlet does, and his actions make sense in the play, but this only happens because Shakespeare wrote the play that way. It is necessarily both. God is the author of creation, but creatures act according to their own unique characters with reasons that make sense for them.

112 Providence is itself a middle position between two reductive extremes: fate and chance. In fate, events are determined but irrational, and so there is no guarantee the good will win out. In chance, there is no rational order to events in the world at all. Both of these positions evacuate life of meaning, for if I am fate's plaything or if the universe has no order, there is no reason to

Yet this providential order does not undermine the real independence of creatures.[113] In order to maximally share his infinite goodness, God creates many different creatures so "that what was wanting to one in the representation of the divine goodness might be supplied by another."[114] The only way to create different creatures is to diversify the act of existence by principles whose potency limits being in a certain way. Thus, creation of many different creatures requires different forms (to diversify species) and matter (to diversify individuals). Moreover, since action follows from being, the form and matter that are the essence of each material creature will be characterized in each creature's unique way of acting according to its distinctive individuality. For example, my actions are always human, but they are also typical of *me*. Thus, each creature has a vocation—God's plan for it in the order of providence—that nevertheless arises wholly on the basis of natural causes (form, matter, substance, accident).

In every action, therefore, God is creating, giving the thing existence, but the nature is also acting. God is utterly free to create what he will as a sign of his love; nevertheless, those natural causes endow the world with an intelligible necessity. Science and natural philosophy have dominion in the natural realm, but why that natural realm exists at all, or is intelligible, requires a metaphysical analysis of the cause of being. We only satisfy all our curiosity when we approach this with a both/and. Thomas has an incisive example of this:

> And so, when we ask the reason *why*, in regard to a natural effect, we can give a reason based on a proximate cause; provided, of course, that we trace back all things to the divine will as a first cause. Thus, if the question is asked: "Why is wood heated in the presence of fire?" it is answered: "Because heating is the natural action of fire"; and this is so "because heat is its proper accident." But this is the result of its proper form, and so on, until we come to the divine will. Hence, if a person answers someone who asks why wood is heated: "Because God willed it," he is answering it appropriately, provided he intends to take the question back to a first cause; but not appropriately, if he means to exclude all other causes.[115]

---

aspire to accomplishment. Providence guarantees both human agency and the assurance that the good will triumph.

113 This argument follows *SCG* III.97.

114 *ST* I.47.1.

115 *SCG* III.97.17. That God and creatures work necessarily work together is another result of the analogy of being, since both act as causes, but in different and complementary ways. This is

Because God and nature work together, Thomas says that "secondary causes are the executors of divine providence."[116] God intends the perfection of the universe in creation, and creatures are the instruments by which that end is accomplished because they have been given the power to act.[117] God thus shares with creatures the dignity of being real causes of order in the universe, even granting creatures a responsibility for bringing the universe to perfection.[118] This is especially true for us. As rational beings, we have a unique responsibility to order the material creation to its perfection.[119] This is the natural law commanding us to act for the universal good in fulfillment of the eternal law.

MIRACLES AND PRAYER

There is one crucial area in which this shared responsibility takes on a different arrangement. This is the fact of miracles and their relation to prayer.

Miracles have become suspect for many modern Christians. Science, they say, proves all causes are natural, and so there is simply no "room" for God to act. Moreover, they insist, a good and omnipotent God would not need to interfere with the world he created. These objections seriously misconstrue the nature of God's action. God can only "interfere" in the world if he is absent from it; but we have seen that the world exists only because of God's constant causal presence. Because God is present in the world by creating the natural causes, it is obvious that he can bring about the same effect as a natural cause

---

commonly denied by philosophers who insist causality is *univocal*, that all causes must act in the same way. The consequence of this assumption is that everything is caused *either by nature or by God* but never both. But as science discovers more and more about natural causality, this leaves a "God of the gaps" who is eventually eliminated as unnecessary to explain causality in nature. Thus, the analogical idea of causality is necessary to defend God's action in the world.

116 *SCG* III.77.1–3. Again, nominalism's denial of real natures would undermine this reasoning which makes God and creature both real causes in the universe.

117 *DP* 3.7. In *DV* 11.1, Thomas corrects the Augustinian tradition's restriction of causal power to God, noting that creatures act as causes in generation of substances, gaining knowledge, and developing virtue.

118 *ST* I.22.3. This cooperative activity extends to the Sacraments and grace. Because Martin Luther had a univocal notion of causality, he assumed that an activity was *either* from grace or from a person. This eliminated human cooperation with grace in the attainment of salvation and leads to the notion of irresistible grace and double predestination. On this, see Charles Morerod, *Ecumenism and Philosophy: Philosophical Questions for a Renewal of Dialogue*, trans. Therese C. Scarpelli (Ann Arbor: Sapientia Press, 2006).

119 *SCG* III.77–78; see also *SCG* II.46; *ST* I.103.6; and *ST* I-II.91.2.

even without the action of that creature.[120] If nature can make wine out of water, as happens in a vineyard over time, God can certainly do the same thing more quickly. God can do anything nature can do, since he makes nature.

This is how to understand miracles. A *miracle* is any effect brought about by God without the normal activity of a natural secondary cause.[121] This clearly departs from the tendentious Humean definition, since a miracle is defined not by what happens but by the causal means by which it happens. Miracles need not be astounding violations of the laws of nature; they can be any small act that God brings to be without the cooperation of a creation. Thomas argues that three kinds of effects might be brought about by a miracle. Most commonly, the effect is something that nature can do, but it is brought about without the operation of nature. For example, a sick person may get well or a storm may dissipate. Yet, when these things occur without nature acting in its usual way, they are miraculous events. Second, a natural event that occurs contrary to the normal order is miraculous. Nature can make a person with sight go blind or a living person die; God, however, can bring sight from blindness and life from death. Finally, and most gloriously, sometimes God will do something that nature cannot do at all. This encompasses such events as making the sun stand still and transforming matter so as to be incorruptible in the Resurrection. These show that God has complete dominion over creation.

God's miraculous activity in the world reveals the importance of prayer for the human role in providence.[122] We must accept that because God is immutable, prayer can never get God to "change his mind." Rather, since he is the creator, creation is utterly dependent on him and his thoughts and will cannot be dependent on our wishes. Nevertheless, even accepting divine immutability, there are two reasons why prayer is essential for the perfection of humanity and of the universe.

First, people pray to change themselves. Just as people change for the better when they attain virtue by habit, prayer changes people by opening them to the gifts of grace in the theological virtues, faith, hope, and love. These gifts illuminate our minds and enflame our hearts, perfecting human nature through supernatural assistance. This will dispose us to accept God's will, which is furthering the order of providence.

---

120 *SCG* III.99 and *ST* I.105.6.
121 *SCG* III.101 and *ST* I.105.7.
122 *SCG* III.95 and 96.

Second, prayer plays a central part in God's *active* providential order. This truth follows from the cooperation of primary and secondary causality. God creates the universe with two causal orders, parallel to one another. There is, of course, the order of nature that science describes so well. But there is also, because God is present in the world, a supernatural order, actions that come about by God's direct action in nature. But these miracles are not the actions of a capricious, willful God. Rather, they are planned by God as part of the providential order of creation from the very start. God has ordained that these miraculous acts be brought about through the intercession of prayer. The faithful, then, in their responsibility to act for the perfection of the universe, have a solemn and profound duty not only to act according to the order of natural causality but also to pray at all times so that the miraculous activity of God might bring about effects necessary for the good of the world.[123] Most of these miracles are never recognized since they often look like natural acts. Nevertheless, God's presence in the world and the efficacy of prayer in bringing about miraculous intervention cannot be doubted. When is a healing natural and due to the skill of a doctor, and when is it supernatural and due to God's action? When does a person reform his ways because of reason and virtue, and when does he do so because of grace? Prayer is the necessary means to bring to actuality the supernatural acts that are an essential aspect of God's providential plan for creation. It is through prayer that primary and secondary causes most intimately cooperate.

Praying so as to fulfill God's providential plan for creation is, in the end, our greatest act of wisdom and love, the purpose for which we were made.

FURTHER READING

Buckley, Michael J. *At the Origins of Modern Atheism*. New Haven: Yale University Press, 1987.

Davies, Brian. *An Introduction to the Philosophy of Religion*, 3rd ed. Oxford: Oxford University Press, 2004.

De Lubac, Henri. *The Drama of Atheist Humanism*. Translated by Edith M. Riley, Anne Englund Nash, and Mark Sebanc. San Francisco: Ignatius Press, 1995.

Feser, Edward. *Five Proofs of the Existence of God*. San Francisco: Ignatius, 2017.

Gilson, Étienne. *God and Philosophy*. 2nd ed. New Haven: Yale University Press, 2002.

Hart, David Bentley. *The Experience of God: Being, Consciousness, Bliss*. New Haven: Yale University Press, 2013.

---

123 Indeed, failing to pray is to introduce a privation into the providential order of creation. As we see in the next chapter, this is precisely what evil is.

Levering, Matthew. *Proofs of God: Classical Arguments from Tertullian to Barth*. Grand Rapids, Mich.: Baker Academic, 2016.

McInerny, Ralph. *Praeambula Fidei: Thomism and the God of the Philosophers*. Washington, D.C.: The Catholic University of America Press, 2006.

Sokolowski, Robert. *The God of Faith and Reason: Foundations of Christian Theology*. Washington, D.C.: The Catholic University of America Press, 1995.

Velde, Rudi te. *Aquinas on God: The 'Divine Science' of the Summa Theologiae*. Ashgate Studies in the History of Philosophical Theology. Aldershot: Ashgate, 2006.

Chapter 9

Evil: The Perennial Objection to the Perennial Philosophy

closed the introduction of this book by noting the importance of correct first principles, since a small error in the beginning can lead to a big error in the end. Throughout, I have tried to show that, when philosophers adopt reductive principles, this leads to conclusions that do not adequately account for the complexity of humankind's experience of creation. In particular, I have argued that a correct appreciation of being, truth, goodness, and beauty not only account for the depth of human experience but also point us toward God as the ultimate source of existence, wisdom, love, and joy. For this reason, reductive ideas of being, truth, and goodness often impede our ability to be open to the fullness of reality.

Perhaps in no other area is this more evident than in dealing with the problem of evil. Many people—not only philosophers—have found the fact of evil so objectionable that they have concluded it disproves the existence of God. I close my argument in this book by showing that this conclusion rests on mistaken notions of being, goodness, and God. If we approach the problem of evil with more adequate first principles, we can come to appreciate the truth of both creation and God more profoundly.

Let us consider why evil is such a problem for the perennial philosophy. The most obvious fact we begin with is that everything in the universe is *in* the universe because it is a being. Being, as we have seen, is convertible with truth, goodness, and beauty. These are the foundational principles of the perennial philosophy. Yet this claim becomes problematic when we recognize that, manifestly, *not* everything in the universe is true, good, and beautiful. A pathetic fact of the human condition is that our reality is marred by falsehood, evil, and ugliness. This problem is all the more perplexing when we insist that all being is created by God. This is why the problem of evil has always been one of the central problems of Christian philosophy: unless we can offer an explanation for the fact of evil, our fundamental claims about the nature of reality, its principles and causes, will remain subject to dispute.[1]

As a prefatory note, it is important to recognize that evil includes both *natural evil* and *moral evil*.[2] That is, sometimes bad things happen to us—we get sick, we go blind, we undergo losses from a hurricane. These natural events are considered evil metaphysically since they clearly are not good, that is, they impede the perfection of being we desire. At other times, though, we commit evil—we sin, we perform bad deeds that hurt another. These moral evils, which also impede our perfection, are things that we are responsible for. Given that God is the creator of both nature and of human free will, the problem of evil concerns both questions. We begin with some general philosophical principles and later make a clearer distinction between the two kinds of evil. But in this chapter *evil* normally refers to both natural and moral evil collectively.

The problem of evil is classically articulated in terms of three inconsistent premises. (1) God creates everything, (2) God is good and omnipotent, and (3) evil exists in the world. We have reason to believe each of these to be true, but we cannot hold all three to be true simultaneously without falling into contradiction. For if God creates everything, and he is omnipotently good, evil ought not exist. Logically, to resolve this inconsistency, you must give up belief in at least one of these premises.

Some people, therefore, will give up the first premise and deny that God creates everything. Some argue that there are two gods—a good God of Spirit and an evil god of matter. This is the position associated with Manicheanism, a heretical religion best remembered as the faith of Augustine's youth. But if there are two such gods, neither is the Supreme Being, and so this fails to answer the question about the origin of reality. Alternatively, as we have seen, others simply deny the existence of any creator at all and assert the material universe is simply a brute fact. This, however, raises problems about why one should expect good to predominate over evil in such a universe (i.e., why evil would be a problem at all) or even what the meaning of good and evil is in a purely material, determinist universe.

Others, however, will give up the second premise and assert that God is not omnipotent but is rather limited in various ways so that he cannot

---

1 The response to the problem of evil is also known as *theodicy*, the justification of God's goodness in light of the fact of evil in the world.

2 *ST* I.48.5.

prevent evil in the universe. A loving God, they argue, will suffer along with his creation. This is the position of the twentieth-century school known as Process Philosophy, associated with Alfred North Whitehead and Charles Hartshorne.[3] The problem with this is that, if God is not omnipotent, it is unclear how he could really be considered the creator. Certainly, this is not the God who has been worshipped in the Judeo-Christian tradition and would not be much better than atheism.

We are left, then, with the third option: denying the third premise that evil exists. But how can we deny that evil exists? Some philosophers, such as Leibniz, suggest that a perfect creator can only create the *most perfect world*.[4] What appears to be evil to us is simply the result of our lack of understanding of the necessary order of a perfect creation. Thus, evil in this view is an illusion because in reality the world is as good as it could possibly be. This answer, however, is completely unacceptable—indeed, offensive— to those who are struggling with evil in their lives.

But there is another way to deny the third premise. This is the way suggested by Plotinus and developed by Augustine and Thomas that has become a central doctrine of Catholic philosophy. This idea is that evil does not exist because it is a *privation* of being. This implies that evil is not an illusion but is a *real lack of being* that ought to be there. It is, therefore, not simply an illusion; it is a recognition of a hole or a wound in the fabric of being.

If evil is a privation of being, however, this returns us to the original problem: if God is an omnipotent and good creator of being, how can such privations of being come about. The answer to this problem begins with the conclusion from the previous chapter: the parallel action of God and creatures as primary and secondary causes. It is clear that evil is a defect in being, but, if God is perfectly good, the defective nature of evil must be attributed to the causal activity of creatures and not to God. Evil is a privation introduced into the world by creatures interacting with one another. This reasoning dissolves the more common objections related to the problem of evil. As Brian Davies observes, "If Aquinas is right, then the problem of evil is not a serious problem at all but rather the result of a confused way of thinking of God."[5]

---

3 The same idea attained some significance in theology in response to the incomprehensible evil of the Holocaust, as in the work of the Protestant theologian Jürgen Moltmann.

4 Leibniz, *The Monadology*, 38–48.

5 Brian Davies, *Thomas Aquinas on God and Evil* (Oxford: Oxford University Press, 2011), 128. The main discussions in Thomas are *ST* I.48–49, *SCG* III.4–15, and *DM* 1.

However, to appreciate this argument correctly, we need to rely on the notions of being, goodness, and God that have been outlined in previous chapters. This is why we have had to wait until now to address this problem: the correct solution to the problem necessarily draws on all our earlier discussions. What is evident from the arguments of many philosophers is that, unless we understand these principles correctly, the problem of evil will appear to be simply insoluble. This is why the resolution to the problem of evil, as framed by the most adequate principles, acts as a sort of capstone recapitulation for the truth of the perennial philosophy. (Because of the way this argument draws on previous chapters, there will be some repetition of arguments made earlier in the book.)

HOW TO THINK ABOUT PRIVATIONS

This solution—that evil is a privation of being—faces an immediate problem. For how can we understand *privation*, something that *lacks* existence? We need to approach this very methodically to understand this claim, for we naturally tend to think of evil as a *thing*, a tendency that will immediately undermine the logic of the solution.

To get a grasp of the meaning of evil as a privation of being, it is helpful to review the great variety of things that we commonly call evil, recalling that this includes both bad things that happen in the world as well as bad things people do. Some evils are easily identified. Murder is evil; slavery is evil; terrorism is evil. Yet, we could also call hunger or cancer or a hurricane or even blighted crops and barren fig trees evil from the perspective of those who suffer because of them. Certainly, that politician (*you know the one*) is evil, and on and on. It is hard to see what all these things have in common. To define a notion, there has to be one common essence that they share; but it is far from clear what all these examples share.

One common rejoinder at this point is to say that in some way all these things cause pain, and so pain is the essence of evil. (This is the principle behind utilitarian ethics.) While this is a widespread belief, there are problems with identifying pain and evil. First, we know some pain is not evil: exercising, raising a child, and breaking a bad habit can all be painful experiences, but they are not evil since they are all intrinsically worthwhile. Another problem is that, if all pain is evil, a reasonable corollary would be that all pleasure is good. But this again is obviously wrong, as pursuing pleasure as the highest good is harmful to us. The real problem, though, is that this thinking misunderstands what pleasure and pain are. According to the perennial tradition, the good is the perfect operation of any substance and pleasure is merely the by-product associated with any natural faculty attaining that perfect operation.[6] Thus, we have many powers to act, and if we do them well and unimpededly, pleasure is the result. Running a race when you are in shape or listening to music when your hearing is good and the playing is done well are both pleasurable. The experience of pain, by contrast, is a by-product of the faculty being frustrated in its operation. Trying to run with a pulled muscle or listening to music with tinnitus or with a lot of ambient noise are painful. But because pain is a sign of a natural operation being frustrated, it can be good if it is understood to be a signal for the person to alter their behavior. This is critical for life. If we lack adequate material comfort, we experience pain; if we have a cavity, we experience pain; if we are wanting for companionship, we experience pain. Pain, then, is the consequence of substances suffering from some kind of disorder that prevents their full perfection in activity. It is that disorder—some lack of proper operation in a faculty—that is the evil; these pains prompt the person to respond to that disordered state of affairs. In this way, pain can serve to move us to the good, the perfection of our nature.

This notion of disorder in the examples just mentioned indicates a *lack* of something we need to flourish. Material goods, health, and friends are things all people should have to realize their potential as a person. For any creature to reach its end, it has to be able to act according to the proper order of its nature. Any disorder in the substance or its operation frustrates that substance's natural tendency for perfection. This is what we mean when we speak of evil as a privation: it is something missing from what ought to be there.

This, however, raises the difficulty of how we can even conceive of a privation. We naturally have concepts about *things*; evil, though, as a privation, is an absence of being.[7] Thinking of evil as a thing is a constant danger for philosophers, for if it is a thing, it has real being and so must be caused by God. This would make God directly responsible for evil. The challenge is to grasp the fact that, if evil is nonbeing, then there is a radical dissymmetry between the being and goodness of creation, on the one hand, and evil, on the other. Beings have independent existence in the world, an active presence that is intelligible and desirable; evil, as non-being, would not have such independent existence and so could not be actively present in the world and could

---

6 Aristotle, *Nicomachean Ethics* X.1–5.

7 *ST* I.48.1.

never be an object of knowledge or desire per se. Since evil lacks being, it has no intelligibility of itself and cannot be defined. Nor can it, lacking all perfection of being, be desired, so evil is never sought for its own sake, but it is only brought about accidentally. This is why evil is always, ultimately, a mystery: as a privation in being, it fails in truth and good. As such it is impossible to talk about directly and can only be grasped indirectly.

Nevertheless, evil is not utterly ineffable. Because it is a privation of being, it can be known indirectly by reference to what is real: active beings in the world that suffer that privation of being. (Indeed, even God knows of evil only by reference to the being to which it is attached as a privation.[8]) For this reason, we say that evil is parasitic on good: it presumes the good of being but indicates a lack of some property expected of that being.[9] This is why our knowledge of being and its goodness must have priority over any intuition of evil: we have to know what something is and what it should do to recognize that it is disordered in any way. For example, it is only because we know what a tooth is, and how it is meant to function, that we can identify a cavity as a privation of being that causes defective operation and so judge it to be evil. Similarly, we know human nature has the capacity to see and to love; disorder in the body or in the soul can deprive a person of these actions needed for human perfection, and so blindness and hatefulness are both evils. Because evil is the lack of some quality that is expected in a given substance, we can employ *absence of expected being* as a stand in for a proper definition.[10] The radical dissymmetry between being and privation, with being and good having absolute ontological priority, shows that the infinite goodness of God is not incompatible with the presence of evil in creation. That is, God's goodness is perfect in his causality, but creatures are imperfect. Consequently, evil is a fact about creatures and not about God.

---

8 *ST* I.14.10.ad 4.

9 *ST* I.48.3. It is for this reason that no being, not even Satan, can be wholly evil, since then they would lack existence completely (*ST* I.48.4).

10 Here again we see the debilitating problems nominalism brings to contemporary philosophy. Since nominalism rejects the existence of universal essences, there is no way to know when a substance is deprived of some property it ought to have. That a person should be able to see and to love, and that blindness and hate are evil, assumes the reality of human nature as a standard for determining what properties an individual should possess. Since nominalists think each substance is radically individual, they have to assume any property attached to it is purely contingent. (Bertrand Russell's influential theory of descriptions is a good illustration of this.) For this reason, they will assume that, if evil can be predicated of a subject, it must be some positive quality in reality, like being blue or tall. These metaphysical assumptions confound attempts to solve the problem of evil.

Still, great confusion about evil persists. This confusion might stem from our need to talk about evil, for our language frames evil as if it were not merely privative. That is, we readily discuss evil as if it were a real quality: "He is evil" or "That act is evil." This use of the verb *is* can lead us too easily into believing that we are asserting the presence of some positive attribute, as would be the case with "He is tall" or "That is loud." The answer is found in the analogy of being. Recall that the very first distinction in being is the difference between real being and beings of reason.[11] Real beings are either substances or one of the nine accidents. Privations, in contrast, do not fall into any of the categories, since they are a denial of being (and, in fact, can be applied to *any* of the categories). We are cognizant of privations, however, and so our talk of evil arises from our mental recognition of the lack of being. We recognize a hole only because we know what a pocket should be; the hole "is" in the pocket as an absence of what should be there. This lack of being is in itself unintelligible; it must be in reference to the pocket, of which it is a privation, to be understood. Since it is difficult to keep our eye upon privation qua privation, we tend to fallaciously reify that absence of being into some positive quality. This is why any proper solution to the problem of evil depends on the convertibility of the transcendental properties and the analogy of being. Without these principles, evil can appear to be a thing in the world, a creature that must be ascribed to the creative action of God.

Let us consider this answer to the problem of evil in more detail. Because evil is intelligible only in light of being, we first briefly review the metaphysical principles of being that are necessary to understand evil as a privation. These include, in particular, the ideas of being, God, and goodness. This will reveal the difference between being and non-being (or privation) that is the critical insight that leads to the true solution to the supposed problem of evil.

METAPHYSICAL BACKGROUND: BEING AND GOD

The existence of evil is not a problem for the Greek philosophical tradition because they assumed a multiplicity of causes, including contrary principles to account for the reality of both good and evil.[12] It is very different with

---

11 *OBE* c.1.

12 The idea of contrary causal principles giving rise to change originates with the Pythagoreans and their famous list of ten pairs of contraries; see Aristotle, *Metaphysics* I.5 (986a22–27); cf. IV.2 (1004b27–30), XII.7 (1072a30–35).

Christian philosophy, which holds there is only one principle of reality, one cause of all that is. The problem is brought home forcefully in the precipitous way in which Saint Augustine begins his dialogue, *On Free Choice of the Will*, where his interlocutor, Evodius, asks, "Please tell me: isn't God the cause of evil?"[13] The Christian reply to this is to emphasize the difference between God as primary cause and creatures as secondary causes. That is, while God is the sole cause of being, and so directly the cause of natural beings, these natural beings act as secondary causal principles by virtue of their own power. It is the operation of these secondary natural causes that is the source of the privation of being in creation; consequently, evil cannot be directly attributable to God. To show how evil can be a privation of being in creatures and not in God, we must begin by reiterating how *being* must be construed in distinctly different ways, so that privation of being will apply in similarly different ways.

The most fundamental metaphysical truth is that the one thing beings have in common is the fact that they *exist*. The act of existence makes things actively present in the world and so intelligible; for this reason, the principle of noncontradiction is the foundation of all rational knowledge. Yet, while it is necessary that everything shares this property of existence, it is equally obvious that there are different kinds of beings; in other words, while *Being* is one, *beings* are many. This unity-in-difference is only possible in light of the analogy of being, since things exercise the act of existence in many different ways.

We first become aware of this analogical difference between beings in reflecting on our own lives. It is obvious that my substantial existence persists throughout my life, while my accidents constantly change. These accidents are real, but they depend on the substance for their existence. My weight or complexion or feelings exist but only if I exist. It is obvious, then, that substances have a more fundamental way of being than accidents. Similarly, though, I realize that my own existence as a substance is not absolute. It is obvious that I needed to be brought into existence and that I will die. There must be, therefore, a mode of being more fundamental than me, something more real that causes me to exist. This cannot be my parents, for their own existence is as contingent as my own; moreover, it is impossible that my existence depends on them because I can go on living even after they are gone. Thus, there must be something whose existence is not contingent and that is the cause of the existence of all other beings. This, of

13 Augustine, *On Free Choice of the Will* I.1.

course, is God, the cause *of the being* of *everything* that exists.[14] Since action follows from being, to be the cause of being, God's essence must be existence itself. Therefore, on the one hand, creatures have imperfect being, in both their substantial and accidental reality, and so can suffer privation (or cease to exist) and experience evil. On the other hand, God, as perfect being, cannot suffer privation. Consequently, evil is utterly foreign to his nature. Moreover, since God's creative activity is to give being, his act cannot be the source of privation, and so he cannot be the cause of evil.

I review this because we cannot unjustifiably assume more than this when we refer to God. From a philosophical perspective, we can only know that God exists as creator. As creator, he is a necessary being that is the cause of the existence; in this way, God and his activity are utterly opposed to privation. This must inform our subsequent discussion of the presence of evil in creation. In particular, we must resist the temptation to add to this idea of God certain arbitrary conditions about what we think God ought to have done. Rather, what we must recognize in God as creator is the unlimited perfection of being that belongs to God alone. This is in fact what we mean when we call God *good*. Since this claim is another source of great confusion, let us now consider the proper meaning of *good*.

BEING AS GOOD

As we have seen, the good is being under the aspect of desirability. Most fundamentally, what all things desire is something better: a more complete mode of existence. Thus, the good that is desired by all things is to possess the state of being that is their perfection.[15] Attaining this perfection is possible only through substances acting, for that action is a realization of their potential for more a more complete state of existence.[16] It is for this reason that desire is able to incite activity (for inaction is, by definition, an absence of being and so something to be avoided). The good as the perfection of being, then, accounts for the dynamism of existence: all entities strive to attain that mode of being the possession of which would make existence better. This understanding of goodness as the perfection of being has three important consequences for the problem of evil.

---

14 This would include all the contrary principles that Greeks pointed to as the natural causes of privation.

15 *ST* I.5.1 and *SCG* I.37.5.

16 *ST* I-II.18.1: "Now in things, each one has so much good as it has being: since good and being are convertible."

First, if goodness is the perfection of being, then every possession of being is good. So, every substance that exists is good, not only because it is created by God but also because being itself is a desired perfection. This is why every creature struggles to maintain itself in existence.[17] But this applies equally to accidental being, since the more a being exists—the more a being possesses those accidents as a perfection of the nature—the more reality the substance has and better that substance is. Therefore, every substance is good and every action is good; no being can be essentially evil.

Second, because being is analogical and possessed in different ways, so goodness, as the perfection of being, will be possessed in equally diverse ways. In other words, *good* is an analogical term. This applies most importantly to the difference just mentioned between merely existing as a substance and the full perfection of being attained when a creature fulfills its potential in second act. This full perfection is the primary signification of the term "good."[18] Thus, that an apple tree exists is good; but an apple tree develops roots and grows limbs and leaves for the sake of its ultimate perfection—growing apples. It is the full fruition of being that manifests the unique goodness of each nature. Similarly, a human being develops through a complex process of gestation, growth, and maturation to attain the perfections of wisdom and love in the context of a well-ordered society. The ultimate good that is desired is always this end-state to which a nature is naturally inclined, and nothing short of that can satisfy.

These examples point to a second important sense of good as analogical. Since the good is the perfection of being, each nature has a mode of perfection appropriate to it. The specific perfection of any being is determined by its nature, and so perfection cannot be reduced to a one simple quality or univocal predicate. It is good for a shark to be a cold-blooded killer, else it would die; it is bad for a person to be a cold-blooded killer, since that is characteristic of ignorance and hate. Thus, the good of any substance has to be specified by reference to the proper operations of the nature of the substance.

This brings us to the third consequence. If good is the perfection of being, then evil, as the lack of goodness, must be the lack of the perfection of being. But this means that evil will be just as analogical as good. Evil can be a privation of first act, as when a substance ceases to exist (I die); or, it

---

17 *ST* I-II.94.2.
18 *ST* I.5.1.ad 1.

can be an absence of second act, as when a substance is deprived of a characteristic proper to it (I go blind or I fail to grow in wisdom).[19] Moreover, what is evil for one nature (a shark lacking gills, which is clearly a defect in light of its nature) is not evil for another (a person lacking gills, which is not defective with respect to human nature).

From this, we can see why evil is not a being at all. All being, both substances and accidents, are good.[20] These beings are knowable, because they have an active presence in the world. Evil, by contrast, is a lack of being, either a substance losing its existence or failing to attain a needed accident. Since all action is for the sake of the good, evil can only be an imperfection that arises *accidentally* in beings that are themselves good.[21] (We return to this shortly.)

Given this understanding of the good, we can reiterate why the problem of evil does not implicate God. As the source of the perfection of being, God is responsible for the good of existence, but can never be directly responsible for evil. Lack of being is not something that Perfect Being can directly cause. Furthermore, we can see that God is himself essentially good. As the source of all perfection, God possesses the complete perfection of being already. Accordingly, God is good necessarily and essentially.[22] This is important for considering the problem of evil because, unlike creatures, God's goodness is not contingent on what he does. As perfect being, God need not—indeed, cannot—do anything to attain further perfection. To assume that God must *do something* to be good is to misunderstand his nature, for he is perfectly good already. This common error, assuming God

---

19 *ST* I.48.5: "Act, however, is twofold; first, and second. The first act is the form and integrity of a thing; the second act is its operation. Therefore, evil also is twofold. In one way it occurs by the subtraction of the form, or of any part required for the integrity of the thing, as blindness is an evil, as also it is an evil to be wanting in any member of the body. In another way evil exists by the withdrawal of the due operation, either because it does not exist, or because it has not its due mode and order."

20 *ST* I-II.18.1: "We must therefore say that every action has goodness, in so far as it has being; whereas it is lacking in goodness, in so far as it is lacking in something that is due to its fulness of being; and thus it is said to be evil."

21 See *SCG* III.10–14.

22 *ST* I.6.3: "God alone is good essentially. For everything is called good according to its perfection. Now perfection of a thing is threefold: first, according to the constitution of its own being; secondly, in respect of any accidents being added as necessary for its perfect operation; thirdly, perfection consists in the attaining to something else as the end. . . . This triple perfection belongs to no creature by its own essence; it belongs to God only, in Whom alone essence is existence; in Whom there are no accidents. . . . Hence it is manifest that God alone has every kind of perfection by His own essence; therefore He Himself alone is good essentially."

should be doing something if he were good, applies a finite human conception of goodness to God.

Although God need not do anything to attain goodness, there is something that God freely does that uniquely manifests his goodness. One characteristic of goodness is that it is self-diffusive: in attaining perfection, a substance's goodness bountifully supplies things needed by other beings.[23] For example, an apple tree, in growing apples, shares its perfection with other creatures in the fruit they eat and even with future generations by way of the seeds in the fruit; a person, in being wise and loving, elevates the experience of others around him who share in his knowledge and charity, which may even enhance the well-being of those in future generations.[24] If the goodness of creatures is self-diffusive, how much more is God's. God is perfect as the infinite act of existence; consequently, he diffusively shares that which is properly his, existence. Thus, in creation, God shares the perfection of his own being by allowing other things to exist and so experience the goodness that is essentially his. Further, he orders creatures to a full participation in goodness by giving them a natural inclination to the perfection of their being in second act. This must be seen as the primary disclosure of God's benevolence: His merciful and gratuitous sharing of existence, which is owed to no creature, for the creature would not *be* without God's goodness.[25] Thus, creation is a manifestation of the Goodness of God. This truth should frame all discussion of evil: to be unmoved by the inestimable goodness of this gift because of some finite defects in being is to forsake the principles of being and goodness themselves.

Yet this fact brings home once again the acuteness of the problem of evil in that very same creation. Why should God allow imperfection in things other than himself? Is this not the real rub of the problem of evil? Does this not reflect poorly upon God's moral nature?

---

23 *SCG* I.37.5. The idea of the diffusiveness of the good comes from Pseudo-Dionysius, *On Divine Names*, IV.1–4, drawing on earlier Platonic sources.

24 *ST* I.19.2: "For natural things have a natural inclination not only towards their own proper good, to acquire it if not possessed, and, if possessed, to rest therein; but also to spread abroad their own good amongst others, so far as possible. . . . It pertains, therefore, to the nature of the will to communicate as far as possible to others the good possessed; and especially does this pertain to the divine will, from which all perfection is derived in some kind of likeness."

25 *ST* I.21.4.

THE PRESENCE OF EVIL IN CREATION

To answer this, let us return to the fact that evil is a privation of being. Now, any being with potency is subject to a possible privation of being. This means that, most generally, *any being subject to change is also subject to evil.* Unlike God, all creatures have such potential. They have a potential to be affected by other creatures and a potential for their own perfection that they may fail to achieve. Evil, then, comes about because of the potential present in all creatures, not because of a failure in God's activity.

Many would object that a good God did not have to create a world with potential, and so God is to blame for evil at least indirectly. Recall, however, that God's goal in creation is to manifest his infinite goodness; to do this, he had to create a great variety of finite creatures. (A universe with only one creature, no matter how good, would still radically fail to represent God's infinite goodness.) This variety would include both unchanging and changing creatures. Indeed, to increase the variety of creatures manifesting goodness, there had to be distinct individuals as well as diverse species. But the form of a species can be individuated only by being received into matter. Since matter is the principle of potency, all those material creatures are necessarily subject to change.[26] Thus, as Thomas concludes, "The perfection of the universe requires that there should be not only beings incorruptible, but also corruptible beings; so the perfection of the universe requires that there should be some which can fail in goodness, and thence it follows that sometimes they do fail."[27] Thus, because some beings will fail—that is, be deprived of some being, either by ceasing to exist (first act) or failing to realize the potential for a perfective accident (second act)—there will be evil in the natural world.

This allows us to better understand the distinction between *natural evil* and *moral evil.*[28] Natural evil is always a failure of being that is good in itself and that is aiming for perfection in its action. Thus, when the creature fails to attain perfection or when it introduces privation into another being, it is bringing about evil *accidentally.* The privation of being and goodness is

---

26 *ST* I.47.1–2.

27 *ST* I.48.2.

28 *ST* I.48.5. Natural evil can also be called evil suffered, or the evil of pain. It is part of the order of nature. The other category of evil is moral evil, which might be called evil done or evil of fault. This category arises from human free will and is outside the order of nature. We take this up below.

wholly dependent on the good of beings seeking the good of perfection. For this reason, we can outline the causes of evil in terms of the four causes. Since nonbeing cannot be a cause—how can something that does not exist bring about an effect?—the cause of evil must be discoverable in the principles of being that in some way go wrong and introduce privation—some damage or defect—into the order of creation.[29] They bring about evil as an accidental effect when their causal activity is deprived of its natural order. Let us consider how the causes can be defective.

A common source of disorder in an effect is when an efficient cause is defective. This occurs when the substance lacks the necessary power to bring about the desired effect, so that that effect is deficient and so evil. For example, when a heart due to illness or malformation is incapable of pumping blood, serious harm, even death, can result. Another common example is when a student who has not studied takes an exam, so his answers are defective simply because he does not have the power to write good ones. Thus, if an agent suffers from a privation of being, it will inadvertently cause defective, or evil, results even when it is acting to attain a good.

A defect can also be introduced from the material cause. This occurs when matter is not properly disposed to receive a certain form, so that the resulting effect will be bad. For example, if a bridge is constructed out of brittle steel, the bridge will be defective even if the blueprints are perfect and the construction crew did their job well. The story of the Three Little Pigs can be seen as a sort of parable about evil that arises due to the use of defective matter in making a house.

Since the soul is the form of the body, and the form is the principle of actuality, it cannot be defective itself. Rather, if the matter composing the body is defective—if there is a genetic mutation of some sort—then the form will not be able to express itself perfectly in the matter of the person. The result is a handicap, a physical, not a moral, evil, which is due to the defect of the matter impeding the form from fully acting on the matter. More broadly, though, the potency of matter is the cause of *all* natural corruption: as the principle of potentiality, matter is always susceptible to change. Natural change—the fact that things eventually wear away—is a natural evil.

This corruption of being points to perhaps the most common experience of evil in the natural world: illness and death. When an organism dies from old age, this means that the body has become disordered to such an

---

29 My summary follows the argument in *SCG* III.10.

extent that it can no longer carry out the functions of life—especially nutrition and hydration by which the body's integrity is maintained. But just as often, illness and death are caused by another creature acting on a victim. For example, antelopes suffer when a lion hunts them, and we suffer when we come down with a cold. This kind of evil can be explained in terms of formal cause. When a substance is deprived of its form by the action of another substance, the one suffers because of that action. Whether it be a lion turning an antelope into lunch, or a virus turning my health into illness, it is the action of one creature causing a change in the state of being (either substantial or accidental) in another creature.

An important aspect of this kind of natural evil is that, in spite of the apparent suffering, there is actually much good being achieved. For in this interaction of creatures, one creature flourishes at the expense of the other who suffers. For example, a lion thrives, and is a good lion, when he kills an antelope, who must suffer; a cold virus thrives when it makes its host sick. In these instances, that change always implies a perfective act in one substance corresponding to the evil of the loss of being in another substance. This is why God allows for this natural evil: because some creature is attaining its perfection, it is part of the overall perfection of the universe. The providential order of the universe does not guarantee that *every* creature succeeds; rather, it is part of the providential order that some creatures will thrive while others suffer as a result, but this is all for the perfection of the universe. As Thomas explains:

> Hence, corruption and defects in natural things are said to be contrary to some particular nature; yet they are in keeping with the plan of universal nature; inasmuch as the defect in one thing yields to the good of another, or even to the universal good: for the corruption of one is the generation of another, and through this it is that a species is kept in existence. Since God, then, provides universally for all being, it belongs to His providence to permit certain defects in particular effects, that the perfect good of the universe may not be hindered, for if all evil were prevented, much good would be absent from the universe. A lion would cease to live, if there were no slaying of animals.[30]

The necessity of natural evil for the perfection of the universe can perhaps be better seen in considering how changes often correlate a growth or

---

perfection in one being with a loss in another.[31] For example, a water molecule is created only when a hydrogen atom forms a chemical bond and loses its existence. This loss of existence is obviously bad for the hydrogen atom, but it is a new perfection of being for the water molecule. Moreover, it seems that the existence of water is good for the world, since water can do so many things hydrogen and oxygen cannot do on their own. In similar fashion, when that water molecule is metabolized by a plant, allowing for the plant's life and fruition, it is bad for the water, which ceases to exist, but good for the plant and wonderful for the world, for plants sustain animals and people. In this sense, the natural evil of substantial change caused by creatures interacting with one another is a necessary constituent of any universe subject to change, for one creature attains perfection by coming to possess the good present in another creature. This also demonstrates how even the natural corruption of death is good for the universe, for that corruption of old beings allows the good of new beings to emerge from that which once was. If prior generations had not passed away, life on earth would be impossible.[32]

Some might question why God's providence includes the fact that one creature can flourish only at the expense of another. Here again we must point to the fact that to manifest his infinite goodness, God had to create many different creatures. But, since action follows from being, the differences in creatures mean that there will be a variety of ways in which creatures attain perfection, each of which represents divine perfection in its own way.[33] Thus, the speed of the antelope and the ferocity of the lion are both

---

31 *SCG* III.4.4: "Therefore, in every change there is a generation and a corruption, in some sense; for instance, when a thing changes from white to black, the white is corrupted and the black comes into being. Now, it is a good thing for matter to be perfected through form, and for potency to be perfected through its proper act, but it is a bad thing for it to be deprived of its due act."

32 *SCG* III.6.10: "Indeed, the change of corruption is never found without the change of generation; neither, as a consequence, is the end of corruption found without the end of generation. So, nature does not intend the end of corruption as separated from the end of generation, but both at once. . . . Thus, privations are not intended by nature in themselves, but only accidentally."

On a larger scale, this is also why the fact of the extinction of 99 percent of all species to have existed is not evil. God allows evolution to express his infinite goodness, and the existence of certain species are incompatible with one another, so it is fitting that God gives them all an opportunity to exist at least for some epoch. It is good the dinosaurs roamed the earth—look at the joy they give both children and adults—but it is better they went extinct so that shrew-like mammals could develop into primates and eventually to humans.

33 Thus, "what was wanting to one in the representation of the divine goodness might be supplied by another [and] the whole universe together participates the divine goodness more perfectly, and represents it better than any single creature whatever" (*ST* I.47.1). Creation achieves complete goodness symbiotically.

manifestations of God's goodness and necessary for the perfection of the universe. For this reason, this kind of natural evil is tolerated by God but not caused by him. God causes the being and goodness of the universe: God causes the goodness of the lion perfecting his nature; though God knows this involves the antelope suffering evil, it is only the perfection of being, and not the privation, that is directly caused by God. Again, this evil, this privation suffered by one creature, is accidental to the good that is actively present in the world.[34]

This leaves only the final cause. However, the final cause is the one cause that cannot be a source of natural evil, even accidentally. This is because the final cause is the second act, the perfection of the being and so good in itself. There is, however, one notable exception to this rule. This is the case of moral evil, those terrible events that we freely cause. Moral evil comes about when a person refuses to act as he ought. Because only humans have free will, only humans are capable of this sort of evil. A tree can be impeded from growing fruit by a blight, but a tree cannot refuse to grow fruit. We, in contrast, can refuse to act for our perfection and happiness. In this refusal, we *fail to change and grow* in a way expected of human nature; we repudiate our final cause in acting for an inferior good like pleasure.[35] Thus, moral evil is an accident of a person acting with a disordered will, thereby depriving himself of the perfection of being.[36]

It is this disordered will that is the source of damage or privation in the world.[37] We are perfected by growing in wisdom and love, to which we are naturally ordered. However, if I *freely choose* to ignore the precepts of the natural law, I deprive myself of the chance to be directed to wisdom and love and so introduce a privation into my own being. Further, being deprived of wisdom and love, my actions will inevitably communicate more disorder into the world. In contrast to natural evil, which includes some movement to perfection, moral evil is pure privation, pure nihilation. There is absolutely no perfective act, either for the agent who deprives himself or

---

34 This reasoning would also apply when one creature injures another, depriving it of some second act, without killing it. Thus, when an alligator maims a deer or when a fungus causes a tree to be barren, that is an accidental privation of an activity flowing from its substantial form.

35 *ST* I-II.18.2.

36 *ST* I-II.19.1.

37 This is the essence of Augustine's argument for the existence of free will in *On Free Choice of the Will*, bk. 1.

for the recipient who suffers due to that person's evil.[38] Unlike the lion killing the antelope, if I murder someone, I suffer by depriving myself of love
and the victim suffers by being deprived of life.

For this reason, these two kinds of evil are related to God in different
ways. Natural evil, since it is suffered only at the expense of some attainment
of perfection, is justified in light of the fact that it is necessary for the perfection of the universe. This is not a utilitarian justification: suffering is
allowed not because more pleasure is brought about or because it most
benefits humankind. Rather, suffering is allowed because the universe as a
whole is ordered to perfection as a gratuitous manifestation of the goodness
of being God has shared with them in creation.

Moral evil is different. Here, no perfection of being occurs at all. It is
permitted by God because it is an unavoidable consequence of free will: if a
person is truly free, he will sometimes choose to do evil. Many have argued
that God should be held responsible for moral evil, because he gave us free
will. But free will follows from our rational nature, and it is we who use it
according to our nature. Neither can God eliminate reason and free will from
the universe, for a universe with wisdom and love clearly better manifests
God's infinite goodness than does a universe without wisdom and love.

Some might object that an omnipotent and good God should intervene
in free choice to prevent evil human acts. This, however, is a violation of
noncontradiction: an act cannot be free if God controls our choice. In fact,
the problematic nature of this objection is obscured when we concentrate
on only the most extreme acts of evil, acts of murder and genocide, which
would appear to be impossible to choose at all. I would suggest, however,
that we remember that the good we desire is *perfection* of human nature,
the best possible state of being. Evil, a privation of being, is any instance in
which we settle for anything less than this perfection. This would in fact
characterize almost all human acts, since very rarely are we perfectly
ordered to the good. An honest person will admit he always has room to
grow. Could God intervene in *all of* these evil choices without violating
human nature as a free secondary cause? When I watch the game instead
of reading philosophy, I am being less than I could be. If God is called on
to prevent our evil choices and actions, he would have to prevent even this
negligible evil. This would be to eradicate nearly every exercise of human

---

38 See *ST* I.48.5–6. Because moral evil is worse than natural evil, Socrates argues that it is better
to suffer evil than to do evil ourselves (*Gorgias* 503c–519e).

agency—we would no longer act with free will, and so we could not accomplish our vocation as secondary causes. Thus, focusing only on the worst forms of evil distracts us from seeing how free will works: in the exercise of choice, it is the human agent who is responsible and is the cause of the failure to do the best he could.

GOD AND EVIL

In fact, God cannot prevent evil completely unless he were to violate the distinction between primary and secondary causes. God is the primary cause of being, and his work in sharing existence is wholly good. Creatures, secondary causes in the universe, cause change according to their nature. Accordingly, God could prevent natural evil only by making a universe without natural change. In other words, God can prevent evil only by eliminating the natural causes of change: the laws of nature and free will. This would be a contradiction of the very notion of creation. Moreover, a universe without change would be a universe in which creatures would never perfect their potentiality, and that would be a universe radically *lacking* in good.[39] Thus, anything except a wholly static universe is bound to suffer natural evil.

More particularly, God's primary causality cannot nullify our free will as a secondary cause. God's action is good; it is we who are responsible for evil. God creates us and orders us to happiness; evil is the result of free will deviating from that divine ordering by negating God's direction and choosing disorder. Thomas compares this to a person with a limp: no matter how hard he tries to walk a straight line, the defect in his leg pulls him off course.[40] (Today we might think of a shopping cart with a bad wheel.) Similarly, it is the defect in the will that deforms human action, not the goodness of God's causal activity. In fact, the evil of the act—as non-being—is the one thing God cannot do.[41] Moreover, God cannot interfere with evil in secondary causes because, as a privation of being, there is nothing to *interfere with*. If God were to act precisely in place of where the human agent is not-acting,

---

39 *ST* I.48.1.ad 5: "Hence evil neither belongs to the perfection of the universe, nor does it come under the order of the same, except accidentally, that is, by reason of some good joined to it."

40 *ST* I.49.2.ad 2 and *DM* 3.2.

41 *ST* I.49.2: "The evil which consists in the defect of action is always caused by the defect of the agent. But in God there is no defect, but the highest perfection. . . . Hence, the evil which consists in defect of action, or which is caused by defect of the agent, is not reduced to God as to its cause."

then clearly it is not the human agent who is acting, but God. This is not preventing an act at all; it is acting-in-place-of, which is a denial of the onto-logical independence of creatures as causes.

Therefore, God creates creatures to be good but permits evil in the created order.[42] His creative act constitutes beings ordered to perfection, but, inasmuch as creatures are subject to change and contingent in their perfection, evil is unavoidably a part of created order.

It might be objected that God has a moral duty to limit suffering. But this is a category mistake. Morality is a standard of human perfection, and so it cannot be applied to God's perfection at all. An act is moral if it fulfills one's nature and gives to others what is owed to them, but, since creation is utterly gratuitous, God cannot owe creatures anything beyond what is essential to the nature they are given.[43] Therefore, having given creatures the gift of existence, God owes them the dignity to act according to their nature. For God to intervene to prevent evil in all cases would be unjust, for then God would violate the very reason for the creature's existence by not allowing it to act for itself.[44] This sharing of causal power is an expres-sion of the generosity of God's goodness, even if the creature realizes that gift imperfectly. So, God cannot, on the pain of contradiction, *both* create independent causal agents *and* simultaneously prohibit them from acting.

Again, it might be objected that even apart from moral obligation, God is said to love us. Would that love not eliminate evil? As we have seen, it is his love that constitutes our independent existence, including our independ-ent agency as creatures and our inevitable failures.[45] Some say a loving God could at least eliminate pain and suffering from human existence. But we have seen that pain is a by-product of a faculty being frustrated in its oper-

---

42 In the *CT* I.142, Thomas gives three reasons for God's permission of evil. First, to have a uni-verse without evil would mean a universe without secondary causes—that is, creatures really acting to cause change. Yet a universe without creatures endowed with the ability to act as real causes would be an impoverished universe. Second, as we have seen, these secondary causes can flourish only by appropriating the good of other beings so as to attain their perfection: I consume apples, and lions consume antelopes, to sustain and flourish as creatures. Third, the experience of evil allows the brilliance of the good to stand out, so that the mind is directed to proper appreciation of the gratuitous gift of being.

43 *ST* I.21.1. To put this another way, God exercises distributive justice in creation but in no sense owes commutative justice to any creature.

44 This is why God is not responsible for the evil of damnation. Hell is not an evil caused by God but an act of justice that is owed to sinners in light of their free choice; *ST* I.49.2 and *DM* 3.1.ad 3.

45 *ST* I.19.2 and I.20.2.

ations. Consequently, God cannot eliminate pain without sacrificing one of the natural signs directing us to perfection.

The argument based on pain reflects a deeper error, for it imposes on God a utilitarian definition of goodness. This assumes that if God is good, he will maximize pleasure for his creatures. It is only in light of this utilitarian definition that Darwin's discovery that nature was "red in tooth and claw" can be a cause for a rejection of theism. If, however, we define goodness in terms of the perfection of being, then God's essential goodness in no way guarantees maximal pleasure for creatures.

This identification of evil and pain also leads to a recursive argument about theodicy. I would argue that an obsession over pain, and a corresponding inability to recognize the priority of goodness over parasitic privations, is itself a defect and a source of evil. The failure to see that evil is parasitic on an immensely good creation is a willful blindness to the good, the true, and the beautiful. This attitude deprives the universe of its transcendent meaning. But, without that presumption of the goodness of the universe, there is no reason to think good should ever triumph over evil.[46] This agnosticism sours into nihilism. It leads to a passivity and makes one indifferent to achieving the good.[47] This overturns not only the Christian appreciation of being over privation but also the Greek idea that order rules over chaos.

Nevertheless, both as Christians and as philosophical realists, we do in fact give precedence to being over nothingness and accordingly to good over evil. Thus, God as the source of being is essentially good; evil characterizes the defective operations of creation.[48] God is not implicated in this evil for, first, creation is primarily a gratuitous goodness and, second, God's goodness is of his essence and not by what he brings about. Thus, God is bound by no obligation to achieve anything more for himself or others, in contrast to the contingent moral actions of human beings.

---

46 On this, see C. S. Lewis, *The Problem of Pain* (New York: Macmillan Publishing, 1962), 37–54. Against the problem of evil, Christians should continually express wonder in the fact that the universe exists at all, that it is intelligibly ordered, that it is replete with desirable things, and that contemplation of it can elicit joy.

47 C. S. Peirce, in "A Neglected Argument for the Reality of God" (*Collected Papers* 1:452–93), makes the observation that a person with a pessimistic constitution will simply not be able to see the logic defending the existence of God (484). Thus, there is a moral defect at the root of much intellectual blindness.

48 See ST I.14.10.ad 3: "Although evil is not opposed to the divine essence, which is not corruptible by evil; it is opposed to the effects of God, which He knows by His essence; and knowing them, He knows the opposite evils."

Evil, then, results from the fact that creatures pursue perfection imperfectly. That we take offense at this wound in the order of creation is understandable; yet to despair our condition and let evil triumph is worse, for that would be to ignore the fact that the same God who makes creation good also offers to us the gift of grace as a path to salvation from every evil.[49]

CONCLUSION: PIETY TO BEING

Evil is a fact of this world, a terrible and often perplexing fact. But, if we understand the world correctly, if we have the correct first principles, we can understand evil and respond to it with equanimity and prudence. Every year, crises pop up—wars, storms, pandemics—and too often people not grounded in the right principles react in ways that only exacerbate the initial evil. They do not understand being, they fail to grasp the truth of the situation. Their philosophical failings make them impotent in the face of an existential challenge.

Western civilization has always been leavened by the confluence of Socrates's claim that what is important is not life but the virtuous life and Christ's revelation that there is no greater love than to sacrifice for one's friends. Human nature calls us not merely to avoid evil but to seek the good, fearlessly and enthusiastically. The perennial philosophy stands as a monument to this, for its first principles insist on a piety to being as the actuality of all acts, into which we must immerse ourselves in all ways. It is these first principles, then, that are our bulwark against the privation of evil, not only today, but in all ages: being as the analogical act of existence dynamically present in the world; truth as the mind's receptivity to that actuality of things in the world; goodness as the perfection of being that motivates activity; and beauty as the gratuitous intelligible harmony of being that induces joyful awe in those who, because they have humbled themselves, can see creation for all it truly has to offer.

We are all called to be philosophers, to perfect the rationality of human nature. But, given the necessary cooperation between nature and grace,

---

49 Theological solutions to the problem of evil are in continuity with philosophy but not provable without revelation. The difference between the two strategies is parallel to the difference between justice and charity: the need to treat people fairly for common good is philosophically provable, but that there is no greater love than to give one's life depends on revelation of the Cross. We can accept the privation of pleasure in fortitude and temperance on basis of reason; but the will to take up the Cross for heroic virtue relies on revelation. There is continuity in perfection here, but theology sees us not simply in terms of human nature but children of God and disciples of Christ.

there is no better way to close than with the prayer with which Saint John Paul II ends his own reflections on philosophy in the Catholic tradition: "May Mary, Seat of Wisdom, be a sure haven for all who devote their lives to the search for wisdom. May their journey into wisdom, sure and final goal of all true knowing, be freed of every hindrance by the intercession of the one who, in giving birth to the Truth and treasuring it in her heart, has shared it forever with all the world."[50]

FURTHER READING

Davies, Brian. *Thomas Aquinas on God and Evil*. Oxford: Oxford University Press, 2011.

Hart, David Bentley. *The Doors of the Sea: Where Was God in the Tsunami?* Grand Rapids, Mich.: Eerdmans, 2005.

Knasas, John F. X. *Aquinas and the Cry of Rachel: Thomistic Reflections on the Problem of Evil*. Washington, D.C.: The Catholic University of America Press, 2013.

Lewis, C. S. *The Problem of Pain: How Human Suffering Raises Almost Intolerable Intellectual Problems*. New York: Macmillan Publishing, 1962.

Maritain, Jacques. *God and the Permission of Evil*. Translated by Joseph W. Evans. Milwaukee: Bruce Publishing, 1966.

———. *St. Thomas and the Problem of Evil*. Milwaukee: Marquette University Press, 1942.

---

50 *Fides et Ratio*, 108. See also the profound meditation on Mary, Seat of Wisdom, in Charles De Koninck, *Ego Sapientia: The Wisdom That Is Mary*, vol. 2 of *The Writings of Charles De Koninck*, trans. Ralph McInerny (Notre Dame, Ind.: University of Notre Dame Press, 2009), 1–62.

Appendix I:
Timetable of Major Philosophers and Key Moments in History

Pre-Socratic Philosophers/Axial Age (600–400 BC)
Thales (625–545 BC)
Anaximander (610–545 BC)
Anaximenes (580–500 BC)
Jeremiah (641–585 BC)
Lao-tzu (604–ca.540 BC)
Zoroaster (dies ca. 550 BC)
Buddha (563–483 BC)
Confucius (551–478 BC)
Second Temple (538 BC)
Ezra and Nehemiah, ca. 450 BC)
Pythagoras (580–500 BC)
Heraclitus (540–475 BC)
Parmenides of Elea (515–450 BC)
Anaxagoras (500–428 BC)
Empedocles (495–435 BC)
Zeno of Elea (490–430 BC)
Leucippus (470–390 BC)
Democritus (460–370 BC)
Protagoras (490–415 BC)

Socratic Period (400–325 BC)
Socrates (469–399 BC)
Plato (427–347 BC)
Diogenes the Cynic (412–323 BC)
Aristotle (384–322 BC)

Hellenistic Philosophy (325 BC–AD 400)
Pyrrho of Elis (365–275 BC)
Epicurus (341–270 BC)
Zeno of Citium (360–260)
Cicero (106–43 BC)
Lucretius (99–55 BC)
+Birth of Christ+

Epictetus (AD 50–130)
Marcus Aurelius (AD 121–180)
Sextus Empiricus (AD 150–225)
Plotinus (AD 204–270)

Medieval and Renaissance Philosophers (AD 400–1600)
Augustine (354–430)
Boethius (480–525)
529 Plato's Academy closed by Justinian and Monte Cassino is founded
John Scotus Erigena (810–875)
Avicenna (980–1037)
Anselm (1033–1109)
Peter Abelard (1079–1142)
Averroes (1126–1198)
Moses Maimonides (1135–1204)
Francis of Assisi (1182–1226)
Bonaventure (1217–1274)
Thomas Aquinas (1225–1274)
Dante Alighieri (1265–1321)
Duns Scotus (1266–1308)
William Ockham (1285–1349)
1453 Fall of Constantinople; Hundred Years' War ends; Gutenberg Bible
Copernicus (1473–1543)
Martin Luther (1483–1546)

Modern Philosophers
Michel de Montaigne (1533–1592)
Francis Bacon (1561–1626)
Galileo Galilei (1564–1642)
Thomas Hobbes (1588–1679)
Rene Descartes (1596–1650)
Benedict Spinoza (1632–1677)
John Locke (1632–1704)

Isaac Newton (1642–1727)
Gottfried Leibniz (1646–1716)
George Berkeley (1685–1753)
David Hume (1711–1776)
Jean-Jacques Rousseau (1712–1778)
Immanuel Kant (1724–1804)
Jeremy Bentham (1748–1832)
Johann Fichte (1762–1814)
G. W. F. Hegel (1770–1831)
Ludwig Feuerbach (1804–1872)
John Stuart Mill (1806–1873)
Charles Darwin (1809–1882)
Soren Kierkegaard (1813–1855)
Karl Marx (1818–1883)

Current Era Philosophers

1859: Darwin's Origin of Species, *Mill's* On
Liberty, *and the birth of Dewey,*
Husserl, and Bergson

C. S. Peirce (1839–1914)
William James (1842–1910)
Friedrich Nietzsche (1844–1900)
Sigmund Freud (1856–1939)
Edmund Husserl (1859–1938)
Henri Bergson (1859–1941)
John Dewey (1859–1952)
A. N. Whitehead (1861–1947)
Bertrand Russell (1872–1970)
Jacques Maritain (1882–1973)
Ludwig Wittgenstein (1889–1951)
Martin Heidegger (1889–1976)
John-Paul Sartre (1905–1980)
W. V. O. Quine (1908–2000)
G. E. M. Anscombe (1919–2001)
John Rawls (1921–2002)
Michel Foucault (1926–1984)
Alasdair MacIntyre (1929–)
Jacques Derrida (1930–2004)

Appendix II:
Natural Knowledge of God

This is a brief list of propositions about God that Thomas Aquinas maintains we can know on the basis of reason alone, independently of all revelation. These questions are from the First Part of the *Summa Theologiae*. Question 1 considers the relation of faith and reason, and then Questions 2 to 26 consider our rational knowledge of God. Questions 27 to 43 are all on the Trinity, which as a mystery of the faith is beyond the capacity of reason and known only in revealed theology. Thomas then returns in Questions 44 to 49 to God's act of creation. Keep in mind that the controlling motif of Aquinas's natural theology is nonetheless negative, that is, what we cannot know about God exceeds by far what we can know.

That God is by Creation
Question 2: That God exists. While the existence of God is not self-evident to us, it can be demonstrated in five ways that argue from effect to God as cause.

What God is like by remotion (that is, how God is *not like* creatures):
Question 3: That God is simple. God is immaterial, noncomposite, and so his essence is the same as his Existence.

Question 4: That God is perfect. As the pure act of existence, God contains all perfections, which is why we can argue from perfections in this world to aspects of God's perfections.

Question 6: That God is good. As perfect, all things desire to imitate God, and so he is purely good as that which all things desire.

Question 7: That God is infinite.

Question 8: That God, as the act of existence, is omnipresent (present in all created things).

Question 9: That God is immutable.

Question 10: That God is Eternal.

Question 11: That God is One (there is only One God).

How we know God
Question 12: Since God transcends human sensate abilities, we know God directly only in the afterlife. However, in this life we know him imperfectly from his effects (creation).

Question 13: We can talk about God from these created perfections by means of analogy.

Positive perfections attributable to God (by analogy)

Of the Intellect:

Question 14: That God is omniscient. As an immaterial being, God's activity must be spiritual; hence, he knows all that is or that could be.

Question 15: That God has Divine Ideas that are the exemplar causes of all that is.

Question 16: That God is Truth.

Question 18: That God is Life (living); thus, God possesses the Neoplatonic triad of being, living, and knowing in exemplary fashion.

Of the Will:

Question 19: That God has a will by which he freely creates the world.

Question 20: That God loves all things (God is love).

Question 21: That God is just and merciful.

Question 22: That God providentially oversees creation.

Question 25: That God is omnipotent (all powerful).

Question 26: That God possesses perfect beatitude.

Concerning Creation

Question 44: That God is the first cause of all things. (God, as good, is also the Final Cause of all things. Thus, God creates all things for himself.)

Question 45: Creation is ex nihilo.

Question 46: While we can prove that there is a Creation, we accept on faith that this occurred in time.

Question 47: That God created many different things for the perfection of the universe.

Question 48: Evil is a privation of the goodness God intends in creating things.

Question 49: The privation that is evil can be caused only by being.

Bibliography

One of the goals of this book is to point the reader to the primary sources so that you can read the arguments firsthand. I have therefore endeavored to include as many references to important philosophers as possible. However, since all the works exist is a great variety of translations and editions and are often available online since they are public domain, I thought it best to provide these references according to standard textual division (such as question and article or chapter and section, and when available, standard pagination) so that the text might be found in any edition. This is most useful to the interested reader who wants to investigate the citation. Below I indicate the particular translation used.

WORKS BY THOMAS AQUINAS

BDT = *Commentary on Boethius's "De Trinitate"*

Faith, Reason, and Theology: Questions I–IV of his Commentary on the "De Trinitate" of Boethius. Translated by Armand Maurer. Toronto: Pontifical Institute of Medieval Studies, 1987.

The Division and Methods of the Sciences: Questions V and VI of his Commentary on the "De Trinitate" of Boethius. Translated by Armand Maurer. 4th rev. ed. Toronto: Pontifical Institute of Medieval Studies, 1986.

CBDH = *Commentary on Boethius's "De Hebdomadibus"*

An Exposition of the 'On the Hebdomads' of Boethius. Translated by Janice L. Shultz and Edward A. Synan. Washington, D.C.: The Catholic University of America Press, 2001.

CM = *Commentary on Aristotle's "Metaphysics"*

Commentary on Aristotle's "Metaphysics." Translated by John P. Rowan. 1961. Reprint, Notre Dame, Ind.: Dumb Ox Books, 1995.

CNE = *Commentary on Aristotle's "Nicomachean Ethics"*

Commentary on Aristotle's "Nicomachean Ethics." Translated by C. I. Litzinger, 1964. Reprint, Notre Dame, Ind.: Dumb Ox Books, 1993.

CP = *Commentary on Aristotle's "Physics"*

Commentary on Aristotle's "Physics." Translated by Richard J. Blackwell, Richard J. Spath, and W. Edmund Thirkel. 1961. Reprint, Notre Dame, Ind.: University of Notre Dame Press, 1995.

CT = Compendium of Theology
Compendium of Theology. Translated by Richard J. Regan. Oxford: Oxford University Press, 2009.

DM = De Malo
On Evil. Translated by Richard Regan. Oxford: Oxford University Press, 2003.

DP = De Potentia
On the Power of God. Translated by the English Dominican Fathers. Westminster, Md.: Newman Press, 1952.

DQDA = Disputed Questions de Anima
Questions on the Soul. Translated by James H. Robb. Milwaukee: Marquette University Press, 1984.

De Reg = De Regimine Principum
Political Writings. Edited and translated by R. W. Dyson. Cambridge: Cambridge University Press, 2002.

DV = De Veritate
Truth. Translated by Robert W. Mulligan, James V. McGlynn, and Robert W. Schmidt, 1954. Reprint, Indianapolis: Hackett, 1994.

OBE = On Being and Essence
On Being and Essence. Translated by Armand Maurer. 2nd rev. ed. Toronto: Pontifical Institute of Medieval Studies, 1968.

PN = The Principles of Nature
Aquinas on Matter and Form and the Elements: A Translations and Interpretation of the "De Principiis Naturae" and the "De Mixtione Elementorum" of St. Thomas Aquinas. Translated by Joseph Bobik. Notre Dame, Ind.: University of Notre Dame Press, 1998.

SCG = Summa Contra Gentiles
Summa Contra Gentiles. Translated by Anton Pegis, James Anderson, Vernon Bourke, and Charles J. O'Neil. Notre Dame, Ind.: University of Notre Dame Press, 1975.

ST = Summa Theologiae
The Summa Theologica of St. Thomas Aquinas. Translated by the Fathers of the English Dominican Province. 1948. Reprint, Allen, Tex.: Christian Classics, 1981.

OTHER WORKS

Adler, Mortimer. *The Difference of Man and the Difference It Makes*. New York: Holt, Rinehart, and Winston, 1967. Reprint, New York: Fordham University Press, 1993.

Aertsen, Jan. *Medieval Philosophy and the Transcendentals: The Case of Thomas Aquinas*. Studien und Texte zur Geistesgeschichte des Mittelalters 52. Leiden, New York, and Cologne: E. J. Brill, 1996.

Anselm of Canterbury. *Basic Writings*. Translated by S. N. Deane. 2nd ed. Chicago and La Salle, Ill.: Open Court, 1962.

Arendt, Hannah. *The Human Condition*. Chicago: University of Chicago Press, 1958.

Aristotle. *The Basic Works of Aristotle*. Edited by Richard McKeon. New York: Random House, 1941.

Ashley, Benedict. *The Way toward Wisdom: An Interdisciplinary and Intercultural Introduction to Metaphysics*. Notre Dame, Ind.: University of Notre Dame Press, 2006.

Augustine. *On the Teacher*. In *Basic Writings of St. Augustine,* edited by Whitney J. Oates and translated by G. C. Leckie, 361–98. New York: Random House, 1948.

———. *The City of God*. Translated by Marcus Dods. New York: The Modern Library, 1950.

———. *The Trinity*. Edited by John E. Rotelle. Translated by Edmund Hill. Brooklyn: New City Press, 1991.

———. *Confessions*. Translated by F. J. Sheed. 1942. Reprint, Indianapolis: Hackett, 1993.

———. *On Free Choice of the Will*. Translated by Thomas Williams. Indianapolis, Ind.: Hackett, 1993.

———. *On Christian Doctrine*. Translated by D. W. Robertson. Upper Saddle River, N.J.: Prentice Hall, 1997.

Bacon, Francis. *Essays, Advancement of Learning, New Atlantis, and Other Pieces*. Edited by Richard Foster Jones. New York: Odyssey Press, 1937.

Baglow, Christopher T. *Faith, Science, and Reason: Theology on the Cutting Edge*. 2nd ed. Woodridge, Ill.: Midwest Theological Forum, 2019.

Barr, Stephen. "Chance, by Design." *First Things*. December 2012. https://www.firstthings.com/article/2012/12/chance-by-design.

Barzun, Jacques. *From Dawn to Decadence: 500 Years of Western Cultural Life 1500 to the Present*. New York: HarperCollins, 2000.

Beckwith, Francis, and Gregory Koukl. *Relativism: Feet Firmly Planted in Mid-air*. Grand Rapids, Mich.: Baker Books, 1998.

Benedict XVI. *Faith, Reason, and the University: Memories and Reflections*. September 12, 2006.

Benestad, J. Brian. *Church, State, and Society: An Introduction to Catholic Social Doctrine*. Washington, D.C.: The Catholic University of America Press, 2011.

Bentham, Jeremy. *The Principles of Morals and Legislation*. Hafner Library of Classics 6. Darien, Conn.: Hafner Publishing, 1970.

Berkeley, George. *A Treatise Concerning the Principles of Human Knowledge*. Edited by Keith Winkler. Indianapolis: Hackett, 1982.

Boethius. *Consolation of Philosophy*. Translated by Joel C. Relihan. Indianapolis: Hackett, 2001.

Bonaventure. *Collationes in Hexaemeron* [Collations on the six days]. Translated by Jose de Vinck. Vol. 5 of *Works of Bonaventure*. Paterson, N.J.: St. Anthony Guild Press, 1970.

———. *Journey of the Mind to God*. Translated by Philotheus Boehner. Indianapolis: Hackett, 1993.

———. *On the Reduction of the Arts to Theology*. Translated by Zachary Harris. Vol. 1 of *Works of Saint Bonaventure*. 2nd ed. St. Bonaventure, N.Y.: Franciscan Institute, 1996.

Brock, Stephen L. *The Philosophy of Saint Thomas Aquinas: A Sketch*. Eugene, Ore.: Cascade Books, 2015.

Buckley, Michael J. *At the Origins of Modern Atheism*. New Haven: Yale University Press, 1987.

Carnap, Rudolph. "Elimination of Metaphysics through a Logical Analysis of Language." In *Logical Positivism,* edited by A. J. Ayer and translated by Arthur Pap, 60–81. Glencoe, Ill.: The Free Press, 1959.

Chesterton, G. K. "St. Thomas Aquinas." *The Spectator*. February 27, 1932.

Chisholm, Roderick. *The Problem of the Criterion*. Milwaukee: Marquette University Press, 1973.

Cicero, *On the Nature of the Gods*. In *Hellenistic Philosophy: Introductory Readings,* translated by Brad Inwood and L. P. Gerson. 2nd ed. Indianapolis: Hackett, 1997.

Clarke, W. Norris. *Person and Being*. Milwaukee: Marquette University Press, 1993.

———. *The One and the Many: A Contemporary Thomistic Metaphysics*. Notre Dame, Ind.: University of Notre Dame Press, 2001.

Collins, James. *A History of Modern European Philosophy*. Milwaukee: Bruce Publishing, 1954.

Comte, Auguste. *Introduction to the Positive Philosophy*. Translated by Frederick Ferre. Indianapolis: Hackett, 1988.

Copleston, Frederick. *A History of Philosophy*. 9 vols. Garden City, N.Y.: Image Books, 1985.

Courtois, Stéphane, and Nicolas Werth, et al., *The Black Book of Communism: Crimes, Terror, Repression*. Translated by Jonathan Murphy. Cambridge, Mass.: Harvard University Press, 1999.

Crowe, Michael Bertram. *The Changing Profile of the Natural Law*. The Hague: Martinus Nijhoff, 1977.

Davies, Brian. *The Thought of Thomas Aquinas*. Oxford: Clarendon Press, 1992.

———. *An Introduction to the Philosophy of Religion*. 3rd ed. Oxford: Oxford University Press, 2004.

———. *Thomas Aquinas on God and Evil*. Oxford: Oxford University Press, 2011.

Deely, John. *What Distinguishes Human Understanding?* South Bend, Ind.: St. Augustine's Press, 2002.

De Koninck, Charles. *Ego Sapientia: The Wisdom That Is Mary*. Vol. 2 of *The Writings of Charles De Koninck*. Edited and translated by Ralph McInerny. Notre Dame, Ind.: University of Notre Dame Press, 2009.

De Lubac, Henri. *The Drama of Atheist Humanism*. Translated by Edith M. Riley, Anne Englund Nash, and Mark Sebanc. San Francisco: Ignatius Press, 1995.

Deneen, Patrick J. *Why Liberalism Failed*. New Haven: Yale University Press, 2018.

D'Entreves, A. P. *Natural Law*. London: Hutchison, 1951.

Descartes, René. *The Philosophical Writings of Descartes*. Translated and edited by John Cottingham, Robert Stoothoff, and Dugald Murdoch. 3 vols. Cambridge: Cambridge University Press, 1985.

Eco, Umberto. *The Aesthetics of Thomas Aquinas*. Translated by Hugh Bredin. Cambridge, Mass.: Harvard University Press, 1988.

Epictetus. *The Handbook (The Encheiridion)*. Translated by Nicholas P. White. Indianapolis: Hackett, 1983.

Fabro, Cornelio. *God in Exile: Modern Atheism from Its Roots in the Cartesian* Cogito *to the Present Day.* Translated by Arthur Gibson. Westminster, Md.: Newman Press, 1968.

Feser, Edward. *Scholastic Metaphysics: A Contemporary Introduction.* Heusenstamm: Editiones Scholasticae, 2014.

———. *Five Proofs of the Existence of God.* San Francisco: Ignatius, 2017.

Feuerbach, Ludwig. *The Essence of Christianity.* Translated by George Eliot. New York: Harper Torchbooks, 1957.

Finley, John. "The Metaphysics of Gender: A Thomistic Approach." *The Thomist* 79, no. 4 (2015): 585–614.

Francis. *Meeting with the Members of the General Assembly of the United Nations Organization: Address of the Holy Father,* September 25, 2015.

Galilei, Galileo. *Dialogue on the Great World System.* Edited by Giorgio de Santillana. Chicago: University of Chicago Press, 1953.

Gilby, Thomas. *The Political Thought of Thomas Aquinas.* Chicago: University of Chicago Press, 1963.

Gillespie, Michael Allen. *The Theological Origins of Modernity.* Chicago: University of Chicago Press, 2008.

Gilson, Étienne. *Reason and Revelation.* New York: Charles Scribner's Sons, 1938.

———. *Being and Some Philosophers.* 2nd ed. Toronto: Pontifical Institute of Medieval Studies, 1952.

———. *History of Christian Philosophy in the Middle Ages.* New York: Random House, 1955.

———. *Elements of Christian Philosophy.* Garden City, N.Y.: Doubleday and Company, 1960.

———. *The Arts of the Beautiful.* New York: Charles Scribner's Sons, 1965.

———. *Forms and Substances in the Arts.* New York: Charles Scribner's Sons, 1966.

———. *Methodical Realism.* Translated by Philip Trower. Front Royal, Va.: Christendom Press, 1990.

———. *The Spirit of Medieval Philosophy.* Translated by A. H. C. Downes. Notre Dame, Ind.: University of Notre Dame Press, 1991.

———. *The Christian Philosophy of St. Thomas Aquinas.* Translated by L. K. Shook. Notre Dame, Ind.: University of Notre Dame Press, 1994.

———. *The Unity of Philosophical Experience.* San Francisco: Ignatius Press, 1999.

———. *God and Philosophy.* 2nd ed. New Haven: Yale University Press, 2002.

Glendon, Mary Ann. *Rights Talk: The Impoverishment of Political Discourse.* New York: Free Press, 1991.

Gould, Stephen Jay. "Nonoverlapping Magisteria." *Natural History* 106 (March 1997): 16–22.

Gracia, Jorge J. E. "Cutting the Gordian Knot of Ontology: Thomas's Solution to the Problem of Universals." In *Thomas Aquinas and His Legacy,* edited by David M. Gallagher, 16–36. Washington, D.C.: The Catholic University of America Press, 1994.

Gregory, Brad S. *The Unintended Reformation: How a Religious Revolution Secularized Society.* Cambridge, Mass.: Belknap Press of Harvard University Press, 2012.

Guthrie, W. K. C. *The Greek Philosophers: From Thales to Aristotle.* New York: Harper and Row, 1975.

Hadot, Pierre. *What Is Ancient Philosophy?* Translated by Michael Chase. Cambridge, Mass.: Harvard University Press, 2002.

Hart, David Bentley. *The Doors of the Sea: Where Was God in the Tsunami?* Grand Rapids, Mich.: Eerdmans, 2005.

———. *Atheist Delusions: The Christian Revolution and Its Fashionable Enemies.* New Haven: Yale University Press, 2009.

———. *The Experience of God: Being, Consciousness, Bliss,* New Haven: Yale University Press, 2013.

Hegel, G. W. F. *Reason in History.* Translated by Robert S. Hartman. Library of Liberal Arts. New York: Pearson, 1995.

Hildebrand, Dietrich von. *The Heart: An Analysis of Human and Divine Affectivity.* Edited by John Henry Crosby. South Bend, Ind.: St. Augustine's Press, 2007.

Hittinger, Russell. *First Grace: Rediscovering the Natural Law in a Post-Christian World.* Wilmington, Del.: ISI Books, 2003.

Hobbes, Thomas. *Leviathan.* Edited by C. B. Macpherson. Harmondsworth: Penguin Books, 1968.

Hume, David. *A Treatise of Human Nature.* Edited by L. A. Selby-Bigge. 2nd ed. Oxford: Clarendon Press, 1978.

———. *An Enquiry Concerning Human Understanding and Concerning the Principles of Moral.* Edited by L. A. Selby-Bigge. 3rd ed. Oxford: Clarendon Press, 1995.

Husserl, Edmund. *Ideas: General Introduction to Pure Phenomenology.* Translated by W. R. Boyce Gibson. London: George Allen and Unwin, 1931.

———. *The Crisis of European Sciences and Transcendental Phenomenology: An Introduction to Phenomenological Philosophy.* Translated by David Carr. Evanston, Ill.: Northwestern University Press, 1970.

Jacobs, James. "The Rational Order of Nature and the Environmental Implications of Natural Law." *Lex Naturalis* 2 (2016): 65–86.

James, William. *Principles of Psychology.* Vol. 53 of *Great Books of the Western World.* Edited by Robert Maynard Hutchins. Chicago and London: Encyclopaedia Britannica, 1952.

———. *Pragmatism and The Meaning of Truth.* Introduction by A. J. Ayer. Cambridge, Mass.: Harvard University Press, 1975.

Jaroszynski, Piotr. *Beauty and Being: Thomistic Perspectives.* Translated by Hugh McDonald. Étienne Gilson Series 33. Toronto: Pontifical Institute of Medieval Studies, 2011.

Jaspers, Karl. *The Origin and Goal of History.* Translated by Michael Bullock. New Haven: Yale University Press, 1953.

Jensen, Steven J. *Good and Evil Actions: A Journey through Saint Thomas Aquinas.* Washington, D.C.: The Catholic University of America Press, 2010.

———. *Knowing the Natural Law: Precepts, Inclinations, and Deriving Oughts.* Washington, D.C.: The Catholic University of America Press, 2015.

———. *Sin: A Thomistic Psychology.* Washington, D.C.: The Catholic University of America Press, 2018.

John Paul II. *Centisimus Annus.* Encyclical Letter. May 1, 1991.

———. *Veritatis Splendor.* Encyclical Letter. August 6, 1993.

———. *Evangelium Vitae.* Encyclical Letter. March 25, 1995.

———. *Homily at Camden Yard, Baltimore, Maryland.* October 8, 1995.

———. *Fides et Ratio.* Encyclical Letter. September 14, 1998.

Jones, Brian. "Breaking Free of Our Metaphysical Winter: On Why Christians Must Study Philosophy." *Homiletic and Pastoral Review,* January 12, 2015.

Kant, Immanuel. *Religion within the Limits of Reason Alone.* Translated by Theodore M. Greene and Hoyt H. Hudson. New York: Harper and Row, 1960.

———. *Critique of Pure Reason.* Translated by Norman Kemp Smith. New York: St. Martin's Press, 1965.

———. *Prolegomena to Any Future Metaphysics.* Translated by Paul Carus. Edited with revisions by Lewis White Beck. Upper Saddle River, N.J.: Prentice Hall, 1994.

———. *Practical Philosophy.* Translated by Mary J. Gregor. Cambridge: Cambridge University Press, 1996.

Kerr, Fergus. *After Aquinas: Versions of Thomism.* Malden, Mass.: Blackwell, 2002.

Kierkegaard, Søren. *The Present Age: On the Death of Rebellion.* Translated by Alexander Dru. New York: Harper Perennial, 1962.

———. *Fear and Trembling.* Translated by Alastair Hannay. Hammondsworth: Penguin Books, 1985.

———. *Concluding Unscientific Postscript to Philosophical Fragments.* Translated by Howard V Hong and Edna H. Hong. Princeton, N.J.: Princeton University Press, 1992.

Kirk, G. S., J. E. Raven, and M. Schofield, eds. *The Presocratic Philosophers.* 2nd ed. Cambridge: Cambridge University Press, 1983.

Klima, Gyula. "*Ancilla Theologiae vs. Domina Philosophorum*: St. Thomas Aquinas, Latin Averroism and the Autonomy of Philosophy." Available at http://faculty.fordham.edu/klima/ANCILLA.HTM.

Klubertanz, George P. *The Philosophy of Human Nature.* New York: Appleton-Century-Crofts, 1953.

Knasas, John F. X. *Aquinas and the Cry of Rachel: Thomistic Reflections on the Problem of Evil.* Washington, D.C.: The Catholic University of America Press, 2013.

Kovach, Francis J. *Philosophy of Beauty.* Norman, Okla.: University of Oklahoma Press, 1974.

Kuklick, Bruce. *A History of Philosophy in America: 1720–2000.* Oxford: Clarendon Press, 2001.

Kupczak, Jarosław. *Destined for Liberty: The Human Person in the Philosophy of Karol Wojtyła / Pope John Paul II.* Washington, D.C.: The Catholic University of America Press, 2000.

Kurtz, Paul, ed. *American Thought before 1900.* New York: Macmillan, 1966.

Lee, Patrick, and Robert P. George. *Body-Self Dualism in Contemporary Ethics and Politics.* Cambridge: Cambridge University Press, 2008.

Leibniz, Gottfried. *Monadology and Other Philosophical Essays.* Translated by Paul and Anne Schrecker. Library of Liberal Arts. Indianapolis: Bobbs-Merrill, 1965.

Leo XIII. *Aeterni Patris.* Encyclical Letter. August 4, 1879.

———. *Rerum Novarum.* Encyclical Letter. May 15, 1891.

Levering, Matthew. *Proofs of God: Classical Arguments from Tertullian to Barth.* Grand Rapids, Mich.: Baker Academic, 2016.

Lewis, C. S. *The Problem of Pain: How Human Suffering Raises Almost Intolerable Intellectual Problems.* New York: Macmillan Publishing, 1962.

———. *The Discarded Image: An Introduction to Medieval and Renaissance Literature.* Cambridge: Cambridge University Press, 1964.

———. *The Abolition of Man*. New York: Touchstone Books, 1996.

———. *Weight of Glory and Other Addresses*. Rev. ed. New York: Harper One, 2001.

Locke, John. *An Essay Concerning Human Understanding*. Edited by John W. Youlton. London: J. M. Dent, 1947.

———. *Two Treatises of Government*. New York: Mentor Books, 1965.

———. *Letter Concerning Toleration*. In *Political Philosophy: The Essential Texts,* edited by Steven M. Cahn, 393–400. 3rd ed. Oxford: Oxford University Press, 2015.

Long, Steven A. *The Teleological Grammar of the Moral Act*. Naples, Fla.: Sapientia Press of Ave Maria University, 2007.

Lucretius. *On the Nature of Things*. Translated by Martin Ferguson Smith. Indianapolis: Hackett, 2001.

Machiavelli, Niccolò. *The Prince*, with Selections from *The Discourses*. Translated by Daniel Donno. New York: Bantam Books, 1966.

MacInerny, Ralph. *Ethica Thomistica: The Moral Philosophy of Thomas Aquinas*. Rev. ed. Washington, D.C.: The Catholic University of America Press, 1997.

———. *Praeambula Fidei: Thomism and the God of the Philosophers*. Washington, D.C.: The Catholic University of America Press, 2006.

MacIntyre, Alasdair. *A Short History of Ethics*. New York: Touchstone, 1966.

———. *After Virtue*. 3rd ed. Notre Dame, Ind.: University of Notre Dame Press, 2007.

———. "On Having Survived the Academic Moral Philosophy of the Twentieth Century." In *What Happened in and to Moral Philosophy in the Twentieth Century,* edited by Fran O'Rourke, 17–34. Notre Dame, Ind.: University of Notre Dame Press, 2013.

———. *Ethics in the Conflicts of Modernity: An Essay on Desire, Practical Reasoning, and Narrative*. Cambridge: Cambridge University Press, 2016.

Manent, Pierre. *An Intellectual History of Liberalism*. Translated by Rebecca Balinski. Princeton: Princeton University Press, 1995.

———. *Natural Law and Human Rights: Toward a Recovery of Practical Reason*. Translated by Ralph C. Hancock. Notre Dame, Ind: University of Notre Dame Press, 2020.

Marcel, Gabriel. *Mystery of Being*. 2 vols. Translated by G.S. Fraser. South Bend, Ind.: St. Augustine's Press, 2001.

Maritain, Jacques. *Art and Scholasticism*. Translated by J. F. Scanlan. New York: Charles Scribner's Sons, 1930.

———. *Theonas: Conversations of a Sage*. Translated by F. J. Sheed. New York: Sheed and Ward, 1933.

———. *Freedom in the Modern World*. Translated by Richard O'Sullivan. London: Sheed and Ward, 1935.

———. *St. Thomas and the Problem of Evil*. Milwaukee: Marquette University Press, 1942.

———. *A Preface to Metaphysics*. London: Sheed and Ward, 1943.

———. *The Philosophy of Nature*. Translated by Imelda C. Byrne. New York: Philosophical Library, 1951.

———. *The Range of Reason*. New York: Scribner's, 1952.

———. *Creative Intuition in Art and Poetry*. New York: Meridian Books, 1954.

———. *Existence and the Existent*. Translated by Lewis Galantiere and Gerald B. Phelan. Garden City, N.Y.: Image Books, 1956.

———. *Scholasticism and Politics*. Translated by Mortimer J. Adler. Garden City, N.Y.: Image Books, 1960.

———. "The Conquest of Freedom." In *The Education of Man: The Educational Philosophy of Jacques Maritain*, edited by Donald and Idella Gallagher, 159–79. Garden City, N.Y.: Doubleday, 1962.

———. *God and the Permission of Evil*. Translated by Joseph W. Evans. Milwaukee: Bruce Publishing, 1966.

———. *The Person and the Common Good*. Translated by John J. Fitzgerald. Notre Dame, Ind.: University of Notre Dame Press, 1966.

———. *Distinguish to Unite, or The Degrees of Knowledge*. Translated by Gerald B. Phelan. Notre Dame, Ind.: University of Notre Dame Press, 1995.

———. *Untrammeled Approaches*. Translated by Bernard Doering. Notre Dame, Ind.: University of Notre Dame Press, 1997.

———. *Man and the State*. Washington, D.C.: The Catholic University of America Press, 1998.

———. *An Introduction to Philosophy*. Translated by E. I. Watkins. Lanham, Md.: Rowman and Littlefield, 2005.

Martin, C. J. F. *An Introduction to Medieval Philosophy*. Edinburgh: Edinburgh University Press, 1996.

Marx, Karl. *Early Writings*. Translated by Rodney Livingstone and Gregor Benton. New York: Vintage Books, 1975.

———. *The Marx-Engels Reader*. 2nd ed. Edited by Robert C. Tucker. New York: W. W. Norton, 1978.

Maurer, Armand A. *About Beauty: A Thomistic Interpretation*. Houston: Center for Thomistic Studies, 1983.

McCoy, Charles N. R. *The Structure of Political Thought: A Study in the History of Political Ideas*. New York: McGraw-Hill, 1963.

Mill, John Stuart. *Utilitarianism, On Liberty, and Considerations on Representative Government*. Edited by H. B. Acton. London: Everyman's Library, 1972.

Miner, Robert. *Thomas Aquinas on the Passions*. Cambridge: Cambridge University Press, 2009.

Morerod, Charles. *Ecumenism and Philosophy: Philosophical Questions for a Renewal of Dialogue*. Translated by Therese C. Scarpelli. Ann Arbor, Mich.: Sapientia Press of Ave Maria University, 2006.

Murray, John Courtney. *We Hold These Truths*. New York: Sheed and Ward, 1960.

Newman, John Henry. *The Biglietto Speech*. May 12, 1879. Available at http://www.newman-reader.org/works/addresses/file2.html.

———. *The Idea of a University: Defined and Illustrated*. Edited by Martin J. Svaglic. Notre Dame, Ind.: University of Notre Dame Press, 1982.

———. *An Essay on the Development of Christian Doctrine*. Notre Dame, Ind.: University of Notre Dame Press, 1989.

———. *An Essay in Aid of a Grammar of Assent*. Introduction by Nicholas Lash. Notre Dame, Ind.: University of Notre Dame Press, 1992.

Nichols, Aidan. *The Shape of Catholic Theology: An Introduction to Its Sources, Principles, and History*. Collegeville, Minn.: The Liturgical Press, 1991.

Nietzsche, Friedrich. *The Birth of Tragedy and The Genealogy of Morals*. Translated by Francis Golffing. Garden City, N.Y.: Doubleday Anchor Books, 1956.

———. *The Gay Science*. Translated by Walter Kaufmann. New York: Vintage Books, 1974.

———. *Thus Spoke Zarathustra*. Translated by Walter Kaufmann. Harmondsworth: Penguin Books, 1978.

———. *The Anti-Christ, Ecce Homo, Twilight of the Idols, and Other Writings*. Edited by Aaron Ridley and Judith Norman. Translated by Judith Norman. Cambridge Texts in the History of Philosophy. Cambridge: Cambridge University Press, 2005.

Nozick, Robert. *Anarchy, State, and Utopia*. New York: Basic Books, 1974.

O'Callahan, John. *Thomistic Realism and the Linguistic Turn: Toward a More Perfect Form of Existence*. Notre Dame, Ind.: University of Notre Dame Press, 2003.

Oderberg, David S. *Real Essentialism*. New York: Routledge, 2007.

Pascal, Blaise. *Pascal's Pensées*. Translated by W. F. Trotter. New York: E. P. Dutton, 1958.

Pegis, Anton C. "St. Anselm and the Argument of the 'Proslogion.'" *Mediaeval Studies* 28 (1966): 228–67.

Peirce, Charles Sanders. *Collected Papers of Charles Sanders Peirce*. 6 vols. Edited by Charles Hartshorne and Paul Weiss. Cambridge, Mass.: The Belknap Press of Harvard University Press, 1931.

Perry, Ralph Barton. *Puritanism and Democracy*. New York: Vanguard Press, 1944.

Pieper, Josef. *Belief and Faith*. Translated by Richard and Clara Winston. Chicago: Regnery, 1963.

———. *The Four Cardinal Virtues*. Translated by Richard and Clara Winston, Lawrence E. Lynch, and Daniel F. Coogan. Notre Dame, Ind.: University of Notre Dame Press, 1966.

———. *Living the Truth: The Truth of All Things and Reality and the Good*. Translated by Lothar Krauth and Stella Lange. San Francisco: Ignatius Press, 1989.

———. *Only the Lover Sings: Art and Contemplation*. Translated by Lothar Krauth. San Francisco: Ignatius Press, 1990.

———. *Guide to Thomas Aquinas*. Translated by Richard and Clara Winston. San Francisco: Ignatius Press, 1991.

———. *In Defense of Philosophy: The Power of the Mind for Good or Evil, Consists in Argumentation*. Translated by Lothar Krauth. San Francisco: Ignatius Press, 1992.

———. *"Divine Madness": Plato's Case against Secular Humanism*. Translated by Lothar Krauth. San Francisco: Ignatius Press, 1995.

———. *Faith, Hope, Love*. Translated Richard and Clara Winston. San Francisco: Ignatius Press, 1997.

———. *Leisure, the Basis of Culture*. Translated by Gerald Malsbary. South Bend, Ind.: St. Augustine's Press, 1998.

Pinckaers, Servais. *Sources of Christian Ethics*. Translated by Mary Thomas Noble. Washington, D.C.: The Catholic University of America Press, 1995.

Pinker, Steven. "The Stupidity of Dignity." *The New Republic,* May 28, 2008.

Pius XI. *Quadrigesimo Anno*. Encyclical Letter. May 15, 1931.

Plato. *The Collected Dialogues of Plato*. Edited by Edith Hamilton and Huntington Cairns. Bollingen Series 71. Princeton: Princeton University Press, 1989.

Plotinus. *The Essential Plotinus*. Edited by Elmer O'Brien, SJ. Indianapolis: Hackett, 1975.

Pluckrose, Helen, and James Lindsay. *Cynical Theories: How Activist Scholarship Made Everything about Race, Gender, and Identity—and Why This Harms Everybody*. Durham, N.C.: Pitchstone Publishing, 2020.

Porphyry the Phoenician. *Isagoge*. Translated by Edward W. Warren. Toronto: Pontifical Institute of Medieval Studies, 1975.

Pseudo-Dionysius. *The Complete Works*. Translated by Colm Luibheid. The Classics of Western Spirituality. New York: Paulist Press, 1987.

Ramos, Alice M. *Dynamic Transcendentals: Truth, Goodness, and Beauty from a Thomistic Perspective*. Washington, D.C.: The Catholic University of America Press, 2012.

Ratzinger, Joseph. *The Ratzinger Report*. With Vittorio Messori. Translated by Salvator Attanasio and Graham Harrison. San Francisco: Ignatius Press, 1985.

———. *On the Way to Jesus Christ*. Translated by Michael J. Miller. San Francisco: Ignatius Press, 2004.

Rawls, John. *A Theory of Justice*. Cambridge, Mass.: Harvard University Press, 1971.

———. *Political Liberalism*. New York: Columbia University Press, 1993.

Reid, Thomas. *Inquiry and Essays*. Edited by Ronald E. Beanblossom and Keith Lehrer. Indianapolis: Hackett, 1983.

———. *Essays on the Intellectual Powers of Man*. Cambridge: Cambridge University Press, 2011.

Reilly, Robert R. *The Closing of the Muslim Mind*. Wilmington, Del.: ISI Books, 2010.

Rist, John M. *Real Ethics: Rethinking the Foundations of Morality*. Cambridge: Cambridge University Press, 2002.

———. *Plato's Moral Realism: The Discovery of the Presuppositions of Ethics*. Washington, D.C.: The Catholic University of America Press, 2012.

———. *What Is a Person? Realities, Constructs, Illusions*. Cambridge: Cambridge University Press, 2020.

Rommen, Heinrich. *The State in Catholic Thought: A Treatise in Political Philosophy*. St. Louis and London: B. Herder Book Co., 1945.

———. *The Natural Law: A Study in Legal and Social History and Philosophy*. Indianapolis: Liberty Fund, 1998.

Roniger, Scott Jude. "Do Friends Need Justice or Do They Just Need Friendship? Natural Law as the Foundations for Justice and Friendship." *Lex Naturalis* 3 (2018): 57–84.

Ross, James. *Thought and World*. Notre Dame, Ind.: University of Notre Dame Press, 2008.

Rousseau, Jean-Jacques. *The First and Second Discourses*. Translated by Roger D. and Judith R. Masters. New York: St. Martin's Press, 1964.

Rziha, John. *Perfecting Human Actions: St. Thomas Aquinas on Human Participation in Eternal Law*. Washington, D.C.: The Catholic University of America Press, 2009.

Saccenti, Riccardo. *Debating Medieval Natural Law: A Survey*. Notre Dame, Ind.: University of Notre Dame Press, 2016.

Sartre, Jean Paul. *Existentialism and Human Emotions*. Translated by Bernard Frechtman and Hazel E. Barnes. New York: Philosophical Library, 1957.

———. *No Exit and Three Other Plays*. Translated by Stuart Gilbert. New York: Vintage International, 1989.

Schall, James. *Roman Catholic Political Philosophy*. Lanham, Md.: Lexington Books, 2004.

Sevier, Christopher Scott. *Aquinas on Beauty*. Lanham, Md.: Lexington Books, 2015.

Simon, Yves R. *Philosophy of Democratic Government*. Chicago: University of Chicago Press, 1951.

———. *A General Theory of Authority*. Notre Dame, Ind.: University of Notre Dame Press, 1962.

———. *The Tradition of Natural Law: A Philosopher's Reflections*. Edited by Vukan Kuic. New York: Fordham University Press, 1965.

———. *Freedom of Choice*. Edited by Peter Wolff. New York: Fordham University Press, 1969.

———. *An Introduction to Metaphysics of Knowledge*. Translated by Vukan Kuic and Richard J Thompson. New York: Fordham University Press, 1990.

Skinner, B. F. *Beyond Freedom and Dignity*. New York: Alfred A. Knopf, 1971.

Smith, Steven D. *The Rise and Decline of American Religious Freedom*. Cambridge, Mass.: Harvard University Press, 2014.

Snell, R. J. *Acedia: Metaphysical Boredom in an Empire of Desire*. Kettering, Ohio: Angelico Press, 2015.

Sokolowski, Robert. *The God of Faith and Reason: Foundations of Christian Theology*. Washington, D.C.: The Catholic University of America Press, 1995.

———. *Introduction to Phenomenology*. Cambridge: Cambridge University Press, 2000.

Spaemann, Robert. *Persons: The Difference between "Someone" and "Something."* Translated by Oliver O'Donovan. Oxford: Oxford University Press, 2007.

———. "Is Brain Death the Death of a Human Person?" In *Love and the Dignity of Human Life: On Nature and Natural Law*, 45–69. Grand Rapids, Mich.: Eerdmans, 2012.

Spinoza, Baruch. *The Ethics and Selected Letters*. Translated by Samuel Shirley. Indianapolis: Hackett, 1982.

———. *Theological-Political Treatise*. Edited by Jonathan Israel. Translated by Michael Silverthorne and Jonathan Israel. Cambridge Texts in the History of Philosophy. Cambridge: Cambridge University Press, 2007.

Strauss, Leo. *Natural Right and History*. Chicago: University of Chicago Press, 1950.

Sullivan, Daniel J. *An Introduction to Philosophy*. Milwaukee: Bruce Publishing, 1957.

Taylor, Charles. *Sources of the Self: The Making of Modern Identity*. Cambridge, Mass.: Harvard University Press, 1989.

———. *A Secular Age*. Cambridge, Mass.: The Belknap Press of Harvard University Press, 2007.

Torrell, Jean-Pierre. *The Person and His Work*. Vol. 1 of *Saint Thomas Aquinas*. Translated by Robert Royal. Washington, D.C.: The Catholic University Press of America, 1996.

Toulmin, Stephen. *Cosmopolis: The Hidden Agenda of Modernity*. Chicago: The University of Chicago Press, 1990.

Trapani, John G. *Poetry, Beauty, and Contemplation: The Complete Aesthetics of Jacques Maritain*. Washington, D.C.: The Catholic University of America Press, 2011.

Vatican Council I. *Dei Filius* II. Dogmatic Constitution. April 24, 1870.

Veatch, Henry B. *Rational Man: A Modern Interpretation of Aristotelian Ethics*. Bloomington, Ind.: Indiana University Press, 1962.

———. *Aristotle: A Contemporary Appreciation*. Bloomington, Ind.: Indiana University Press, 1974.

Velde, Rudi te. *Aquinas on God: The 'Divine Science' of the Summa Theologiae*. Ashgate Studies in the History of Philosophical Theology. Aldershot: Ashgate, 2006.

Voegelin, Eric. *The New Science of Politics*. Chicago: University of Chicago Press, 1952.

Weaver, Richard. *Ideas Have Consequences*. Chicago: University of Chicago Press, 1984.

Weber, Max. *The Vocation Lectures: "Science as a Vocation" and "Politics as a Vocation"*. Edited by David Owen and Tracy B. Strong. Translated by Rodney Livingstone. Indianapolis: Hackett, 2004.

Weigel, George. *Witness to Hope: The Biography of Pope John Paul II*. New York: HarperCollins, 1999.

Weinreb, Lloyd L. *Natural Law and Justice*. Cambridge, Mass.: Harvard University Press, 1987.

Whitehead, Alfred North. *Process and Reality: An Essay in Cosmology*. Edited by David Ray Griffin and Donald W. Sherburne. Corrected ed. New York: The Free Press, 1978.

Wippel, John. "Metaphysics." In *The Cambridge Companion to Thomas Aquinas*, edited by Norman Kretzmann and Eleonore Stump, 85–127. Cambridge: Cambridge University Press, 1993.

———. *Medieval Reactions to the Encounter between Faith and Reason*. Milwaukee: Marquette University Press, 1995.

———. *The Metaphysical Thought of Thomas Aquinas: From Finite Being to Uncreated Being*. Washington, D.C.: The Catholic University of America Press, 2000.

Wojtyła, Karol. *The Acting Person*. Edited by Anna-Teresa Tymieniecka. Translated by Andrzej Potocki. Dordrecht: D. Reidel, 1979.

———. *Love and Responsibility*. Translated by H. T. Willetts. San Francisco: Ignatius Press, 1981.

———. *Person and Community: Selected Essays*. Translated by Theresa Sandok, OSM. New York: Peter Lang, 1993.

Wood, Robert. *Placing Aesthetics*. Athens, Ohio: Ohio University Press, 1999.

Wootton, David. *Power, Pleasure, and Profit: Insatiable Appetites from Machiavelli to Madison*. Cambridge, Mass.: The Belknap Press of Harvard University Press, 2018.

Index

abortion, 172n2, 179, 267, 292, 295

abstraction, 163–70, 275, 279, 341

accidents: in the analogy of being, 121–22; Aristotle's theory, 71–72, 74–75, 76, 78, 94–95, 97n11; as created by God, 360; and division of being, 115, 118–20, 378; and evil, 383–84, 386–87; God's lack of, 354–55; goodness of, 250–51, 268, 380–81; individuating, 113, 114, 200; of a moral act, 258; as object of knowledge, 155, 161, 163, 168n96; sex as, 212–13; unity as, 191n49, 287–88. *See also* action follows from being; categories

acedia, 27n14, 278

act and potency: in the analogy of being, 119, 122–23; Aristotle's principle of change, 70–75, 78–79, 94, 328–29; in art, 268, 274; double composition of, 111–13; essence and existence, 104–8; in ethics, 249–53, 255, 274, 316–18; and evil, 383–84; God and, 348–55; and human nature, 199–201; as principle of knowledge, 130, 157, 162–64, 274

act, first and second. *See* action follows from being

action follows from being: in Aristotle, 71, 74–75, 76, 80; art, 268; essence and, 110, 364, 365; ethics and, 221, 223n4, 250–52, 257, 317; evil and, 379, 380–81, 383, 386; in God, 348–49, 350n64, 359–62; human nature, 190, 196, 199, 200–1; Hume's rejection of, 231; in the ladder of being, 124; knowledge of, 157n70, 161, 164; natural law and, 260, 304

Adler, Mortimer, 65n20, 187n44

Aertsen, Jan, 273n160

aesthetics, 277–80, 346

analogy of being: 121–24, 126–27, 325, 377–78, 392; beauty, 275; causality, 366n115; and God, 332, 345, 349, 350n64, 358–62; good as, 380; life as, 196; love as, 206–7

analytic philosophy, 17n25, 144n44

Anaxagoras, 61, 326

Anaximander, 57–58

Anaximenes, 58

angels, 112, 125, 140n29, 200n64, 206n84, 210, 359

animals, 33, 213, 249n74, 254n9; as a genus, 77, 112, 121; human nature as, 176, 185, 187n46; and powers of the soul, 125–26, 158–61, 191, 195–96, 202–4, 208, 245, 264

Anscombe, G. E. M., 17n25

Anselm, 6, 139n27, 346–47

appetite, 116, 174, 185, 195, 201–5, 206, 208, 224, 232, 245–46, 254–55, 259, 272–73, 360n96. *See also* love; will

Aquinas, Thomas. *See* Thomas Aquinas

Arendt, Hannah, 27n12

argument: from design, 335–36, 353n70; dialectical, 33–34; ontological, 139, 340, 346–47, 353n69

Aristophanes, 45n53

Aristotle, 57, 61, 68–80, 85, 86n67, 94, 95n3, 96, 103n21, 112, 185n34, 201n67, 224n7, 375n6; on ethics, 242–48, 249, 253, 255, 259, 262n129, 267, 268n145, 271n155, 273, 274n168; on God, 39, 328–30, 349n62, 351n66; on justice, 297n35, 298n39, 299n41, 306n64; on knowledge, 130, 131n5, 156, 168n97, 176n16; on the nature of philosophy, 24–28, 63n14; in the perennial tradition, 5, 8, 24–48, 81, 83–84, 110; on politics, 283–84, 295n28, 300n45, 307n66, 308n68, 315n82; and the soul, 191

art, 16, 269–72

Ashley, Benedict, 96n9, 100n16

atheism, 16, 184, 332, 334n26, 335, 341n35, 343–45

atomists, 61–62, 327n5. *See also* psychological atomism

Augustine, 7, 8, 10, 39n38, 82–83, 139n25, 169n99, 237n38, 255, 258n111, 261n121, 268n147, 270n150, 270n153, 284, 303n56, 346, 356n83, 366n117, 373, 378, 387n37

authority, 84, 88, 121, 248, 261, 265, 284, 298, 306–11